THE STORY
of the
GARDEN

Books by Eleanour Sinclair Rohde
published by The Medici Society

A GARDEN OF HERBS	1920
THE SCENTED GARDEN*	1931
THE STORY OF THE GARDEN*	1932
GARDENS OF DELIGHT	1934
SHAKESPEARE'S WILD FLOWERS	1935
HERBS AND HERB GARDENING	1936
VEGETABLE CULTIVATION & COOKERY	1938
THE WARTIME VEGETABLE GARDEN	1940

* Republished by the Medici Society in 1989

An eighteenth-century garden scene
(From the original at Nymans, Sussex, destroyed in a fire)

THE STORY
OF THE GARDEN

By

ELEANOUR SINCLAIR ROHDE

WITH A CHAPTER ON AMERICAN GARDENS
by MRS. FRANCIS KING

Love lays out a garden on the Earth

LONDON
THE MEDICI SOCIETY, LTD.

First published in 1932 by The Medici Society.
Now reprinted from the 1933 edition
with additional colour illustrations

Published by The Medici Society Ltd, London, 1989

British Library Cataloguing in Publication Data:

Rohde, Eleanour Sinclair
  The story of the garden
  1. Gardens – History
  I. Title
  712'.6'09   SB451

ISBN 0-85503 145 X

Distributed by B. T. Batsford Ltd, PO Box 4, Braintree,
Essex CM7 7QY,   *Telephone* 0376 21276

Set in Garamond type and printed on 'Cranham Lodge' Laid,
made specially to match the paper of the original edition.

Printed and bound in Great Britain at the University
Printing House, Oxford.

TO

' SSO '

WITH LOVE FROM

E. S. R.

PREFACE

The frontispiece of this book is from the original picture in Colonel Messel's collection and reproduced with his kind permission. I am delighted to be able to include a chapter on American gardens by Mrs. Francis King, whose books are as great a source of pleasure to English as to American garden-lovers. Parts of this book have appeared in article form in *The Field* and *The Bookman* and are reproduced by kind permission of the editors. I am indebted for the illustration of one of the patron saints of gardening—Saint Fiacre—from a miniature in a manuscript in the Bibliothèque Nationale, to Mrs. Roy Hunt of Pittsburgh, Pennsylvania, who most kindly sent me a reproduction of it.

The vignette on the title-page—'Love lays out a garden on the Earth'—is from an eighteenth-century gardening book—not merely a charming 'conceit' of that period, but a beautiful ideal which I think appeals to us all.

ELEANOUR SINCLAIR ROHDE

CRANHAM LODGE,
REIGATE, SURREY.
November, 1932.

CONTENTS

LIST OF ILLUSTRATIONS

LIST OF ILLUSTRATIONS

LIST OF ILLUSTRATIONS

THE STORY OF THE GARDEN

CHAPTER I

THE TRADITIONAL INFLUENCE OF ANCIENT GARDEN LORE

It is a curious fact that all the knowledge we have of the most ancient gardens is of pleasaunces of great splendour. Of the humble beginnings of the art of gardening there are no records. This is true not only in regard to the civilizations of the ancient East, but also those pleasure grounds whose architectural remains in Mexico testify to a garden-craft of great magnificence, and deriving from what antiquity can only be conjectured. The old belief that these great civilizations of the East and West had a common origin in Atlantis certainly makes a stronger appeal to the imagination than the modern theory that the earliest civilizations of the American continent were drawn ultimately from Egypt and Babylonia, India and Indonesia, China, Japan and Oceania, and date back to a time when Europe was in the Neolithic phase of culture.

Whatever their ultimate source may be, our gardens are not only of an ancient lineage, but both in architecture and symbolism their origin was ' exceeding magnifical '. There is little in the modern world to compare with the splendour of the gardens of ancient Egypt, the pleasure grounds of Babylon, the Chinese gardens of antiquity, the gardens of the early Mexican civilization, or even those made by the Emperor Bābār. The beauty of the old symbolism—the little we understand of it—is as interesting as the gardens themselves. To the Eastern mind symbolism has always been of paramount importance; it is a more striking feature of some of the finest monuments of antiquity—at least to some minds—than their grandeur. Symbolism nowadays is conspicuous by its absence, but it was not until the landscape school destroyed the beautiful formal gardens that we lost the ancient traditions of the craft together with the symbolism.

The garden architecture of the greater part of two

B   I

continents—Europe and Asia—was for centuries dominated by traditional forms deriving apparently from the two oldest civilizations—Egypt and Babylon, and to these, owing to the discoveries during the last two years in Sind and Punjab, must now be added a third—prehistoric India. That this last-mentioned civilization was no mere provincial off-shoot of Mesopotamian culture but was developed ' for countless generations '[1] on the banks of the Indus and its tributaries, is becoming more and more manifest. Who the peoples were who evolved it is still an open question, but it seems reasonable to suppose that they were the Dravidian people described in the Vedas as the Dasyus or Asuras, whose culture was largely destroyed in the second or third millenium B.C.

The civilizations of Egypt and Babylon depended entirely on irrigation, a fact which is of dominating importance in the history of gardening. For every illustration of a mediæval, Tudor, or Stuart garden, every book in the whole range of mediæval, sixteenth and seventeenth-century garden literature, whether English, French, Italian, or Dutch, points to the influence of garden-craft based on the necessity for continual irrigation. The simplest, the most definite and possibly the earliest of all garden plans—a garden divided in four by four rivers issuing from a source in the centre of the garden—is depicted (to quote but a few examples) in the Hindu Vedas, in the Persian garden carpets and in the gardens made by the Emperor Bābār, following probably a traditional plan dating back to what far distant past we do not know. This plan derives ultimately no doubt from the simple lines of the cosmic cross. The most beautiful written record of such a garden plan, i.e. a four-fold field plot divided by four rivers, is that in the second chapter of Genesis. In the symbolism of numbers four is the number of creation, the symbol of nature. The river that ' went out of Eden ' was divided into four heads, there are four corners of the earth, four winds of heaven, four seasons of the year. We find the survival of the ancient four-fold field plot in the plans of Tudor gardens that have come down to us. A still more remarkable example of the force of

[1] I quote from an article in *The Times*, February 26, 1926, by Sir John Marshall, Director-General of Archæology in India.

PERSIAN GARDEN CARPET
(Eighteenth-century)
Victoria and Albert Museum

tradition, even in such a detail as the shapes of garden beds, may be noted in the chess-board arrangement of the beds in the old formal gardens of Western Europe. It is not natural to lay out beds in squares, but in the East this was necessary to facilitate the continual irrigation needed during the dry season, and in western Europe we maintained this traditional lay-out, although with our frequent rainfall it was unnecessary. The revival of the art of gardening in Western Europe coincided with the Crusades, a period when every class of society was brought into close contact with the East, and consciously or unconsciously imbibed much of the garden lore of the unchanging East.

In one of the earliest Egyptian garden plans (from the tomb of a general of Amenophis III, *circa* 1500 B.C.) we find an interesting development of the ancient four-fold field plot. The more one studies this plan the more one is struck with its beauty and symmetry. Instead of four, this vast enclosure is divided into eight gardens, the whole arrangement being remarkable for its balance. The plot surrounded by a wall (probably of crude brick) and surmounted with rounded tiles is four-square, it contains eight gardens (each surrounded by a wall), four of them being water-gardens—the water-fowl and lotuses are clearly depicted. There are two orchards, two summer-houses and four vine pergola walks leading to the house. Apart from the magnificent main entrance there are two small side entrances. Outside one of the outer walls of the garden is a shady avenue running parallel with the wall, and beyond is a canal, a beautiful approach to a desert garden. The entrance is shown through a lofty doorway covered with hieroglyphic inscriptions. This entrance house probably contained a reception-room for guests apart from rooms for the porter, head-gardeners, etc. From the entrance one passes into an enclosure wholly occupied with vine pergolas running in parallel lines. A path in the middle leads directly to the house. The vines are trained on pillars with rafters overhead—the pillars and rafters may have been decorated in colour—and shade the walks. It is easy to visualize the beauty of these four long pergola-shaded walks, especially when the vines were in fruit. The house itself is comparatively small; like the villas of the ancient Romans it is overshadowed by the importance of the garden. Flowers, it will be noted, adorn the rooms on every floor. The four water-gardens are all shown surrounded by grass plots. Two of them are depicted with flower beds on opposite sides and overlooked by summer-houses and shady avenues of trees on two sides; the other two water-gardens with flower beds on one side and shady avenues of trees on three sides. Shady avenues are depicted all round the inner side of the enclosing wall. Beyond date palms and dom palms (the latter easily distinguishable by their bifurcated trunks) the trees in the garden are not specified, but there were doubtless sycomores, figs, and pomegranates.

As in all Eastern gardens water and shady trees are the dominating features. The gardens of the earliest civilizations were water-gardens in every sense. Water was the soul of the eastern paradise; water, both seen and heard, the source of beauty, rest and perpetual freshness. Water figures largely in the Bible, and special emphasis is laid on the power of 'living waters' as distinct from waters stored up during the rainy season. Both the Garden of Eden and Ezekiel's paradise (Ezekiel xxviii. 13, 17) were fertilized by living waters, and one recalls the lines in the Canticles—'a fountain of gardens, a well of living waters and streams from Lebanon' (Cant. iv. 15). The life-giving, purifying power of water was not only the dominant factor in garden planning, not only the central feature of the garden, but the background of the earliest garden symbolism. Throughout Eastern symbolism water has a feminine significance. Even in the earliest Egyptian hieroglyphics a water pot represented womanhood.

Here again the force of tradition is evident, for even in small mediæval and sixteenth-century gardens, fountains were as a rule the central features. It was not till the seventeenth century that the sundial replaced the fountain of olden times.

Shade was second in importance only to water in the gardens of the ancient civilizations. We look down upon the flowers in our gardens, but they looked up to behold the beauty of the trees. Trees are more frequently mentioned than flowers in the Bible, and greater importance is attached to them. To cite but a few instances—the laws concerning trees (Levit. xix. 23 ;

4

xxvii. 30; Deut. xx. 19), Jotham's parable of the trees (Judges ix. 8), Nebuchadnezzar's dream (Daniel iv. 10). Moreover, such records as have come down to us show that the garden-loving rulers and nobles of the early civilizations were enthusiastic collectors of trees. Of the ancient Egyptian rulers, Queen Hatshepsut, Thothmes III and Rameses III were particularly famed in this respect. Queen Hatshepsut's name is always associated with the incense trees brought back by the expedition she sent to 'the land of Punt' (probably Somaliland); Thothmes III, who claimed that he ruled from the fourth cataract of the Nile to the Euphrates and who seems to have been a great flower and garden lover, recorded in one of the halls of Karnak the flowers, trees and animals he brought back with him from his Syrian conquests. Like Solomon, he had a menagerie, and lions, apes, and giraffes were brought to stock it. One of Rameses III's inscriptions states that he imported foreign plants in honour of the god Amon. When he made a new foundation at the delta of the Nile, he made great pleasure gardens 'wide places for walking with all kinds of sweet fruit trees, laden with fruit, a sacred way, beautiful with flowers of all lands, with lotus and papyrus countless as the sands'. Among the gifts to Heliopolis:

'I give thee great gardens, planted with trees and vines in the temple of Atuna. I grant thee grounds with olive trees in the city of On. I provided them with gardeners and numerous people to prepare pure oil of Egypt, to kindle the lamps in thy glorious temple. I grant thee groves and copses with date-palms, ponds planted with lotus flowers, rushes, grasses, and flowers of all lands for thy beautiful face'.

As in all ancient civilizations, certain plants were specially sacred. To the Egyptian the sycomore[1] was the sacred 'solitary' tree. Traditionally, it was the tree which stood at the vault of heaven beside the rising and the setting sun, and that it was fashioned of malachite indicated perhaps that it was for ever green. There is a wealth of literature on the subject of tree worship in general. In connection with gardens it is interesting to note how frequently a solitary tree figures in the records of early pleasaunces. We are carried back in thought to the mystic tree of Accadian literature, the Yggdrasil of Norse

---

[1] *Sycomorus antiquorum syn ficus sycomorus.*

mythology, the Kalpadruma of the Vedas and the Persian *haoma*. The oldest description of a sacred artificial tree is perhaps that to be found in the Mahāwamsa—the imitation of the sacred pipala (fig tree) made by King Duthagamini and set up in Ceylon two centuries before Christ—a tree whose roots were made of coral fixed in an emerald floor, its trunk of silver, its fading leaves of gold, the young leaves and fruit of coral, and above the tree a canopy. Eight lucky signs were depicted on the trunk and in the rows of vases arranged before the tree were four different kinds of sweet perfumes. The date tree has always had a masculine significance, with a further meaning of life, and it was frequently opposed to the cypress, the emblem of death. The most familiar Indian design shows the entwined fruit tree and cypress—emblems of life and death. In the gardens of ancient Byzantium the symbolism of the tree was emphasized by the decorative cone surmounting the fountain—the cone representing probably the cone of the male date palm. One is reminded also of the 'House of the Tree' in old Bagdad, the palace which derived its name from the mystic tree of gold and silver standing in the midst of a great circular pool, and of the tree-fountains made in far-distant parts of Asia.

The interesting point in connection with the traditional influence of this ancient symbolism on Western garden lore is the striking fact that in the gardens described in mediæval fabliaux and romances we find again the symbolic solitary tree and water. For instance, in the mystic garden depicted in the *Romaunt of the Rose*, the most noted piece of garden literature of the Middle Ages, the conspicuous features of the garden are the solitary tree and the fountain beneath it.

Amongst the most attractive of Egyptian garden scenes are those depicting the 'fields of peace' as they so beautifully described the future paradise. Of these much has been written. To flower and garden lovers, however, it is the plant symbolism in the tomb paintings which is of the deepest interest. For the ancient Egyptians saw in the burial of the seed, its germination and growth, the springing up of the glorified resurrection body, the same symbolism, in fact, that S. Paul used (1 Cor. xv. 36–38, 42–44). Another type of plant symbolism is shown in

6

the 'Gardener's tomb' at Thebes.[1] This is the tomb of Sen-nofer, who held various high offices at Thebes during the XVIII Dynasty. Besides being *Erpa* (Hereditary Noble) and *Ha* (Prince or Chief) of Thebes, he was also Overseer of the garden, fields, and granaries of the god Amon. Sen-nofer describes himself as being greatly beloved by the King (Amenhotep II, *circa* 1449–1423 B.C.) and in the tomb he is once styled by the extraordinary title of Zat of Amen. The plant symbolism in the inner chamber is beautiful. The two jackals on pylons facing each other represent Anubis the guardian of tombs—Anubis on the right representing the west or the setting sun, the life that is over; Anubis on the left, the east or the new day, the new and more glorious life. In this inner chamber (as in the outer) a luxuriant vine overspreads the whole of the ceiling and in the inner chamber the vine on the one side is shown stripped of fruit (the life that is over) while on the other side it is loaded with clusters of ripe grapes, setting forth the richness of the life to come. It is notable that the vine is absent above the representation of the funeral ceremonies, but the vine is shown immediately over the figure of Osiris, the source of the new life of the deceased. Amidst the branches a vulture is depicted with outspread wings, holding the symbol of life in each talon. Most beautiful of all, perhaps, is the symbolism on the pillars. Here in the last pair of pictures Sen-nofer in his new life is represented as growing like a tree. In the last picture he is seated, arrayed magnificently with gold ornaments, holding his official baton in his right hand and in his left a lotus flower, which he smells. It is significant that in this picture he is both enveloped by the sycamore and the branches of the tree seem to be growing out of all parts of his head and body—representing his perfect growth in Osiris. Beside him kneels his wife Meryt and before them is a table with three vases wreathed with lotus buds and above the vases is one fully opened lotus flower and two in bud. Overhead are inscribed long prayers, including the petition 'May he (Osiris) grant that his (Sen-nofer's) dead body may germinate like a seed in the Netherworld'; and in the prayer along the angle at the left-hand wall there is the petition that 'Sen-nofer may

[1] See *The Gardener's Tomb*, by C. Campbell, D.D.

behold the disc of the sun and smell the sweet breeze of the North '.

If it is in the Egyptian tomb paintings that we find the earliest illustrations of the rectangular formal garden, it is in the records of ancient Babylon and Assyria that we find the earliest accounts of the park and the terraced garden. In the Gilgamesh epic we find the first mention of a park, though not a park in the modern sense, for it was not enclosed, nor was it a park in the early Eastern sense, in that it was not a plantation on formal lines. That parks from the earliest times were laid out on formal lines is shown by the Chaldaic word, *kiru*, signifying ' a row of trees ', the word used in the most ancient times to denote a formal plantation as distinct from *qister* (a wood).[1] Tiglath Pileser I was the first to record (*circa* 1100 B.C.) that he had enriched the Assyrian parks with foreign trees.

' Cedars and Ukarin (box) Allakanu wood have I brought from the lands which I conquered, trees which none of the kings my fore-fathers had planted ; these trees I took and planted them in the parks of my country, these trees I planted in the parks of Assyria '.

Parks were not the only type of pleasure ground even in ancient Assyria, for as early as 2340 B.C. it is recorded of King Gudea that he planted vineyards and made fish ponds bordered with reeds. Sennacherib made both a magnificent park beyond the precincts of his palace and gardens of vast extent. ' At the command of the gods the gardens with vine and fruit plantations, and herbs flourish mightily '. He states that he levelled mountain and field, and that these parks and gardens were filled with the choicest products of the mountains and countries around—' all spice plants from the land of the Hittites, myrrh which grows better in the gardens than in its native country, plantations of vines from the hills, fruits from every land '.

To Babylon is always ascribed the origin of the terraced garden, in the ' hanging gardens of Babylon '. Although one of the seven wonders of the ancient world, the exact nature of these gardens has always been a source of discussion. Nor have they ever been satisfactorily explained, for although they

---

[1] See *A History of Garden Art*, by M. L. Gothein.

The Emperor Babar laying out The Garden of Fidelity

(From the Emperor Babar's Memoirs)

Victoria and Albert Museum

INDIAN GARDEN PAVILION

SHAH JEHAN RIDING IN A FORMAL GARDEN
(Late Moghul, c.1730)
Museum of Fine Arts, Boston, Mass

were described in antiquity as the most remarkable feature of a great city, no remains have ever been excavated which could be identified with them. During Mr. Woolley's excavations at Ur, structural arrangements were found in the masonry of the temple of the Moon-god, which could only be explained as having been made to drain the layers of soil on the terraces of the temple. Presumably, therefore, these terraces were planted with trees and shrubs and possibly flowers. The terraces of the temple of Bel-Marduk at Babylon were probably similarly planted with trees and must have presented a magnificent spectacle when each terrace was massed with bloom. Strabo (XVI. 1, 5) states that the 'hanging gardens' of Babylon 'consist of vaulted terraces raised one above another'. Diodorus Siculus (II. 10, 2–6), who denies that they were made by Semiramis, describes them as being square, and each terrace provided with earth of sufficient depth to grow trees, and that the whole looked like a mountain. Berosus (260 B.C.) states that this wonderful erection was made by Nebuchadnezzar II for his Median wife.

The ancient veneration for 'high places' is probably the origin of the 'hanging garden', which may be seen also in the *ziggurats* of Babylonian times, the 'high places' of the Bible, the 'mountain of the pure sons of Adam' in Apocryphal literature, and in the Vedas the sacred Mount Meru, whence flowed north, south, east, and west the four fertilizing streams. Paradise, in early tradition, was frequently associated with a high mountain, and it is interesting to recall that Milton describes an elevated paradise. There is no example to-day of an artificial 'mountain' laid out in garden terraces, but in the seven-terraced Bagh-i-takt (literally the 'Garden of the Throne') near Shiraz, which even in its present mournful condition is one of the great gardens of the world, and the terraced gardens of Italy, we see a faint reflection of those made in the past. In the case of the terraced Italian garden, however, as in that of the Bagh-i-takt, it is only one side of a natural slope that is transformed by terraces—not an artificial 'mountain'.

It seems curious that the tradition of a mount should have been so faithfully copied, although apparently only on a small scale, as late as Tudor and Stuart times. They seem to have been more commonly made in gardens in these islands than on the continent. Bacon, in his famous essay, mentions a mount 'in the very middle of the garden '. The best illustrations of mounts in Stuart times are those depicted in New College garden and Wadham garden in Loggan's *Oxonia illustrata* and Queen's garden and Pembroke garden in his *Cantabrigia illustrata*. Although we have no definite evidence of the influence of traditional garden lore in these islands until early mediæval days, it is interesting to remember that mounts and probably mazes figured strikingly in the days of the ancient Britons.[1]

[1] It has long since been amply proved that our British ancestors were a highly cultured people. Their astronomical knowledge has never been disputed; legal authorities (Fortescue and Coke. See *De Laudibus Legum Angliæ*; Coke, Preface to third volume of Pleadings) assert that the Molmutine laws promulgated by the British king Molmutius are the foundation of British liberties and have remained the unwritten laws of this island; the headquarters of the Druidic order, the oldest religious and educational system in Europe, was in Britain, and the youths, not only of Britain but also of Gaul, were sent to British universities; the majority of their thirty-one universities give their names to this day to the capitals of our counties; the Druidic Triads are ' the oldest literature in the oldest living language in Europe '; splendid specimens of British art may be seen in the British Museum, notably their bronze shields and enamelled horse-trappings (British craftsmen were taken to Rome to teach the art of enamelling), and British justice, patriotism and humanity were always a source of profound admiration even to their enemies. Until the last century the authority of the oldest British historians, Gildas and Nennius, was never questioned, and it was only German scholars who stated (with no definite proof) that the coming of Brutus to Britain was a ' fable '. The discoveries of Professors Schliemann and Sayce have thrown light on the subject of Trojan influence on British civilization which goes far to disprove that the coming of Brutus was ' fabulous '. Traditions, as Disraeli said, can neither be made nor destroyed, and we may yet learn that the ancient traditions, notably those concerning the first settlement in this island by Britains led by Hu Gaderu about the time of Abraham, embodied in the Triads and the Mabinogion, are historical facts. For fifteen hundred years, traditions of British civilization were unquestioned, and now there is every reason to believe that the citizens of London, Winton, and Caerleon-on-Usk, to mention but a few, were citizens of no mean cities. Nothing indeed could be more striking than the difference between the rude remains of the aborigines who inhabited these islands and the stupendous monuments of the early Britons whose origin was apparently in Accadia, the southern province of Babylonia.

Their artificial ' mounts ' and ' holy hills ' in these islands are amongst the most famous in the world—notably Silbury (artificial, except where a natural hillock was partly utilized), Glastonbury Tor, St. Katherine's Hill at Winchester, the Round Table Mound at Windsor ('the holy mound of the ruler' to give it its Welsh name, a mound which has been proved to be indisputably artificial) and the Eton ' Montem ', which has now partially lost its original form. Like the *ziggurats* of Babylon, the British mounts were terraced, and as modern research has shown, the lines were drawn by men who were skilled astronomers. Further, it is interesting to recall the symbolism of dry land appearing above the sea connected with these ancient British mounds. A British Gorsedd (Supreme Seat) was always associated with a symbolic trench. Like the *ziggurats* of Babylon these mounts were prototypes of the mounts which were so curious a feature of gardens in mediæval, Tudor, and Stuart days.

How remarkable it is that the very name of London commemorates one of these ' holy hills '—Llandin (*llan*=sacred, *din*=eminence).[1] The highest of the prehistoric ' holy hills ' was Parliament Hill. To this day anyone may see the vestige that remains of the old symbolic trench in the ponds, now used for bathing and boating. The ' Llandin ' is sometimes called the ' Areopagus ' of Britain, for there is the tradition that S. Paul preached from its summit. (For this reason he became the patron saint of our capital and his emblem, the sword of martyrdom, is incorporated in the arms of the City.) On the Bryn Gwyn (*bryn*=hill, *gwyn*=white or holy) now stands the White Tower of the Tower of London, from time immemorial associated with our Kings. Traditionally the White Mound (the site of the White Tower) was the burial place of Brutus and Imogene, *circa* 1100 B.C., also of Molmutius, the great law-giver King. This mound is also associated with King Belin, whose name lingers to this day in Billingsgate, and his descendant, Lludd (founder of Ludgate). The summit of the ancient mount is now crowned by the Conqueror's Norman chapel. Penton (*pen*=head, *ton*=sacred mound) is to this day known by its ancient name. It has long since lost its circular

[1] See *Prehistoric London*, by E. O. Gordon.

contour, and it seems impossible to visualize it as it was even in Elizabethan days, when, as Gerard tells us in his Herbal, white saxifrage grew abundantly on it, but even now one may realize from its summit what a magnificent view it commanded of the ancient city. It was probably the site of an observatory, for no one has yet estimated the date of the well under Sadlers' Wells Theatre. Like the holy well in Deans Yard, Westminster, it was doubtless used by the ancient astronomers.[1] On Thorney Island was the Tothill (sacred mound). No trace of the old 'Mount' remains now, but we know from John Norden, the topographer of Westminster in Elizabeth's reign, that it existed then—'Tothill Street, lying in the west part of the cytie, taketh name of a hill near it which is called Toote-hill'. This mount is also marked in Rocque's map (1746) on Toothill Fields at the bend of the ancient causeway, Horseferry Road. In the opinion of Dean Buckland, the Druidical College stood on the site of the present College Gardens. In the vicinity was an ancient sanctuary, of which the privileges were confirmed by Edward the Confessor, and to this day the open space in front of the west doors of the Abbey is known as the Broad Sanctuary.

Mounts indeed seem to have been the most prominent features of prehistoric London and the most ancient traditions of our capital are those associated with the worship of the Most High. Druidism, as many authorities have emphasized, was not only one of the most ancient, but one of the purest religions. No graven images have ever been found in connection with the religious monuments of our British ancestors, but only unwrought stones. In 1901 when the great trilithon of Stonehenge

---

[1] Strabo, it will be remembered, mentioned a well of this type at Syene, and in the modern observatories at Wilson and Potsdam, wells of the same type, arranged with mirrors, are used by distinguished astronomers of to-day. Merlin's Cave in Penton, associated with the Druid astronomer of King Arthur's reign, was a fashionable resort even as late as the eighteenth century. In connection with this 'astronomer's well' it is interesting to recall that in the grounds of Greenwich Observatory is a well of unknown antiquity. As an old print in the observatory testifies, it was used by Flamsteed, the first Astronomer Royal, for making daylight observations, probably in precisely the same way as the Druid astronomers in ancient times.

was raised, flint hammers were found, which confirmed the old tradition that in making cuttings for religious purposes the Druids used only flints. (Cf. And there shalt thou build an altar unto the Lord thy God, an altar of stones : thou shalt not lift up any iron tool upon them. Deut. XXVII. 5.) The mounts of the heathen nations seem to have been closely connected with their sacrificial groves, so frequently mentioned in the Bible and never without condemnation. There is no mention of sacrificial groves in ancient British literature and their mounts are suggestive rather of the holy mounts of the Bible, notably Mount Sinai and the Mount of Olives. Like the Israelites the ancient Britons worshipped the One God, the Three in One, the second Person of the Druidic Trinity being Esu or Yesu. To quote but one of their utterances :

Let God be praised in the beginning and the end,
Who supplicates Him, He will neither despise nor refuse.
God above us, God before us, God possessing (all things),
May the Father of Heaven grant us a portion of mercy.

It is indeed striking that for centuries the most remarkable features of gardens in these islands were mounts which perhaps commemorated the 'high places' or 'holy hills' connected with the religion of our ancestors.

Mazes have captivated human imagination for wellnigh four thousand years, and Pliny, it will be remembered, described them as 'the most stupendous works on which mankind has expended its labours'. In pleasure grounds they were apparently first made to recall the splendour of those vast and curious works, and as features of gardens they have persisted through the centuries to this day. To our race they are peculiarly interesting, for in these islands the numerous Troy towns or mazes, cut in the turf from time immemorial, commemorated originally the ancient city of Troy, and Brutus (leader of the second colonization of this island by Britons), the prince who tradition says was crowned king in Britain *circa* 1185 B.C. Modern research has gone far to prove the truth of this ancient 'fable'. Further, more than one distinguished authority has commented on the fact that the Saffron Walden Maze, the maze on St. Catherine's Hill, Winchester, and the Alkborough

Maze, are precisely the same as the three types of mazes portrayed on the Cretan coins, and Crete, according to Virgil, was once the home of the Trojan race. According to Fitz-Stephen, the Troy Game was played in the streets of London in Plantagenet days by the youths of the Royal household every Sunday in Lent, the King and his courtiers being present. According to many authorities on street games, some of those played by children to-day resemble the old Troy Town game. Mazes, like mounts, were indeed a significant and interesting feature of the old formal gardens.

Apart from the dominant influence of Eastern tradition in garden architecture, it is, I think, a little difficult for us to realize that even the types of gardens in mediæval days had more in common with Eastern than with modern types. The earliest records of mediæval pleasure grounds of importance show that they were primarily tree gardens, copies of the ' paradises ' of the older civilizations. The tradition had been notably maintained by the Medes and Persians, who were famed not only for their hunting parks, but also for those adorned with trees as desirable for their fruit as for their beauty, and enclosures filled with rare animals. Charlemagne's garden (see his *De villis et curtis*) was essentially of the nature of a Persian park. He too had a menagerie, which contained even an elephant. (This unfortunate animal—a gift from the Sultan of Bagdad—was made to walk the whole distance to Aix-la-Chapelle, a journey which took seven years.) Henry I, of England, the first English King who is recorded to have made a pleasaunce, established a park at Woodstock, and for his amusement kept ' lyons, leopards, strange spotted beasts, porcupines, camells and such like animals ' which were sent him from ' divers outlandish Lands '. Petrus Crescentius, the thirteenth-century author of the most noted mediæval treatise on gardens, describes a menagerie as an essential feature of a royal garden. Moreover, it is noteworthy that in the ' royal ' section flowers are not even mentioned. ' The gardens of royal personages, and powerful and wealthy lords ' were to be tree gardens, enclosed with lofty walls and adorned with fountains, pavilions and fish-pools. In fact, a true Eastern paradise, in spite of the fact that shade (on which he lays great emphasis) is not as essential in Western as in Eastern lands. We seem to be returning to the tree gardens of olden days, for the most notable gardens to-day are chiefly collections of trees and shrubs rather than of herbaceous plants and annuals.

The gardens of moderate size in mediæval and even early Tudor days in this country were of the same types as in Biblical times. Solomon had every kind of Eastern garden, his orchards, herb gardens, and vineyards being those on which most emphasis is laid in the Canticles. Orchards, herb gardens and vineyards were the representative gardens, not only in these islands but in western Europe generally. It is impossible even to visualize correctly the various types of mediæval gardens if one looks at them from a modern standpoint. It is essential to bear in mind their Eastern nature. Our orchards and herb gardens to-day bear little resemblance to those of mediæval, Tudor, or even Stuart days. Orchards in those days, as in Biblical times and in the days of the most ancient civilizations, were pleasure gardens, laid out on formal lines and adorned with fountains, pavilions, grass plots, etc. Herb gardens were not only for use, but for beauty; roses, lilies, gillyflowers, primroses, violets, irises, and many other flowers being grown in them, and the gardens themselves laid out in formal beds. Vineyards in Biblical times, as in the days of ancient Egypt and Assyria, were pleasure gardens, and so apparently were the vineyards belonging to large houses in these islands even in Shakespeare's time. Further, as in Egyptian days, vines in England were trained to poles and rafters. Both Shakespeare and Gerard refer to this as the common method of growing them. Solomon commented on the sweet smell of vine blossom. So did Bacon; and the latter reckoned 'vine flowers' among the 'things of beauty in season' in May and June.

Garden-houses, again, in mediæval and Tudor times were Eastern in their magnificence. The Persians delighted in these costly pavilions, and the most magnificent garden-house described in literature is surely that mentioned in the Book of Esther as belonging to the Persian King Ahasuerus. With its divans of gold and silver, its gorgeous hangings 'white, green, and blue, fastened with cords of fine linen and purple to silver rings and pillars of marble' and its pavement of red, blue, and white, and black marble ' (Esth. i. 6), this pavilion must have been worthy of the garden in which the King entertained ' the power of Persia and Media, the nobles and princes of the provinces '. Garden-houses in Tudor days were frequently erected for great banquets, and even those of a permanent nature were larger than the few examples seen to-day.

Further, it is curious to find traces of the survival of the old Eastern double enclosure of vineyards and gardens. The hedge of thorns and the wall (the one a living, the other a dead material) are mentioned by Isaiah—' And now go to ; I will tell you what I will do to my vineyard ; I will take away the hedge thereof and it shall be eaten up and break down the wall thereof.' (Isa. v. 5.) The most interesting example of the survival of the old double enclosure in mediæval gardens is in Pinturicchio's fresco of about 1495 in the Vatican. This shows a small garden surrounded by a brick wall, also an inner fence of gilded reeds. The inner fence is obviously unnecessary and merely a traditional feature. (See illustration.)

Of the culture of prehistoric India we as yet know but a fragment, and nothing that sheds any light on the gardens. There is an almost limitless field for the excavator ; for between 3000 and 4000 miles of river bed wait to be unearthed. But wherever trenches have been dug at Mohenjo-daro they have disclosed the remains of a finely built city of the third millenium B.C. and beneath layer after layer of earlier structures. The future may disclose the similarity of this culture with that of Egypt and Babylon, and of their plant lore we may learn much. Amongst the numerous seals found at Mohenjo-daro was one showing the sacred pipal tree of India with twin heads of antelope springing from its stem.

Apart from tree worship, the most ancient plant symbolism apparently is that connected with the lotus flower, and to students of ancient garden lore it is of profound interest that the symbolism of the lotus is intimately connected with the symbolism of the purity and beauty of water. No authority has yet stated whether the original centre of the World Lotus was in the mountains of Upper Egypt or the Himalayas. One distinguished authority[1] tells us that all Indian poetry and

[1] E. B. Havell.

mythology point to the Himalayas as the centre of the world and the throne of the gods, that the feeling of awe and adoration which their majesty inspired is the chief clue to the meaning of Indian symbolism. As the ancient Egyptians venerated the remote mountains of Upper Egypt as the source of the life-giving Nile, so to the Himalayan people in Vedic times the lofty peaks were holy, not merely for their own majestic beauty but because they guarded the worshipful sources of life, the pure sources of the mighty rivers which made the lowlands fertile. Most sacred of all was Lake Mānasarovara, about 15,500 feet above sea level, near the centre of the Himalayas, the lake near which the Indus, the Brahmaputra and the Ganges have their sources. Of this region, Vishnu Purāna says it is the place where Brahma has his throne 'like the seed vessel of a lotus'. In ancient Vedic symbolism Asia was a four-petalled lotus flower; China being the eastern petal, Persia and the regions beyond the western, Turkestan the northern, the southernmost of the four great outer petals being the plains of India. The upturned petals of the flower were the snowy peaks of the Himalayas. The mighty peaks of the 'Roof of the World' were the inner circle of the World Lotus, and here the Devas themselves had their palaces and lotus thrones. The seed vessel of the World Lotus was Brahma's holy city near Mount Kailāsa and the blue waters of Lake Mānasarovara. There was the further mystic symbolism of the lotus—the root Brahma, the source of all creation, the stalk Māyā, the phenomenon of this world and the flower the world itself, and the fruit the soul when liberated. In Indian art, the Buddha's throne is nearly always represented with the outer fringe of petals turned downwards, frequently the whole flower is shown with the petals turned down. As Mr. E. B. Havell has pointed out:

'This symbolism is so characteristically Indian and so widely diffused in early Buddhist art, that the mere coincidence of "bell shaped" capitals occurring in Persia hardly justifies the name which archæologists have given them. Perhaps Persia borrowed the idea from India, the land of the lotus, together with the flower itself. But it is much more probable that it was evolved by the carvers of the sacrificial posts in Vedic times, when the Aryans occupied the valley of the Euphrates and were in contact with Egypt and Assyria and with their relatives in Iran '.

The traditional plan on which the far-famed Moghul gardens were planned may be in origin as ancient as the symbolism of the World Lotus. As his Memoirs show, the Emperor Bābār laid out his Char-Bagh (four-sided garden) on a plan resembling the four-fold field plot of Vedic literature, the symbolic central raised platform corresponding to the sacred Mount Meru. The chief pleasaunce which for twenty years he laboured to beautify was surrounded with a high enclosing wall and the site divided into four parts by walks paved with stone or marble. Each of these walks led to a gateway or pavilion placed in the centre of one of the walls. The four rectangular plots were divided into still smaller plots by paths parallel with the main walks. It was a ' watered garden ', for down the centre of each walk on each side stone channels were cut whereby the water could be conveyed to his plantations of trees. During his ten years of wandering, when his life had been a series of hairbreadth escapes, Bābār never seems to have failed to observe any unusual plant or any rare bird. The Central Asian highlands were so familiar to him, that he knew whence to fill his garden with treasures and no gift pleased him so much as that of a rare tree or seeds of plants unknown to him. No sooner had Bābār made himself ruler of the vast territories stretching from the Himalayas to the Vindhyas than he established the garden at Agra which must have been one of the wonders of the age. Six hundred and eighty masons and thousands of labourers worked under not only overseers but the Emperor's vigilant eyes and when he held his first great durbar in the palace garden the ambassadors from sovereign potentates were amazed at its splendour. The gardens made by his descendants—notably those of the Taj and the Shalimar Bagh— give some indication of the grandeur of those made by the founder of the Moghul dynasty. In Europe a faint reflection of the beauty of ancient symbolic garden architecture is preserved in the Moorish gardens in Spain.

To what similar if not same ancient origin may be ascribed the oldest gardens in America, of which any records have come down to us ?

INFLUENCE OF ANCIENT GARDEN LORE

According both to the Spanish accounts of them and the remains of the Texcoan pleasaunce which exist to this day, the gardens of ancient Mexico were of a splendour comparable only to those of the great civilizations of the East. The detailed descriptions given by Spanish eye-witnesses in the early sixteenth century testify to a garden tradition of great magnificence, already established for many centuries and dating back to what remote past can only be imagined. Further it is noteworthy that in the language of the Nahuas there are words describing different types of gardens, ranging from the humble *xochichinancalli*—literally 'flower place enclosed by a cane or reed fence'—to *xochitecpancalli*—literally 'palace of flowers', a beautiful name to designate a lordly pleasure ground.[1] Most striking of all surely is the fact that in ancient Mexico there was apparently the same cult for gardens on high places as in ancient Babylon. Not only Montezuma but the Lords of Texcoco and the Tarascan rulers built these terraced gardens. The ruler of Mexico, being both high priest as well as King, was obliged to rise at midnight to 'observe the north star, the Pleiades and other constellations'. Dr. Cervantes de Salazar, writing in 1565, states briefly that the Indians preferred to build their gardens on hills rather than on plains. It is at least possible that when the astronomer priests were engaged in the worship of the Moon-god on the *ziggurat* of ancient Babylon, astronomer priests in ancient Mexico on similar 'high places' were engaged in performing similar rites.

Magnificent as were Montezuma's own gardens, the records show they they were not comparable to those of his ancestors. Montezuma the Elder, soon after his accession about 1450, decided to restore the gardens of his ancestors at Huaxtepec 'where there were rocks with carved effigies of his forefathers, fountains, gardens, trees with flowers, and trees yielding fruit'. The monarch sent Pinotetl, his chief overseer, with orders to restore the irrigation system, the fountains and reservoirs. At the same time he sent an embassy to the Lord of Cuetlaxtla, on the tropical coast region, requesting him to send the vanilla orchid, magnolia, and cacao trees and other rare plants, together

[1] See *The Gardens of Ancient Mexico*, by Z. Nuttall. (The Smithsonian Report for 1923.)

with native gardeners to plant and tend them. The Lord of Cuetlaxtla not only sent a vast number of plants and trees with their roots in earth, but the bundles were wrapped in exquisitely woven mantles. On arrival the gardeners begged permission to observe certain ceremonies before planting. They fasted for eight days, drew blood from their ears, and anointed the plants, and to the god of flowers they offered many dead quail, after sprinkling the soil and the plants with blood. They predicted that none of them would be lost after observation of these ceremonies. Within three years everything they had brought was growing so luxuriantly that they themselves were amazed and said that not even in their native soil had they flowered so soon. It was of this tropical garden at Huaxtepec that Cortes wrote to Charles V, in a letter dated May 15, 1522, that it was ' the finest, pleasantest, and largest that ever was seen, having a circumference of two leagues '. A stream, he added, with high banks ran through it and for the distance of two shots from a crossbow there were arbours and refreshing gardens and an infinite number of different kinds of fruit trees, many herbs and sweet-scented flowers. The historian Torquemada adds the information that besides the beautiful groves, fountains, rest houses, gardens filled with flowers, fruit and game, there were bowers, oratories, and observatories with the steps leading to them cut in the solid rock.

The gardens of his successor and namesake Montezuma are described thus by Dr. Cervantes de Salazar in 1565 :

' This great monarch had many pleasaunces and spacious gardens with paths and channels for irrigation. These gardens contained only medicinal and aromatic herbs, flowers, native roses and trees with fragrant blossoms, of which there are many kinds. He ordered his physicians to make experiments with the medicinal herbs and to employ those best known and tried as remedies in healing the ills of the lords of his court. These gardens gave great pleasure to all who visited them on account of the flowers and roses they contained and of the fragrance they gave forth, especially in the mornings and evenings. It was well worth seeing with how much art and delicacy a thousand figures of persons were made by means of leaves and flowers, also the seats, temples, and the other constructions which so greatly adorned these places '.

In these flower gardens Montezuma did not allow any vegetables or fruit to be grown, saying that it was not kingly to cultivate plants for utility or profit. Vegetable gardens and orchards, he said, were for slaves or merchants. At the same time he owned such, but they were at a distance and he seldom visited them. Outside the city of Mexico he had houses in extensive groves of trees surrounded by water, so that the game could not escape and he could be certain of his quarry.

During his captivity Montezuma frequently begged permission from Cortes to visit those of his gardens which were situated within two leagues of the capital, a request which Cortes never denied.

Of the ancient 'Athens of America'—Texcoco—much has been written. The splendour of the gardens there seems to have exceeded even those made by Montezuma the Elder.

The great Nezahualcoyotl, king, law-giver, poet and philosopher, who was born in 1403, not only inherited many gardens from his ancestors, but being an ardent flower-lover, he created eight new pleasaunces, adorned with canals, fountains, baths, and other water-works, and with flowers and trees brought from remote places. Many of the walls of his palace were adorned with pictures of tropical species he was unable to grow. Doctor Hernandez, the sixteenth-century Spanish physician who saw them, comments on the botanical accuracy of these paintings. Friar Matilinia, writing in the middle of the sixteenth century, described as particularly worth seeing the poet king's palace and its 'enclosed garden, containing more than a thousand very large and very beautiful cypress trees', and another palace with 'many gardens and an immense pool'. Two modern writers, Brantz Mayer and Professor E. B. Tylor, describing the ancient grove of cypresses, comment on the fact that the trees were arranged in a square corresponding with the points of the compass. Mayer, writing in 1850, says :

'The grove is formed by double rows of gigantic cypresses, about 500 in number, arranged in a square corresponding with the points of the compass and enclosing an area of about ten acres. At the north-western point of this quadrangle another double row of lordly cypresses runs westwardly toward a dyke, north of which there is a deep oblong tank neatly vaulted and filled with water. . . . Along the raised banks and beneath the double line of the majestic trees were the walks and orchards in which Nezahualcoyotl and his courtiers amused themselves '.

Professor E. B. Tylor, who visited the place in 1856, records :

' This is a grand square, looking towards the cardinal points and composed of ahuehuetes, grand old deciduous cypresses, many of them forty feet around and older than the discovery of America '.

A sixteenth-century map shows that at that time there was another grove planted in a circle beyond the square enclosure. Many of the grand old trees are still living, silent witnesses of the stately splendour of the ancient Mexican pleasure gardens.

Of the king's ' hanging garden ' on the hill of Texcotzinco overlooking the lake of Texcoco, there are to this day the architectural remains, which testify to its former magnificence. Mayer says :

' the hill of Texcotzinco is connected with another hill on the east by a tall embankment about 200 feet high, upon whose level tops, which may be crossed by three persons on horseback abreast, are the remains of an ancient aqueduct built of baked clay, the pipes of which are now as perfect as the day they were first laid '.

There are still the remains of a small palace on the crest of the hill, also of a building with flights of steps which may have led to the tower, which according to the native historians was nine stories high, another which may have been an outdoor theatre, a large circular bathing pool and small circular fountain on a platform at the base of a flight of steps, all hewn out of the solid rock. Most remarkable of all is the large circular bath cut out of an enormous block of porphyry and projecting into space. W. Bullock described it as ' standing out like a martin's nest from the side of a house '. It is not only an extraordinary bath but still more extraordinarily placed. It is a beautiful basin about 12 feet long by 8 feet wide, having a well 5 feet by 4 feet deep in the centre, surrounded by a parapet or rim 2 feet 6 inches high, with a throne or chair such as is represented in ancient pictures to have been used by kings.

' There are steps into the basin or bath, the whole cut out of the living porphyry rock with the most mathematical precision and polished in the most beautiful manner '.

If the gardens of ancient Mexico originated from the same source as those of the great civilizations of the East, it is at least possible that labyrinths may some day be traced to the same origin. In the Old World labyrinths and mazes were constructed, as far as we know, in the first instance, in connection with the mysteries, particularly the mysteries of Isis and the Eleusinian mysteries. Little is as yet known of labyrinths in connection with the ancient civilizations of America, but they, in common with the gardens of the great civilizations of both the Old and New World, may trace back to an origin of strange antiquity.

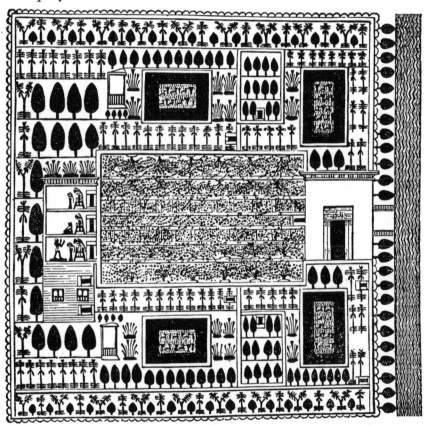

Plan of an Egyptian garden (*circa* 1500 B.C.), from the tomb of a general of Amenophis III. (See p. 4).

23

There has been only one period in history when the gardens of western Europe were alike—during the supremacy of Rome. In the provinces, even so far apart as North Africa and Britain, luxurious villas compensated their owners for their lengthy exile from the capital. At least in the southern part of this island there were doubtless gardens which were reproductions of the ordered beauty of those in Italy, though they probably never equalled the most splendid—for instance, those attached to Nero's Golden House, which must have extended from above the Baths of Trajan to the gardens of Mæcenas; or Pliny's winter villa at Laurentinum. The gardens of Rome in early days were apparently of marked simplicity, but those of imperial Rome were imitations of the splendours of the pleasure grounds of the East. Foreign wars, especially the conquest of Greece, and the influence of semi-Oriental customs, fatally affected the old simplicity and the new civilization was soon reflected in the gardens. Imperial Rome was circled with a girdle of magnificent pleasure grounds—terraces with marble colonnades, nymphæa, rose gardens, fountains and fish ponds, avenues of ilex and cork trees, cool retreats shaded by cypress, stone pines, chestnuts, planes, bay-laurels, walnuts and acacias, and adorned with the absurd but skilled work of the topiarists. No city in the outlying parts of the Roman dominions could have vied with the magnificence and luxury of the gardens of imperial Rome, not only the vast pleasaunces, but the courtyards, balconies, and roof-gardens, and the forcing-houses where roses bloomed in winter under the protection of mica.

It is more likely that the Roman gardens in these islands were similar to those depicted in the Pompeian frescoes—enclosures laid out on formal lines, with flower-beds both round and rectangular edged with box, and overlooked by a colonnade, generally with three wings with pavilions at each corner. Then perhaps on another terrace paths bordered with topiary work, a form of horticulture apparently purely Roman in origin. The origin of topiary work is not known for certain,

A dance in a garden

(From a fifteenth-century copy of *Le Roman de la Rose*)
British Library

but according to Pliny it was invented by one Cnæus Martius, and even in Pliny's day the art was so advanced that fleets of ships and hunting scenes were shown in clipped evergreens. Above all flowers the Romans loved roses, violets, narcissi and hyacinths.   The rose belongs to their earliest traditions and they spread its culture wherever they conquered.   They were skilled in grafting, budding, pruning, and fumigating.   In Rome itself they cultivated the Campanian, the scented Milesian rose, the monthly blooming Carthaginian roses, the Pæstum rose (highly valued for its two periods of blooming), the musk rose and the gallica.   If the gallica rose were not already known in this island, it would surely have been introduced by them. *Narcissus poeticus* is described as a native of Britain in *Hortus Kewensis*, but Phillips in his *Flora Historica* (1824), says :

'This narcissus seldom produces seed in England, even by the assistance of cultivation, and we are therefore of opinion that the few plants which have been found at Shorne between Gravesend and Rochester as well as those discovered in Norfolk are the offsets from imported plants, probably of as early a date as the time of the Romans, who, we may naturally conclude, would not fail to plant the flower of their favourite poet, when we discover that they paved the floors of their dwellings with *tessellæ* that represented his tales '.

The 'hyacinth' of the classics is probably *h. orientalis*, for Homer mentions it amongst the fragrant flowers of spring, and Pliny describes it as having grass-like leaves and the scent of the grape flower.   Other poets speak of its sapphire, crimson, purple, and white bells.   Their hyacinths, however, can have borne little resemblance to the coarse florists' types of to-day. Even the illustrations of 300 years ago show them as far more delicate and graceful flowers.   Although no definite information has come down to us it is more than probable that even in these islands vegetables and fruit were grown in abundance, for the wealthy Roman spared neither money nor pains to have the best of both.   Cabbages were highly valued in Rome ; indeed, Cato regarded them as the best of all vegetables ; good both cooked and raw dressed with vinegar.   Asparagus, endive, lettuce, beet, fennel, and leek may have been amongst their introductions.   Tacitus states that all vegetables and fruits could be grown in Britain, save the olive and the vine. He wrote in the first century and the introduction of vines into this country is usually ascribed to the Emperor Probus. The wild cherry is indigenous, but Pliny says the cherry was introduced during the first half of the first century ; he referred probably to a cultivated type. Figs were amongst the most valued fruits in ancient Rome, and according to tradition figs were first grown in this island in the sheltered parts of the Sussex coast in Roman days. According to another tradition, however, an abbot of Fécamp introduced the culture of the fig into that country in Norman days, and his memory remains in the name Sompting Abbots. Yet another tradition says that Thomas à Becket planted the first fig tree in England at Tarring on his return from a pilgrimage to Rome. To the Romans also is ascribed the introduction of the sweet chestnut, the ' Sardinian nut ' so much esteemed in southern Europe.

During the decline of the Roman Empire, and still more after its dissolution, the art of gardening sank to a low ebb, and it is certainly to the monasteries that we owe the maintenance, at least to some extent, of the old traditions, although on a much humbler and more utilitarian scale. Yet during the Dark Ages, when garden-craft in the greater part of Europe was at its lowest ebb, the Moors in Spain were making gardens, the remains of which are to this day amongst the most remarkable in the world. Their beauty and interest in those far-off days we can only imagine. The first of the Omeyyad Sultans, Abd-er-Rahman (ninth century), spared no pains to procure rare plants and seeds even from lands as far distant as India to adorn his garden. He introduced from Damascus the pomegranate, still the emblem of Andalusia. The palaces and gardens of Cordoba (under the Omeyyads the city measured twenty miles across) have long since disappeared, but the remains of the ancient splendours of Granada, ' the goblet of silver full of emeralds ', as the Arabs described it, testify to what the Alhambra and the Generalife must have been in Moorish times. It is at least possible that there were Moorish gardens in southern France. Five times Saracen emirs guided their hosts into the heart of Aquitaine, subjugating the inhabitants as much by the peaceful influence of arts and industries as by the force of arms.

26

THE MEDIÆVAL GARDEN

That their invasions were by no means transient is proved by what remains, even to this day, of their mines and subterranean engineering works. There are picturesque glimpses of royal and other pleasaunces in France in the Middle Ages as early as the sixth century—for instance, Saint Radegonde, queen of Clothair, King of the Franks, who fled from the court to Poitiers, where she founded a nunnery and laid out a garden on the sunny slopes beneath the city walls. Here she and her nuns toiled with their own hands, and here Fortunatus, the bishop-poet, delighted to wander and compose his poems. Even thirteen centuries ago the violet was the symbol of humility, for when Fortunatus sent violets and other sweet-scented flowers to the queen he wrote :

' He who offers violets must in love be held to offer roses. Of all the fragrant herbs I send none can compare in nobleness with the purple violet. They shine in royal purple : perfume and beauty unite in their petals. May you show forth in your life what they represent '.

We read too of Childebert's queen, whose garden ' was balmy with the perfume of roses of Paradise ' and that through this pleasaunce she and the king were wont to walk on their way to the church of Saint Germain des Près. Charlemagne was apparently a garden lover and his capitulary *De villis et curtis* laying down what should be grown in fine orchards and gardens is one of the most important mediæval documents pertaining to gardens that has come down to us.

No account of a royal pleasaunce in this island as early as Charlemagne's time has been preserved, but there is the charming legend of Saint Maurilius, who worked in the garden of a British prince four hundred years before Charlemagne's reign. Saint Maurilius was a native of Milan, who studied under Saint Ambrose. He followed Saint Martin to Tours and was ordained by Saint Martin. The Bishop of Angers sent Saint Maurilius to Chalons to convert the heathen there and blessed him before his departure. At Chalons Saint Maurilius (or Saint Maurille, to give him his French name) prayed that God would destroy the heathen temple and idols, and according to the legend fire came down from heaven and consumed them. Saint Maurille was subsequently made Bishop of Angers in succession to Saint

Apothême, but feeling that this honour was too great for him, he fled and took ship for Britain. According to another account the Saint was overcome with grief at having seen Saint Réné die without receiving the chrism, and, attributing this calamity to his own negligence, secretly took the keys of the holy relics and made his way to the sea-coast, where he embarked for Britain. The powers of evil, to add to his distress, caused him to drop the keys of the holy relics into the sea. Saint Maurille vowed he would never return to his own city unless God caused the keys to be restored. He changed his garments and, without letting his name be known, presented himself before one of the British princes in this island and offered himself as a gardener. The prince received him joyfully and took him into his service, but a stranger visiting the court recognized him and he was induced to return to his bishopric at Angers. Unfortunately we are not told which prince, but this would have been just at the time when the Romans were withdrawing their legions, a period of which we have very little information. Two scenes from this legend are beautifully depicted in one of the celebrated Angers tapestries made in 1460. (See illustration.) One half of this tapestry (all that remains of this series) shows Saint Maurille with a halo and wearing a violet-coloured robe, working with a long-handled spade. The enclosure is planted with fruit trees and gooseberry bushes and a small bed is planted with flowers. On the other half the prince and princess, wearing their crowns, are depicted seated in a simple but beautiful pavilion, the table before them is spread with viands and near by is another table with gorgeous dishes. Saint Maurille offers a dish filled with fruits to the Queen. Above is the inscription : LA MER LUI . . . LES CLEFS DU RELIQUAIRE DE L'EGLISE ET DEPUIS A LE ROY DENGLETERRE QUI JOYEULSEMENT LE RECEUT ET RETINT. Another inscription beneath has been so torn that it is unreadable.[1] Saint Maurille, Bishop of Angers, died in 543 and to this day his memory is specially venerated in Anjou.

The earliest records of monastic gardens date from the

---

[1] This tapestry is thus described in the inventory of 1467—*Item tapiceria de vita sancti Maurilii continens tres species.* It disappeared during the Revolution, but this piece was found in 1874, nailed up in a corn-loft. It was in a pitiable condition, but it has been carefully restored.

ninth century, and the earliest known plan of a garden—that of St. Gall near the Lake of Constance—is of that date. The monastery is particularly interesting to English-speaking folk, for the founder, Saint Gall, was an Irishman of noble family, and at one time he was in a monastery in County Down under the rule of Saint Comgal. In 585 he was one of the twelve monks who followed Saint Columban on his mission to the Franks. He spent his life preaching to the heathen tribes, and when he was eighty-five he founded the monastery of St. Gall. He ruled this monastery for ten years, and for a hundred years after his death the rule of Saint Columban was followed, and then the rule of Saint Benedict was adopted. Saint Benedict, it will be remembered, attached great importance to manual work, and it is especially to the Benedictines that the art of gardening owed so much during the Middle Ages. The plan of the abbey garden at St. Gall is remarkably interesting for it shows that the monasteries maintained the traditional lay-out of the Roman *villa rusticus*, the largest spaces being devoted to apples, pears, plums, medlars, figs, peaches, mulberries, hazels, walnuts and almonds and a kitchen garden.

Not only has the earliest plan of a garden been handed down to us from St. Gall, but the first-known gardening book of mediæval days comes from that monastery. It is of the same century as the plan. Walafred Strabo (a monk when Grimwald was abbot), the author of the poem, *The Little Garden*, was also a biographer of Charlemagne (he wrote the biography at the request of the Emperor Charles III, who spent three days at the monastery). His life of Charlemagne is his most famous work, but *The Little Garden* is a touchingly human book, and how vividly it portrays a ninth-century garden and the old monk toiling in it. The treatise begins with a charming dedication ' to the beloved Father Grimaldus '.

' This book ', says Walafred Strabo, ' is humbly offered in token of love and admiration. When you sit beneath the apple tree, where you are often surrounded by the boys from your school, some of them running to show you apples they have gathered, so large they can scarcely hold them in one hand, perchance you will peruse it. May God make you abound more and more in goodness and crown you with life everlasting '.

THE STORY OF THE GARDEN

The description of the making of a little garden is as true to-day as it was a thousand years ago :

' The gardener must not be slothful but full of zeal continuously, nor must he despise hardening his hands with toil '.

' When last winter had passed and spring renewed the face of the earth, when the days grew longer and milder, when flowers and herbs were stirred by the west wind, when green leaves clothed the trees, then my little plot was overgrown with nettles. What was I to do ? Deep down the roots were matted and linked and riveted like basket-work or the wattled hurdles of the fold. I prepare to attack, armed with " the tooth of Saturn ", tear up the clods and rend them from the clinging network of nettle roots. . . . I plant my seeds and the kindly dew moistens them. Should drought prevail, I must water it, letting the drops fall through my fingers, for the impetus of a full stream from the water pot would disturb my seedlings. Part of my garden is hard and dry under the shadow of a roof ; in another part a high brick wall robs it of air and sun. Even here something will at last succeed ' !

Herbs for healing were naturally grown in abundance in this little monastic garden—sage,' of good scent it is and full of virtue for many ills ' ; rue, ' with its blue-green leaves and short-stemmed flowers, so placed that the sun and air can reach all its parts, great is its power over evil odours ' ; ' southernwood of the hair-like leaves cures fever and wounds ; it has wellnigh as many virtues as leaves ' ; ' the pumpkin casts its tendrils far and wide . . . slim is the stem from which it hangs, but huge the bulk which it attains ' ; Wormwood, ' what can equal this for fever and gout, for headache use an infusion of it and plaster your head with a crown of the wet leaves ' ; Horehound, ' it is bitter to the palate yet its scent is sweet. Drink horehound hot from the fire if you are poisoned by your stepmother ' ; fennel, ' deserves high praise both for its taste and smell and is good for weak eyes ' ; ' mint I grow in abundance and in all its varieties. How many they are ; I might as well try to count the sparks from Vulcan's furnace beneath Etna '.
But above all Walafred Strabo loved his roses and lilies :

' Better and sweeter are they than all the other plants and rightly called the flower of flowers. Yes, roses and lilies, the one for virginity with no sordid toil, no warmth of love, but the glow of their own sweet scent, which spreads further then the rival roses, but once bruised or crushed turns all to rankness. Therefore roses and lilies for our church, one for the martyr's blood, the other for the symbol in his hand. Pluck them, O maiden, roses for war and lilies for peace, and think of that Flower of the stem of Jesse. Lilies His words were and the hallowed acts of His pleasant life, but His death re-dyed the roses '.

In regard to English monasteries, we know that books on herbs were studied at least as early as the eighth century, for Boniface, the Apostle of the Saxons, received letters from England asking him for more books on simples and complaining that it was difficult to obtain foreign herbs.[1] The oldest Saxon book dealing with the virtue of herbs is the Leech Book of Bald, *circa* 900–950. This Leech Book was evidently the manual of a Saxon doctor and it is the oldest existing Leech Book written in the vernacular. The MS. was apparently written shortly after Alfred's death, and is probably a copy of a much older manuscript, for what is known as the third Book of the Leech Book is a shorter and evidently much older work incorporated by the scribe, Cild by name. Bald, who ordered Cild to transcribe the MS., may have been a personal friend of King Alfred, and at any rate he had access to the King's correspondence, for one chapter consists of prescriptions sent by Helias, Patriarch of Jerusalem, to the King. It would be interesting to know the names of the successive owners of this thousand-year-old book, but we only know that for a time it was in the library of Glastonbury Abbey. It is impossible to handle this beautifully penned manuscript without thinking of the scores of similar MSS. which must have been thoughtlessly destroyed. If only Mary Tudor had carried out Dr. John Dee's suggestion to form a Royal Library of the ancient MSS. dispersed from the monasteries at the Dissolution what treasures might have been preserved! Other Saxon MSS. include four copies of the translation of the Latin *Herbarium Apuleii Platonici*, and the

---

[1] *Nec non et si quos sæcularis scientiæ libros nobis ignotos adepturi sitis, ut sunt de medicinalibus, quorum copia est aliqua apud nos, sed tamen segmenta ultra marina quæ in eis scripta comperimus, ignota nobis sunt et difficila ad adipisandum.* Bonifac. Epistolæ, p. 102.

Lacnunga, an original work of early, but unknown, date. It has been pointed out by eminent authorities that the Anglo-Saxons had names for and used a far larger number of plants than the continental nations. In the *Herbarium of Apuleius,* including the additions from Disocorides, only 185 plants are mentioned, and this was one of the standard works of the early Middle Ages. In the *Herbarius* of 1484, the earliest herbal printed in German, only 150 plants are recorded, and in the German *Herbarius* of 1485 there are 380. But from various sources it has been computed that the Anglo-Saxons had names for and used at least 500 plants.

The earliest glimpse we are afforded of an English monastic or, rather, convent garden is the well-known story of William Rufus going to visit Romsey. Eadmer, who records this incident, was told it by Anselm, who had it direct from the Abbess. Maud, who afterwards became the wife of Henry I, was being educated at the nunnery under the charge of her Aunt Christina, the Abbess. Rufus wished to see her and gave as his pretext that he wished to see the roses, and other flowering herbs. Her aunt, fearing his purpose, made the child, then only twelve years old, put on a nun's veil, and with the other nuns she passed through the garden and subsequently the King left peaceably.

The earliest plans of a monastic garden in this country that have been preserved are those included in the plans of Canterbury made about 1165. These are bound up with the Great Psalter of Eadwin and are now in the library of Trinity College, Cambridge. In one of these plans nearly half the space (surrounded by cloisters) between the dormitory and the infirmary is occupied by the herbarium and trees are shown near the fish-pond. The other plan shows the orchard and vineyard beyond the walls. What a pleasure the herbarium must have been to those inmates of the infirmarium who could walk in the cloisters. One is reminded of the word-picture in the description of Clairvaux by a contemporary of Saint Bernard—the garden where the monks rested in their leisure hours, a garden intersected with rivulets dividing the plots and a great basin of water stocked with small fishes and the orchard which was a delight to the sick in the infirmarium, who could see the trees and hear

Orchard scene

(From a fifteenth-century copy of *Le Livre de Rustican*)
British Library

SAINT MAURILLE WORKING IN HIS GARDEN AND
OFFERING THE FRUITS OF HIS LABOURS TO THE QUEEN
(Fifteenth-century tapestry)
Angers Cathedral

SAINT FIACRE, A PATRON SAINT OF GARDENS
(From the original miniature in a Book of Hours)
Bibliothèque de l'Arsenal, Paris

the birds singing. The Canterbury plan does not extend far enough to show the historic garden overlooked by the Archbishop's palace, where the knights who murdered Becket ' threw off their cloaks and gowns under a large sycamore in the garden, appeared in their armour and girt on their swords '.[1]

The principal gardens of a monastery in early as in late mediæval days were the herb garden, the orchard and the vineyard. No definite information is available as to the herbs grown in Saxon and early Norman days, but our Saxon ancestors had names for and were evidently familiar with kale (they called March ' sprout kale month '), beet, radish, onion, leek (leeks were so commonly grown that ' leac tun ' was one of the names for a kitchen garden ; in the same way we describe a small plot as a ' cabbage patch '), parsley, fennel, linseed, mallow, mint, coriander, cumin, lovage, feverfew, chervil, lettuce, turnip, rue, mustard, wormwood, and hemp. Their herb gardens were not devoid of the more beautiful flowers, for roses, madonna lilies, irises (*I. germanica*), peonies (*p. officinalis*), and poppies (*p. rhœas*), were all used as herbs. What roses did they grow ? Here again we do not know for certain. But the Romans surely introduced R. *centifolia* (the old cabbage rose) brought in some immemorial time from the Caucasus. That it was the hundred-leaved rose extolled by Homer is probable though not certain. According to Loiseleur-Deslongchamps the damask was a rose grown in France centuries before Crusading days and would probably have been brought to England. Also R. *gallica*, which is a native of central and southern Europe and eastward as far as the Caucasus. The origin of the white rose of England (R. *alba*) and the red variety, the red rose of England, is unknown, but they have been associated from time immemorial with our island. Pliny, writing in the first century, said ' The isle of Albion is so called from its white cliffs washed by the sea, or from the white roses with which it abounds '. In a political poem *circa* 1460–1471, the white rose of England is mentioned :

' the white rose of England that is freshe and wol not fade,
Both the rote and the stalke that is of great honoure '.[2]

[1] See Dean Stanley's *Hist. Memorials of Canterbury*.
[2] *Early English Text Society*, Vol. IV.

Parkinson, in his *Paradisus* (1629), describes the white rose and the red rose of England as

'the most ancient and knowne Roses to our Countrey, whether naturall or no I know not, but assumed by our precedent Kings of all others, to bee cognizances of their dignitie the white rose and the red'.

Peonies are one of the oldest cultivated flowers, not only in the West but in the Far East. The plant was used by our Saxon ancestors for flavouring purposes and the seeds were carried as a charm against evil, a custom which survived until at least as late as the last century. The Madonna lily appears to have been grown from equally far-off days. One of the earliest illustrations of this flower is in a miniature in the Benedictional of Saint Ethelwold of Winchester (tenth century). The Saxon queen Etheldreda, foundress of Ely Cathedral, is depicted holding in one hand a book of the Gospels and in the other a Madonna lily. In an eleventh-century Saxon translation of the *Herbarium Apuleii Platonici* there is a painting of the whole plant with the stamens standing out beyond the petals, looking like rays of light emanating from the flowers and as it were crowning them. Until Tudor days the Madonna lily was styled simply 'the lily', and in sixteenth-century herbals 'the white lily'. Irises (*I. germanica*) and poppies were also grown in very early days. Walafred Strabo, writing in the ninth century, mentions both as growing in his garden.

One of the most attractive illustrations of a mediæval herb garden is a miniature in the fifteenth-century copy of Petrus Crescentius' *Opus Ruralium Commodorum*. (See illustration.) The miniature shows the herbs growing in square plots in a walled garden, and beyond the narrow streets of a mediæval town, The herbalist is being consulted by a patient, the herbalist's wife stands at the shop door, a woman in the foreground smells a herb and small boys are carrying about baskets of herbs.

Orchards were naturally of great importance to the monasteries. Apples, pears and cherries were required in large quantities for eating and apples for cider. It is interesting to remember that the Wardon pear (mentioned in the twelfth century by Alexander Necham), for centuries the most commonly grown pear in this country, originated at the Cistercian monastery of Wardon, in Bedfordshire. Three Wardon pears figured as the arms of the house. The cherry is one of our indigeneous trees. The popularity of this fruit is evident from the fact that it was grown in sufficient quantities to require separate 'cherry-yards'. In Lydgate's time cherries and strawberries were hawked in the streets of London.

> Then unto London I dyd me hye
> Of all the land it beareth the pryse.
> 'Hot pescodes' one began to crye
> 'Strabery rype' and 'cherryes in the ryse'.

Mulberries, peaches, quinces, plums, figs, and medlars were probably introduced in Roman times if not before. Both the common mulberry and the quince have been grown in Europe from time immemorial. Peaches were certainly known in this country as early as King John's reign, for, according to the chronicler, Roger of Wendover, he died from a surfeit of peaches and ale. In the fourteenth century both Lydgate and Chaucer mention them among the common fruits. In the *Romaunt of the Rose* they are classed with quinces, apples, medlars, plums, pears, chestnuts and cherries.

> And many homely trees there were
> That peches, coynes and apples bere ;
> Medlers, ploumes, peres, chesteynes,
> Cheryse, of which many one fayne is,
> Notes, aleys and bolas
> That for to seen it was solas.

According to Mr. Bean, the wild medlar which is found in the south of England is not believed to be truly indigenous. In mediæval days as now, the fruits were stored until 'bletted' (partially decayed). Chaucer refers to this custom in the Prologue to the Reeve's Tale[1] and his description of a goldfinch 'leaping pretilie' about in the branches of a medlar in bloom is one of the most charming of his garden word-pictures.

[1] But if I fare as doth an open-ers
That ilke fruit is ever lenger the wers
Til it be roten in mullock or in stie.

' And as I stood and cast aside mine eie
I was ware of the fairest medlar tree,
That ever yet in all my life I sie.
As full of blossomes as it might be.
Therein a goldfinch leaping pretilie
Fro bough to bough ; and as him list, he eet
Here and there of buds and floures sweet '.[1]

The extent to which vines were grown in England in early days is striking. The Saxons called October ' Wyn moneth '. Vine in Hampshire is said to derive its name from the vines planted there during the reign of the Emperor Probus. Writing in the early eighth century, Bede says that vines were grown in some parts of Britain, and in King Alfred's laws it was enacted that any who damaged ' the vineyard or field of another ' should give compensation. In Domesday about thirty-eight vineyards are mentioned, the largest—twelve arpends in extent —being at Betesham on Henry de Ferriere's property. (An arpend is roughly equal to an acre.) Ely in the eleventh century was famed for its vines—the Normans dubbed it ' Isle des Vignes ', and according to the old rhyme :

Foure things of Elie towne, much spoken are.
The Leaden Lanthorn ; Marie's chappell rare,
The mighty Milhill in the Minister field
And fruitful vineyards which sweet wine do yield.[2]

The Bishops of Ely also had a vineyard at Ely Palace, their house in Holborn, and to this day Vine Street commemorates the site of it. Gloucestershire also was a noted vine county. William of Malmesbury writing in the twelfth century says :

' This county (Gloucestershire) is planted more thickly with vineyards than any other in England, more plentiful in crops and more pleasant in flavour. For the wines do not offend the mouth with sharpness since they do not yield to the French in sweetness '.[3]

The traditional sites of these old vineyards may still be seen

---

[1] *The Flower and the Leaf.*
[2] The old Latin rhyme runs thus :
  Quatuor sunt Eliæ : Lanterna, Capilla Mariæ
  Et Molendinum, nec non claus vinea vinum.
[3] *De Gestis Pontif,* Book IV.

A king and queen playing chess in a garden

(From a fifteenth-century copy of Marco Polo's travels written and illuminated in England)

Bodleian Library

LOVERS IN A CASTLE GARDEN
(From a Book of Hours)
British Library

SUSANNAH AND THE ELDERS
(From the fresco by Pinturicchio)
Borgia Apartments, Vatican Museums

in the Cotswolds in many places, where there are curiously narrow and obviously artificially made terraces. At Hereford too the 'Vinefields' terraces can still be distinguished.

Giraldus Cambrensis, who was tutor to Prince John (afterwards King John), mentions in his *Itinerarium Cambriæ* that the beautiful garden at his birthplace, the Castle of Manorbia, was enclosed on one side by a vineyard and on the other by a wood. Necham, in his *De Naturis Rerum*, devotes a chapter to the vine. He says little of practical vine culture, but he refers to the usefulness of growing vines against walls. He makes an interesting statement to the effect that when the grape gatherers reach the last row they sing a song of rejoicing, but unfortunately he does not give the words.

Apart from the chief gardens many of the various officeholders in monasteries had their own gardens. As a rule the Abbot or Prior had a privy garden. At Abingdon, the accounts, which date from the thirteenth century, show that the Precentor and the 'Custos operum' each had a garden and paid rent to the gardenarius.[1] At Norwich the Sacristan had 'S. Mary's garden' and the 'green garden' and the cellarer rented the 'little garden' or 'garden within the gates'.[2] At Winchester the Almoner had a separate garden and another garden was known by the charming name of 'Le Joye'. As early as the ninth century there was a sacristan's garden at Winchester and in the Lady Chapel there is a fifteenth-century doorway (now bricked up) which formerly led into this garden, the site of which is to this day called 'Paradise'. It was in the sacristan's garden that the flowers for the decoration of the church were grown and it is impossible for any imaginative person to look at this doorway without catching a fleeting vision of this 'paradise' full of flowers of past centuries. Churches were far more lavishly decorated than they are now. For the festivals the shrines were lovingly adorned with flowers; sweet-scented rushes and herbs were strewn on the floor; even the candles were wreathed with flowers and the priests wore garlands of

[1] Camden Society, *Accounts of the Obedientiars of Abingdon Abbey*, R. E. G. Kirk, 1892.
[2] See *An Introduction to the Obedientary and Manor Rolls of Norwich Cathedral Priory*, by H. W. Saunders.

flowers. Henry VI in his will left to Eton College a piece of ground for the express purpose of growing flowers for the decoration of the chapel. 'The space between the wall of the church and the wall of the cloister shall conteyne 38 feet which is left for to sett in certaine trees and flowers, behovable and convenient for the same church'. Further the King directed, that this garden should be surrounded by a good high wall ' with towers convenient thereto '.[1] This is, I believe, the only record of a garden in England having walls with towers.

If horticulture in early days owed much to the monasteries, it must be remembered that the inmates had opportunities denied to others of improving their knowledge. In those troublous times they enjoyed at least comparative peace ; unlike the majority of folk, the monks could read and the frequent intercourse with the continental monasteries must have helped the importation of new plants. To the Hospitaller Orders, the Templars and the Knights of Saint John, we doubtless owe the introduction of many treasures from the East, and they owned numerous gardens in various parts of England. For instance, Hampton Court gardens are on the site of a house, with gardens, which belonged to the Hospitallers. London in mediæval days contained many monastic gardens. Most have long since disappeared, but the Temple garden recalls the memory of the Knights Templars who once owned this land, and Black Friars, the property owned by the Dominicans when they moved from Holborn to the riverside. One of the oldest, if not quite the oldest garden in England, is the ' College Garden ' of Westminster Abbey, once a herb garden. For this was the infirmary garden attached to Edward the Confessor's buildings and in mediæval days it was joined to the ' grete garden '. The Little Cloister was the cloister of the infirmary and the vaulted sombre entrance to it (leading from the ' Dark Entry ') was the entrance used by the monks in the Confessor's reign.

The earliest English illustration of a royal garden that has come down to us is a miniature in a copy of Marco Polo's travels (now in the Bodleian Library) written and illuminated in England in the fifteenth century. In this a king and queen, wearing their crowns, are depicted playing chess, seated in a garden surrounded

[1] Nields' *Wills of the Kings and Queens of England.*

by a castellated wall. The gardener, who is either pruning or grafting, watches them over the wall. (See illustration.)

There are notices of royal gardens long before this date, however. Henry I built a palace at Woodstock and made a park fourteen miles in circumference where he kept 'lyons, leopards, strange spotted beasts, porcupines, camells and such like animals ', which were sent to him from ' divers outlandish Lands '. Woodstock, however, is chiefly associated with Henry II's name, for at this palace was the famous labyrinth and bower connected with the tragedy of Fair Rosamond. The labyrinth, however, contrary to popular belief, was apparently not a hedge maze, but an elaborate architectural labyrinth, similar probably to the labyrinth ' containing recess within recess, room within room, turning within turning ',[1] built by Louis of Bourbourg, at Ardres, for Count Arnold in the same century. John Brompton, Abbot of Jervaulx, describes the Woodstock labyrinth in his Chronicle under the year 1151 and it is clear he refers to a labyrinth building in the park. John Aubrey in his *Remaines* (1686) quotes an old ballad in which Fair Rosamond's bower is described as built ' most curiously of stone and timber strong ', with one hundred and fifty doors and so intricate that no one could find the way but with ' a clue of thread '. Samuel Croxall and Thomas Hearne, both writing in the early eighteenth century, describe the remains as still standing in their day.

The first mention of gardens at Woodstock is in Henry III's reign. In 1250 the King commanded the Bailiff of Woodstock to encircle the Queen's garden with two walls, ' well built and high with a good herbary in which the same Queen may be able to disport herself; and a gate from the herbary next the chapel of Edward our son, into the aforesaid garden '.[2] The ' herbary ' may refer to an enclosure where herbs were grown, but it is more likely that it was a herber (arbour), in this case a royal pavilion or possibly the elaborate type of ' arbour ' consisting sometimes of several rooms made with living trees skilfully pleached. The fact that two years later an order was

---

[1] Lambertus Ardensis. *Historia Comitum Ardensium et Guisnensium*, A.D. 800-1200, in *Reliquiæ Manuscriptorum of Petrus de Ludewig*, 1727.
[2] Liberate Roll, 34 Hen. III. m.6.

given to turf 'the great herbary' confirms this possibility. Arbours of all sizes were usually turfed in the Middle Ages.

Apart from Woodstock, entries in the Pipe Rolls, Exchequer Rolls and Liberate Rolls show that there were gardens attached to the royal residences of Windsor, Westminster, Clarendon, Charing and the Tower in the twelfth and thirteenth centuries. No description of an English royal garden in the thirteenth century has been preserved for us, but Henry III's order to his Bailiff at Woodstock, together with the earlier account of the park and the menagerie, indicate that royal gardens in England were similar to the type described by Petrus Crescentius in his *Opus Ruralium Commodorum* (written in the latter half of the thirteenth century). It is a curious fact that this book, which occupies a unique place in garden literature, and was one of the earliest books to be printed and was subsequently translated into Italian, French and German, has never been translated into English. His description of a garden suitable for royal personages and powerful and wealthy lords is certainly suggestive of an Eastern park or paradise and (translated) runs thus :

Let it be a place where the pleasant winds blow and where there are fountains of waters . . . it should be enclosed with lofty walls. Let there be in some part a wood of divers trees where the wild beasts may find a refuge. In another part let there be a costly pavilion where the king and his queen or the lord or lady may dwell, when they wish to escape from wearisome occupations and where they may solace themselves.

Let there be shade and let the windows of the pavilion look out upon the garden but not exposed to the burning rays of the sun. Let fish-pools be made and divers fishes placed therein. Let there also be hares, rabbits, deer and such-like wild animals that are not beasts of prey. And in the trees near the pavilion let great cages be made and therein place partridges, nightingales, blackbirds, linnets and all manner of singing birds. Let all be arranged so that the beasts and the birds may easily be seen from the pavilion.

Let there also be made a pavilion with rooms and towers wholly made of trees where the king, the queen or the lords and ladies may resort in fine weather. This pavilion may be made in this manner. The spaces and rooms may be measured out and where there would be walls there plant fruit-bearing trees which can easily be interlaced, such as cherries, and apple trees ; or else olives, or poplars which will grow quickly. Or this pavilion may more easily be made of dead wood and planted with vines which will cover the building. The trees may be grafted with divers fruits by the diligent gardener. It will be needful for him to know all the different kinds of trees and herbs, so that he may perform his work diligently and that no fault may be found by the king or lord.

When this work is accomplished, then the king may delight himself in this garden, thanking and glorifying God the Sovereign Lord of all, the Cause and Author, the beginning and the end of all that is good.

The most charming description of a royal garden in this country that has come down to us is that of the 'garden fair' of Windsor Castle, in the early years of the fifteenth century, penned by James I of Scotland. Captured when only twelve years old (when the ship in which he was being sent to France was becalmed off Flamborough Head), he spent nine years as a prisoner at Windsor (1413–1424). His description of the garden is brief, yet it is a vivid picture of this secluded close, with its arbours, its shady alleys, its hawthorn hedges, so thick that within 'scarce any wight might espy', and the song of 'the little sweet nightingale'.

> 'Now was there made, fast by the Towris wall,
> A garden fair ; and in the corners set
> An arbour green, with wandis long and small
> Railed about and so with trees set
> Was all the place, and Hawthorne hedges knet,
> That lyf was none walking there forebye
> That might within scarce any wight espy.
> So thick the boughes and the leaves green
> Beshaded all the alleys that were there,
> And mids of every arbour might be seen
> The sharpe greene sweet Juniper
> Growing so fair with branches here and there,
> That as it seemed to a lyf without,
> The boughes spread the arbour all about.
> And on the small greene twistes sat
> The little sweet nightingale, and sung
> So loud and clear, the hymnis consecrat
> Of loris use, now soft, now loud, among,
> That all the gardens and the wallis rung
> Right of their song '.

41

It was while walking beneath the tower that he first saw and fell in love with 'Cupid's own princess', his future wife, Jane Beaufort (granddaughter of John of Gaunt), whom he saw in the garden.

> 'Ah sweet! are ye a worldly creature
> Or heavenly thing in likeness of nature?
>
> Or are ye god Cupides own princess
> And comin are to loose me out of band?
> Or are ye very Nature the goddess
> That have depainted with yr heavenly hand
> This garden full of flowers as they stand?'

Even as early as the twelfth century, Londoners were garden lovers, for FitzStephen, who lived in Henry II's reign, tells us in his Life of Becket that the citizens had large and pleasing gardens. One of the most famous in the thirteenth century was that belonging to the Earl of Lincoln in Holborn. Besides the garden there was a fish-stew and a vineyard, both dating from the time when the Dominicans owned the place. By the fourteenth century and possibly long before, large gardens were sufficiently numerous in London for a special market to be held for the sale of the surplus herbs and fruits. This market was held opposite the church of St. Austin, near the gate of St. Paul's Churchyard. This market became

'a nuisance to the priests who are singing Matins and Mass in the church of St. Austin and to others, both clerks and laymen, in prayers and orisons there serving God, as also, to other persons passing there both on foot and horseback; as well as to the people dwelling in the houses of reputable persons there, who by the scurrility, clamour and nuisance of the gardeners and their servants, there selling pulse, cherries, vegetables, and other wares to their trade pertaining are daily disturbed'.[1]

The Mayor and Aldermen were petitioned and the gardeners also made a petition.

'Unto the Mayor of London shew and pray the Gardeners of the Earls, Barons, and Bishops, and of the citizens of the same city. May it please you Sire, seeing that you are the chief guardian of the said

[1] Edward III, A.D. 1345. Letter Book F, fol. cxi (Guildhall) quoted in *Memorials of London and London Life*, by H. T. Riley.

Mediæval herb garden

(From a fifteenth-century copy of *Le Livre de Rustican*)
British Library

city and of the ancient usages therein established, to suffer and to maintain that the said gardeners may stand in peace in the same place where they have been wont in times of old; in front of the Church of St. Austin, at the side of the gate of St. Paul's Churchyard in London; there to sell the garden produce of their said masters, and make their profit, as heretofore they have been wont to do; seeing that they have never heretofore been in their said place molested, and that, as they assert, they cannot serve the commonalty, nor yet their masters, as they were wont to do;—as to the which they pray for redress '.

Finally it was ordained that all gardeners of the City ' as well aliens as freemen ' should sell their goods in ' the space between the South gate of the said church (St. Austin) and the garden-wall of the Friars Preachers at Baynard's Castle . . . and no-where else '.

Apart from the Saxon herbals, the earliest English writings on gardens date from the twelfth century. Both Alexander Neckham, Abbot of Cirencester, and Grosseteste, Bishop of Lincoln, touch on the subject in their books. Neckham, who was born in 1157, spent the early part of his life at St. Alban's; he became head of the school belonging to the Abbey at Dunstable, by 1180 he was teaching at the University at Paris, returned to Dunstable before 1190, and ultimately went to the Augustinian Abbey of Cirencester, where he became Abbot in 1213. In both his books Neckham touches on the subject of gardens. In *De Naturis Rerum* he sets forth what should be grown in a ' noble garden ', but in common with the majority of the writers of that day, he copied largely from classical sources, and as he includes oranges, lemons, pomegranates, myrrh, etc., it is impossible to know how far his list of flowers, herbs, and fruits accurately represents what was generally grown in large gardens in his day. His list of flowers and herbs includes roses, lilies, peonies, violets, poppies, and daffodils, mandrake, turnsole, parsley, costmary, fennel, southernwood, coriander, sage, savory, hyssop, mint, rue, dittany, smallage, pellitory, lettuce, garden cress; of pot herbs, beet, mercury, orach, sorrel, and mallows, and of fruits, medlars, quinces, Wardon pears, and pears of St. Regula. (The last-named pears probably took their name from Saint Regolo, Bishop of Arles.) In his other book, the poem entitled *De laudibus divinæ Sapientiæ*, two

43

of the ten parts into which it is divided are devoted to the praises of various herbs and fruits. Grosseteste's writings on husbandry are largely based on Palladius' *De Re Rustica*, and are of less interest than Neckham's.

The most important original treatise by an Englishman describing garden flowers, is the seventeenth book of Bartholomæus Anglicus' monumental *De Proprietatibus Rerum*, the source of common information on Natural History throughout the Middle Ages. Batman, writing in 1582, describes Bartholomew as being 'of the noble familie of the Earles of Suffolk'. His book was first printed at Basle about 1470 and the esteem in which it was held may be judged from the fact that it went through at least fourteen editions before 1500, and besides the English and French translations it was also translated into Spanish and Dutch. There is fresh air and the beauty of living flowers in all Bartholomew the Englishman's writings, but there is only space here to quote from his descriptions of a few. The lily and the atmosphere of the lily he describes in a phrase of unforgettable simplicity and beauty; so simple indeed that one feels only a child or a great scholar could have written it :

'The lily is an herb with a white flower. And though the leaves of the flower be white yet within shineth the likeness of gold '.

The section on the rose is longer than most. To quote a few phrases :

'The rose of gardens is planted and set and tilthed as a vine. . . . The tame rose hath many leaves set nigh together, and be all red ; other almost white with wonder good smell. . . . And the more they be bruised and broken, the vertuouser they be and the better smelling. . . . The rose arrayeth her thorn with fair colour and good smell . . . and when they be full grown they spread themselves against the sun rising. . . . Among all flowers of the world the flower of the rose is chief and beareth the prize. And by cause of vertues and sweet smell and savour. For by fairness they feed the sight ; and pleaseth the smell, by odour, the touch by soft handling '.

Of the violet he says :

'Violet is a little herbe in substance and is better fresh and new than when it is old. And the flower thereof smelleth most. . . . And the more vertuous the flower thereof is the more it bendeth

A mon seul désir

(From the tapestries: *La Dame à la Licorne*)
Musée de Cluny, Paris

the head thereof downward. Also flowers of springing time springeth first and sheweth summer, The littleness thereof in substance is nobly rewarded in greatness of savour and of vertue '.

His description of the apple tree is strikingly fresh, and how accurately the word ' merry ' describes the taste of an apple !

' The apple tree maketh shadow with thick boughs and branches, and fair with divers blossoms and flowers of sweetness and liking : with good fruit and noble. And is gracious in sight and in taste and vertuous in medicine . . . some beareth sourish fruit and hard and some right sour and some right sweet with a good savour and merry '.

Judging from the number of manuscript copies and translations in this country the most popular of the classical treatises on plants was Macer's herbal. The earliest copies date from the twelfth century, two of these being in the British Museum, two in the Bodleian and one in the library of Lincoln Cathedral. The book was translated into English as early as the twelfth century with the addition of ' A fewe herbes wyche Macer tretyth not '. Both this and the translation by John Lelamour, Schoolmaster, of Hereford, are in the British Museum. (British Museum, Sloane 84 and 5). Other early manuscripts in the vernacular include a fourteenth-century poem of forty-three couplets ' of diverse herbis ' in the Ashmolean Museum (Ashmole, 1397, III-IV), a fourteenth-century list of herbs which once belonged to John Argenteux, Provost of Kings (now in the library of Gonville and Caius College, Cambridge, 198. III), a fourteenth-century treatise of herbs in the Pepys Library, Magdalene College, Cambridge, the fourteenth-century Meddygon myddfai—by the physicians of Myddvai, co. Caermarthen (British Museum Addit. 14912. I), and a treatise on rosemary, written by a clerk of the school of Salerno and sent by the Countess of ' Henawd ' (Hainault) to her daughter, Philippa, wife of Edward III. This last-named is in the library of Trinity College, Cambridge, and it is obviously the original of the lengthy and poetical passage on rosemary in Bancke's Herbal (1525), the earliest English printed herbal. In his ms. the translator ' danyel bain ' says that rosemary was unknown in England until the Countess of Hainault sent some to her daughter. Many curious old beliefs about this herb, not to be found in any of the other early treatises on plants, are to be found in this manuscript. Amongst others that rosemary never grows higher than the height of Christ when he was a man on earth, that after thirty-three years the plant increases in breadth but not in height and that it is a holy tree and with folk that be 'juste and Rightfull gladlye it groweth and thryveth'.

Another interesting English work of the fourteenth century is a medical poem, of which there are several copies in this country and one in the Royal Library at Stockholm. This treatise deals with twenty-four herbs and the writer states that he learnt about them in a book he borrowed from the priest to a lady 'of great name'. The poem begins with a description of betony, 'powerful against wicked spirits' and then treats, amongst other herbs, of centaury, marigold, celandine, pimpernel, motherwort, vervain, periwinkle, rose, lily, henbane, agrimony, sage, rue, fennel and violet. Of marigold he says, that only to look on it strengthens the eyesight, that it must be picked only when the moon is in the sign of the Virgin and not when Jupiter is in the ascendant. And the gatherer, who must be out of deadly sin, must say three Pater Nosters and three Aves. Vervain must be picked 'at Spring of day in ye monyth of May'. Under sage we find a variation of the old proverb 'How can a man die who has sage in his garden'. Of the rose he says :

> Of ye rose yt spryngeth on spray
>   Schewyth hys flowris in someres day
> It nedyth nogt hym to descrie
>   Everi man knowyth it at eye.

Lilies 'white as milk' he says should be plucked when the sun is in the sign of Leo—that is to say 'fro mydde July to mydde Awgust'. And of violets :

> ' Vyolet an erbe cowth
> Is knowyn in ilke manys mouthe,
> Oyle of hys floure is profitable
> And w^t oyle of rose medicinable,
> Ye oyle of hys fayre floures
> In man distroith wycked humoris
> Wherefore it is meche of pris
> And meche in Boke comendid is '.

46

THE MEDIÆVAL GARDEN

The earliest known original work on practical gardening written in English is the poem *The Feate of Gardening*, by Mayster Ion Gardener (Library of Trinity College, Cambridge). To quote Lady Cecil, who transcribed it and made the glossary, 'this work is invaluable, as it gives incontrovertible evidence of the plants then actually to be found in an English garden (i.e. in the fifteenth century) and the way in which they were cultivated'. Nothing is known of the author, the copy in the library of Trinity College was apparently written about 1440, but the poem is probably older. The title *The Feate of Gardening* was probably added by a later hand. Jon Gardener was certainly a practical gardener, his poem gives clear and sensible instructions for growing the fruits, flowers, and herbs he mentions, and it is entirely free from superstitious beliefs and absurd statements about grafting and rearing fruit trees prevalent in most writings of this period.[1]

With increasing prosperity gardens naturally became larger and those belonging to wealthy folk in the fourteenth and fifteenth centuries must have been singularly attractive. Indeed in the old romances and exquisite miniatures and illuminations in mediæval manuscripts we see the pleasaunces of those days as through magic casements and look into a fairyland of the past in springtime. There was little in the way of comfort indoors in mediæval days to compensate for the long gloomy winters when communication with the outer world was slow. But when the earth donned afresh her robe of green embroidered with flowers, it was a time of universal rejoicing. Mediæval art and literature alike are permeated with the joy of spring, when life was transformed by the sunlight and social festivities were held on meads starred with flowers and beneath fruit trees gay with blossoms.

The orchard, as in the ancient East, was a pleasure garden, and, as in the smaller enclosures, the grass was planted with flowers and the whole plot surrounded with a crenellated wall.

---

[1] See *On a Fifteenth Century Treatise on Gardening*, by Mayster Jon Gardener ... with remarks by The Honourable Alicia M.Tyssen Amherst. *Archæologia*, LIV. In the plant lists at the end of this book I have quoted (with Lady Cecil's kind permission) the list of plants of which Jon Gardener writes with her glossary.

An orchard of this type is depicted in the fifteenth-century copy of the *Romaunt of the Rose* in the British Museum. (See illustration.) Here a dance is shown taking place on the 'lawn' of the orchard. The 'lawns' of mediæval days were imitations of the natural meadow and like the natural meadow they were bright with flowers. Illustrations in mediæval romances, missals and books of hours all bear mute testimony to the fact that a dark green tapestry adorned with a profusion of flowers formed the ideal mediæval pleasure garden. It was a 'flowery mead' of this description that Boccaccio described in the *Decameron*.

'What seemed more delightful than anything else was a plot of ground like a meadow, the grass of the deepest green, starred with a thousand various flowers. All around were orange and lemon trees laden with flowers and fruit and in the centre of the grass plot a carved fountain of pure white marble'.

Maerlant in his *History of Troy* writes of an orchard :

'The grass was not very high
But moderate ; on it were all kinds of flowers
On which the dew still sparkled.
The orchard was walled in all round,
In the centre stood a beautiful fountain,
A fine tree blossomed there
So full grown that its green leaves
Cast their shadow on the fountain and on
The greater part of the orchard'.

The description of a flowery mead in Chaucer's version of the *Romaunt of the Rose* is familiar to all :

'Ther sprang the violete al newe,
And fresshe pervinke riche of hewe,
And floures yelowe, whyte and rede :
Swich plentee grew ther never in mede,
Ful gay was al the ground and queynt
And poudred, as men had it peynt,
With many a fresh and sondry flour
That casten up a ful good savour'.

Flowery meads are nowhere more beautifully depicted than in the old tapestries. The flowers are not easy to identify, for

48

they are frequently conventionalized and others are purely fanciful. But in their beauty and fresh effect the flowery meads of olden times are immortalized. Few perhaps are more fascinating than those in the wonderful series of tapestries commonly known as ' The Lady of the Unicorn ' (Cluny Museum). Apart from their superb colouring, their varied interest and beauty of detail, these tapestries have the charm of mystery and picturesque tradition. According to the legend, Pierre d'Aubusson, lord of Boussac, took these tapestries with him as a reminder of his lady-love to solace him during his exile. All that is actually known of their origin is that they were woven probably in Tournai, about 1480. In the first tapestry (see illustration) the ' Lady of the Unicorn ', richly apparelled, is depicted standing before a tent sprinkled with tears and bearing the romantic motto, ' A mon seul desir ' ; she is taking a jewelled necklace from a casket held by her maiden ; on either side are a lion (emblem of courage) and a unicorn (emblem of chastity). In the background are the arms of the Le Viste family, the whole setting of the scene being a flowery mead thickly planted with flowers and trees amongst which play rabbits, dogs, foxes, goats, birds, and wild beasts. The Lady and her maiden, the lion, the unicorn, the arms and the animals all appear in different positions in each of the tapestries and in each the setting is a different flowery mead. The other five tapestries are said to represent the five senses. In one she picks up morsels of food from a beautiful vessel held by her maiden to give to the bird perched on her left hand ; in the second she toys with fragrant flowers ; in the third she holds the unicorn's horn ; in the fourth she plays an archaic musical instrument ; in the fifth she holds a mirror before the unicorn. It is difficult to identify even the majority of the countless flowers and one is reminded of the vague descriptions of the early writers. For instance, Gauthier de Coinci (1183–1236) when choosing the miracles of the Madonna, says :

' I do even as he who seeks flowers in a meadow ; the which is all spring-like and bedecked with flowers, and who sees all around him many divers ones, crimson and violet, and yellow and dark blue, that he knows not which to pluck first '.

E

There appear, however, to have been exceptions in very early days to the planting of turf with flowers, for Albertus Magnus (thirteenth century), in his *De Vegetabilius*, describes a green plot in a garden as

'a plot of grass carefully weeded and trampled under foot, a true carpet of green turf with no projections on its uniform surface. . . . Behind the grass plot are planted in quantity aromatic and medicinal herbs'.

A beautiful type of pleasure garden is depicted in another well-known miniature in the *Romance of the Rose*. (See illustration.) This shows skilful division of a small piece of ground into three enclosed gardens. We certainly have much to learn from our mediæval ancestors of the art of making gardens within gardens and a plan such as this could easily be copied. One plot being on a different level adds to the charm and interest. In one enclosure the central feature is a globe-shaped fountain with water flowing out of animal masks and passing by a small canal into the lower garden. The turf is planted with flowers. Some of the company are singing accompanied by a musician, whilst others sit and listen. The enclosure is lattice-work with a doorway leading into a further garden. In the latter there are raised flower-beds, and in the distance a long bed thickly planted with carnations. The lower plot is surrounded by a castellated wall with a door similar to the wooden door in the upper garden.

Fountains seem as a rule to have been the central features of gardens of any size; those depicted in mediæval illustrations are as a rule exceptionally fine and the variety of them is remarkable. The description of the fountain in the mystic garden of the *Romance of the Rose* is singularly beautiful:

'Without the door.
Of paradise the blest, I ween,
No sight more beauteous may be seen
Than this bright well. The gushing source
Springs ever fresh and sweet. Its course
It takes through runnels twain, full deep,
And broadly trenched; it knows no sleep

Mediæval garden

(From a fifteenth-century copy of *Le Roman de la Rose*)
British Library

KING RENE OF ANJOU WRITING HIS BOOK
MORTIFIEMENT DE VAINE PLAISANCE
(From the *Book of Hours of Isabella of Portugal*)
Bibliothèque Royale Albert Ier, Brussels

THE MEDIÆVAL GARDEN

By day or night, for ne'er 'tis dried
By wasting drought of summer tide,
Nor hath stern winter's iron hand
The power to make its waters stand
Immovable, but out the ground
Its babble calls, the whole year round
Close, tender herbage, which doth push
Unceasingly, strong, thick, and lush.

Fast in the fountain's pavement shone
Two sparkling spheres of crystal stone,
Whereon my gaze with wonder fell

     .   .   .   .

When that the sun which searcheth all
The things that live on earth, lets fall
His rays within this fount, we see
An hundred colours gorgeously
Shine forth within the water bright,
Vermilion, azure, silvery white,
And richest gold. Such virtuous power
These crystals have that every flower
And tree within this pleasaunce seen,
Reflection finds in their sweet sheen '.[1]

The vast, mystic pleasaunce described in this poem is probably an ideal and not an actual pleasaunce, but it is the most remarkable described in mediæval literature and it is noteworthy that, like the pleasure grounds of the East, it is a tree rather than a flower garden.

              such skilful art
Had planned the trees that each apart
Six fathoms stood, yet like a net
The interlacing branches met ;
Through which no searching rays could pass
To sear the sward, and thus the grass
Kept ever tender, fresh and green
Beneath their cool and friendly screen.

As in the *Chanson de Roland*, the pine tree is the ' solitary ' tree and as conspicuous a feature as the fountain.

[1] From the translation of *The Romance of the Rose*, by F. A. Ellis.

a glorious pine,
Ne'er since great Charles of Pepin's line
Was born, hath mortal eye e'er seen,
In any garden as I ween,
A spine so tall, straight-grown, and fair.

The typical fifteenth-century garden-seat was built of brick
and cushioned with turf or some low-growing plant, such as
violets. But this was by no means the only type; indeed, it is
doubtful whether garden seats have ever been so magnificent
as they were in the fifteenth century. To quote but one
example; in the *Garden of the Guild of Antwerp Archers*, by an
unknown fifteenth-century artist, in the Musée Royal des
Beaux Arts, at Antwerp, a magnificent stone seat with a
canopy, in which the Master sits, is depicted. (See illustration.)
In the left foreground of the miniature of ' good King René '
writing in his study is the earliest illustration I know of a
movable garden-seat. It would be a charming model for
anyone wishing to make a garden-bench of this type. (See
illustration.)

Turfed seats were the commonest, however, and a marked
feature of gardens in mediæval days. They were usually made
along the enclosing wall and sometimes round trees. They
were supported by wattle fencing or faced with brick or stone,
and the earth planted with turf or turf and flowers or with low-
growing plants, such as daisies, violets or camomile.[1] These
turfed seats were also made in arbours. Chaucer, in *The Flower
and the Leaf*, says :

' Thought I, this path some whider goth, parde,
And so I followed, till it me brought
To a right pleasaunt herber well y wrought.

[1] The directions in gardening books of the period show that turfed
seats planted with grass and flowers were undoubtedly a common feature
as late as the early seventeenth century. In Richard Surflet's translation
of *La Maison Rustique* we find : ' These sweet herbes and flowers for nosegaies shall be set in order upon beds and quarters of such like length and
breadth as those of the kitchen garden, and some of them upon seats'.
William Lawson (*The New Orchard and Garden*, 1618) says : ' In all your
Gardens and Orchards bankes and seats of Camomile, Penny-royall,
Daisies and Violets are seemely and comfortable '.

Maugis et la belle Oriande
(From *Le Roman de Renaud de Montauban*)
Bibliothèque de l'Arsenal, Paris

THE TREE OF JESSE

(Jan Mostaert, c. 1474)

Rijksmuseum, Amsterdam

That benched was and with turfes new
Freshly turved, whereof the grene gras,
So small, so thicke, so short, so fresh of hew
That most like unto green wool wot I it was.
The hegge also that yede in compas
And closed in all the greene herbere
With sicamour was set and eglatere.

And shapen was this herber roofe and all
As a pretty parlour : and also
The hegge as thicke as a castle wall,
That who that list without to stond or go
Though he would all day prien to and fro,
He should not see if there were any wight within or no '.

Chaucer here describes a somewhat elaborate arbour, but they varied from simple affairs made with poles, with roses, jasmine, etc., trained over them to magnificent pavilions. Even as early as the thirteenth century covered galleries were a common feature. These galleries—sometimes vine-covered— were enlarged at the four corners into pavilions, and there was occasionally also a pavilion in the centre.

The raised beds were faced with brick or stone in the same fashion as the turfed seats, and it is interesting to note that they are sometimes depicted planted with grass as well as flowers. A raised bed of this type figures prominently in the small enclosed garden in Jan Mostaert's *Stem of Jesse*. (See illustration.) A raised bed faced with brick is depicted behind the sleeping Jesse, from whose body springs the stem of the tree. On the branches, scattered about as fruit, are the ancestors of the Mother of Our Lord, who is shown at the top. The lowest figure (with a harp) is David. On either side of the garden stand prophets. On the bed is a peacock, the emblem of eternity—' Of the increase of his government and peace there shall be no end, upon the throne of David and upon his kingdom . . . from henceforth even for ever '. (Isaiah IX. 7.)

Illustrations of the topiary work of the Middle Ages are rare, more curious than beautiful, and interesting as the immediate prototypes of the later topiary work, which reached an absurd climax in the eighteenth century. The art is said to have originated with the Romans, but it may be of far more ancient origin.

That the art was preserved through the Middle Ages is probably due to the monks, but there is no definite proof of this. An interesting illustration of topiary work is depicted in the prayer book of Juana de Castile. Another may be noted in the garden beside King René's study. The King is depicted seated beneath a canopy writing his book, *Mortifiement de Vaine Plaisance*, and outside is a small garden enclosed with a crenellated wall. There are several raised beds and in one of them a piece of topiary work is the important feature; beyond is a small fountain. Outside the garden a path between two walls leads to the bridge over the river. (See illustration.) This miniature is from the *Book of Hours of Isabella of Portugal* (Royal Library, Brussels). Isabella was the third wife of Philippe le Bon of Burgundy and their initials are shown interlaced and there are the charming mottoes—' Autre Nauray '; ' Mon joye '; and ' Tant que je vie '. Illustrations of miniature topiary work are still rarer, the most interesting perhaps being that depicted in the *Romance of Reynaud de Montauban* (Arsenal Library, Paris). Here a diminutive shrub, suggestive of Japanese dwarfed shrubs, and cut in tiers, is shown in a pot in the centre of the raised bed. (See illustration.)

There are numerous illustrations of the curious custom of placing pots of growing flowers on beds already planted with flowers. Carnations were apparently the favourite flower grown in this fashion. In the *Romance of Reynaud de Montauban* (cited above), Maugis and la belle Oriande are depicted seated in a castle garden; the inner enclosure being surrounded with lattice-work. The turf is planted with flowers and on the right is a simple but charming fountain. Behind the lovers is a three-sided raised bed faced with brick, planted with turf and flowers, and beside Oriande a large pot of carnations in bloom. In the prayer book of Juana of Castile, illuminated by Gheraert David (*circa* 1498), there are two attractive courtyard scenes. In both, courtyards leading into a narrow street are depicted and in the confined space of the courtyard there are six raised beds, two of them being much higher than the others. A lady in the costume of the period tends the flowers in the central beds. There are flower-pots on the window-ledges (one of Madonna lilies) and three pots of carnations on the raised bed underneath the window. The earthenware or metal pots were frequently very ornate and in various mediæval manuscripts they appear as decorations in the floral surrounds of the pages in missals and Books of Hours.

The best contemporary illustrations of the flowers grown in mediæval gardens are to be found in the *Book of Hours of Anne of Brittany* (*Bibliothèque Nationale*). Few Books of Hours can be compared with this masterpiece, in which Jean Bourdichon (one of the greatest painters in France during the reigns of Charles VIII, Louis XII and François I) depicted, at the Queen's command, the flowers of the gardens, fields, and woods of Touraine; 300 species of plants were painted with inscriptions in gothic lettering, giving the names in Latin and French. The work took about six years and for over 400 years now these lovely pages have been admired by generations of flower-lovers. By a mandate dated 14th March, 1508, the Queen (Anne of Brittany) ordered 600 crowns to be paid to Jean Bourdichon for having ' richement et sumptueusement historie et enlumyne les Grandes Heures destinees au service de la reine'. One page shows Anne of Brittany herself seated in a small castle garden; she is engaged in making a garland of flowers and an attendant kneels before her, holding a basket of flowers. Another attendant, standing on a raised bed planted with flowers, gathers roses. Beyond is a castle, which in appearance is certainly suggestive of Langeais, where she spent her honeymoon. (See illustration.)

Of the ideal gardens of the Middle Ages the ' Mary gardens ' are amongst the most lovely and especially interesting inasmuch as the illustrations of them embody so much of the old flower symbolism. The beauty of holiness, symbolized by the beauty of flowers, is a characteristic of some of the most notable works by the great artists, and to all flower lovers their use in symbolism is of deep interest. We are accustomed to associate flower symbolism with paintings, yet some may be found in the writings of even pre-mediæval days. The Venerable Bede, it will be remembered, wrote of the lily as the emblem of the Virgin, the white petals symbolizing her pure body and the golden anthers the beauty of her soul. There is a legend told of Saint Augustine, that when in England he rejoiced in the beauty of her flower-starred meadows, and seeing one day a field agleam with daisies, he compared them to the spirits of the blessed, shining in the gardens of Heaven and reflecting, at least in small measure, the beauty of the Source of all light. Meeting children with daisy chains, he showed them the sun in the centre of each flower and the white rays spreading from it; so, he said, should the Sun of Righteousness reign in their hearts, radiating from them purity and goodness.

Amongst the works of the early masters, few are so full of flower symbolism as the ' Mary Garden ' by an unknown master of the fifteenth century in the Frankfort Gallery. (See illustration.) The Mother of Our Lord is depicted seated in a mediæval enclosure thickly planted with flowers and surrounded by a castellated wall. Instead of a jewelled crown she wears a coronet of upstanding conventional leafy sprigs, exquisitely depicted. The Holy Child is being taught to play an instrument of music by an angel with flowers in her hair. Saint Michael (adorned with flowers) and Saint George (in armour) sit talking to each other by a tree and beside stands a young man listening to them. An attendant gathers cherries and another is getting water from a small well or fountain—'A garden enclosed is my sister, my spouse . . . a fountain of gardens, a well of living waters and streams from Lebanon '. Note in this picture the insignificance of the little ape-like Devil in the shadow of the ' rod of Jesse ' the vine-stock with young vigorous growth (to the right of the Holy Child). The Devil is seated just beyond Saint Michael's feet, and listens apparently with intense envy and malice to the two saints who ignore his presence. The sinister figure looks dark and insignificant, utterly overshadowed by the exceeding brightness and glory of the Holy Child, from whose head emanate rays of light.

The vine-stock is a reference to Isaiah's prophecy—' There shall come a rod out of the stem of Jesse and a branch shall come out of his roots '. The prophet has just been speaking of the cutting down of the mighty cedars of Lebanon, symbolizing the power of Assyria. The phrase ' cut down like a cedar ' signified total extinction, for none of the conifers (with the exception of one or two species, such as the Canary Island pine) send out shoots when once cut down. With this symbol of evil the prophet contrasts the low-growing vine. The word translated 'rod' means literally a 'brilliant' or 'shining' bough. The vitality of the vine has been famed from time immemorial and it is the oldest symbol of the royal house of Judah. 'Binding his foal unto the vine and his ass's colt unto the choice vine; he washed his garments in wine and his clothes in the blood of grapes'. (Gen. XLIX. 11). And it is the most sacred of Christian symbols, for ever hallowed by Our Lord's words 'I am the true vine'. (S. John xv. 1). In this picture it will be noted that the vine-stock is very prominent to the right of the Holy Child in the centre of the foreground.

Behind the Madonna is a raised bed and it is planted with irises, hollyhocks, marigolds, and a flower which is obviously one of the *cruciferæ*, but it is impossible to say which. The iris has always symbolized royalty and Dante, it will be remembered, crowned his four-and-twenty signori with irises. In Christian art, the iris refers to the royal birth of Our Lord, Who was of the house and lineage of David. In Ghirlandaio's *Adoration of the Shepherds*, irises, violets and daisies are depicted growing outside the stable. In Palmezzano di Forli's *Madonna and Child* (in the Brera, Milan) the Holy Child seated on His Mother's knee holds an iris flower. In Luca della Robbia's *Adoration* (in the Bargello) a crown of irises is held by angel hands over the Virgin's head. In Hugo van de Goes' *Adoration of the Shepherds*, one of the vases (adorned with a design of vine leaves and grapes) is filled with purple and white irises and orange lilies. The royal significance of the irises in this picture is emphasized by the lilies of the field, for even Solomon 'was not arrayed like one of these'.

At the feet of the Holy Child a daisy is depicted, symbolizing His innocence. We exclude this humble little flower from our gardens, but our mediæval ancestors loved its fresh beauty, and Chaucer called the daisy 'the floure of floures'. Near Saint Michael grow wild strawberries. These symbolize the fruits of righteousness, and they figure notably in Giovanni di Paolo's *Paradise*, also in several of Botticelli's pictures.

Madonna lilies figure behind the two saints and the young man. The symbolism of this flower is a large subject. In early days they were the flowers of celestial joy, but for their radiant

purity they were adopted as above all the flower of the Madonna.
The early Sienese artists retained the older meaning of the lily
as the flower of Paradise. Pictures of the Annunciation are
curiously rare before the fourteenth century, but even in the
earliest lilies are seldom absent, placed either beside the Madonna
in a vase or as a wand in the hand of the angel Gabriel. To
Dante the pale lily could not express the glowing mystery of the
Incarnation. Only the splendour of the rose could symbolize the
flame of Divine Love drawn down to earth. To him the Virgin
was 'the rose wherein the Divine Word was made incarnate' :

> ' la rosa, in che il Verbo divino
> Carne si fece '.

The rose symbolized also for Dante the very soul and centre
of his faith. When he reaches Heaven his soul blossoms forth
with love and adoration 'full blossomed as a rose before the sun' :

> ' Come il Sol fa la rosa, quando aperta
> Tanto divien, quant'ell'ha possanza '.

The infinity of the blessed in Paradise were as a white rose
' in a circle spread so far that the circumference were too loose a
zone to girdle in the sun '. (Paradiso XXXI. 103.)

In the Mary Garden a rose tree in full bloom is depicted as
prominently as the lilies near the cherry tree. In early days the
rose signified the blood of the martyrs, and Saint Bernard of
Clairvaux declared the rose to be the symbol of Our Lord's
Passion. Gradually, however, the rose came to signify the
Divine Love whereby the Son of God became Perfect Man as
well as Perfect God. In Hubert van Eyck's *Adoration of the
Lamb*, in Ghent Cathedral, there are bushes covered with roses in
full bloom. Carnations had much the same meaning as the rose.
In Hugo van der Goes' *Adoration of the Shepherds*, one of the vases
contains carnations and columbines, the carnations symbolizing
Divine Love, the columbines the seven gifts of the Holy Spirit,
and the transparency of the vase the Immaculate Conception.

The most conspicuous flowers in the foreground are lilies of
the valley, symbolizing humility, a peony with a butterfly on an
open blossom, and to the right, ' the dragon slain '. I do not
know of any other instance of a peony figuring in a sacred

picture; it is prominent in this, and it would be very interesting to know its significance. Violets and cowslips may be discerned near the Holy Child; the former symbolizing His humility and the cowslips possibly may signify the keys of Heaven.

The fruit symbolism in this picture is confined to cherries and apples. The cherry signifies the joys of Heaven and the apple the sorrows of this earth. In Memling's picture in the Uffizi, the Holy Child seated on His Mother's knee holds cherries in His left hand, whilst with the other He takes an apple from the hand of an angel. In the Mary Garden the apple is depicted significantly near the Bread and Wine on the table. It will be noted that no less than eleven different birds are shown in this garden. Surely there is symbolism connected with these, but apart from the Dove and the peacock (the symbol of eternity) the significance of birds appears to be unknown. Here and there it seems possible to discern the plants of evil repute—nettles and hellebore—but unlike the other flowers they are obscure and seem to fade into insignificance in the presence of the Light of the World.

The subject of Mary gardens is a large one, for illustrations of them range from early woodcuts to the works of the great masters. There is no space here, however, to cite more than one or two of outstanding interest and varied types—the Mary Garden in the Grimani Breviary in the library of St. Mark's, Venice; Stefano da Zevio's *Virgin of the Rose Garden*, at Verona, the Virgin in the Garden in the Rheims tapestry, the *Virgin of Dordrecht*, at Dordrecht.

And what of the patron saints of gardens? Two were venerated throughout the Middle Ages—Saint Phocas and Saint Fiacre—and it is pleasant to realize that we can claim Saint Fiacre, for in spite of his French name he was either a Scotch or an Irish prince. Saint Phocas is, however, the earliest patron saint of gardening. He lived in the third century outside the city of Sinope in Pontus. His life was divided between prayer and work in his little plot, where he grew vegetables for the poor and flowers. In a time of persecution two strangers came and craved his hospitality, and the Saint bade them welcome and gave them of his best, as he did all poor travellers. That night they told him they were searching for Phocas, a Christian, and that they had orders to slay him. The Saint did not reply, but after his devotions he went into his little garden and dug a grave. Next morning, when the strangers were about to depart, he told them he was Phocas. They were overcome with horror, but the Saint led them into the garden and bade them fulfil their orders. They cut off his head and he was buried in the grave among the flowers he had tended. Saint Phocas is represented outside the cathedral of Palermo, and among the mosaics in St. Mark's, Venice.

Saint Fiacre, who lived in the seventh century, left his home to preach to the heathen Gauls, near Meaux. He was welcomed by Saint Faro and lived as an anchorite in the midst of the great forests there, where he made a garden and dwelt unharmed by the wolves and wild boars. According to one tradition, his garden was miraculously enclosed, and a woman told his bishop that it was with the help of the Evil One. The bishop wisely went himself to see the saint who had made a garden in the midst of the forest, and found that what the woman had told him was untrue. After that, no woman dare go near his oratory, lest she should be smitten with blindness, and even in the seventeenth century no woman would enter his chapel in the Cathedral of Meaux. It is on record that in 1648 Anne of Austria declined to enter it.

There is a miniature of Saint Fiacre in a Book of Hours in the Bibliothèque Nationale, showing the saint with a spade in his hand in his garden, and in the background the Cathedral of Meaux. (See illustration.) The page is surrounded with a design of flowers and leaves, and butterflies. Beneath is written part of the office for his day, which translated runs thus :

'This Saint according to the law of his God struggled even unto death and was not terrified by the words of the wicked, for he was founded on the firm rock of Christ.

The just man will grow like the lily.
Response. And he will flourish in the sight of God.

A Mary garden
(Fifteenth-century, unknown)
Städelsches Kunstinstitut, Frankfurt

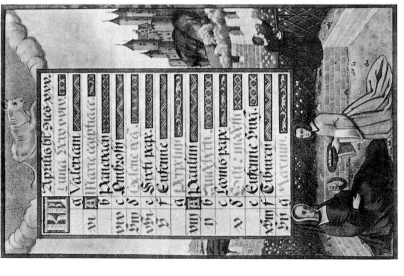

GARDEN OF THE GUILD OF ANTWERP ARCHERS

(Fifteenth-century, unknown)

Musées Royaux des Beaux-Arts de Belgique, Brussels

ANNE OF BRITTANY IN HER GARDEN

(From the *Book of Hours of Anne of Brittany*)

Bibliothèque Nationale, Paris

CHAPTER III

The 'garden fayre by musikes tower', depicted by Stephen Hawes in his *Historie of graunde Amoure and la bell Pucell,* is, I think, the most charming description of the transitional type of garden, partly mediæval in character and partly Tudor. The pleasaunce is depicted 'at VI at clocke' in the morning.

> 'When the little byrdes swetely did sing
> With tunes musicall in the faire morning.'

At this hour Amour and Good Counsell went to the ' garden fayre by musickes tower, walled most goodly '. At the gate they met the portress ' that was right gentle and called Curtesy '. She saluted them and ' with words of meekness ' asked of their coming. ' Truly ', they replied, ' a little to speake with la bell Pucell '.

' Truly ', quoth Courtesy :

> ' Truly quoth she in the garden grene
> Of many a swete and sundry flower
> She maketh a garland, that is very sheen
> With true loves wrought, with many a coloure,
> Replete with swetenes, and dulcet adoure
> And all alone, withouten company
> Amiddes an harber, she sitteth pleasauntly '.

Then Courtesy bade them wait a little space and anon returned with a gracious reply from la bell Pucell. Then the gate of the pleasaunce, ' walled most goodly ', was opened and they entered to behold the curious knot gardens laid out in rampant lions and dragons ; the four-square inner enclosure ' to Paradise right well comparable ' with its dulcet spring, its gold and azure fountain made in the similitude of a dragon with three heads spouting water into a silver pool and beside the fountain la bell Pucell, with hair like refined gold and arrayed in blue and ermine, making a chaplet of flowers.

THE STORY OF THE GARDEN

                          ' The garden glorious
Like to a place of pleasure most solacious,
With Flora paynted and wrought curiously
In divers knottes of marveylous greatness.
Rampande Lyons stode up wonderfly
Made all of herbes with dulcet swetenes,
With many dragons of marveylous likenes
Of divers floures made, full craftely
By Flora coloured, with colours sundry.

Amiddes the garden so much delectable
There was an harber, fayre and quadrant,
To Paradise right well comparable,
Set all about with floures fragrant,
And in the middle, there was resplendishaunt
A dulcet spring, and marveylous fountains
Of gold and azure made all certaine.

In wonderfull and curious similitude
There stode a dragon, of fine gold so pure
Upon his tayle, of mighty fortitude
Wrethed and skaled, all wyth asure
Having thre heades, divers in figure
Whiche in a bathe, of the silver great
Spouted the water, that was so dulcet.

Beside whiche fountaine, the most fayre lady
La bell Pucell, was gayly sittyng
Of many floures, fayre and royally
A goodly chaplet, she was in makynge.
Her heere was downe so clearely shinyng
Like to the golde ; late purified with fire,
Her heere was bryght as the drawen wyre.

Like to a ladye, for to be right true
She wore a fayre and goodly garment
Of most fine velvet, all of Indy blewe
With armines powdred, bordered at the vent,
On her fayre handes, as was convenient
A payre of gloves, right slender and soft
In approaching nere, I did beholde her oft.'

The ornate fountain is both mediæval and Tudor, but the knotted garden dates in this country only from early Tudor times. It would be interesting to know the origin of this curious type of flower-bed and it is at least possible that it is a development of the Arabian custom. It was introduced apparently very early in the sixteenth century or before, for Cavendish, writing of the Hampton Court gardens in 1520, says :

> ' My garden sweet, enclosed with walles strong
> Embanked with benches to sytt and take my rest,
> The Knots so enknotted it cannot be espres't,
> With arbors and alyes so pleasant and so dulce.'

Nearly all sixteenth and seventeenth-century garden books give numerous plans for these ' knots ', some of the simplest being, oddly enough, in the later books and some of the most complicated in the early. The beds were either raised, though not so high as in mediæval times, and supported by tiles, etc., or they were on the same level as the path. The broad lines of the geometrical design were planted in some low, close-growing shrub or herb such as hyssop, box, thyme, thrift, etc. Parkinson speaks of lavender cotton (*santolina chamæcyparissus*) for laying out knots as being ' of the highest respect for late daies, accepted both for the beauty and forme of the herbe . . . the rarity and novelty of this herbe being for the most part but in the gardens of great persons, doth cause it to be of the greater regard '. Yet Hyll, in his *Profitable Arte of Gardening* (1568), speaks of lavender cotton as commonly used in the making of dwarf shrub mazes. Thrift Parkinson describes as ' the most anciently received ' for making knots. He lists also hyssop, germander, marjoram, savory, thyme, juniper and yew (' juniper and yew . . . soon grow too great ') and dwarf box he highly commends. This edging was then apparently a novelty, for he describes it as being ' only received into the gardens of those that are curious '. It is interesting to note his statement that the clippings of the sweet-scented herbs can be used for strewing rooms. The interstices of the design were filled with flowers. We usually plant beds all of one colour and are only now beginning to imitate our Tudor ancestors' posy-like arrangement of flowers of different colours

63

' so that the place will seem like a piece of tapestry of many glorious colours to encrease every one's delight '.[1] Sometimes the interstices were covered with different coloured sands instead of plants. Bacon condemned these—' As for the making of knots or figures with divers coloured earths . . . they be but toys ; you may see as good sights many times in tarts '. Other knots were more elaborate and instead of geometrical designs low growing herbs were planted to form heraldic animals. This is the type described in the *Historie of graunde Amoure and la bell Pucell.* The flowers most frequently grown in the interstices of these knots were the spring flowers—daffodils, cowslips, primroses, bachelors' buttons, jacinths (hyacinths) and so forth. The popularity of the ' curiously knotted garden '[2] in mediæval and Tudor days is the more comprehensible when one realises how dull gardens would otherwise have been, not only during winter but even autumn. The flowers and shrubs which give us colour and interest during the darkest months of the year were unknown then and, except for marigolds, flowers were indeed few from the time the hollyhocks faded till the first snowdrops appeared. The varying shades of green of the dwarf evergreen shrubs, ranging from the pale grey of lavender cotton to the dark green of box and yew, together with the interest of the design, made the knots and dwarf shrub mazes a delightful winter garden. How attractive this type of garden can be when well made may be judged from the fact that a knot garden won the gold medal at the last International Flower Show (held in New York). It was the outstanding feature of the Garden Club of America's exhibition.[3]

Carved wooden figures of animals were another interesting feature of Tudor gardens. They figured conspicuously in the Hampton Court pleasure grounds which were much enlarged after Henry VIII took possession in 1529. There must have been an extraordinary number of these ' beasts ', for Edward More (of Kingston) alone was paid 20s. a piece for carving 159 and

[1] John Parkinson . . . *Paradisus* (1629).
[2] *Love's Labour's Lost.* Act I, Sc. 1.
[3] This knot garden was the joint exhibit of the Garden Clubs of Litchfield (Conn.), Millbrook (N.Y.), and Morristown (N.J.).

PLATE 18

A 'herber', with Garden seats and Table, from *The Gardener's Labyrinth* (1577), by Thomas Hyll.

Scene from *The Gardener's Labyrinth* (1577), shewing a 'wall herber' and the raised beds and sparse planting characteristic of Elizabethan gardens.

PLATE 19

AND here I also place the other Maze, whiche may be lyke ordred and vsed, as I spake before, and it may eyther be set with Isope and Tyme, or with winter Sauery and tyme.
For these do well endure, all the winter through grene. And there be some, whiche set their Mazes with Lauender Cotton, Spike, Maierome, and such lyke.

Design for a dwarf shrub maze, from *The Proffitable Arte of Gardening* (1568).

there are various other entries in the royal accounts for the making of these curious ornaments—lions, greyhounds, dragons, hinds, bulls, antelopes, griffins, leopards, tigers, harts, badgers, some of them 'bearing shields with the Kinges arms and the queene's'. Many of them were placed in the 'pond garden' (now the Privy garden). In Holbein's well-known picture of Henry VIII and his family (Hampton Court), Simon the Jester (jester to the King) and his wife, Jane the Fool, are depicted on either side of the royal group, and in the background these carved beasts are shown sitting on their haunches on pillars and holding aloft vanes.[1] Queen Elizabeth had thirty-four carved heraldic beasts in her privy garden at Whitehall. Leopold von Wedel, who visited this country in her reign, gives a brief description of the royal pleasaunce with its tennis court and bowling green, and in the privy garden he was chiefly impressed with the great sundial and the carved and painted wooden figures of animals on wooden pillars. The animals, he says, were finely carved, they had gilded horns and held aloft vanes with the Queen's arms. Heraldic beasts were as much a feature of French and Italian as of English gardens and in the Bargello at Florence there are now the magnificent bronze animals which formerly adorned one of the Medici gardens.

Another interesting feature of this period is also shown in Holbein's picture, namely, the railed beds. Even in late medi-æval days, the illustrations show that flower-beds were frequently railed with trellis-work, but this fashion of enclosing the beds became less common in Tudor times and rails took the place of the older elaborate trellis-work. In Holbein's picture oblong flower-beds are shown enclosed with rails painted green and white. Green and white are the Tudor colours, the colours of the leek with a further significance of purity (white) and eternity (green). Beds merely planted with flowers and not laid out in a complicated design (or 'enknotted') were called 'open knots' and they were railed or if raised from the ground they were supported with oak boards, tiles, shank bones of sheep, or lead. Parkinson says 'Oaken inch boords . . . foure or five inches broad', which shows how much lower the beds

[1] The garden depicted is that of Whitehall.

were than in mediæval times. Tiles he says, ' keepe up the edge of the beds in a pretty comely manner ', but they are apt to get broken. When shank bones of sheep were used they were stuck into the ground the small end downwards, and Parkinson says that they become white in time ' and prettily grace out the ground '. Lead, he says, is used by ' some that are curious ', the upper edge being either plain ' or cut out like unto the battlements of a Church ; this fashion hath delighted some, who have accounted it stately (at the least costly) and fit for their degree '. But he adds that the lead is too hot in summer and too cold in winter. All these edgings he describes as in use ' for raised ground be it knots or beds '. He describes as ' the latest invention ' the edging of beds with ' whitish or blewish pebble-stones of some reasonable proportion and big-nesse '. But this edging he considers suitable only for beds on a level with the path and ' is accounted both for durability, beauty of the sight, handsomnesse in the worke and ease in the working and charge to be of all other dead materials the chiefest '. The custom of edging beds with jaw-bones ' used by some in the Low Countries and other places beyond the Seas ' he condemns as ' too grosse and base '.

Gardens in Tudor times were still ' gardens enclosed ' but the castellated walls and strong defences of earlier times were no longer necessary. The strong rule of the Tudors gradually ushered in a period of prosperity and security and pleasure grounds increased in size. In Dr. Andrew Borde's *Boke for to lerne a man to be wyse in buylding of his house* (*circa* 1500) we are given a brief glimpse of the type of garden of the middle years of the sixteenth century. ' It is a commodious and pleasant thing in a mansyon ', says Borde, ' to have an orcharde of sundrye fruytes, but it is more commodyous to have a fayre garden repleated with herbes of aromatyke and redolent savoures; in the garden may be a poole or two for fysshe; yif the pooles be clene kept '. He mentions also a dovecote, a pair of butts for archery and a bowling alley as ' necessary and pleasant '.

The pleasure garden of early Tudor days became in course of time the elaborate garden of Elizabethan times and planned in conjunction with the house. It became customary for the same architect to design both house and garden and there are extant drawings by John Thorpe, the celebrated architect of Elizabeth's reign, of houses with their gardens, which he designed. According to Bacon, the planning of a garden required the greater skill; 'And a man shall ever see that when ages grow to civility and elegance men come to build stately sooner than to garden finely, as if gardening were the greater perfection'. The Elizabethan garden, like the Elizabethan house, was stately. It is, of course, difficult to estimate to what extent we were influenced by Italian ideas. Italian influence was strong in Elizabethan days, Queen Elizabeth herself spoke the language fluently and a visit to Italy was considered essential in the education of young men of any standing. Those who went to Italy would certainly not have failed to see the splendours of the gardens, notably those made as early as 1417, by Cosimo de Medici, from the designs of Michelozzo Michelozzi, the Boboli garden begun by Eleanora de Medici in 1549, the architects being Il Tribolo and Buontalenti; Poggio a Cayano, designed by Giulio di San Gallo, was famed for its menagerie and aviary, established by Lorenzo de Medici and his villa at Careggio, for its collection of rare plants. Many of the princely Roman gardens were designed by the greatest artists of the day. Raphael and San Gallo designed the gardens of the Villa Madama, for Margaret Duchess of Parma, and Bramante those of the Vatican. Falda's *Li Giardini di Roma* is a remarkable record of the gardens which must have been familiar to the majority of English travellers in those days. Incidentally it is interesting to note in these drawings that mounts were rare features in Italian gardens. The magnificence of fountains in Elizabethan gardens was doubtless due to Italian influence, but other features we modified to suit our climate and our national preference for homelike rather then princely gardens. Further it is a striking fact that although some two hundred English translations of Italian works were published between 1547 and 1600, on subjects ranging from theology to cookery, no Italian gardening book was translated into our language.

In England square gardens, divided again into four, were common. 'The garden', says Bacon, 'is best to be square, encompassed on all four sides with a stately arched hedge'.

THE STORY OF THE GARDEN

In the *Paradisus* (1629) we find :

'The foure square forme is most usually accepted with all and doth best agree to any man's dwelling. . . . Yet if it bee longer than the breadth and broader than the length, the proportion of walks, squares, and knots may be soone brought to the square forme, and be so cast, as the beauty thereof may bee no lesse than the foure square proportion '.

Gardens were usually enclosed by high brick walls, as the illustrations in Thomas Hyll's works show ; they suggest the ' garden circummured with brick ' in *Measure for Measure*.[1] Hentzner tells us that walls in England were ' exceedingly commonly ' covered with rosemary. Sometimes the enclosures were hedges, but it is not likely that these were frequently like the ' stately arched hedge ' described by Bacon, with little turrets and cages of birds ' and over every space between the arches some other little figure with broad plates of round coloured glass gilt for the sun to play upon '. The approach to a stately garden was usually from a terrace in front of the house, from which the greater part of the garden could be surveyed. Flights of steps led from the terrace and broad, straight walks called ' forthrights ' led at right angles from the terrace across the garden, these walks being intersected at intervals by other walks parallel with the terrace. The plots between these walks were laid out in knots, flower-beds, mazes, topiary work, etc., and the knots frequently reproduced the geometric tracery which was a feature of many Elizabethan houses.

The Elizabethans paid great attention to walks. ' The fairer and larger your allies and walks be, the more grace your garden shall have '.[2] There were broad open walks turfed or sanded or planted with sweet-smelling herbs—' those which perfume the air most delightfully not passed by as the rest, but being trodden upon and crushed are three—that is burnet, wild thyme, and water-mints ; therefore you are to set whole alleys of them to have the pleasure when you walk or tread '.[3] Then

[1] *Measure for Measure*, Act IV, Sc. 1.
[2] John Parkinson, *Paradisus*, 1629.
[3] Lord Bacon, *Of Gardens*.

there were the shady alleys with trees meeting in an arch over-head (willows, limes, sycamores, and whitethorn were commonly used). 'The thick-pleached alley' wherein Antonio saw Don Pedro and Claudio walking (*Much Ado about Nothing*) was probably the type of alley described by Bacon—'a covert alley upon carpenter's work, about twelve foot in height, by which you may go in shade into the garden'. In regard to walks between hedges, Parkinson says that privet, sweetbriar, whitethorn, 'enlaced together', were all used, 'and roses of one or two or more sorts placed here and there amongst them'. Low hedges were made of lavender, rosemary, sage, southern-wood, or lavender cotton. Others, he says, 'plant Cornell trees and plash them or keep them low to form a hedge'. Others again used pyracantha 'which in time will make an evergreen hedging and when it beareth fruit, which are red berries like unto hawthorn berries, makes a glorious shew among the green leaves in winter time'.

Other walks were made along the enclosing wall with the plants trained to form an arch overhead. Hyll calls these walls 'herbers', and he suggests the use of fragrant plants—rosemary, jasmine, and musk roses. In wall herbers of any length he suggests the making of windows 'whereby they might the more fully view and have delight of the whole beautie of the garden'. Galleries, which were such a feature of late mediæval and Tudor gardens, were even more sub-stantial than wall herbers and were 'privy ways' for the members of the household to reach the chapel and the garden. They were frequently adorned with arbours or 'roosting places'. Galleries of this sort are mentioned in the description of Thornbury Castle, which in Henry VIII's reign passed into the hands of the ill-fated Duke of Buckingham.

'On the south side of the ynner warde is a proper gardeyn, and above the same a goodly gallery conveying above and beneth from the principall lodgings boothe to the chapel and parish church, the utter part of the said gallery being of stoon imbattled and the ynner parte of tymbre covered with slate.

On the este syde of the said Castle or Manor is a goodly gardeyn to walke inne cloosed wt high walls imbattled. The conveyance thither is by the galery above and beneath and by other privie wayes,

Beside the same privie gardeyn is a large and goodly orcharde full of young graftes well laden wt fruite and many roses and other pleasyres : and in the same orcharde are many goodly alies to walke yn openly : and round about the same orcharde is covered on a good height, other goodly alies wt roosting places, coverede thoroughly wt white thorne and hasill, and wt oute the same ; on the utter parte the said orcharde is inclosed wt sawn pall and wt out that ditches and quick set hegges '.

Garden-houses as in mediæval days varied from arbours of the simplest type—Shakespeare's ' pleached bowers where honey-suckles ripen'd by the sun forbid the sun to enter '—to brick or stone buildings. The summer-house (a building open on all sides with slender pillars supporting the roof) erected by Bacon in the garden of Gray's Inn, remained till the middle of the eighteenth century. It stood on a small mount with a view over the neighbouring fields to the hills of Highgate. In London indeed garden-houses were apparently a fashionable cult and Hall, the Tudor chronicler, condemned these ' faire summer houses like Midsummer Pageants, with Towers, Turrets and Chimney tops ' with great severity. According to him they were ' not so much for use or profit, as for shew and pleasure, and bewraying the vanity of men's mindes, much unlike to the disposition of the ancient Citizens, who delighted in building of Hospitals and Almeshouses for the poore '. Parkinson, in the *Paradisus*, mentions the plants he considers best for arbours and banqueting houses—' the Jacimine, white and yellow, the double Honeysocke, the Ladies' Bower, both white and red and purple, single and double . . . to set by arbours and banquetting houses that are open before and above, to help to cover them, and to give both sight, smell and delight '. Humbler structures were sometimes covered with scarlet runners which ' do easily and soone spring up and growe into a very great length ; being sowen neere unto long poles fastened hard by them or hard by arbours and banquetting places '.

The custom of making arbours in trees dated at least from mediæval days, for a miniature in a fifteenth-century Italian Book of Hours shows a man seated in a ' roosting-place ' of this kind, writing a book. As in Holland lime trees were commonly trained to make elaborate arbours, two and even three stories high. Parkinson, in his *Paradisus*, says of the lime, ' it is planted both to make goodly Arbours and Summer banquetting houses . . . a second above it and a third also '. He describes a three-story arbour of this kind he had seen at Cobham, in Kent, which was so roomy that there was space for at least 50 men in each of the first two stories :

' And I have seene at Cobham in Kent, a tall or great bodied Lime tree, bare without boughes for eight foote high, and then the branches were spread round about so orderly, as if it were done by art, and brought to compasse that middle Arbour : And from those boughes the body was bare againe for eight or nine foote (wherein might be placed halfe an hundred men at the least, as there might be likewise in that underneath this) and then another rowe of branches to encompasse a third Arbour with stayres made for the purpose to this and that underneath it : upon the boughes were laid boards to tread upon, which was the goodliest spectacle mine eyes ever beheld for one tree to carry '.

Mounts were a conspicuous feature of English gardens throughout the sixteenth and seventeenth centuries and they are mentioned in the descriptions of nearly all the great gardens. The mounts were usually crowned with a substantial building. Bacon describes a mount as the central feature of a ' prince-like ' garden.

' I wish ', he says, ' in the middle a fair mount, with three ascents, and alleys enough for four to walk abreast ; which I would have to be perfect circles, without any bulwarks or embossments : and the whole mount to be 30 feet high, surmounted by a fine banquetting house with some chimneys neatly cast '.

In Henry VIII's reign an immense mount was constructed in the ' King's New Garden ', at Hampton Court, and it was crowned with a magnificent summer-house. Sometimes there were several mounts in one garden and if near the park Lawson suggests ' you may shoot a Buck ' from the mount. They were sometimes planted with fruit trees :

' When you behold in divers corners of your Orchard, Mounts of stone or wood, curiously wrought within and without, or of earth covered with Fruit Trees, Kentish Cherries, Damsons, Plums, etc., with stairs of precious workmanship : and in some corner (or more) a true Dial or Clock, and some Antick works ; and especially silver-sounding Musick, mixt Instruments, and Voices, gracing all the rest; How will you be wrapt with Delight ' ?[1]

Mazes and topiary work are mentioned in nearly all sixteenth- and seventeenth-century gardening books. The word ' maze ' suggests a hedge-maze to modern ears, but with few exceptions the mazes described by Elizabethan and Stuart writers were dwarf mazes made of hyssop, lavender cotton, winter savory, thyme, germander, etc. Thomas Hyll gives two designs for them (see illustration), ' that who so listeth, having such room in their garden may place the one of them . . . for the only purpose to sport in them at times '. Lawson, in his *New Orchard and Garden* (1618), describes a hedge maze—' Mazes well framed a man's height may perhaps make your friend wander in gathering of Berries till he cannot recover himself without your help '.

Topiary work is depicted in a few illustrations of mediæval gardens, but it seems to have become common even in small gardens in Tudor times. Bacon condemned the art. ' I, for my part, do not like images cut out in juniper or other garden stuff—they be for children. Little low hedges round like welts, with some pretty pyramids I like well, and in some places fair columns '. According to Parkinson privet was commonly used ' to be cut, led and drawn into what forme one will either of beasts, birds or men armed or otherwise '. Yew was naturally adapted for topiary work, and rosemary was ' sette by women for their pleasure to grow in sundry proportions as in the fashion of a cat, a peacock, or such things as they fancy '.[2] ' Your Gardener ', says Lawson, ' can frame your lesser wood to the shape of men armed in the field, ready to give battle : of swift-running Grey-hounds, or of well-sented and true running Hounds to chase the Deer or hunt the Hare. This kind of hunting shall not waste your Corn nor much your Coyne '.[3]

[1] W. Lawson, *A New Orchard and Garden* (1618).
[2] Barnaby Googe, *Foure Bookes of Husbandry* (1577).
[3] W. Lawson, *A New Orchard and Garden* (1618).

Bacon evidently disliked vases and statues in a garden as much as topiary work—' Great Princes sometimes add statues and such things for state and magnificence, but nothing to the true pleasures of a garden '. Statues and vases were apparently unknown in mediæval gardens. The fashion for them is said to have been revived by Cardinal d'Este early in the sixteenth century. He built his villa near Rome on the site of that of the emperor Hadrian, and distributed the statues found (whilst digging the foundations, etc.) in various parts of the grounds. Francis I, of France, imitated him and thence the custom became common in western Europe.

Fountains, as in mediæval days, were an important feature and contemporary accounts show they were very ornate. The fountains at Hampton Court, Whitehall and Nonsuch were celebrated. Norden, writing in 1598 of Hampton Court, says ' Queen Elizabeth hathe of late caused a very beautiful fountaine there to be erected in the second court, which graceth the Pallace, and serveth to great and necessarie use ; the fountain was finished in 1590 not without great charge '. Frederick, Duke of Wurtemburg, who visited the place in 1592, wrote : ' In the middle of the first and principal court stands a splendid high and massy fountain, with an ingenious water-work, by which you can, if you like, make the water to play upon the ladies and others who are standing by and give them a thorough wetting '. A similar type of fountain was noted by Hentzner in 1596 in the gardens of Whitehall. In the privy gardens at Nonsuch he remarks on several—two that spurted water one round the other, small birds being perched on each and the water streaming out of their bills, in the ' Grove of Diana ' a fountain with Actæon turned into a stag and sprinkled by the goddess and her nymphs ; and another with concealed pipes which spurted water on all that came near. The fountain at Kenilworth stood in an octagonal basin large enough for carp, and in the centre were two athletes standing back to back ' carrying a ball " 3 feet over " with the Earl of Warwick's heraldic device, the Bear and Ragged Staff, at the top. The sides of the great basin were carved with Neptune, Thetis in her chariot drawn by dolphins, there Triton by his fishes, here Proteus herding his sea-bulls, then Doris and her daughters solacing on sea sands . . . whales, whirlpools, sturgeons, tunnys, conches, and wealks '.

Parkinson says a garden should be embellished with ' a fountain in the midst thereof to convey water to every part of the garden either in pipes under the ground, or brought by hand and emptied into large cisterns or great Turkey Jars, placed in convenient places '. Apart from fountains, pools (condemned by Bacon) and ' fair receipts of water ' were common and as the essay *Of Gardens* shows the latter were very elaborate.

' For fountains, they are a great beauty and refreshment ; but pools mar all and make the garden unwholesome and full of flies and frogs. Fountains I intend to be of two natures ; the one that sprinkleth or spouteth water, the other a fair receipt of water of some 30 or 40 foot but without fish slime or mud. . . . As for the other kind of fountain, which we may call a bathing pool, it may admit much curiosity and beauty wherewith we will not trouble ourselves ; as that the bottom be finely paved, and with images ; the sides likewise and withal embellished with coloured glass and such things of lustre encompassed also with fine rails of low statues.'

In Sir Philip Sidney's *Arcadia* there is a delightful description of an Elizabethan garden with a pond ' whose shaking crystal was a perfect mirror to all the other beauties '.

' They came into a place curiously set with trees of the most taste-pleasing fruits ; but scarcely had they taken that into their consideration but that they were suddenly stept into a delicate green ; on each side of the green a thicket, and behind the thickets again new beds of flowers which being under the trees, the trees were to them a pavilion and they to the trees a mosaical floor. In the midst of all the place was a fair pond, whose shaking crystal was a perfect mirror to all the other beauties, so that it bare show of two gardens ; one in deed and the other in shadows ; and in one of the thickets was a fine fountain '.

At the time of the Dissolution most of the monastic properties passed into secular hands, and the gardens suffered many changes. But to this day many of the old monks' pools and fish stews remain, the only survivals of the old monastic enclosures. Among the most noted are those at Newstead Abbey and at Hatton Grange in Shropshire. At the latter the pools are still called by the old names—Abbot's Pool, Purgatory, Hell, and Bath Pool. Gardens on the sites of old monastic gardens have a charm peculiarly their own and those on the sites of old nunnery gardens preserve, I think, even more of their old character. At Carrow Abbey, for instance, the atmosphere still seems dominated by the generations of quiet nuns who from Stephen's reign to the Dissolution must have loved this secluded place. Above all, one is conscious there of the personality of that radiant laughter-loving saint, the Lady Julian of Norwich, who must often have frequented this garden. It was only a few hundred yards away that the 'Sixteen Revelations' were made known to her, the inspiration of her *XVI Revelations of Divine Love*, which is by many held to be the most beautiful of all English mystical writings. The peace of centuries haunts gardens such as these, and it will be a sad day indeed, not only for those of us who live in these islands, but for all those who come from the remotest parts of the Empire and America, and who love, as we do, the quiet hidden beauties of the old country, if they should ever be destroyed.

Sundials date back at least to the days of our Saxon ancestors. The oldest in England is one on a monolith in the Bewcastle churchyard, which dates from A.D. 670, and the names inscribed on the shaft are those of the princes who fought against the heathen invaders. There are no actual records of sundials in mediæval gardens, but in Tudor days they were apparently common and some are still in existence. Amongst the most interesting are the four-sided dial at Manington Hall, Shropshire, with the inscription :

> These shades do fleet
>   From day to day :
> And so this life
>   Passeth Awaie.
>   1595
>   Deus Mihi Lux
>   God is my Light.
>
> Finis Itineris sepulchrum
> The grave is the end of the journey.

THE STORY OF THE GARDEN

Fui ut es, eris ut sum.

I was as thou art, thou wilt be as I am.

Ut hora, sit vita.

Life is as an hour,

and the dial supposed to have been erected by Sir Francis
Nethersole, who acquired the Benedictine nunnery at Poles-
worth in 1539. (This nunnery was founded by Egbert, King
of the West Saxons, and his daughter Edith was the first abbess.)
The curious suggestive inscription on the dial runs thus :

Hortus utramque tulit, nos et meditemus in horto.

The garden bore both, let us also meditate in the garden.

Other Tudor sundials are those on the triangular lodge at
Rushton, built by Sir Thomas Tresham in Elizabeth's reign.
The building is symbolic of the Trinity and there are sundials
on each of the three gables, one inscribed ' Respicite ' ; another,
' non mihi ', and the third, ' soli laboravi ' ; the dial at Cordell's
Hospital at Long Melford dated 1573, and the dial at the Priory,
Warwick, dated 1556.

Amongst the most famous gardens of Tudor days were those
of Sion, Sir Thomas More's at Chelsea, Theobald's, Hampton
Court, Nonsuch, Kenilworth, and Sir Hugh Platt's.

Even in the sixteenth century Sion was an old garden and
many of the cypresses which are still there may have been planted
long before. (Turner refers to these cypresses in his Herbal,
1540.) The religious house or rather houses were founded by
Henry V on his accession, one for monks and the other for nuns
of the Swedish order of St. Bridget.

' and I have built
Two chantries, where the sad and solemn priests
Sing still for Richard's soul '.[1]

The King laid the foundation-stone in person. These houses
were known as the Monastery of St. Saviour and St. Bridget ;
there were eighty-five Religious (commemorating the seventy-
two disciples and thirteen apostles), sixty of the Religious being

[1] *Henry V*, Act IV, Sc. 1.

76

Sisters and of the twenty-five Brothers thirteen were priests. The chapels were under one roof, separated by a grille. It was a wealthy community, for Henry V gave them the Manor of Isleworth and, later, Henry VI endowed them with lands in many counties. For over a hundred years it was one of the most notable foundations; ' at the head of all the convents for women in England, in learning, riches and piety ', but at the time of the Dissolution the ' Daughters of Sion ' had to leave their peaceful abode and, carrying, it is said, the keys of Sion with them, they finally took refuge in Lisbon. Henry VIII kept the wealthy monastery in his own hands, and there his fifth queen, Katherine Howard, was imprisoned before her trial, and execution, and there too the King's body rested when being taken to Windsor, where he was buried. Edward VI gave the property to his uncle, the Lord Protector Somerset, who built the present house on the foundations of the old buildings, which he partially destroyed. Mary Tudor restored the place to the ' Daughters of Sion ', but on Elizabeth's accession they were again dispersed; like her father she kept the rich property in her own hands till her death, when Sion was bestowed on Henry Percy, ninth Earl of Northumberland.

This old garden has many memories—Henry V, Archbishop Chichele, the gentle nuns, the Lord Protector Somerset, John Dudley, Duke of Northumberland, who was executed on the accession of Mary Tudor, Lord Guildford Dudley and Lady Jane Grey (they spent their honeymoon at Sion), William Turner, the ' Father of English Botany ', Charles I's children (who were taken from Sion to St. James' Palace to see their father before his execution), Charles II (he took refuge at Sion when the Plague was raging in London in 1665), John Evelyn, and Queen Anne (as Princess she stayed at Sion). John Evelyn, who visited Sion in 1665, to attend the Council when Charles II was there, did not admire the garden which had been famed for over a century. He describes the place as ' built out of an old Nunnerie of stone, and faire enough but more celebrated for its garden than it deserves; yet there is excellent wall fruite, and a pretty fountaine; nothing else extraordinary '.

The interest of the gardens, however, centres in Tudor

days, when they were laid out by the Lord Protector Somerset and there is little reason to doubt that the work was done under the superintendence of Dr. William Turner, 'the Father of English Botany'. Somerset was keenly interested in botany, and when on Edward VI's accession Turner was able to return to England, the Protector made him his chaplain and physician. Turner dated his *Names of Herbes* (1548) from Sion, he frequently refers to the Sion garden, and he dedicated the first part of his noted Herbal to Somerset :

' To the mighty and christiane Prince Edward Duke of Summerset, Erle of Hertford, Lord Beauchampe and Uncle unto the Kynges Maiesty, Wyllyam Turner his servant wysheth increase in the knowledge of Goddes holy worde and grace to live thereafter '.

On the east and west sides of Sion there were originally large walled gardens and in the angle where they met there was a high mount whence there must have been a beautiful view of the river, but when Somerset was attainted for high treason, this mound was declared to be a fortification. The mound on the south-east side of the house is said to mark the site of the old 'fortification'. It was the opinion of the late Colonel Eustace Balfour that the walls and hedges shown in Bush's print dated 1737 (reproduced in Walford's *Greater London*) show the layout of the garden as designed by Somerset and Turner, two centuries before. This old formal garden was destroyed when the grounds were laid out afresh by Capability Brown. All that survives of the Tudor garden is the mulberry tree, said to be the oldest in England, and brought from Persia in 1548.

Probably no garden in Henry VIII's reign was so frequently visited by the foremost men of the age, both English and foreign, as the garden at Chelsea, belonging to that ' dauntless soul erect who smiled on death '—Sir Thomas More. The house dated from the early sixteenth century and is described by Erasmus as ' neither mean nor subject to envy yet magnificent and commodious enough '. The only and all too brief description of the garden that has come down to us is that by Heywood :

' Wonderfully charming, both from the advantages of its site . . . and also for its own beauty ; it was crowned with almost perpetual verdure ; it had flowering shrubs, and the branches of fruit trees interwoven in so beautiful a manner that it appeared like a tapestry woven by Nature herself'.

An avenue led to the river-side and the stairs descending to the eight-oared barge wherein Sir Thomas was wont to go to Whitehall or the City. There was also a great terrace walk running eastwards from the house. How often More must have walked on this terrace with the King (Henry VIII), Erasmus, Colet, Linacre, Tunstall, John Heywood, the early English playwright, to mention but a few of those who thronged the place which Erasmus describes as :

'a university of Christian religion, for though there is none therein but readeth or studieth the liberal sciences, their special care is piety and virtue ; none seem idle ; that worthy gentleman doth not govern with proud and lofty words, but with well-timed and courteous benevolence ; everybody performeth his duty, yet is there always alacrity ; neither is sober mirth anything wanting '.

Henry VIII frequently visited More at Chelsea, spending whole days there. Faulkner indeed says that the King probably bought Chelsea Manor ' from having observed in his frequent visits to Sir Thomas More the pleasantness of the situation on the bank of the Thames ; and from the salubrity of the air, deeming it a fit residence for his infant daughter, the Princess Elizabeth, then between three and four years of age '. In spite of the King's many visits More understood his royal master's temper all too well. One day the King came unexpectedly and dined with him, and after dinner walked in the garden with him for an hour with his arm about the Chancellor's neck. As soon as the King had taken his departure Sir Thomas' son-in-law observed to him that he should be very happy, for the King had treated no person with such familiarity save Cardinal Wolsey. ' I thank our Lord ', answered Sir Thomas, ' I find his grace my very good lord indeed . . . however, son Roper, I may tell thee I have no cause to be proud thereof, for if my head would win him a castle in France, it should not fail to go off '. After Sir Thomas's execution his former home became at times a royal residence. Anne of Cleves died there in 1557, and Katherine Parr, after Henry VIII's death, occupied it after her remarriage with Admiral Seymour, having charge of Princess

Elizabeth, then a child of thirteen. In Elizabeth's reign the property belonged for a time to Lord Burleigh, and until the latter part of the nineteenth century an elm in the park was commonly known as the 'Queen's Elm', under which it is said the Queen with Lord Burleigh sheltered during a storm. In 1615 part of the property was walled in and until 1876 was generally known as Chelsea Park—a park where the old mulberry trees and cedars remained till turned into the wilderness of bricks and mortar now know as Elm Park Estate.

Of Theobald's, the garden which is supposed to have inspired Bacon's essay *Of Gardens*, we know little beyond the fact that Gerard tells us in his Herbal that he had supervised both the gardens at Theobald's and those belonging to Lord Burleigh in the Strand for twenty years. Hentzner, who visited Theobald's in 1591, gives a singularly dull description of the gardens ; he barely mentions the plants and seems to have been impressed chiefly by the water garden, the labyrinths and the summer-house.

'We left London in a coach in order to see the remarkable places in its neighbourhood. The first was Theobald's, belonging to Lord Burleigh, the Treasurer. In the gallery was painted the genealogy of the Kings of England. From this place one goes into the garden, encompassed with water, so that with a boat one may wander among the fruit groves and have much pleasure and row between the shrubs ; here are a great variety of trees and herbs, labyrinths made with a great deal of labour, a fountain with its basin of white marble, columns also and pyramids of wood and other materials in various parts of the garden. After seeing these we were led by the gardener into the summer house and in the lower part, which is built semicircularly, are the twelve Roman Emperors in white marble and a table of Lydian stone ;[1] the upper part of the summer house is set with cisterns of lead into which the water is conveyed through pipes so that fish may be kept in them, and in summer-time they are very convenient for washing oneself in the cool water. In a banqueting room very near this and joined to it by a little bridge was an oval table of red marble '.

Peak, in his *Desiderata Curiosa*, said of these gardens, ' One might walk two myle in the walkes before he came to their

[1] Frederick, Duke of Wurzburg, who visited Theobald's in 1592, described this table as being 14 spans long, 17 wide, and 1 thick.

PLATE 20

Scene from *The Gardener's Labyrinth* (1651), by Thomas Hyll

Watering from a pump, from *The Gardener's Labyrinth* (1651).

PLATE 21

A MOST BRIEFE

and pleasaunt treatyse, teachynge
howe to dreff, sowe, and set a Garden,
and what propertyes also these few her
bes heare spoken of, haue to our como-
dytie: With the remedyes that may be
vsed àgainst such beasts, wozmes, flies
and such lyke, that commonly noy
gardēs, gathered out of the prin
cipallest Authors in this art
by Thomas Hyll
Londyner.

Title page (exact size) of the first gardening book printed in
the English language. *A most briefe and pleasaunt Treatyse*
(1563).

ends '. When James I, in 1603, made his ' Southern Progress ' to be crowned King of England, he visited Theobald's and in the labyrinth ' recreated himself in the meanders compact of bays, rosemary and the like overshadowing his walk '. He so coveted the garden that a few years later (1607) he gave Cecil Hatfield in exchange for it.

Although we have so little information concerning the magnificent garden which was under Gerard's supervision, of his own garden we have abundant information in his Herbal. Holborn was almost a village then and wallflowers and stone-crops grew on the houses. Gerard tells us that in Gray's Inn Lane he gathered mallow, shepherd's purse, sweet woodruff, bugle, and in the meadows near by red-flowered clary, white saxifrage, the ' sad-coloured ' rocket, yarrow, lesser hawkweed and trefoil. Gerard's own garden was probably on the slope of the hill between Ely Place and the Fleet Hill ; where he was surrounded by meadows, fields, and woods. This garden was full of rarities, for how often in his Herbal we read of various plants, ' these be strangers in England yet I have them in my garden', and sometimes he triumphantly adds ' where they flourish as in their natural place of growing '. In 1596 he published a catalogue of twenty-four pages of the plants he grew—the first complete catalogue of the plants in any garden, public or private. The only known copy of the first edition is in the Sloane Collection in the British Museum. The second edition was published in 1599 and is excessively rare. Is it not at least probable that Shakespeare visited Gerard's garden ? They were near neighbours for many years, for Shakespeare lived in the house of a Huguenot refugee (Mountjoy by name) 1598–1604. This house was at the corner of Mugwell Street (now Monkswell Street) and Silver Street and almost opposite was the Barber-Surgeons' Hall. In 1598, the year after the publication of his Herbal, and again in 1607, Gerard was ap-pointed examiner of candidates for admission to the freedom of the Barber-Surgeons' Company. Except in the herbals there is more old English herb lore in Shakespeare's works than in those of any other writer, and it is difficult to believe that the man whose works are so full of traditional plant lore did not visit the garden of the greatest herbalist of the day.

THE STORY OF THE GARDEN

Kenilworth, being in Warwickshire, must have been known to Shakespeare and a vivid contemporary account of it is to be found in a letter dated 1575, from Robert Laneham to Master Humphrey Martin, mercer of London. The letter was written during Queen Elizabeth's visit to the castle, and certainly no other contemporary description gives so clear an idea of the beauty of a great garden of Elizabethan times, with its spacious grassy terrace, ' with arbors at either end ', ' redolent by sweet trees and flowers ', the view from it of a vast enclosure divided into four plots, the carved beasts, the aviary, the fountain in an octagonal basin, the beauty and scent of the flowers, the songs of the birds and the animated scene with all the people passing to and fro for the pageant.

' His Honor's the Earl of Leicester's exquisite appointment of a beautiful garden, an acre or more in quantity, that lieth on the north. Whereon all along the Castle wall is reared a pleasant terrace, ten feet high and twelve feet broad, even under foot and fresh of fine grass, as is also the side thereof towards the garden, in which by sundry equal distances with obelisks and spheres and white bears all of stone upon their curious bases by goodly shew were set.

To these two fine arbors, redolent by sweet trees and flowers, at each end one. The garden plot under that, with fair alleys green and some (for change) with sand, smooth and firm, pleasant to walk on as a sea-shore when the water is avoided.'

He describes the garden itself as being divided into four large quarters and in the centre of each ' upon a base of two feet square and high ' obelisks of red porphyry. There were plantations of all pleasant fruits and in the middle of the wall furthest from the terrace a great aviary 30 feet long, 14 broad and 20 high, in the centre of the garden a fountain in an octagonal basin, ' wherein pleasantly playing to and fro carp, tench, bream, and for varietie pearch and eel '.

' A garden then so appointed, as wherein aloft upon sweet shadowed walk of terrace, in heat of summer to feel the pleasant whisking wind above, or delectable coolness of the fountain-spring beneath, to taste of delicious strawberries, cherries and other fruits, even from their stalks ; to smell such fragrancy of sweet odours, breathing from the plants, herbs and flowers ; to hear such natural melodious music and tunes of birds ; to have in eye for mirth sometime these underspringing streams ; then the woods, the waters (for both pool and chase were hard at hand in sight), the deer, the people (that out of the East arbour in the base Court, also at hand in view), the fruit trees, the plants, the herbs, the flowers, the change in colours, the birds flittering, the fountain streaming, the fish swimming, all in such delectable variety, order and dignity ; whereby at one moment, in one place, at hand, without travel, to have so full fruition of so many God's blessings, by entire delight unto all senses (if all can take) at once ; for etymon of the word worthy to be called Paradise ; and though not so goodly as Paradise for want of the fair rivers, yet better a great deal by the lack of so unhappy a tree.'

A London pleasaunce, with interesting associations and dating from Tudor days, remained a garden until this century, when it was sold (except a very small part) by the Drapers' Company, to whom it had belonged since Henry VIII's reign. Before that it was the property of Thomas Cromwell, Secretary of State to Henry VIII. The garden then was much smaller and he enlarged it by the simple process of removing his neighbours' palings (without even giving them warning), encroaching in each case 22 feet and erecting a high brick wall. Stowe, who records this in his *Survey of London*, writes with feeling on the subject, for his father was one of those whose property was filched in this forcible manner. ' My Father had a garden there, and there was a house standing close to his south pale ; this house they loosed from the ground and bare upon Rowlers into my Father's garden 22 foot ere my Father heard thereof '. Cromwell, however, was second only to the King and Stowe states that no one ventured to utter a protest. When Cromwell fell from favour and was executed, the Drapers' Company bought the property from the King.

Other well-known gardens were those belonging to that great gardener, Sir Hugh Plat. Sir Hugh Plat, who came of a well-known Hertfordshire family, was the son of a wealthy brewer, and was educated at St. John's College, Cambridge, and thence went to Lincoln's Inn, but we never hear of him practising as a lawyer. Throughout his life he seems to have been an amateur in the true sense of the word, keenly interested both in gardening and mechanical inventions, but having ample means he never appears to have pursued these interests with any commercial purpose. He was in fact the Sir Kenelm Digby of Elizabethan days. It was for his mechanical inventions that he was knighted by James I (there are many unpublished notes by him on scientific subjects among the MSS. in the British Museum, *Collections relating to alchemy, Secrets of Physicke and Surgery*, etc.), but even among his contemporaries he was chiefly noted for his knowledge of all that pertained to gardening. He had his own gardens at Bishops' Hall, Bethnal Green and Kirby Castle, and judging from his books he both visited and was in communication with the leading gardeners of his day. All the information he gleaned seems to have been most carefully noted, for in each case he mentions the name of his informant—' Mr. Pointer of Twickenham ' ; ' Parson Simson ' ; ' Andrew Hill ' ; ' Colbourne ', and so forth.

His first book was *The Jewel House of Art and Nature* (1594), but his claim to fame rests on the section of the book devoted to distillation, which was subsequently enlarged and published separately with the attractive title *Delightes for Ladies to Adorn their Persons, Tables, Closets and Distillatories with Bewties, banquets, perfumes and Waters* (1602). In this dainty little volume every page of the early editions is surrounded with a charming woodcut border and even the blank pages at the end of the book have the same. The borders vary considerably ; that in the 1602 edition being the best. In the later editions they are poor. Some of the most pleasing have conventional designs with the Tudor rose, the fleur de lis of France and the Queen's initials, E.R., interlaced with the design at the top and bottom of the page; others with roses, violets, gilliflowers and marigolds, worked into the design. The dedicatory poem must have been very pleasing to the ladies for whom these ' delightes ' were collected, but it is too long to quote more than a few lines :

> With painful pen I whilom writ at large
> But now my pen and paper are perfum'd,
>
> .   .   .   .   .
>
> Rosewater the inke I write withall :
> Of sweetes the sweetest I will now commend,

To sweetest creatures that the earth doth beare
These are the Saints to whom I sacrifice
Preserves and conserves both of plums and peare.

The recipes themselves are full of the fragrance of an Elizabethan still-room—damask petals in abundance, rose-water,
elecampane roots (it was elecampane that Helen of Troy had
in her hand when carried off by Paris—hence the name), 'clipt
violets', gilliflowers, and marigold petals, candied rosemary
flowers, borage flowers, sucket of lettuce stalks, candied nut-
megs, oranges 'preserved after the Portugall fashion', paste
of cowslips, cinnamon water, distilled waters of thyme, lavender
and rosemary, 'spirit of honey', eglantine water, 'Scottish
handwater' marigolds candied in wedges 'Spanish fashion',
sweet hand waters, rose, cowslip and violet vinegars, damask
powders, 'sweet and delicate pomanders, washing balls, paste
royal in spices', 'Muskadine confits', 'sweet powder for
sweet bags', balm water, angelica water, rosa solis, 'Conserve
of red and damask roses', conserves of violets, borage, flowers,
rosemary and bugloss flowers, syrup of horehound, of maiden
hair and hyssop.

The most important plan of an Elizabethan garden that has
come down to us is that of All Souls College, Oxford. Robert
Hovenden, who was Warden at the time of Queen Elizabeth's
second visit to the city, made the garden at his own expense.
The plan is preserved in the first of the five large volumes
of his *Typus Collegiæ*, and it is full of interesting details, but
unfortunately no reproduction gives an idea of the charm and
attractive colouring of the original. Knot gardens were the
dominating feature, and one of the two large 'knots' east of
the old cloisters Hovenden had laid out in a design taken
from the arms of the Founder—Archbishop Chichele. For
this 'knot' is the college chevron between three cinquefoils
gules. The other is in a design similar to one in Hyll's *Gardener's
Labyrinth* (1574). Beyond there is a terrace with a summer-
house. The hedges between the cloister and the knot garden
and on the south side are elaborately cut to resemble a castellated
wall. Near the High Street are two more knot gardens surrounded on three sides by a wall and on the south side by a spiked
wooden fence. The site of All Souls garden was given by Sir

William Petre, who was successively Secretary of State to Henry VIII, Treasurer to Edward VI, Secretary to Queen Mary, and Privy Councillor under Elizabeth.

Of the gardens of humbler folk the most vivid word-pictures are those to be found in Tusser's *Five Hundred Points* (1573). For here we find the typical English farmhouse garden, a garden overflowing with fruit and fragrant with delicious scents—of roses, carnations and sweet-scented herbs. Tusser's lists are full of the names of the old-fashioned flowers country house-wives have always cherished—red and damask roses, sweet Williams, 'sops in wine' (carnations), eglantine, snapdragons, pinks, pansies, hollyhocks, wallflowers, bachelors' buttons, columbines, daffodils, rosemary, primroses, lily of the valley, marigolds, lilies, lavender, valerian, Star of Bethlehem, peonies, poppies, and he takes it for granted that the garden is the special province of the housewife and gives her excellent practical instructions in digging, weeding, sowing seeds, etc. In those days, when seedsmen were scarce, it was the housewife's duty to collect her own seeds and to exchange with her neighbours.

> Good huswifes in Sommer will save their owne seedes
>   against the next yere, as occasion nedes.
> One seede for another, to make an exchange
>   with fellowlie neighbourhood seemeth not strange.

It is interesting to remember that Mr. Rudyard Kipling found the motive for his *An Habitation Enforced* in Tusser's homely book. Much has been written about old Tusser and Fuller summed up his life thus:

'He was successively a musician, schoolmaster, serving man, husbandman, grazier, poet, more skilful in all than thriving in any profession. He traded at large in oxen, sheep, dairies, grain of all kinds to no profit. Whether he bought or sold he lost, and when a renter impoverished himself and never enriched his landlord. Yet hath he laid down excellent rules in his book of husbandry and houswifry, (so that the observer thereof must be rich) in his own defence. He spread his bread with all sorts of butter, yet none would stick thereon. Yet I hear no man to charge him with any vicious extravagancy or visible carelessness, imputing his ill success to some occult cause on God's counsel.

Tusser died in 1580 and was buried in St. Mildred's in the Poultry. His grave has this inscription:

> Here Thomas Tusser,
>   Clad in earth doth lie,
> That sometime made
>   The Points of Good Husbandrie.
> By him then learn thou mayest
>   Here learn thou must
> When all is done we sleep
>   And turn to dust.
> And yet through Christ
>   To heaven we hope to go,
> Who reads his bookes,
>   Shall find his faith was so.[1]

In Shakespeare's and Spenser's works, to say nothing of the lesser writers, such as Herrick, the beauty, the fragrance and the ' atmosphere' of the flowers and gardens of sixteenth-century England are immortalised, above all the homely flowers which for centuries have been grown in this country alike in princely and cottage gardens. In what foreign literature can one gather such handfuls of flowers, described in so few words and showing such intimate knowledge as in the works of the Elizabethans?

What lovelier than the lyric of sunrise in a garden, the marigolds opening their ' golden eyes', and the garden so full of dew that the horses of the sun can be watered at the ' springs on chaliced flowers'?

> Hark! Hark! the lark at heaven's gate sings
> And Phœbus 'gins arise;
>   His steeds to water at those springs
>   On chaliced flowers that lies;
> And winking Mary-buds begin to ope their golden eyes.
> With everything that pretty is—My lady, sweet, arise;
>   Arise, arise.

A miniature picture of early morning is suggested in the

---

[1] See *Five Hundred Points of Good Husbandry*, by Thomas Tusser, with an introduction by Sir Walter Scott, and a Benediction by Rudyard Kipling, incorporated in a foreword by E. V. Lucas.

brief phrase ' the morn's dew on the myrtle leaf ',[1] the ' soft myrtle ' of *Venus and Adonis*. Whose garden, one wonders, is depicted in Spenser's matchless word-picture[2] of a butterfly flitting about in the sunlight of an Elizabethan pleasaunce full of ' odors and alluring sights ' ?

> To the gay gardins his unstaid desire
>   Him wholly carried, to refresh his sprights ;
> There lavish nature in her best attire,
>   Powres forth sweete odors and alluring sights.

> There he arriving round about doth flie,
>   From bed to bed, from one to other border,
> And takes survey, with curious busie eye.
>   Of every flower and herbe there set in order :
> Now this now that he tasteth tenderly
>   Yet none of them he rudely doth disorder ;
> Ne with his feete their silken leaves deface,
>   But pastures on the pleasures of each place.

> And then again he turneth to his play,
>   To spoyle the pleasures of that Paradise ;
> The wholesome Saulge, and Lavender still gray,
>   Rank-smelling Rue, and Cummin good for eyes,
> The Roses raigning in the pride of May,
>   Sharpe Isope, good for greene woulds remedies,
> Faire Marigoldes, and Bees-alluring Thyme,
>   Sweet Marjoram, and Daysies decking prime.

> Coole violets and Orpine growing still,
>   Embathed Balme, and cheerfull Galingale,
> Fresh Costmarie, and breathfull Camomile,
>   Dull Poppie, and drink-quickening Setuale,
> Veyne, healing Vervein, and head-purging Dill,
>   Sound Savourie, and Basil hartie-hale,
> Fat Colworts, and comforting Perseline,
>   Colde Lettuce and refreshing Rosmarine.

---

[1] *Antony and Cleopatra*, Act III, Sc. 12.
[2] E. Spenser, *Muiopotmos*.

Then when he hath both plaid and fed his fill,
In the warme sunne he doth himself embay,
And there him rests in riotous suffisaunce
Of all his gladfulness and kingly joyaunce.

How much there is in both Shakespeare and Spenser's writings of the loved spring flowers ' the sweet o' the year ' !

Fresh Spring, the herald of Love's mighty King,
In whose cote-armour richly are displayed
All sorts of flowers, the which on earth do spring,
In goodly colours gloriously arrayed.[1]

Of the joyous time :

When proud-pied April dress'd in all his trim
Hath put a spirit of youth in every thing.[2]

Primroses, *Primulæ silvarum*, which Ben Jonson called ' the glory of the spring ', and so named, says Parkinson, because ' they shew by their flowering the new Spring to be coming on, they being as it were the first Embassadors thereof '. How perfectly Shakespeare describes their rare combination of pale sweetness and merry radiance !

Primroses, first born child of Ver
Merry Springtime's harbinger
With her bells dim.[3]

Daffodils :

That come before the swallow dares and take
The winds of March with beauty.[4]

Cowslips 'so plentiful in the fields but many take delight in them and plant them in their gardens . . . the smallest are usually called throughout all the North Country Birds Eyen because of the small yellow circle in the bottoms of the flowers resembling the eye of a bird '.[5]

[1] E. Spenser.
[2] W. Shakespeare. Sonnet XCVIII.
[3] *The Two Noble Kinsmen*, Act I, Sc. 1.
[4] *Winter's Tale*, Act IV, Sc. 3.
[5] J. Parkinson, *Paradisus*.

> The Cowslips tall her pensioners be,
> In their gold coats spots you see :
> These be rubies, fairy favours,
> In these freckles live their savours.[1]

'Pensioners' to our modern ears suggest old men, but Queen Elizabeth's pensioners were a guard of the tallest and noblest born men in the prime of their youth, arrayed in resplendent 'gold' liveries encrusted with jewels. In the *Merry Wives of Windsor* we realize that 'pensioners' were more important than earls ; 'There have been knights and lords and gentlemen with their coaches, letter after letter, gift after gift ; smelling so sweetly (all musk) and so rustling I warrant you in silk and gold ; and yet there has been earls and what is more pensioners'. And the 'cowslips tall' of Titania's court were the fairy queen's pensioners wearing rubies—'fairy favours'—on their golden liveries. Spenser too loved cowslips :

> Strowe me the ground with Daffadowndillies
> And cowslips and Kingcups and loved Lillies,
> The pretty Pawnce
> And the Chevisaunce
> Shall match with the fayre flowre Delice.[2]

The many other spring flowers—'Puck's broom',[3] 'to sweep the dust behind the door', the plant which gave its name to the Plantagenet family and as a herb was valued throughout the Middle Ages for its medicinal properties as well as its beauty and fragrance—'sweet is the broome-flowre but yet soure enough' ;[4] 'daisies smell-less yet most quaint', 'daisies pied' beloved also of Chaucer ; 'ladysmocks all silver white',[5] 'bold oxlips and the crown imperial',[6] 'violets blue' whose scent Bacon thought the sweetest of all flowers—'that which above all others yields the sweetest smell is the violet and next to that the musk rose '—

---

[1] *A Midsummer Night's Dream*, Act II, Sc. 1.
[2] Edmund Spenser, *The Shepherd's Calendar*.
[3] *A Midsummer Night's Dream*, Act V, Sc. 2.
[4] E. Spenser. Sonnet XXVI.
[5] *Love's Labour's Lost*, Act V, Sc. 2.
[6] *Winter's Tale*, Act IV, Sc. 3.

THE TUDOR AGE

'The violets that strew
The green lap of the new-come Spring '[1]

abound in Shakespeare's writings :

'Violets dim,
And sweeter than the lids of Juno's eyes,
Or Cytherea's breath '.[2]

To the scent of the sweet south wind blowing over violets, the Duke in *Twelfth Night* compares ethereal music :

That strain again ! It had a dying fall.
O it came o'er my ear like the sweet south
That breathes upon a bank of violets
Stealing and giving odour.[3]

'Nodding violets' with thyme and oxlips clothed the bank where Titania slept, and in one of the sonnets we read :

'The forward violet thus did I chide :
Sweet thief, whence didst thou steal the sweet that smells
If not from my love's breath ? The purple pride
Which on thy soft cheek for complexion dwells
In my love's veins thou hast too grossly dyed '.[4]

The violet is the old English symbol of constancy. In a book of songs published in Elizabeth's reign, entitled *A Handful of Pleasant Delights* (1566), there is a quaint poem, 'A Nosegay always Sweet for Lovers to send Tokens of Love at New Years Tide or for Fairings as they in their minds shall be disposed to write'. One verse begins :

'Violet is for faithfulness
Which in me shall abide.'

In Anthonye Askham's *Herball* (1550) there is this charming recipe for sleeplessness. 'For them that may not slepe for sickness seeth this herb in water and at even let him soke well hys feete in the water to the ancles ; when he goeth to bed

---

[1] *The Two Noble Kinsmen*, Act I, Sc. 1.
[2] *Winter's Tale*, Act IV, Sc. 3.
[3] *Twelfth Night*, Act I, Sc. 1.
[4] Sonnet XCIX.

bind of this herbe to his temples and he shal slepe wel by the grace of God '.

Purple anemones, the ' azured hue ' of bluebells, columbines (one of the flowers given by Ophelia), the flower de luce, which adorned Joan of Arc's sword :

> ' here is my keen-edged sword
> Deck'd with fine flower de luces on each side '.[1]

Then the wealth of the summer flowers above all roses—' roses do comfort the heart '.[2] The rose, as Gerard tells us, ' beeing not onely esteemed for his beautie, vertues and his fragrant and odoriferous smell ; but also because it is the honour and ornament of our English Scepter as by the conjunction appeareth in the uniting of those two most royall houses of Lancaster and Yorke. Which pleasant floures deserve the chiefest places in Crownes and garlands '. Shakespeare's ' morning roses newly washed with dew ' :

> ' So sweet a kiss the golden sun gives not
> To those fresh morning drops upon the rose '.

In Shakespeare alone there are sixty passages fragrant with roses—the true old roses. For his roses were the red rose of England, ' the red rose on triumphant briar ', the white rose of England, Damask roses, the musk roses and eglantine of Titania's bower, the cabbage rose, the York and Lancaster rose. And in one of his sonnets their scent lives for ever.

> ' The rose looks fair but fairer it we deem
> For that sweet odor which doth in it live.
> The canker blooms have full as deep a dye
> As the perfumed tincture of the roses
> Hang on such thorns and play as wantonly.
> When summer's breath their masked buds discloses.
> But for their virtue only is their show,
> They live unwoo'd and unrespected fade ;
> Die to themselves. Sweet roses do not so ;
> Of their sweet deaths are sweeter odours made '.

---

[1] *King Henry VI*, Part I, Act I, Sc. 2.
[2] William Langham, *The Garden of Health* (1579).

Then Perdita's 'lilies of all kinds', the flowers to which Shakespeare refers over twenty times and which Spenser described as 'lady of the flowering field'.[1] Then the 'fairest flowers o' the season'—Ben Jonson's 'rich Carnations' and the 'streaked gilliflowers' beloved by Spenser:

> 'Bring hither the pink and purple columbine
> With gillyflowers
> Bring Coronations and Sops in wine
> Worn of paramours'.

The 'lark's heels trim'; the marigold 'that goes to bed with the sun and with him rises weeping'; the 'pinks of courtesy' and 'pansies for thoughts'—'pray God give thee but one handfull of heavenly hearts ease, which passeth al the pleasant flowers that grow in this worlde',[2] and the monkshood of Romeo's 'dram of poison'.[3] Sweet clover and burnet, which Bacon esteemed so highly for perfuming the air when trodden upon, the sweet-scented honeysuckle, the 'luscious woodbine' of Titania's bower, the flowers which grew so thickly over the bower where Beatrice and Benedick met:

> 'the pleached bower
> Where honeysuckle ripened by the sun
> Forbid the sun to enter'.[4]

The aromatic herbs—rosemary, 'that's for remembrance; pray you love, remember', the herb of which Sir Thomas More wrote 'As for rosemarie I lette it runne all over my garden walls, not onlie because my bees love it, but because it is the herb sacred to remembrance and to friendship, whence a sprig of it hath a dumb language'. Of this herb William Langham in his *Garden of Health* (1579) says: 'Carry powder of the flower about thee, to make thee merry, glad, gracious and well-beloved of all men . . . the conserve of the flowers comforteth the heart marvellously'. The aromatic sharp hyssop, good for 'green

---

[1] *Faerie Queene*, II. 6. 16.
[2] *Bullein's Bulwarke of defence . . . which Bulwarke is kepte with Hillarius the Gardiner* (1562).
[3] *Romeo and Juliet*, Act V, Sc. 1.
[4] *Henry V*, Act V, Sc. 2.

wounds remedies '; and rue, which, like rosemary, keeps its
' seeming and savour all the winter long ' :

> ' There's rue for you ; and some for me ;
> We may call it herb of grace o' Sundays.
> Oh, you must wear your rue with a difference '.[1]

It was rue the gardener in *King Richard II* set to com-
memorate the sad queen :

> ' Here had she fall a tear ; here in this place,
> I'll set a bank of rue, some herb of grace ;
> Rue, even for ruth, here shortly shall be seen,
> In the remembrance of a weeping queen '.[2]

Perdita's ' hot lavender ', thyme and savoury, Titania's bank
' where the wild thyme blows ', fennel and mint, camomile,
' the more it is trodden on the faster it grows ', the ' sweet
marjoram of the sallet ', sweet balm, wherewith the elves were
commanded to rub the chairs in Windsor Castle :

> ' The several chairs of order look you scour
> With juice of balm, and every precious flower ',

and ' Dian's bud ' (*artemisia*) used by Puck at Oberon's command to undo the charm laid on Titania by ' love in Idleness ' :

> ' Be as thou wast wone to be,
> See as thou wast wont to see ;
> Dian's bud on Cupid's flower
> Hath such force and blessed power '.

John Lyly too in his *Euphues and his England* gives us a
charming glimpse into an Elizabethan garden and the courtly
folk in it :

' Gentlemen, what floure like you best in all this border, heere be
faire Roses, sweete Violets, fragrant Primroses, heere wil be Jilly-
floures, Carnations, sops in wine, sweet Johns, and what may either
please you for sight or delight you with savour ; Loth we are you
should have a posie of all, yet willing to give you one, not that which
shal looke best, but such a one as you shal lyke best.

[1] *Hamlet*, Act IV, Sc. 5.
[2] *King Richard II*, Act III, Sc. 4.

Lady, of so many sweet floures to chuse the best, it is harde, seeing they be all so good. If I should preferre the fairest before the sweetest you would happely imagine that either I were stopped in the nose, or wanton in the eyes : if the sweetnesse before the beauty, then would you gesse me eyther to live with savours, or to have no judgement in colours ; but to tell my minde (upon correction be it spoken) of all floures I love a faire woman '.

A unique record of the flowers grown in Elizabethan gardens is to be found in the collection of exquisite flower and fruit paintings[1] by Jacques Le Moyne. Le Moyne, who, according to Brunet, was a native of Dieppe, escaped the massacre of Saint Bartholomew and fled to this country. It is generally presumed that he became a member of the Sidney household, possibly in a tutorial capacity, for his book, *La Clef des Champs*, published at Blackfriars in 1586, is dedicated to Lady Mary Sidney, mother of Sir Philip Sidney. Whether a member of the household or not, he was certainly on terms of the friendliest intimacy, for the dedication is signed ' vostre très affectionné '. Le Moyne states that his book (of which there are only two known copies) was published for the use of those engaged in the arts of printing, sculpture, goldwork, embroidery and tapestry and some of the drawings were utilized as illustrations. The original drawings are very beautiful and the colours as fresh and clear as though painted yesterday.

The earliest gardening book printed in the English language that has come down to us is *A Most Briefe and pleasant treatyse teachynge how to dress, sowe and set a Garden . . . by Thomas Hyll, Londyner* (1563). The only known copy of this tiny volume, which is a compilation chiefly from classical sources, is in the British Museum. The subsequent enlarged editions of the book were issued with the title *The Profitable Arte of Gardening*, the known editions being those of 1572, 1574, 1579, 1586, 1593, and 1608. Hyll's later book, *The Gardener's Labyrinth* (1577), is incomparably his best and it contains attractive woodcuts depicting Tudor gardens with people in the costumes of the period, either working in the garden or enjoying the beauty of it. Hyll died before he completed this book, and he left the editing of it to his friend Henry Dethicke, who prefaced

[1] Now in the Victoria and Albert Museum.

the book with a dedicatory letter addressed to William Cecil, Lord Burghley, Lord High Treasurer of England. Hyll's name is also associated with that rare little volume, *The newe Jewell of Health* (1576), by George Baker, who was ' chirurgian ' to Queen Elizabeth. In his preface, Baker states : ' Thomas Hyll dyd also take paynes in this worke, but before it coulde be brought to perfection, God tooke him to his mercie'. The attractive preface to this book concludes thus :

' So finishing this my simple Preface, desiring God to further the studie of all those which faithfully and truely meane in the exercise of this so noble an Arte, desiring all those which shall find any fault, that they will friendlye admonish me thereof, or else to note them in the margent of their owne bookes for their private use and commoditie, till such time as it shall be newe printed agayne, and then if it shall please them to give me their old Bookes so corrected, I will deliver them newe for them. And as for those finde faultes which will doe nothing themselves, I wey them not, for I had rather be serviceable to my Countrie than to please some particular persons, as the Lorde doth knowe, who rules and guydes us all in the right way. Amen.

From my house in Bartholomew's Lane beside the Royall exchange in London this XVI day of Februarye 1576.'

The first book devoted entirely to kitchen gardens is that excessively rare little volume, *Profitable Instructions for the Manuring, Sowing and Planting of Kitchen Gardens . . . by Richard Gardiner of Shrewsberie* (1599). The only copy in this country is one of the second edition (1603), and that is in the British Museum. The only copy of the first edition (1599) I know was formerly in the library of the late Mr. J. Jacobs. It came into the market a few years ago, and fetched £100. I believe it is now in a private library in America. *Profitable Instructions* is a pamphlet thirty pages long, and the author was a Shrewsbury linen draper. He treats of cabbage, carrots, parsnips, turnips, lettuces, beans, onions, cucumbers, artichokes, and leeks. Potatoes are not even mentioned, for though Gerard was growing them in his garden in Fetter Lane, the novelty was apparently still unknown in Shropshire. Gardiner was an enthusiast on the subject of lettuces and carrots. His lettuces, he declared, were better than those grown in London. His dissertation on carrots is lengthy and concludes thus :

March

(A calendar miniature by Simon Bening of Bruges, c.1530)
British Library

'Carrets are good to be eaten with salt fish. Therefore sowe Carrets in your Gardens and humbly praise God for them, as for a singular "great blessing" . . . Admit if it should please God that any City or towne should be besieged with the Enemy, what better provision for the greatest number of people can be then every garden to be sufficiently planted with carots?'

Two other Elizabethan books of kitchen garden and orchard interest are *A Short Instruction very profitable and necessary* . . . (1592) and *The Orchard and the Garden* (1597). The only known copy of the former diminutive treatise is in the Marquis of Crewe's library.[1] It is the only gardening book I know in which the instruction is given to make the sign of the cross when planting. 'Coleworts white and greene must be sowen in February or March in an old moon and in such a sygne X it is good to replant them'. Both these books are translations, the former from the French original and the latter on the title page is described as 'gathered from the French and Dutch'. The important translations of this period were those by Leonard Mascall, Barnaby Googe and Richard Surflet. The best known of these are the two latter—Barnaby Googe's *Foure Bookes of Husbandry* (1577), written throughout in a very lively dramatic fashion and in dialogue, and Richard Surflet's *Countrie Farme* (1600). Leonard Mascall's *Booke of the Art and manner howe to plant and graffe . . . With divers other new practise, by one of the Abbey of Saint Vincent in Fraunce practised with his owne handes . . . with an addition of certaine Dutch practises* (1572), was the first book translated into English and is dedicated to 'my very good Lorde Sir John Pawlet, Knight, Lorde S. John'. The epistle dedicatory to the reader is charming:

'Gentle Reader thou shalt understand, I have taken out of divers Authours this simple worke, into our Englishe tongue, praying thee for to accept it in good part : in so dooing thou shalt holden me to traveyle further therein . . .

Wherefore, gentle Reader, let us nowe leave of from all wanton games and ydle pastimes, and be no more children which seeke but theyr owne gayne and pleasure, let us therefore seeke one of us for another all good workes for the common wealth, whereby those that doe come after us may so enjoye our workes and travell herein,

---

[1] An earlier edition has recently come into the market. See page 276.

as we have done of our predecessors, that therein God may be glorified, praysed and honoured in all our workes of planting and graffing : and we therefore may be thankefull, from age to age, during this mortal lyfe. Amen '.

Mascall (*circa* 1546–1605) came of a family said to have established themselves in Sussex shortly after the Conquest and there is still a farm called Mascall's. The name is supposed to be a corruption of the Norman Marescal, and members of the family were sheriffs of the county in the reigns of Richard Cœur de Lion and John. Leonard Mascall's home was Plumpton Place and in the moat which formerly surrounded it he is said to have put the first carp brought to England. With the exception of the ' Dutch practises ' the book is a translation of David Brossard's *L'Art et Manière de semer de faire Pepinières*, which is chiefly concerned with grafting. This art was considered of paramount importance in mediæval, Tudor and Stuart times, and Mascall states that it was the Romans who first taught it. The most interesting passage in the book is the beautiful old gardening prayer, which the author quotes :

' And, whensoever ye shall plant or graffe it shall be mete and good for you to saye as foloweth.

In the name of God the Father, the Sonne and the holy Ghost, Amen. Increase and multiplye, and replenishe the earth : and saye the Lordes prayer, then say : Lord God heare my prayer, and let this my desire of thee be hearde. The holy spirite of God which hath created all things for man and hath given them for our comfort, in thy name O Lorde we set, plant, and graffe, desiring that by thy mighty power they maye encrease, and multiply upon the earth, in bearing plenty of fruite, and the profite, and comfort of all thy faithfull people, thorow Christe our Lorde. Amen '.

CHAPTER IV

STUART TIMES

During the latter half of the sixteenth and the first half of the seventeenth century, gardens were continually being enriched by new treasures. Indeed, it is interesting to realize how many of what are now our most familiar plants were introduced during this period—the crown imperial, tulips, everlastings, love-in-a-mist, dittany, martagon lilies, honesty, the annual candytuft, lychnis, the Persian fritillary, the Persian ranunculus, lilacs, laburnum, the yellow crocus, double hepaticas, African marigolds, Sweet Sultan, annual and perennial sunflowers, Marvel of Peru, Michaelmas daisies, evening primrose, tobacco, nasturtium, *lilium canadense rubrum, lobelia cardinalis,* acacia, the American plane, the tulip tree, the red maple, and amongst vegetables Jerusalem artichokes and the potato. It requires very little imagination to realise the keen interest taken in the numerous plants sent from the New World, quite apart from the rarities continually being received from Constantinople and Persia. Parkinson, who received so many treasures, says :

' And I doe wish all Gentlemen and Gentlewomen, whom it may concerne, to bee as careful, whom they trust with the planting and replanting of these fine flowers, as they would be with so many Jewels '.

De l'Écluse was the first to introduce the crown imperial into western Europe. He sent it to Vienna in 1576 and as it grew wild in Persia it was first named the Persian lily. The name ' crown imperial ' has a pathetic association with the fair and learned Julie for whom the *Guirlande de Julie*[1] was painted. It is said Gustavus Adolphus would have offered her his hand

[1] *The Garland of Julia.* This manuscript was presented to the beautiful Julie de Rambouillet, by the Duke de Montausier, on their wedding-day. The greatest artists of the day depicted all the most beautiful cultivated flowers on vellum and the most famous poets wrote the verses. Corneille wrote those in praise of the orange flower and the everlasting. During the French Revolution this seventeenth-century manuscript was sent to Hamburg, where it was sold in 1795, but to whom has never been discovered.

had he gained the imperial crown and hence the name of the flower. Parkinson, however, indicates that the name was first given by Alphonsus Pancius (physician to the Duke of Florence), 'who first sent the figure thereof unto Mr. John de Brancion'. The name 'crown imperial' was adopted in all the European languages. When it was first introduced into England is uncertain. Shakespeare mentions it, but Gerard speaks of it as a rare and strange plant. Parkinson chose the flower for the subject of his first chapter and says of it: 'The Crowne Imperiall for his stately beautifulnesse deserveth the first place in this our Garden of delight'.

Some species of everlastings are native in this country, but the Eastern 'everlasting' used for crowns and garlands in classical times was sent to England in a dried condition in Elizabeth's reign, for Gerard, in 1597, records he saw them 'in the handes of Master Wade, one of the clerkes of his Majesties Counsell, which was sent him among other things from Padua in Italie'. He describes the flower as 'of a yellow colour glittering like gold'. Parkinson, in the *Paradisus*, speaks of them as being cultivated in gardens.

Few plants have caused so much sensation as the tulip, when first introduced into western Europe. It was cultivated in Turkey before 1550 and Conrad Gesner, the botanist, was the first to record seeing a tulip flowering in western Europe. He saw them in a garden at Augsburg and describes the flower as being 'like a red lily having eight petals of which four are outside and just as many within with a pleasant smell, soothing and delicate which soon leaves it'. According to Hakluyt, in his *Remembrances of Things to be Endeavoured at Constantinople*, tulips were introduced into England before 1582. They rapidly became very popular, and Parkinson in his *Paradisus* describes flower lovers as being

'more delighted in the search, curiosity and rarities of these pleasant delights than any age I think before. But indeede this flower, above many others, deserveth his true commendation and acceptance with all lovers of these beauties, both for the stately aspect and for the admirable varieties of colours that daily doe arise in them. . . . But above and beyond all others, the Tulipas may be so matched, one colouring answering and setting of another, that the place where they stand may resemble a piece of curious needlework or a piece of painting, and I have knowne in a Garden, the Master as much commended for this artificial form in placing the colours of Tulips, as for the goodnesse of his flowers or any other thing. . . . But to tell you of all these sorts of Tulipas (which are the pride of Delight) they are so many and as I may say, almost infinite, doth passe my ability and as I believe the skill of any other. . . . Besides this glory of variety in colours that these flowers have, they carry so stately and delightfull a forme, and do abide so long in their bravery (enduring above three whole months from the first unto the last) that there is no Lady or Gentlewoman of any worth that is not caught with this delight or not delighted with these flowers.'

Amongst lilies the important introduction during this period was the martagon or Turks-cap lily. Gerard says:

' it was sent among many other bulbs of rare and daintie flowers by Master Harbran, ambassador there, unto my honourable good lord and master the Lord Treasurer of England, who bestowed them upon me for my garden '.

Gerard calls the martagon the ' red lillie of Constantinople ', and another old name was ' the lily of Nazareth '. The name ' martagon ' Gerard says was given to these lilies by Matthiolus. Gerard also states that smaller varieties were given him by James Garret. Parkinson describes a dozen different kinds of martagon lilies. *Lychnis Chalcedonica* was probably introduced from Constantinople in Elizabeth's reign, for Gerard calls it also ' flower of Constantinople ' and ' Campion of Constantinople '. It was probably introduced long before, during the Crusades, for in many languages its old name is Cross of Jerusalem. Cross of Jerusalem is one of the old English names for the flower; in French, Spanish, and Italian it is similarly named. An old Portuguese name is Cruz de Malta, possibly because the shape of the flower is suggestive of a Maltese cross.

The pleasant old-fashioned honesty, *lunaria biennis*, is generally believed to have been introduced in Elizabeth's reign and was given its familiar name probably from the transparent seed-vessels. Parkinson says it was also called Penny-flower and he states that the roots were eaten in salads ' both in our owne Country and many places beside '. The annual candytuft dates from the same reign, but the broad-leaved shrubby candytuft, which is a native of Persia and Sicily, was not introduced till 1679, and the following year it was cultivated in the Oxford Physic Garden. (The narrow-leaved species from Candia was introduced in 1731 and grown in the Chelsea Physic Garden in 1739.) The dog's-tooth violet is described by Gerard as of recent introduction and Lobel is generally supposed to have been the first to grow it, possibly in Lord Zouch's garden at Hackney, which was under his charge. The European species is a native of France, Switzerland, Germany, Italy and Siberia. The various American species were not introduced till much later. Fritillaries are natives of most parts of Europe and Gerard is the first to record the introduction of any foreign species. He says that plants were sent him ' by the curious and painful herbarist Jean Robin ', and that the flowers were greatly esteemed ' for the beautifyling of our gardens and bosoms of the beautiful '. The Persian fritillary was introduced before the crown imperial, and Parkinson says, ' it was first brought from Persia into Constantinople and from thence sent unto us by the means of divers Turkie merchants and in especial by the procurement of Mr. Nicholas Lete, a worthy merchant and a lover of all fair flowers '.

The Persian ranunculus (R. *asiaticus*) was another introduction of Elizabethan times, though there has always been the tradition that it was brought to France as early as the thirteenth century by Louis IX from Palestine. Gerard says plants were frequently brought

' by divers persons, but they have perished by reason of the long journey, and want of skill of the bringers, that have suffered them to lie in a boxe, or such like so long, that when we have received them, they have been as drie as ginger ; notwithstanding Clusius saith, he received a plant fresh and greene, the which a domesticall theefe stole foorth of his garden ; my lord and master the Right Honourable, the Lorde Treasurer,[1] had divers plants sent him from thence, which were drie before they came as aforesaide. The other groweth in Alepo and Tripolis in Syria naturally, from whence we have received plants for our gardens, where they flourish as in their owne country '.

At least one species of spring-flowering crocus was apparently

[1] William Cecil Lord Burghley.

introduced in Elizabeth's reign, for Gerard says, 'That pleasant plant that bringeth foorth yellow flowers was sent unto me from Robin of Paris'. Parkinson devotes no less than ten pages to crocuses introduced from many parts, 'and now by such friends helpes as have sent them, they prosper as well in our Gardens, as in their naturall places'. The anemone hepatica was evidently known before Gerard's day, but though he mentions the double kind, he says they were strangers to England. Parkinson, who describes hepaticas as 'welcome early guests', states that according to Clusius the double hepatica was sent by Alphonsus Pansius from Italy, and that according to the same authority it had been found wild in parts of Austria. African marigolds, which are natives of Mexico, were also introduced in Elizabeth's reign. Gerard says the 'African' marigold was first received 'when Charles the Emperor made a famous conquest of Tunis; wherefore it was called *Flos Aphricanus* or *Flos Tunetensis*. Possibly therefore they were called 'African' in compliment to the Emperor, who had just returned from Tunis. The Sweet Sultan, which is a native of Persia, was introduced during Charles I's reign and Parkinson describes it as 'but lately obtained from Constantinople'. He states further that the Turks called it 'the Sultan's flower', for the monarch on first seeing the plant took a fancy to it and wore it. *Lobelia cardinalis* (a native of North America) was introduced early in the seventeenth century. Parkinson describes it as a 'brave plant', and James Justice, writing more than a hundred years later, says of it, 'it excells all other flowers I ever knew in the richness of its colour'. The name lobelia was bestowed on this genus by Charles Plumier, the great French botanist of Louis' XIV's reign, in honour of Matthias Lobel. *Convolvulus minor*, a native of Barbary, was introduced in Charles I's reign. Parkinson describes it as being 'of a most excellent fair skie-coloured blew, so pleasant to behold that often it amazeth the spectator'. He says he received the seeds of *convolvulus minor* 'out of Spain and Portugal from Guillaume Boel'. The American bindweed he describes as a rare plant seldom flowering in this country 'because our cold nights and frosts come so soone, before it can have comfort enough of the Sun to ripen it'.

Both the annual and the perennial sunflowers were introduced from America in Elizabeth's reign. In the religious ceremonies of the ancient Peruvians the virgins who officiated in the Temple of the Sun were crowned with sunflowers made of pure gold and carried golden sunflowers in their hands, a spectacle which made a deep impression on the Spaniards who witnessed the ceremony. Annual sunflowers are first mentioned by Gerard, who calls them ' the Flower of the Sunne ' or ' the Marigold of Peru '. He says that in his Holborn garden he had them growing 14 feet high and that in Spain they had been known to grow to a height of 24 feet. He also grew the perennial sunflower, which is a native of Virginia. Gerard states that he had never seen the seed, but the perennial sunflower rarely produces seed in this country and is propagated by root division. Marvel of Peru was amongst the earliest introductions from South America, De l'Écluse gave it the name by which it is still commonly known and it was probably cultivated in this country quite early in Elizabeth's reign, for Gerard, writing in 1597, says he had had it many years in his garden and that in favourable seasons the seed ripened. He says of the plant that it should be called ' rather the Marvell of the World than of Peru alone '. The Michaelmas daisy (*aster Tradescantia*) was brought direct from Virginia by John Tradescant the younger. The American golden rod, or ' Aaron's rod ' as cottagers used to call it, was not introduced till 1648. The evening primrose (*oenothera biennis*) is one of the most familiar flowers introduced from Virginia. It was first sent to Padua in 1619, but the date of its introduction into this country is uncertain. Parkinson is the first English writer to mention it and he describes it as ' the tree Primrose of Virginia '.

Tobacco (*nicotiana affinis*) was amongst the most noted introductions from America and valued at first not so much as a garden flower as for its medicinal qualities. Nicolas Monardes, a Spanish doctor living in Seville, wrote his famous book, *Dos libros el veno que trata de todas las cosas que traen de nuestras Indias Occidentales*, in 1569, and it was translated into English by John Frampton in 1577 (*Joyfull newes out of the newe founde worlde*). John Frampton's book contains the first illustration of tobacco to be found in an English book. According to Monardes, tobacco was a herb of great antiquity among the

Red Indians and they taught the Spaniards its medicinal virtues. The natives called it Picielt and the name tobacco was given it by the Spaniards, whether from the island which still bears the name Tobago, or from a native word connected in some way with the use of the dried leaves for smoking. Monardes says it was first introduced into Spain ' to adornate Gardens with the fairenesse thereof and to give a pleasant sight, but nowe we doe use it more for his mervelous medicinable virtues than for his fairenesse '. On its first introduction into Europe tobacco was apparently regarded as a new all-heal and Monardes says that in the city of Seville

' they know not what other to doe, having cut or hurt themselves but to run to the Tabaco as to a most readie remedie. It doth mervellous workes, without any need of other surgery, but this only hearbe '.

Monardes tells us further that the name Nicotiana was given to the plant in honour of Nicot ' my very friend ye first author inventor and bringer of this hearbe into France '. Monardes' own name is perpetuated in the genus Monarda. *Monarda fistulosa*, however, was not introduced into England till 1656, and then by John Tradescant the younger. *Monarda didyma*, the scarlet bergamot commonly grown in gardens, was introduced by Peter Collinson in 1744. It was formerly commonly known as Oswego tea because it was drunk as a beverage by the people of Oswego. Monardes' name is also associated with the humble nasturtium (*tropæolum majus*). Parkinson, who describes it as being ' of so great beauty and sweetness withall that my Garden of delight cannot be unfurnished of it ', says,

' this goodly plant was first found in the West Indies, and from thence sent into Spaine unto Monardus and others from whence all other parts have received it. It is now very familiar in most Gardens of any curiosity ', . . . Monardus and others call it Flos sanguineus of the red spots in the flowers, as also Mastnerzo de las Indias, which is Nasturtium Indicum, by which name it is now generally knowne, and called and wee thereafter in English Indian Cresses '.

The first American rose to be sent to Europe, R. *virginiana*, must have been introduced fairly early in the seventeenth century, for Parkinson writes of it in his *Theatrum Botanicum*

(1640). The flowers he describes as being ' of a pale purple or deep incarnate colour like unto those of the sweet brier'. This rose with its deep-toothed leaves is still grown in our gardens and we have also the double-flowered variety Rose d'Amour, introduced by Philip Miller in 1768. As early as Gerard's day, *Yucca gloriosa* and *Thuya occidentalis*, both from America, were grown in this country, for Gerard writes of them. The American plane was introduced by John Tradescant the younger. He also introduced the American walnut, the tulip tree, the deciduous cypress (*taxodium distichum*), the red maple and the acacia. The first acacia was sent to France in 1601 and it was planted by Vespasien Robin in the Jardin des Plantes (Paris). The stump of it remains still. The most beautiful American tree introduced in the seventeenth century was *taxodium distichum*, of which one of the finest specimens may be seen close to the entrance of the Oxford Botanic Garden.

In regard to the kitchen gardens of this period it is difficult to balance the conflicting evidence. According to Holinshed, writing in Elizabeth's reign, vegetables were plentiful ' in this land in the time of the first Edward ', but he says they were neglected from Henry IV's reign till Henry VIII's reign, remaining ' either unknown or supposed as food more meet for hogs and savage beasts to feed upon than mankind '. But, in his own lifetime he states rich and ' the poore commons ' alike were again eating ' melons, pompions, gourds, cucumbers, radishes, skirrets, parsnips, carrets, cabbages, navewes, turnips, and all kinds of salad herbes '. His statements seem untrustworthy, for it is not at all likely that ' the poore commons ' grew melons or cucumbers. In regard to ' salad herbes ' even during Elizabeth's reign we imported these as well as onions, cabbages, carrots, etc. Tusser, in his *Five Hundred Points*, speaks of beans, runcivall peas, cabbages, carrots, gourdes, ' pompions ' (marrows), beets, parsnips, onions, and turnips as commonly grown and Richard Gardiner, writing in 1599, treats of the same vegetables with the addition of artichokes and cucumbers. Yet Samuel Hartlib, writing in 1659, says :

' About fifty years ago this art of gardening began to creep into England, into Sandwich and Surrey, Fulham and other places. Some old men in Surrey, where it flourisheth very much at present, report that they knew the first gardeners that came into those parts to plant cabbages, colleflowers, and to sow turnips and carrets and parsnips, and raith-rape peas, all which at that time were great rarities, we having few or none in England but what came from Holland and Flanders. These gardeners with much ado procured a plot of good ground and gave no lesse than eight pounds per acre ; Yet the gentleman was not content, fearing they would spoil his ground because they dud use to dig it, so ignorant were they of gardening in those days '.

We certainly owed much to the Huguenot refugees from France and the Low Countries, especially the weavers and gardeners who came to this country during the latter half of the sixteenth century. The market gardens they established, notably those at Battersea and Bermondsey, became celebrated. They settled chiefly at Norwich, ' a place very much addicted to the flowry part ', Colchester and the Cinque Ports. The Dutch gardeners were highly esteemed and invited by the local landowners to advise them about their gardens. In Gage's *Hengrave* there is a reference to a Dutch gardener who was paid 3s. 4d. ' for his travayle from Norwich to Hengrave to viewe ye orchardes, gardyns, and walkes ', and again ' Paid to the Duchman for clypping the Knotts, altering the alleys, setting the grounds, finding herbs and bordering the same 40s.' According to the old couplet it was the refugees also who popularized hop-growing.

> Hops, Reformation, Bayes and Beere
> Came into England all in one yeare.

It was the Huguenots also who started the first flower societies in England, the earliest is said to have been established in Spitalfields. The most noted seem to have been those at Norwich. Sir James Smith mentions a play called *Rhodon and Iris*, which was acted at the Florists' feast at Norwich in 1637.[1]

---

[1] *Transactions of the Linnæan Society*, Vol. II, p. 296. Mr. Stephen, City Librarian of Norwich, kindly sent me an extract from the *Norwich Mercury*, July 1736, showing that these flower feasts were still held during the eighteenth century under the same name.

' THE SONS OF FLORA intend to hold their Annual Feast at the Maid's-Head in St. Simon's in Norwich, on Wednesday the 21st of this Instant July : where all Admirers of Nature are desir'd to come and view this Year's Produce, which will consist of as great a Variety of new and well-

Although there had been market gardeners in and around London since early mediæval times, it was not till the third year of James I's reign that the Gardener's Company of the City of London was founded and established by Royal Charter. A second Royal Charter was granted in the fourteenth year of his reign. The Company was empowered to examine all 'plants, stocks, setts, trees, seedes, slippes, roots, hearbes and other things . . . in any market within the Cittie of London and six myles about', to burn anything 'deceitfull or unprofitable', and no person was allowed to exercise the art of gardening without their permission.

Amongst vegetables the most important introduction by far was the potato. Gerard was one of the first to grow the plant and he proudly states, 'I have received hereof from Virginia roots which grow and prosper in my garden as in their own native countrie'. Gerard was in fact the originator of the popular but incorrect epithet—'Virginia potato'. The potato (*solanum tuberosum*) is not a native of Virginia, though it may have been introduced there in the sixteenth century. Sir Walter Raleigh and Thomas Herriot brought back the potato from the New World in 1585 or 1586, whether from Virginia or not is unknown. The Spaniards had brought it from Quito as early as 1580. The potato to which Shakespeare refers (*Troilus and Cressida*, V. 2. 534, and *Merry Wives of Windsor*, V. 5. 20 and 21) is of course the sweet potato which had been introduced into Europe long before. This potato (*ipomæa batatas*) is generally believed to have been brought back by Christopher Columbus, and it was cultivated in Spain early in the sixteenth century. It was so commonly grown in England in Elizabethan days that Gerard speaks of it as 'the common potato', which is somewhat confusing to modern readers. Parkinson also grew the sweet potato and says that both these and the potato of Virginia were cooked with sack and sugar or baked with marrow, sugar and

blown Flowers, as ever were seen in this City. And for the greater Satisfaction of the Gentlemen who shall Dine there, and the preserving of an agreeable Order, it is determin'd, that no Person be admitted without a Ticket, and that Dinner be ready at Two a-Clock. Tickets at 3s. each to be had of either of the Stewards, and of the Printer hereof, at the Maid's-Head aforesaid, or at Mr. LEO. WISCARD's, Hatter, in the Market place.'

spice, ' a daintie and costly dish for the table ', and that the ' Comfit-makers ' preserved and candied them for banquets. Although the ' potato of Virginia ' aroused so much interest when it was first introduced, it was not grown to any extent and the working people did not eat them for another two hundred years. Gilbert White, writing late in the eighteenth century, says :

' They have prevailed by means of premiums within these twenty years only, and are much esteemed here now by the poor, who would scarcely have ventured to taste them in the last reign '.

As early as 1664, however, the first book devoted entirely to the potato was published, with this comprehensive title— *England's Happiness Increased, or A Sure and Easy Remedy against all Succeeding Dear Years. By a Plantation of the Roots called Potatoes, whereof (with the Addition of Wheat Flower) excellent good and wholesome Bread may be made every Year, eight or nine Months together, for half the charge as formerly. Also by the Planting of their Roots, Ten Thousand Men in England and Wales, who know not how to Live, or what to do to get a Maintenance for their Families, may of One Acre of Ground make Thirty Pounds per Annum. In-Invented and Published for the Good of the Poorer Sort. By John Forster, Gent.* Anyone in search of ' new ' ways of cooking potatoes would be well advised to consult this little volume, for the receipts are excellent. He gives methods of stewing potatoes in wine with butter and sugar, baking them in pies with marrow sugar, and spice, making potato bread, puddings, custards, cheesecakes ' and others dress them other wayes, every man according to his own taste and liking ; all which ways they are a very wholesome and strengthening Food '.

The ' Jerusalem ' artichoke, whose native habitat stretches from the North American plains to the lake districts of Canada and as far south as the middle of Georgia, was an article of food amongst the Indians, from whom the early explorers learnt the use of it. In 1617 Goodyer, the great Hampshire botanist, was sent roots of it by Franqueville—' the one I planted, the other I gave to a friend : mine brought me a peck of roots wherewith I stored Hampshire '. That same year Goodyer wrote an account of the plant for Dr. Johnson, who printed it in his enlarged edition of Gerard's Herbal (1633). Previous to this the plant had been figured and described by Parkinson in the *Paradisus* (1629), and he calls them ' Potatoes of Canada ', and he adds that ' some ignorant and idle head ' called them Artichokes of Jerusalem because the taste of the roots was similar to the bottom of a Globe artichoke. He says of them that they had ' growne to be so common here with us at London, that even the most vulgar begin to despise them, whereas when they were first received among us, they were dainties for a Queene '. We certainly have not improved on seventeenth-century methods of cooking them, for they used to boil them and then serve them sliced and stewed in butter with a little wine—' a dish for a Queene '.

Broad beans were still a staple dish amongst poor folk. Kidney beans Parkinson describes as ' a dish more oftentimes at rich men's tables than at the poore '. In writing of peas we find that Parkinson heads his list of varieties with the old ' runcivall pea ' and he mentions also the green hasting, sugar peas, spotted peas, grey peas, white hasting peas, peas without skins, Scottish peas and ' the early or French pease which some call Fulham Pease, because those grounds thereabouts doe bring them soonest forward for any quantity, although sometimes they miscarry by their haste and earlinesse '. Chick peas never became popular in England though Parkinson describes them as being regarded in Spain ' as the most dainty kinde of Pease that are '.

Skirrets, which have disappeared from modern gardens, figured largely in Tudor and Stuart kitchen gardens and Parkinson, who places them first among root vegetables, describes the taste as ' very pleasant, far beyond any Parsnip, as all agree that taste them '. No less an authority than John Evelyn describes them as ' exceedingly nourishing, wholesome, and delicate '. He adds that they were so valued by the Emperor Tiberius that he accepted them for tribute. Possibly they were amongst the numerous vegetables grown in these islands in Roman days and then lost again until introduced in Tudor times. Skirret (*sisum sisarum*) is a native of China and is generally believed to have been introduced into this country in Henry VIII or Edward VI's reign. But we have no definite information on this point. In sixteenth, seventeenth, and eighteenth-century books they figure as a common vegetable. Gerard solemnly observes, 'Tis reported they were heretofore something bitter; see what culture and education effects'. Joseph Cooper, who was cook to Charles I, gives a recipe for skirret pie, made with boiled skirrets dipped in yolks of egg, cooked chestnuts and slices of hard-boiled eggs with butter and flavoured with lemon, cinnamon, and nutmeg. Skirrets were also fried in batter, flavoured with ginger or cinnamon and nutmeg. John Evelyn, in his *Acetaria*, gives a recipe for skirret milk, also highly recommended by Tryon in *The Good Housewife* (1692), as 'an excellent restorative to people who have suffered through long illness'.

Scorzonera (Viper's grass), a native of the south of Europe, was introduced in the sixteenth century. Parkinson says that Monardes was the first to write about it and that 'the roots preserved in sugar as I have done often doe eate almost as delicate as the Eringus roote'. Parkinson tells us that it was the refugees from the Low Countries who taught us how to cook spinach, a method which is still the best.

'Spinach is an hearbe fit for sallets . . . many English that have learned it of the Dutch people, doe stew the herbe in a pot or pipkin without any moisture than its owne, and after the moisture is a trifle pressed from it they put butter and a little spice unto it and make therewith a dish that many delight to eate of. It is used likewise to be made into Tartes and many other varieties of dishes, as Gentlewomen and their Cookes can better tell than myselfe'.

Mustard as in earlier times was grown not as a 'salad' but for the seeds to make mustard sauce and for medicinal purposes. Asparagus is first mentioned by Gerard, but it had probably been cultivated in this country in Roman days. Parkinson describes it as 'a principal delectable sallet herb'.

I do not think we appreciate to what an extent vegetables in those days were served in salad form, even root vegetables, such as carrots, turnips and skirrets. Gervase Markham, in his *English Housewife*, describes as a 'humble Feast which any good man may keep in his Family for the entertainment of his true and worthy friends', a sixteen course banquet in which vegetables in our modern sense of the word are conspicuous by their absence, but salads figure largely. 'Simple salads' consisted of chives, boiled carrots, turnips, lettuces, asparagus, purslane, etc., chopped and served with vinegar, oil and sugar. 'Compound salads' were adorned with the young leaves of red sage, mint, lettuce, violets, marigolds, spinach, etc. He describes a compound salad fit 'for Princes' tables' as first a layer consisting of blanched and shredded almonds, raisins shredded and figs, capers, olives, currants, finely-chopped red sage, spinach with vinegar, oil and sugar; then a layer of oranges and lemons finely sliced and covered with 'the fine thin leaf of the red Cole-flower', then a layer of olives, slices of pickled cucumber and shredded lettuce, this layer being adorned with slices of oranges and lemons. There were also 'preserved sallets' consisting of violets, primroses, gillyflowers, cowslips, broom flowers, etc., preserved in vinegar and 'sallets for shew only'. The latter consisted of carrot or other roots cut into fantastic shapes 'as some into Knots, some in the manner of Scutcheons and Arms, some like Birds and some like Wild Beasts, according to the art and cunning of the Workman'.

Kitchen gardens, however, were still more largely planted with herbs than with what we call vegetables. For instance, in *The Countrie Farme*, translated by Richard Surflet in 1600, the list of 'pot herbs' runs thus: coleworts, endive, sow thistle, succory, globe artichokes, sorrel, burnet, marigolds, beets, blites, arrach, spinach, borage, bugloss, leeks, purslane, onions, chives, garlic, parsley, rocket, tarragon, smallage, chervil, costmary, asparagus, cress, saffron, turnips, radishes, parsnips, carrots, skirrets, mustard, poppies, cucumbers, gourds. The herbs in the physic garden are mallows, hollyhocks, gentian, eyebright, elecampane, dittany, celandine, valerian, angelica, blessed thistle, scabious, betony, water germander, comfrey, coltsfoot, cinquefoil, periwinkle, peonies, agrimony, mullein, mercury, milfoil, adders' tongue, goosegrass, Solomon's seal, stinging and dead nettle, plantain, pellitory of the wall, shepherd's purse, crowfoot, germander, fumitory, centaury, honeysuckle and tobacco. Parkinson, in his *Paradisus*, gives the virtues of nearly all the plants mentioned in his 'Garden of Pleasant Flowers'. It is but rarely, he says, 'these flowers serve only

THE SPRING GARDEN

(From *A Garden of Flowers*, 1615,
translated from the Netherlandish original of Crispin de Pass)

Royal Horticultural Society Library

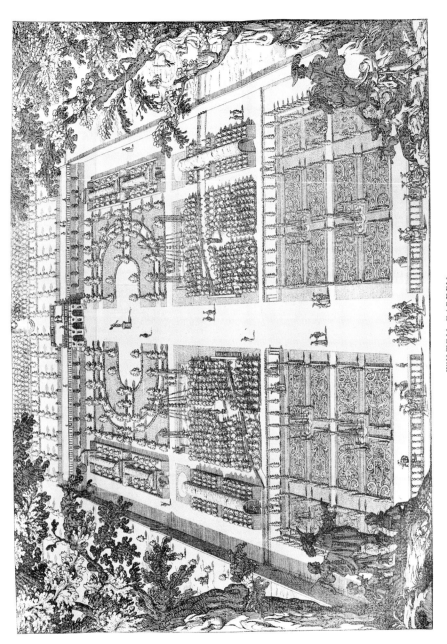

WILTON GARDEN

(From *Wilton Garden*, by Isaac de Caus)

Royal Horticultural Society Library

to decke up the Gardens of the curious ', or to quote another of his charming phrases :

' the chiefe or onely use thereof is to be an ornament for the Gardens of the curious lovers of these delights, and to be worne of them abroad, which for the gallant beauty of many of them, deserveth their courteous entertainment among many other the like pleasures '.

In connection with kitchen gardens it is difficult for us to realize to what an extent flowers and sweet-smelling herbs were grown, not only for decoration but for strewing on the floor. Levimus Lemnius, a Dutchman who travelled in this country in 1560, wrote of the English people that

' their chambers and parlours strawed over with sweet herbes refreshed mee ; their nosegays finely intermingled with sundry sorts of fragraunte flowers, in their bedchambers and privy rooms, with comfortable smell cheered me up, and entirely delighted all my senses '.

Meadowsweet was highly esteemed for strewing. Gerard says :

' The leaves and flowers of meadowsweet farre excelle all other strowing herbs for to decke up houses, to strowe in chambers, halls and banqueting houses in the summer time, for the smell thereof makes the heart merrie and joyful and delighteth the senses '.

And Parkinson tells us (in his *Theatrum Botanicum*) that ' Queene Elizabeth of famous memorie did more desire meadow-sweet than any other sweete herbe to strewe her chambers withall '.

Houses were adorned not only at Christmas time, when rosemary, bay, ivy, holly, and mistletoe were used, but also at other festivals.

> When yew is out, and birch comes in,
>   And many flowers beside
> Both of a fresh and fragrant kin
>   To honour Whitsuntide,
> Green rushes then, and sweetest bents
>   With cooler open boughs,
> Come in for comely ornaments
>   To re-adorn the house.[1]

[1] R. Herrick.

Flowers also were grown in window-boxes and indoors and Sir Hugh Platt makes many suggestions on the subject in his *Floræs Paradise* : ' In every window you may make square frames either of lead or of boards well pitched within ; fill them with some rich earth and plant with flowers or hearbs therein as you like best '. For growing over doors he suggests sweet-briar, rosemary, etc. And the chimney-place in summer time, he suggests, ' may be trimmed with a fine bank of mosse or with aspen . . . or the white flower called everlasting. And at either end Rosemary pots '.

In many gardens plots were devoted to flowers for the making of nosegays (which Parkinson calls by the delightful name of tussie-mussies) and garlands. In Lawson's *Countrie Housewife* we find :

' The Garden shall be divided into two equall parts. The one shall containe the hearbes and flowers used to make nosegaies and garlands of, as March Violets, Provence Gillo-flowers, Purple Gillo-flowers, Indian Gillo-flowers, small Paunces, Daisies, yellow and white Gillo-flowers, Marigolds, Lily-convally, Daffodils, Canterburie-bells, Purple velvet flower, Anemones, corne-flag, Mugwort, Lillies and other such-like as may be called the Nosegay Garden. Also in it you shall plant all sorts of strange flowers, as is the Crowne imperiall, the Tulippos of sundrie kindes, Narcissus, Hyacinthes, Helletropians, and a world of other of like nature, whose colours being glorious and different, make such a brave checked mixture, that it is both wondrous pleasant and delactable to behold.

The other part shall have all other sweet-smelling hearbes, whether they be such as beare no flowers, or if they beare any, yet they are not put in Nosegaies alone, but the whole hearbe with them, as Soothern-wood, Wormewood, Pelletorie, Rosemarie, Jesamine, Marjerom, Balme, Mints, Penneroyall, Costmarie, Hyssope, Lavander, Basell, Sage, Savourie, Rue, Tansey, Thyme, Cammomile, Mugwort, bastard Marjerom, Nept, Sweet Balme, All-good, Anis, Horehound and others such like, and this may be called the Garden for hearbes of a good smell '.

Great attention was paid to fruit trees in Tudor days, the royal orchard at Tenham in Kent was famous and the best varieties could be bought there. The history of this orchard is recorded in that rare little pamphlet, *The Husbandman's Fruitful Orchard* (1609) :

'One Richard Harris, of London, Borne in Ireland, Fruiterer to King Henry the eight, fetched out of Fraunce great store of graftes, especially pippins, before which time there were no pippins in England. He fetched also out of the Lowe Countries, cherrie grafts and Peare graftes of divers sorts : Then tooke a peese of ground belonging to the King in the Parrish of Tenham in Kent, being about the quantitie of seaven score acres : whereof he made an orchard, planting therein all those foreign grafts. Which orchard is and hath been from time to time, the chiefe mother of all other orchards, for those kinds of fruit in Kent and divers other places. And afore that these said grafts were fetched out of Fraunce and the Lowe Countries although that there was some store of fruite in England, yet there wanted both rare fruite and lasting fine fruite. The Dutch, and French, finding it to be so scarce, especially in these counties neere London, commonly plyed Billingsgate and divers other places, with such kinde of fruite, but now (thankes bee to God) divers gentlemen and others . . . have planted many orchards fetching their grafts out of that orchard which Harris planted called the New Garden'.

Yet when Tusser wrote in Elizabeth's reign, farmhouse gardens were evidently plentifully stocked with fruits, nuts, and vines.

> ' Good fruit and good plentie doth well in the loft,
> then make thee an orchard and cherish it oft :
> For plant or for stock laie aforehand to cast,
> but set or remove it er Christmas be past.
> Set one fro other full fortie foote wide,
> to stand as he stood is a part of his pride.'

Tusser's list of fruits is lengthy—apples, of all sorts, apricots, barberries, bullaces, cherries, ' red and blacke ', and cornel cherries, damsons, gooseberries, grapes, ' white and red ', green ' or grasse plums ', whortleberries, medlars, mulberry, peaches, ' white and red ', pears ' of all sorts ', quince, raspberries, ' reisons ', strawberries, ' red and white ', service trees, wardens, ' white and red ', and ' wheat plums '. Like Parkinson, he includes nuts amongst his fruits—chestnuts, filberts, ' small nuts ' and walnuts. The ' reisons ' were probably currants of sorts. Gerard, writing in 1597, describes red currants, not by name but as small fruit like gooseberries, but red in colour and without ' prickles '. Gerard classes ' currans ' (the currant of

Corinth) with grapes. Parkinson describes red, white and black currants. The white currant he describes as having ' a pleasant winie taste and daintie' ; the black currant as having branches, leaves and fruit with ' a stinking scent . . . but the berries are eaten of many without offending either taste or smell '.

Strawberries, as in mediæval days, were the wild strawberries improved by cultivation.

> Wife unto thy garden and set me a plot
> With strawberry rootes of the best to be got ;
> Such growing abroade, among thornes in the wood
> Wel chosen and picked proove excellent good.

Hyll, in his *Gardener's Labyrinth*, says that the strawberry ' by diligence of the Gardener, becommeth so great that the same yeeldeth faire and big Berries as the Beries of the Bramble in the hedge.' Parkinson mentions ' the white Strawberry and the Bohemian Strawberry.' The last-named he describes as ' the goodliest and greatest . . . for beauty farre surpassing all. Master Quester the Postmaster first brought them over into our Country as I understand, but I know no man so industrious in the carefull planting and bringing them to perfection as Master Vincent Sion, who dwelt on the Banck side, near the old Paris garden stairs '. Parkinson also praises highly a wild kind : ' No great bearer but those it doth beare are set at the toppes of the stalks close together, pleasant to behold and fit for a Gentlewoman to weare on her arme, etc., as a raritie instead of a flower '.

Quinces were far more valued in those days than they are now. Gerard mentions three varieties and Parkinson, who gives six, says : ' There is no fruit growing in this land that is of so many excellent uses as this, serving as well to make many dishes of meate for the table as for banquets and much more for the Physicall vertues. . . . And being preserved whole in Sugar, either white or red, serve likewise, not only as an after dish . . . but is placed among other Preserves by Ladies and Gentlewomen and bestowed on their friends to entertain them. . . . Codimacke also and Marmilade jelly and Paste are all made of Quinces '. Apples were grown in large quantities, chiefly for the making of cider, but the best sorts were served as dessert.

To quote Parkinson, ' The best sort of apples serve at the last course of the table in most men's houses of account, where, if they grow any rare or excellent fruit it is then set forth to be seen and tasted '. Judging by the number of varieties, pears were even more popular than apples, the best known being the old Wardon and ' Bon Crétien '.

The most important introduction amongst fruit trees in Tudor days was the apricot. According to Mr. Bean[1] this tree is believed to have been cultivated by the Chinese many centuries before the Christian era, gradually spreading westwards to Europe. It is generally thought to have been introduced into England early in the sixteenth century, but it may have been known long before. Turner mentions ' apricocks ' both in his *Names of Herbes* (1548) and his Herbal. In the former he says : ' We have very fewe of these trees as yet ', and in his Herbal (1551) : ' I have sene many trees of thys kinde in Almany and som in England '. Tusser includes ' apricocks ' in his list of fruits to be planted or moved in January. Cherries, plums, damsons, peaches, nectarines, apricots, figs, medlars, mulberries, were grown in variety. Nuts—almonds, walnuts, horse and sweet chestnuts, and filberts—were included in the ' orchard '. Parkinson refers to hazels, but the only hazel he includes in his section on ' The Orchard ' is the Virginian hazel, of which he says : ' I know not if any hath planted of them, or if they differ in leafe or any thing else '. The Virginian nuts he describes as being smaller, rounder, browner, thinner shelled and more pointed at the end than our native kind. All fruits were grown not merely for food or drink but for their medicinal uses and for distilled waters, and of apples ' a fine, sweet oyntment called " *pomatum* " was made '. The small fruits too were used in many ways. The leaves of black currants were put into sauces, the leaves and distilled water of raspberries were used medicinally and so forth.

James I made a great effort to popularize mulberry culture in order to establish a silk industry. A circular letter, *Instructions for the increasing of Mulberie Trees . . . Whereunto is annexed his Majesties Letters to the Lords Liefetenants*, was sent to the Lords-Lieutenants of all the counties in 1609 ordering them to announce

[1] W. J. Bean, *Trees and Shrubs hardy in the British Isles.*

that the following March a thousand mulberry trees would be sent to each county town to be sold at three-farthings a plant or six shillings the hundred. All who were able were required to buy them. Seed was also distributed, but the seed was that of *M. nigra*, which is less suitable for silkworms than *M. alba*. The King himself established a mulberry garden, four acres in extent, outside the 'King's park' (i.e. the park attached by Henry VIII to his palace of St. James). W. Stallenge was paid £955 to wall, establish and plant 'The Mulberry Garden' and £120 a year for providing mulberry leaves for silkworms. The scheme failed, but it left a fine walled garden and the building afterwards known as Mulberry Garden House. The old mulberry trees which still adorn so many old gardens in this country probably date from James' reign. Possibly the King had been inspired to make this effort to establish the silk industry in England by the publication in 1607 of *The Perfect use of silk-wormes and their benefit. . . . Done out of the French originall by D'Olivier de Serres, Lord of Pradel, into English by Nicholas Geffe Esqre. With an annexed discourse of his owne for to have abundance of fine silke by feeding of silke-wormes with-in the same.*

Vineyards alone suffered a decline in early Stuart times. In Elizabethan times vineyards were still of great importance and, as in ancient Egypt, the vines were trained to poles and rafters. Shakespeare refers to this custom in the brief phrase 'thy pole-clipt Vineyard'.[1] This method of growing them is described by Gerard, who says :

'The Vine is held up with poles and frames of wood and by that means it spreadeth all about and climbeth aloft ; it joyneth itselfe unto trees, or whatsoever standeth next unto it'.

Sir Hugh Platt frequently refers to vineyards and asserts there is no reason why English wine should not be as good as that made on the Continent. Failure he ascribes to 'blockish ignorance of our people who do most unjustly lay their wrongful accusations upon the soil'. Parkinson lists twenty-three varieties but he states frankly that the cultivation of vines was declining and he ascribes the cause to the Dissolution of the

[1] *The Tempest*, Act IV, Sc. 1.

Monasteries (the monks being the skilful growers) and to the change in the climate.

' I have read that manie Monasteries in this Kingdome having Vine-yards, had as much wine made therefrom as sufficed their convents yeare by yeare : but long since they have been destroyed, and the knowledge how to order a Vineyard is also utterly perished with them. For although divers, both Nobles and Gentlemen, have in these later times endeavoured to plant and make Vineyards and to that purpose have caused French men . . . to be brought over to performe it, yet either their skill failed them, or their Vines were not good, or (the most likely) the soile was not fitting, for they could never make anie wine that was worth the drinking, being so small and heartlesse that they soone gave over their practise. . . . I think it a fruitlesse labour for any man to strive in these daies to make a good Vineyard in Eng-land in regard not only of the want of knowledge . . . but most chiefly and above all others that our years in these times do not fall out to be so kindly and hot to ripen the grapes, to make anie good wine as formerly they have done '.

It was during this period that the first efforts were made to protect delicate plants during the winter and to force plants into early bloom. Judging from the references in his writings Sir Hugh Platt was deeply interested in these efforts and makes various suggestions. For instance, he suggests the growing of plants against a concave wall lined with lead or tin. ' Quaere ', he adds, ' if these walls did stand so conveniently as they might also be continually warmed with kitchen fires ; as serving for Backs unto your chimneys, if so, they should not likewise finde some little furtherance in their ripening '.

The earliest account of these primitive efforts to shelter ' dainty flowers ' and ' delicate fruits ' is that given by Gervase Markham in his *English Husbandman* (1613) :

' I have seen diuers Noblemen and Gentlemen, which have beene very curious in these dainty flowers (daffodils and columbines, hya-cinths, narcissi and tulips) which have made large frames of wood (with boards of twenty inches deepe), standing upon little round wheeles of wood, which being made square or round according to the Master's fancie, they have filled with choyse earth, such as is most proper to the flower they would have grow, and then in them sowe their seedes, or fixe their Plants, and so placing them in such open places of the Garden, where they may have the strength and violence of the Sunne's heate all the day, and the comfort of such moderate showers, a fall without violence or extraordinaire beating, and at night draw them by man's strength into some low vaulted gallery ioyning upon the Garden, where they may stand warme and safe from stormes, windes, frosts, dewes, blastings, and other mischiefes which ever happen in the Sunne's absence and in this manner you may not onely have all manner of dainty outlandish flowers, but also all sorts of the most delicatest fruits that may be, as the Orange, Limond, Pomegranate, Cynamon-tree, Olive, Almond, or any other, from what clime as ever it be derived, observing onely but to make your frames of wood, which containes your earth, but deeper and larger, according to the fruit you plant in it, and that your Alleys through which you draw your Trees when you house them be smooth and levell, least being rough and uneven, you iogge and shake to rootes with the waight of the Trees, which is dangerous. And least any man may imagine this is but an imaginery supposition, I can assure him that within seaven miles of London, the experiment is to be seene where all these fruits and flowers with a world of others grow in two Gardens most abundantly '.

Even in Parkinson's time oranges were grown only ' with some extraordinary looking and tending ' of them.

' If therefore any be desirous to keepe this tree, he must so provide for it, that it be preserved from any cold, either in the winter or spring, and exposed to the comfort of the sunne in summer. . . . Some keepe them in great square boxes, and lift them to and fro by iron hooks on the sides, or cause them to be rowled by trundels, or small wheels under them, to place them in an house, or close gallerie for the winter time : others plant them against a bricke wall in the ground and defend them by a shed of boardes, covered over with seare-cloth in the winter, and by the warmth of a stove, or other such thing, give them some comfort in the colder times : but no tent or meane provision will preserve them '.

An event of great importance was the establishment of the Oxford Physic Garden in 1621, the land being the gift of Henry, Earl of Danby, a Christ Church man, who in his youth had been page to Sir Philip Sidney and later served as captain of a man-of-war. He was described by the Lord High Admiral as one of the best captains in the Fleet. (It is interesting to recall that Danby's younger brother, John, has always been credited

with having introduced 'the Italian garden' into England.)
The beautiful gateway (built by Nicholas Stone from a design
by Inigo Jones) was finished in 1632 and the wall by 1633.
According to tradition the first gardener to be appointed was
John Tradescant the elder, but he died and the post was given
to Jacob Bobart the elder.

In the galaxy of great names associated with the history of
gardening in early Stuart times the Tradescants[1] hold a unique
place. John Tradescant the elder, gardener to Robert Cecil,
first Earl of Salisbury, is first heard of in 1607, at Meopham.
(The Cecils owned the manor of Shorne near Meopham.) In
his master's service Tradescant went abroad several times to
Haarlem, Brussels, Leyden, and Paris, and many of the original
bills for the plants he brought back are still preserved at Hatfield. He was an enthusiastic searcher for fruit trees of merit,
and amongst his most notable introductions was a fine black
cherry known as 'Tradescant's cherry', which was grown in
England even as late as the nineteenth century, although George
Brookshaw, in his *Pomona Britannica* (1817), says it was then
'very scarce and little known'. This cherry is figured in the
seventeenth-century book of water-colour paintings of fruits
known as '*Tradescants' Orchard*, in the Bodleian. Tradescant
passed into the service of Lord Wotton (probably on Cecil's
death in 1612). Lord Wotton had acquired St. Augustine's
Palace, Canterbury, from Cecil and the garden of which Tradescant was put in charge was doubtless what is now the garden of
the Warden and Fellows of St. Augustine's Missionary College.
When Captain Argall was raising funds to take out a band of
settlers to Virginia, Tradescant contributed £25, a large sum
for those days. Although he did not go to Virginia himself,
his name is associated with the Virginian spiderwort (*tradescantia virginica*) which Parkinson, to whom he gave some
specimens of it, named after him. In 1618 Tradescant accompanied his friend and neighbour, Sir Dudley Digges, on the
mission sent by James I to the Emperor of Russia.[2] They
landed at Archangel and Tradescant was able to explore the

[1] See *The Tradescants and their Times*, by D. Gardiner, R.H.S. Journal,
July 1928.
[2] See Hamel's *Tradescant der Aeltere, 1618 in Russland*.

islands in the delta of the Dwina in one of the Emperor's boats ; the result of his observations being the first list that has come down to us of Russian flora. In 1620 he again went in a ship commanded by Argall, this time on an expedition led by Sir R. Mansell against the Algiers pirates. He brought back with him ' the Argier Apricocke ', which was soon grown in every garden of any size. Before Lord Wotton's death Tradescant had passed into the service of the ill-fated Duke of Buckingham and accompanied his master on the expedition to the Ile de Rhé. Owing to the Duke's influence Tradescant was appointed head-gardener to Charles I, although the post had been promised to James Haydon. It was about this time that Tradescant settled in Lambeth, where he established his Physic garden and ' Tradescant's Ark ', the first museum so far as is known in this country. His garden and museum were visited by all the celebrities of the day—Charles I and Henrietta Maria, Arch-bishop Laud, the Duke of Buckingham, the Earl of Salisbury (son of the Salisbury whom Tradescant had served), and Sir Thomas Herbert, the explorer.

The date of Tradescant's death is unknown (probably 1637). He left everything to his son John, who had inherited his father's tastes. In 1637 the younger John was in Virginia collecting plants and after his father's death he returned and took charge of the Physic Garden and the ' Ark '. In 1652 his only son, also named John, died, aged nineteen, and was buried with his grandfather in Lambeth Churchyard. The catalogue of treasures both in his garden and ' Ark ' was published in 1656 with portraits by Hollar of the elder and the younger Tradescant, both of whom had been ' gardeners to the rose and lily queen '. Throughout the Commonwealth days Tradescant remained peacefully at Lambeth, but a year after the Restoration a warrant was issued for his arrest ' for making a shew of severall strange creatures, without authority from his Maiesties Office of the Revells '. Tradescant appealed straightway to the King. Charles II could be a good friend when he chose, and amongst the State Papers is preserved the royal reply to Tradescant's enemies :

' Our express pleasure is that the said Tredeskyn be suffered freely and quietly to proceed as formerly in entertaining and receiving all persons whose curiosity shall invite them to the delight of seeing his rare and ingenious collection of Art and Nature '.[1]

Tradescant the younger died in 1662. His rarities passed to his friend Ashmole, and ultimately to the University of Oxford. It has frequently been pointed out that the Ashmolean Museum unjustly commemorates the name of Ashmole, who merely added to the collection, instead of Tradescant, the original founder of the ' Ark ' of rarities. But there is now a memorial window to Tradescant in the Old Ashmolean Museum (re-opened in 1923), the gift of the Garden Club of Virginia. The window represents Tradescant's coat-of-arms, surrounded by a wreath of *tradescantia virginica*.

The garden at Lambeth has long since disappeared but the name ' Tradescant ' lives in the glorious double daffodil, grown alike in princely and cottage gardens, the daffodil which Gerard called *Narcissus roseus Tradescanti* and of which Parkinson wrote : ' This Prince of Daffodils belongeth primarily to John Tradescant as the first founder thereof that we know and may well be entitled the Glory of Daffodils '.

The tombstone of the three generations of Tradescant may still be seen in Lambeth churchyard with its epitaph :

> ' Know, stranger, ere thou pass beneath this stone
> Lye John Tradescant, grandsire, father, son.
> The last died in his spring ;—the other two
> Liv'd till they had travelled Art and Nature through.
>
> .   .   .   .   .   .
>
> Those famous Antiquarians that had been
> Both gardeners to the Rose and Lily Queen,
> Transplanted now themselves, sleep here, and when
> Angels shall with their trumpets waken men,
> And fire shall purge the world, these hence shall rise,
> And change this garden for a Paradise '.

The most elaborate plan of a garden of this period that has come down to us is that of Wilton garden. (See illustration.) The plan shows first a series of plots ' embroidered ' with flowers with shrubs at the corners of each plot, four elaborate

---

[1] *Dom. State Papers*, Ch. II, XXX, VII, 74. Public Records Office.

fountains and at the further end a terrace (with shrubs at regularly spaced distances along the further side), ' for the more advantage of beholding those Platts '. Then in the second garden the river Nader flowing through woods and groves, the bridge spanning it being the breadth of ' the greate Walke ', two long tunnelled arbours 300 feet long, ' diverse allies ' and two great statues. Between the second and third gardens two ponds with fountains and ' two Columnes in the middle casting water all their heigth which causeth the moving and turning of two Crownes att the top of the same '. Beyond the great lawn planted with cherry trees and in the centre the brass Gladiator, ' the most famous statue of all that Antiquity hath left ', at each side of the lawn tunnelled arbours with elaborately cut entrances, and at the further end of the great walk a great stone Portico and on either side a stairway leading up to the terrace, the stairway having, instead of balusters, ' Sea Monsters casting water from one to the other from the top to the bottome '. All the details in the artist's description can be identified in the plan.

' This Garden within the enclosure of the New Wall is a Thousand foote long and about Foure hundred in breadth devided in its length into three long Squares or Parallelograms, the first of which divisions next the building hath ffoure ffountaines with Statues of marble in their midle, and on the sides of those Platts are the Platts of fflowers, and beyond them is the little Terrass rased for the more advantage of beholding those Platts, this for the first division. In the Second are two Groves or woods cutt with divers walkes and thorough these Groves passeth the river Nader haveing of breadth in this place 44 foote upon which is built the bridge of the breadth of the greate walke, in the midest of the aforesayd groves are two great Statues of white marble of eight ffoote heighth, the one of Bacchus and the other Flora, and on the sides ranging with the Plotts of flowers are two coverd Arbors of 300 ffoote long and diverse allies. Att the beginin of the third and last division are on either side of the great walke two Ponds with ffountaynes and two Collumnes in the midle casting water all theire heigth which causeth the moveing and turning of two Crownes att the top of the same, and beyond is a comparttment of greene with diverse walke planted with cherrie trees and in the medle is the great Ovall with the Gladiator of brass the most famous Statue of all that Antiquity hath left on the sides of this compartment and answering

124

the platts of fflowers and long arbours are three arbours of either side with turning Gallaryes communicating themselves one into another, att the end of the greate walke is a Portico of stone cutt and adorned with Pilasters and Nyches within which are ffigures of white marble of 7 ffoote high; of either of the sayd portico is an assent leading up to the terrasse upon the steps whereof instead of Ballasters are Sea Monsters casting water from one to the other from the top to the bottome and above the sayd portico is a great reserve of water for the Grotto '.

Evelyn in his Diary said of Wilton that it was ' heretofore esteemed the noblest in England '.

Another plan of remarkable interest is that of Holyrood, drawn, *circa* 1646, by James Gordon of Rothiemay. The gardens now are wind-swept, but the plants in those old days were well sheltered, for the plan shows no less than ten separate gardens enclosed by high walls. This was the garden as it had been in Mary Queen of Scots' time, and two of the knot gardens, north of the palace, are laid out in the design of fleur-de-lis, which must have recalled to her her beloved France. Beyond Croft-an-Righ House is a large enclosure planted with trees, and to the east there is another enclosure similarly planted. Of the two largest gardens one was evidently the kitchen garden and the other elaborate knot gardens divided by an avenue of trees. The fine old sundial, about 10 feet high, dating from Charles I's reign, was discovered in a very neglected condition in Queen Victoria's reign, when it was restored. It has twenty facets, each with its dial. This sundial was made by John Milne, who in Charles I's reign executed the magnificent stone staircase and many of the finest carvings both inside the palace and without.

The earliest plan of a Yorkshire garden is that in William Lawson's *New Orchard and Garden* (1618). Of the author of this delightful book we know little, save that he was a Yorkshireman, and that county may well be proud of ' the Izaak Walton of garden writers ', the author of the first book on the subject of North-country gardens, of the first book (*The Countrie Housewife's Garden*), written for women gardeners, and the most attractive of the early bee books. He was an old man before he ventured to set forth his experiences of labouring 'forty and eight years' in a garden, and indeed he writes as only an old man could write, whose life-long companions had been flowers, fruit-trees, birds and bees. With all the humility characteristic of one who had had great experience he 'gathered these Rules and set them down in writing, not daring to hide the least Talent given me of my Lord, and Master, in Heaven'. His book is permeated throughout with a spirit of reverence and humility. Lawson immortalized the small homely English garden, full of the old-fashioned flowers we English folk have always loved, and gladdened with the hum of bees and the songs of the birds—'the principallest delight of an Orchard'.

The garden depicted in his plan (see illustration) and described by him with such loving enthusiasm is on three terraces—on the first terrace a square garden planted with fruit trees with flowers growing 'in spaces betwixt the trees and in the borders and fences', and in the left-hand space a man with a drawn sword and a prancing horse suggests topiary work—'your Gardner can frame your lesser wood to the shape of men armed in the field ready to give battell'. Steps on either side lead down to the next terrace, with another fruit garden, and on the right a knot garden laid out in the form of the Yorkist rose combined with the six-pointed masonic star. In the centre of the terrace is an ornate fountain. On the lowest terrace kitchen gardens laid out on formal lines. Stillrooms with triumphant little flags flying from them are depicted in the four corners of the garden and next the two most sheltered there are beehives. Note that the garden as a whole still represents the ancient 'four-fold field plot'.

In the north of England it was customary to surround gardens with earth walls, planted with wallflowers, etc., but Lawson condemns these picturesque walls, preferring 'a stone enclosure, handsome, high and durable'. Parkinson also preferred brick or stone walls.

'It shall hardly availe you', Lawson adds, 'to make any fence for your Orchard, if you be a niggard of your Fruit. For as liberalitie will save it best from noisome neighbours (liberalitie I say is the best fence) so Justice must restrain rioters'. Within the garden Lawson directs mounts 'curiously wrought within and without' to be placed, mazes to be made, 'a pair

126

of Buts to stretch your Arms ', and ' in mine own opinion ', he adds, ' I could highly commend your Orchard, if either through it or hard by it, there could run a pleasant River with silver streams ; you might sit in your Mount and angle a peckled Trout, sleighty Eel or some other daintie Fish '. Lawson writes at greater length of fruit trees than of flowers, but he enumerates the favourite flowers of those days—roses, lilies, violets (' nothing behind the best for smelling sweetly '), primroses, ' the faire and sweet-scented woodbine ', rosemary, and sweet eglantine (' seemly ornaments about a doore or window '), lavender, hollyhocks, flower-de-luce, wallflowers, stock-gilliflowers, marjoram, pansies, mallows, valerian, etc. Above all he loved his carnations—' I may well call them the King of flowers except the Rose, and the best sort of them are called Queen July-flowers. I have of them ', he adds with a childlike confidence in his readers' interest, ' nine or ten several colours, and divers of them as big as Roses, of all flowers (save the Damask Rose) they are the most pleasant in sight and smell '.

Few gardening books, old or modern, give any space to the gardener, but Lawson devotes the whole of the first chapter to him, and a delightful chapter at that. ' The gardener ', he says :

' must be Religious, Honest, Skilful and therewithal Painful . . . by religion I mean (because many think Religion but a Fashion or Custom to go to Church) maintaining and cherishing things Religious . . . above all things and God's word. . . .

The Gardener had not need be an idle or lazy Lubber . . . there will ever be something to do. Weeds are always growing . . . moles work daily . . . in Winter your Trees and Herbs would be lightened of Snow and your Allies cleansed. . . . When Summer cloath your Borders with Green and speckled colours your Gardener must dress his Hedges and antick works : watch his Bees and hive them : . . . now begin Summer Fruits to ripen and crave your hand to pull them . . . you must needs allow him good help to end his labours which are endless. . . . Such a Gardener as will conscionably, quietly and patiently travel, God shall Crown the labours of his hands with Joyfulness and make the Clouds drop fatness. . . . If you be not able nor willing to hire a Gardener, keep your profits to your self, but then you must take all the pains '.

THE STORY OF THE GARDEN

Seventeenth-century garden writers say little of garden pests and the absurd beliefs dating from classical times which figure so conspicuously in Hyll's books are not even mentioned. Lawson, however, gives an entire chapter to the subject of ' Annoyances ', under which comprehensive title he includes diseases such as canker, wounds, insect pests, animals (deer figure in the list of these), ' boisterous blasts of winds ', cold, weeds, worms, moles, filth, ' poysonful smoak ', evil neighbours, ' a careless Master ', and ' an indiscreet negligent or no Keeper '. ' See you here ', he says, ' an whole Army of mischiefs banded in troops against the most fruitful trees the earth bears, assailing your labours ! Good things have most enemies '. Against beasts he says, ' besides your out-strong fence, you must have a fair and swift Grey-hound, a Stone-bow, Gun, and if need require an Apple with an hook for a Deer, and an Hare-pipe for an Hare '. Against birds he can recommend a ' Stone-bow '. Against evil neighbours, ' Justice and liberality will put away evil neighbours, or evil neighbourhood. And then (if God bless and give success to your labours) I see not what hurt your Orchard can sustain '.

How Lawson loved his birds :

' One chief grace that adorns an Orchard I cannot let slip : a brood of Nightingales, who with several notes and tunes with strong delight-some voice out of a weak body, will bear you company night and day. . . . The gentle Robin-red-breast . . . will help her, and in winter in the coldest storms will not keep apart. Neither will the silly Wren be behind in Summer, with her distinct whistle (like a sweet Recorder) to cheer your spirits.

The Blackbird and Throstle (for I take it the Thrush sings not but devours) sing loudly in a May morning and delight the ear much and you need not want their company if you have ripe Cherries or Berries. . . .

What shall I say ? A thousand of pleasant delights are attending an Orchard. . . . And by the senses, as Organs, Pipes and Windows, these delights are earned to refresh the gentle, generous and noble mind.

What joy may you have that you shall see the blessing of God on your labours while you live, and leave behind you to heirs (for God will make heirs) such a work that many ages after your death shall record your love to their Country '.

Lawson's *Countrie Housewife's Garden* is a charming picture of a garden belonging especially to the lady of the house. He divides it into two parts :

' The Summer Garden '—roses, lavender, rosemary, bee-flowers, hyssop, sage, thyme, cowslips, peony, daisies, clove-gilliflowers, pinks, southernwood, lilies.

The Herb Garden with ' comely borders of roses and lavender ' and with ' your herbs of biggest growth by walls or in borders '. Under ' Herbs of great growth ' he lists fennel, angelica, tansy, hollyhock, lovage, elecampane, French mallows, lilies, French poppy, endive, succory, and clary. Under ' Herbs of middle growth ', borage, bugloss, parsley, sweet Cicely, flower-de-luce, stock gilliflowers, wallflowers, aniseed, coriander, fether-few, marigolds, oculus Christi, langdebeef, Alexanders, carduus-benedictus ; and under ' Herbs of smaller growth ', pansies, marjoram, savory, strawberries, saffron, licoras, daffodils, leeks, chives, chibbals, skirrets, onions, bachelors' buttons, daisies, pennyroyal.

This little treatise concludes with the sage advice that should the mistress have her maids to help her weeding the garden, ' withal I advise the Mistress either to be present her self, or to teach her maids to know herbs from weeds '.

Lawson was a great bee-lover, and his *Husbandry of Bees* (the first of the seventeenth century bee-books) forms the second part of his *Countrie Housewife's Garden* : ' And I will not account her any of my good Housewives that wanteth either Bees of skilful-nesse about them '. It is indeed difficult for us to realize the importance of bee-keeping during the centuries when sugar was a luxury so costly that only the wealthiest could afford it for medicine. Bees supplied the only sweet food, also drink and light for all from the king to the peasant. Lawson's little treatise is full of the wisdom of one who had known and loved bees all his life. He emphasizes their need of cleanliness, warmth, and dryness ; he prefers straw hives to wood—' straw hives are in use with us which I commend for nimbleness, closeness, warmness and driness '. Further he advises all to place their hives near an orchard—' your bees delight in wood . . . therefore want not an Orchard. A May's swarm is worth a mare's foal : if they want wood they be in danger of flying away '.

The most notable of the early seventeenth-century bee-books was Charles Butler's *Feminine Monarchie* (1623), and one edition of this was dedicated to Queen Henrietta Maria. This edition is written in 'simplified' spelling, probably the first effort at 'simplified' spelling made in this country. The attractive feature of Butler's book is the bee-music associated with the after-swarms, elaborated into four pages of 'bees madrigal', a typical seventeenth-century conceit.

Gervase Markham in *The English Husbandman* gives a plan for a small country house and a garden larger than Lawson's terraced garden. Markham depicts, in fact, a typical Jacobean country-house with the big hall in the centre and the chief rooms looking on to the garden on the south side. A Stuart pleasaunce with an orchard laid out in the formal fashion of the period, the trees ' all planted in such rowes that, which way soever a man shall cast his eyes yet hee shall see the trees every way stand on rowes, making squares, alleys and devisions, according to a man's imagination'. In the centre a fountain and ' some curios and arteficiall banquetting house', he adds, ' would give luster to the Orchard '. Then a ' garden of pleasure ' consisting of a series of square enclosures, some of them laid out in knots and dwarf shrub mazes. He describes both elaborate knots laid out in the form of coats-of-arms ' to be seene in the Gardens of Noblemen and Gentlemen which may beare coate armor ', and simple knots where the housewife may spread out her linen cloths to dry on broad close-clipped hedges of lavender or box. It is interesting to note his statement that the old-fashioned knots were being given up by the wealthy in favour of 'novelties'. He does not use the word ' parterres ' but these were evidently the ' novelties ' to which he refers. He mentions the French custom of tiling paths or covering them with ' powder of marble ', but he notes that this is costly and that gravel or sand is as pleasant to the eye. Grass walks, he sagely observes, are only for those hours of the day when there is no dew, otherwise ' you must provide shoes or bootes of extraordinary goodnesse '. Moreover in his opinion they do not afford sufficient contrast to the green of the plants.

The most important by far of all seventeenth-century gardening books was the matchless *Paradisus* (1629). It is generally acknowledged to be the most beautiful gardening book in the English language. Of the author we know very little, save that he was born in 1567, probably in Nottinghamshire, and that before 1616 he was practising as an apothecary and had a garden in Long Acre ' well stored with rarities '. He was Apothecary to James I and after the publication of his *Paradisus* Charles I bestowed on him the title of Botanicus Regius Primarius. He died in 1650 and was buried at St. Martin in the Fields. But though the facts concerning his life are so meagre, his character shines through every page of his book. The *Paradisus* is a typically English book, permeated with a spirit of reverence and humility and simple delight in the beauty of flowers. Parkinson, as we know from a pathetic passage in *Theatrum Botanicum* (1640), was a childless man and he seems to have lavished all his love and tenderness on his flowers. Above all he loved the spring flowers. How delightfully he writes of the ' stately beautifulness ' of the Crown Imperial, of ' this delightfull plant ' the fritillary and its varieties, of tulips ' the pride of delyght ', of ' beautifull and goodly Daffodils ', of Jacinths and muscari, of crocuses, which he calls ' Medowe Saffron of the Spring ', of ' bulbous flower-de-luce ', of anemones ' so dainty, so pleasant and so delightsome ', of bears' ears, ' those delights of nature ', of primroses and cowslips, ' the Embassadors of Spring '. Of his summer flowers he seems to have loved most his gilliflowers, especially ' the great Harwich or old English Carnation ' and the ' Clove Gilliflower ' and the white carnation Delicate, which he describes as ' a goodly delightfull fair flower ', his lilies, and chiefly perhaps his roses—the white rose of England, the red rose of England, the carnation rose (how seldom one sees this charming old rose now), the damask, the cabbage rose, the double yellow rose, the York and Lancaster, the velvet rose, the Cinamon rose, the musk rose, the sweet briar, and others too numerous to mention. And ' after all these faire and sweete ' flowers he includes in his Garden of Pleasant Flowers ' a few sweete herbes both to accomplish this Garden and to please your senses by placing them in your Nosegays, or else whereas you list '—lavender, lavender cotton, basil, sweet marjoram, thyme and hyssop. This ' Speaking Garden ', as the author himself describes the book, is dedicated to Queen Henrietta Maria :

' Accept, I beseech your Maiestie, this speaking Garden, that may informe you in all the particulars of your store, as well as wants, when you cannot see any of them fresh upon the ground, and it shall further encourage him to accomplish the remainder ; who in praying that your Highnesse may enjoy the heavenly Paradise, after the many yeares fruition of this earthly, submitteth to be

Your Maiesties

in all

humble devotion

Iohn Parkingson '.

The *Paradisus*, written throughout in the dignified phraseology of the seventeenth century, is not a book to be read in our hurried modern fashion ; it is impossible to describe and a lifetime's friendship with this stately volume serves only to increase one's love for the devout, simple-minded author. I think he is best described by a paragraph in his own book :

' That as many herbes and flowers with their fragrant sweet smels doe comfort and as it were revive the spirits and perfume a whole house : even so such men as live vertuously, labouring to doe good and to profit the Church of God and the Commonwealth by their paines or penne, doe as it were send forth a pleasing savour of sweet· instructions, not only to that time wherein they live, and are fresh, but being drye, withered and dead, cease not in all after ages to doe as much or more '.

Like Gerard, Parkinson refers to many notable folk in the garden world, and to personal friends, and in each case with a courtly dignity which is very charming. Both in the *Paradisus* and *Theatrum Botanicum* there are references to John Tradescant, ' that painfull industrious searcher and lover of all nature's varieties ', John Gerard, Guillaume Boel, the de Franquevilles (both father and son), Thomas Johnson (the eminent botanist and editor of the enlarged edition of Gerard's Herbal), Captain John Smith of Virginian fame, Jean Robin of Paris (Keeper of the King's gardens in Paris, to whom Gerard in his Herbal so frequently refers as ' my loving friend John Robin '), John Goodyer (the Hampshire botanist), and James Cole (described by Gerard as ' a learned Merchant of London '). One of the most celebrated gardeners of the day, mentioned by both Gerard and Parkinson, was Nicholas Leete. Nicholas Leete, to whom Elizabeth and Stuart garden-lovers owed much, was a member of the Worshipful Company of Ironmongers and Master of it in 1616, 1626, and 1627. (The portrait of him, arrayed in his gorgeous furred Master's robe and Elizabethan ruff, hung in Ironmongers' Hall until the building was destroyed by a German bomb in 1917.) Gerard wrote of him, ' He is greatly in love with rare and faire flowers, for which he doth carefully send unto Syria, having a servant out there at Aleppo and in many other countries for the which my selfe and likewise the whole land are much bound unto him '. Amongst other treasures he sent Gerard an ' orange tawnie gilliflower ' from Poland. This was the yellow Sops-in-wine, a carnation hitherto unknown in England. From his ' servant at Aleppo ' many rarities were sent. His most important introduction was the yellow Provence rose (R. *sulphurea syn* R. *hemispherica*) which Parkinson accurately describes as ' very tender '. He says that this rose

' was first procured to be brought into England by Master Nicholas Lete, a worthy merchant of London and a great lover of flowers ; from Constantinople, which (as we heare) was first brought thither from Syria ; but perished quickly both with him and with all others to whom he imparted it ; yet afterwards it was sent to Master John de Franqueville, a Merchant, also of London, and a great lover of all rare plants, as well as flowers, from which is sprung the greatest store that is now flourishing in this Kingdom '.

Ralph Tuggie, to whom there are various references both in Johnson's edition of Gerard's Herbal and in the *Paradisus*, had a celebrated garden at Westminster. He was especially noted for his carnations, and some of the best were named after him— ' Master Tuggies Princesse ' and ' Master Tuggie his Rose Gilliflower '. After his death his widow kept up his garden, as we know from Johnson, who in writing of carnations in his enlarged edition of Gerard's Herbal, advises his readers to consult ' the oft mentioned Worke of my friend Mr. John Parkinson ', and adds :

' If they require further satisfaction, let them at the time of the yeare repaire to the garden of Mistress Tuggie (the wife of my late deceased friend Mr. Ralph Tuggie) in Westminster, which in the excellencie and varietie of these delights exceedeth all that I have seene, as also, he himself, whilst he lived exceeded most, if not all, of his time, in his care, industry and skill, in raising, increasing and preserving of these plants '.

During the troublous years of the Civil Wars there was scant time for the ' retired leisure ' of gardens. But at least one of the great Parliamentarian generals was an enthusiastic flower-lover —General Lambert. He was lord of the manor of Wimbledon and his garden was noted for tulips and gilliflowers. In a pack of satirical playing-cards, published during the Commonwealth, the Eight of Hearts is depicted with a full-length ' portrait ' of him holding in his right hand a tulip and beneath, ' Lambert Kt. of ye Golden Tulip '.

Under the Commonwealth régime, however, considerable attention was given to the utilitarian side of gardening, notably orchards. Amongst the many names associated with this movement that of the Oxford nurseryman, Ralph Austen, is of paramount importance. A contemporary, Anthony Lawrence,[1] wrote of him :

' He hath by his labours and experiments, done more good for Oxford and thence for England than is yet done by many gaudy Gallants, who spend more in a day than this honest Nurseryman can can spare in a year '.

Austen's best-known book, *A Treatise of Fruit-Trees* (1653), was written with the avowed object of encouraging fruit growing in England. It is interesting to remember that as early as 1601 John Taverner, in his *Certaine Experiments*, advocated that all hedgerows in this country should be planted with fruit-trees and he added the sensible suggestion that if anyone picked the fruit merely to satisfy his own hunger he should go unpunished, but that if he carried it away he should be dealt with as a thief. Long before the publication of Austen's book, however, the Worcestershire and Herefordshire orchards were famed, and Austen emphasizes that if those who pretended that the north parts of England were too cold would attend to their fruit trees

[1] *Nurseries, Orchards, Profitable Gardens, and Vineyards Encouraged . . . In several Letters . . . the first letter from Anthony Lawrence . . . 1677.*

as diligently as the West-country folk, they would have as fine fruit. Like Lawson, Austen counsels liberality as the best means of 'defending' an orchard.

'Above all, let those that have much fruit spare a part to them that have but little or none of their own, and be no niggards but liberate to their neighbours; and this bounty will bring a double blessing, first from God, to increase the fruits; secondly from men, not to diminish them'.

And in another passage:

'Oh how sweet and pleasant is the fruit of those trees which a man hath planted and ordered with his owne hand, to gather it and largely and freely to bestow and distribute it among his kindred and friends'.

The first part of Austen's book is eminently practical, but according to Anthony à Wood the second part, *The Spiritual Use of an Orchard of Fruit Trees*, damaged the sale of the book, 'being all divinity and nothing therein of the practice part of gardening many refused to buy it'. This statement seems exaggerated, for subsequent editions of the whole book appeared in 1662 and 1667, and the *Spiritual Use of an Orchard* was reprinted separately in 1847. Certainly to modern readers the most attractive part of Austen's book is the chapter entitled 'The Pleasures of an Orchard'. In this he writes with naïve charm of the appeal an orchard makes to all the five senses— the songs of the birds, the 'soft and gentle aires' of the wind moving the boughs, and the leaves, the cool touch of the leaves, and fruits, the pleasure of beholding the 'decent formes' of the trees, 'the well compos'd allies, walkes, seats and arbours', the delicate colours of leaves, blossoms, and fruits.

'Is it not a pleasant sight to behold a multitude of trees round about; bespangled and gorgeously apparelled with greene leaves, bloomes and goodly fruits, as with a rich robe of imbroidered work, or as hanging with some pretious and costly jewels or pearls, the boughs laden and burdened bowing downe to you and freely offering their ripe fruits?'

Then the pleasure to the sense of smell in the 'most precious and pleasant odor' of the blossoms 'perfuming the ayre throughout all the orchard and the sense of taste enjoying not only the fruits themselves but ' dainties made from them '.

' There is a rejoycing in earthly blessing which God allowes to us Deut. 26. II. Thou shalt rejoyce in every good thing which the Lord thy God shall blesse thee in all thy increase, and in all the workes of thy handes, therefore thou shalt surely rejoyce : And when our waies please God he saies : Goe eat thy bread with joy and drink thy wine with a merry heart '.

In The *Spiritual Use of an Orchard* Austen tells his readers that the ' World is a great Library and Fruit-Trees some of the Bookes wherein we may read and see plainly the Attributes of God, his Power, Wisdom and Goodnesse'. He had evidently lived through a time of great spiritual distress, a time he describes as ' walking in darkness, seeing neither Sunne nor Starres for many Months together, out of which the Lorde (I will speake it to his praise) hath delivered me with great advantages '. It was his earnest desire that fruit trees should speak to others as they had to him of the love and wisdom of God and hence this little volume of *Similitudes*.

' Our Eyes (Especially on the Sabbath day) ought as little Bees fall upon severall Objects, and from them (as from so many Flowers), gather hony and bring it into the hive ; That is, sweet heavenly wholsome Meditation for magnifying the Creator in all his Attributes '.

Austen's other book, *A Dialogue between the Husbandman and Fruit-Trees* (1676), is excessively rare.[1] Several of the early gardening books were written in dialogue form, the most noted being Bullein's *Bulwarke of defence* (1562) and *The Solitary Gardener* (1706), but Austen's volume is the only one in which the plants (in this case fruit trees) take their share. The dialogue is between the ' Husbandman ' and the ' Fruit-Trees ' and begins with an enquiry from the former as to what language the trees speak. The dialogue is delightful, but there is only space to quote one paragraph.

Fruit Trees : ' Many people (of all sorts) come from time to time and walk among us, and look upon us, and commend us for brave

---

[1] There is no copy in the British Museum.

handsome Trees, lovely and beautifull especially when we are in our Gallantries; full of beautifull blossomes and pleasant wholesome Fruits; and some greedily pluck us and tear us, and sometimes break off some of our Branches to get our Fruits; and so go their waies; But speak never a word to us, neither do they understand what we say to them '.

Interest in American plants increased with greater knowledge. Several important books were published during the seventeenth century, amongst them *Canadensium Plantarum Aliarumque Nondum Editorum Historia* (1635), by the French botanist Jacques Cornutus; John Joscelyn's *New England's Rarities Discovered* (1672); and William Hughes' *The American Physitian; or a Treatise of the Roots, Plants, Trees, Shrubs, Fruits, Herbs, etc., growing in the English Plantations in America* (1672). Unlike Cornutus, who apparently had not visited America, but only described the plants from specimens sent him, both Joscelyn and Hughes wrote from personal knowledge of the living plants. Hughes visited the West Indies and Joscelyn had spent eight years in America, chiefly in the neighbourhood of Boston. Even as late as 1663 the country had been very imperfectly explored, for Joscelyn states that he cannot say whether New England is an island or not. He was also not very sure whether America was an island, but quite confident that the Indians were closely allied to the Tartars.

The outstandingly interesting features of his book are the notes on plants used medicinally by the Indians, the list of English weeds unknown in America before, but introduced by the new settlers: (the list includes couch-grass, shepherd's purse, dandelion, groundsel, sow-thistle, stinging nettle, mallows, plantain, wormwood, chickweed, mullein, knot-grass, and comfrey—the Indians, he states, called plantain ' Englishman's Foot, as though it were produced by their treading ', and perhaps, most interesting of all, the earliest list that has been preserved of the English garden-plants which the early settlers tried to grow. What visions this list conjures up of plants and seeds taken carefully on the long voyage (it took three months in those days), and the pathetic, futile efforts to cherish such favourites as rosemary, lavender, and southernwood through the rigours of a New England winter. Truly, wherever our race goes, and they have been to all the accessible (and most of the inaccessible) parts of the globe, they establish gardens and always gardens of the type they left in the Old Country. How pleasant to remember that entry recorded in John Winthrop's diary that before they even set foot on land the settlers were greeted with *the smell of a Garden*—their first greeting in the New World:

' We had now fair Sunshine Weather and so pleasant a sweet Aire as did much refresh us, and there came a smell off the Shore like the Smell of a Garden '.

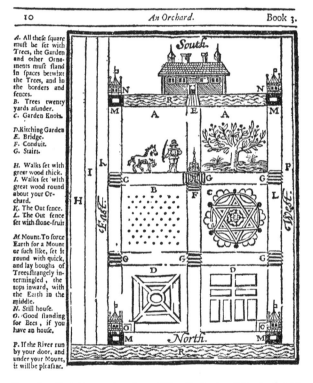

Plan of a Yorkshire garden, from *A New Orchard and Garden* (1618), by William Lawson. (See page 125.)

CHAPTER V

The Restoration gave a great impetus to gardening, and from this period onwards pleasure gardens may be roughly divided into two very different types—those made in 'the grand manner' in imitation of French gardens, and the old-fashioned pleasaunces belonging to folk who either could not afford to follow the royal example or who preferred the older and homelier type of garden. Whether Le Nôtre ever came to England is still a vexed question, but there is no doubt that French influence was paramount in this country during the latter half of the seventeenth century. Charles II, during his exile, had been vastly impressed by the splendours of French gardens; on his return he appointed André Mollet head-gardener at St. James's Park and he did his utmost to secure the services of De la Quintinye, 'Director General of the Fruit and Kitchen Gardens of all the Royal Houses', who twice visited England, but De la Quintinye remained faithful to Louis XIV.

St. James's Park was the first place to be altered in accordance with the new French ideas. Charles II entirely changed its appearance by making the canal and planting avenues, the work being done by French gardeners. The Park began to be fashionable in James I's reign, but in Charles II's time it was thronged, for though only a few had the privilege of driving through it, it was open to all on foot. Crowds used to watch the King and his courtiers playing paille-maille[1] (a game like croquet) on the site of the present Mall, the King being noted for his skill. The popularity of the Park with people of all classes was undoubtedly due to Charles himself, for he was constantly there and delighted to roam about unattended. There were always groups watching with profound interest whilst the King, invariably accompanied by his numerous dogs, amused himself feeding the ducks, flirting with fair ladies and bandying

[1] In James I's reign the game was played on the north side of the street, now called Pall Mall. Subsequently the game was played within the Park, and the Mall, like Pall Mall, preserves the name of the game.

witticisms with all and sundry. His dull solemn brother, James, remonstrated with him once for risking his life by going about so freely unattended. Charles, with his usual ready wit, retorted : ' No one would be such a fool as to kill me to put you on the throne '. It is easy to visualize the King with his dogs and the crowds of spectators, but it is not so easy to visualize the Park as it was then, with the beautiful gardens of St. James's Palace occupying the whole of the north side of the Mall, the deer and the cows under the trees beyond the Mall and the milk-women selling mugs of milk. Charles had laid out the park on French lines, but in spite of that it must have looked very homely and pleasant, characteristically English and wholly lacking in the frigid grandeur of Versailles.

It is far more difficult to estimate the importance of Le Nôtre's influence in this country than that of De la Quintinye. Le Nôtre occupies a unique place in the history of gardening and he is the only man of whom it can be said that not only did he introduce a wholly new type of garden architecture, but that his powerful influence was felt almost immediately in the gardens of all the leading European countries. He found gardens Gothic in character, he created vast pleasaunces which were perfect settings for the palaces designed by the greatest architects of his day. That he could rely on the almost boundless wealth of his royal master for the fulfilment of his magnificent plans was his good fortune.

During the early years of Louis XIV's reign French gardens had been of the mediæval type. Fontainebleau was the exception, for François I introduced many Italian features there, and Henry IV also enlarged the boundaries of the domain and added canals and avenues. He employed an Italian architect, Francini, chiefly celebrated for his mechanical contrivances in connection with water-works. Du Cerceau's interesting collections of plans, *Les plus excellants Bastiments de France* (1576), shows in remarkable detail the gardens attached to the great châteaux built chiefly during the sixteenth century. French gardens during that period must have been both gay and magnificent— square flower parterres surrounded by low balustrades with heraldic animals on posts, the animals and posts being as in England painted or gilded, magnificent fountains (the fountains at Château Gaillon were particularly fine, one with three immense basins, the water pouring from one to the other through satyr masks, and the lowest basin beautifully sculptured) ; tunnelled arbours, ornate pavilions and labyrinths both square and round. Bernard Palissy, the great garden designer and author of *Récepte véritable* (1563),[1] was an enthusiast on the subject of elaborate natural arbours—trees planted closely and trained to form summer-houses. The Mollets, who for three generations were famed as gardeners, were horticulturists rather than designers, and the elder Mollet made a collection of rare flowers at the Château d'Anet. Two innovations in garden design are usually, however, ascribed to them—Claude Mollet the younger, who planned the royal gardens for Henry IV and Louis XIII, is said to have invented *parterres à compartiments de broderie*, i.e. box laid out in imitation of embroidery, and his younger son, André, was the first writer to advocate the planting of avenues of trees on an extensive scale.[2] Herein they foreshadowed, though but dimly, the splendours of Le Nôtre's designs.

Like so many French artists, Le Nôtre was of humble birth. His father, who began as an under-gardener at the Tuileries, became superintendent of the royal gardens and it is interesting to remember that his godmother was the wife of Claude Mollet, then head-gardener of the Tuileries. There has always been the tradition that Le Nôtre studied painting in his youth and met Le Brun and Le Vau, who were afterwards associated with him in his work at Versailles. He certainly worked under his father in the Tuileries gardens and possibly even as a boy he dreamt of the gardens he would fill with his ' peculiar magic of infinite perspectives ', to quote Cousin. It was not till he was nearly forty that Le Nôtre was given his first great opportunity—at Vaux-le-Vicomte, where the splendour-loving, ostentatious Fouquet spent eighteen million francs in making the most magnificent house and gardens in the realm of France. Fouquet invited the King to a fête in the gorgeously illuminated gardens, and the capricious monarch was infuriated to find that his host's

---

[1] *Récepte véritable par laquelle tous les hommes de la France pourrent apprendre a augmenter leurs Trésors avec le Dessin d'un jardin délectable et utile* (1563).

[2] André Mollet. *Le Jardin de Plaisir* (1651). The only known copy of the English translation—*The Garden of Pleasure*—is in Lord Newton's library.

new abode was far statelier than the royal palace of St. Germain and Fontainebleau. Three weeks later Fouquet was imprisoned for life, and Le Nôtre was thenceforward occupied almost entirely in the King's service, for Louis XIV had been swift to recognize his genius. At Versailles he made the gardens which to this day reflect something of their ancient splendour, though how different they must have looked when thousands of guests in the picturesque costumes of the period attended the fêtes given by the 'Roi Soleil', when the great canal was gay with brilliantly coloured Venetian gondolas, and banquets and dances were illuminated by countless torches held aloft in gilded *torchères*. The ghosts of former days still haunt the Tuileries, Chantilly (Le Nôtre altered Chantilly for the great Condé), Fontainebleau, the Grand Trianon and St. Cloud, but the splendour has gone. It is difficult to understand how all this magnificence, superb vistas, gorgeous fountains, canals, immense parterres, etc., appealed to English flower-lovers, much as they must have admired Le Nôtre's architectural genius. For flowers were conspicuous by their almost complete absence, at any rate in the immediate vicinity of the palace. It would have been impossible to fill flower-beds in such vast gardens, when nurserymen were few, and in winter the great beds would have looked dull and empty. Le Nôtre, therefore, laid out immense *parterres de broderie*—box planted in intricate designs on beds very slightly raised in the centre, with a surface covering of coloured sands, brickdust, and so forth and with clipped shrubs at intervals. Flowers, however, were grown in considerable abundance in the *parterre fleuriste*, which corresponded to our modern 'picking garden', for the flowers were used for indoor decoration. Louis XIV took the keenest interest in the flowers grown for the royal table and frequently visited the *parterre fleuriste*, which was under the supervision of De la Quintinye, the head of the royal kitchen-gardens.

Immediately after his accession, Charles II, who 'loved planting and building', began the alterations at Hampton Court on French lines. He planted the great avenue of limes round the semicircular parterre (nine and a half acres in extent) and the avenues radiating from it, he constructed the canal, three-quarters of a mile long, he adorned the parterre with 'a rich and noble fountaine' and statues cast in copper by Fanelli. Evelyn, who saw the place two years later, describes the park and garden thus :

'Hampton Court is as noble and uniforme a pile and as capacious as any Gotiq architecture can have made it. . . . The park formerly a flat naked piece of ground, now planted with sweete rows of lime trees ; and the canall for water now neere perfected ; also the hare park. In the garden is a rich and noble fountaine, with syrens, statues, etc. cast in copper by Fanelli, but no plenty of water. The cradle-walk of horne-beame[1] in the gardenes, for the perplexed twining of the trees, very observable. There is a parterre which they call Paradise, in which is a pretty banquetting house, set over a cave or cellar.[2] All these gardens might be exceedingly improved, as being too narrow for such a place '.

Amongst the most notable gardens of early Restoration days were those belonging to Lord Capel, created Earl of Essex in 1661, and his brother, Sir Henry Capel, created Baron Capel of Tewkesbury in 1692. The Earl of Essex's garden at Cassiobury was under the care of Moses Cooke, author of *The Manner of Raising, Ordering and Improving Forest-Trees* . . . (1676). Evelyn, in his Diary, says, ' No man has been more industrious than this noble Lord. . . . The gardens at Cassiobury are very rare, and cannot be otherwise, having so skilful an artist to govern them as Mr. Cooke, who is, as to the mechanical part, not ignorant in mathematics and pretends to astrology '.

Sir William Temple, in his *Gardens of Epicurus*, states that ' the perfectest figure of a garden ' he ever saw was that of Moor Park in Hertfordshire, made by the Countess of Bedford. His vivid description is particularly interesting, as it portrays the type of seventeenth-century terraced garden made before the introduction of French ideas. A terraced garden with the ' great parlours ' of the house opening on to the broad gravel walks, flights of steps leading to the parterre with its fountains and statues, its shady stone-paved cloister walks, one being

---

[1] Evelyn says horn-beame, but they are wych-elms. In William and Mary's reign this was called ' Queen Mary's Bower', and for over two centuries the walk has been known by this name.

[2] This was probably the old Water-gallery.

covered with vines, the lowest terrace all fruit trees ('ranged about the several quarters of a wilderness') with green walks.

'Because I take the garden I have named to have been in all kinds the most beautiful and perfect, at least in the figure and disposition, that I have ever seen, I will describe it for a model to those that meet with such a situation, and are above the regards of common expense. It lies on the side of a hill (upon which the house stands) but not very steep. The length of the house, where the best rooms, and most of use or pleasure are, lies upon the breadth of the garden, the great parlours open into the middle of a terrace gravel-walk that lies even with it, and which may be, as I remember, about three hundred paces long, and broad proportion ; the border set with standard laurels, and at large distances, which have the beauty of orange trees out of flowers and fruit : from this walk are three descents by many stone steps, in the middle and at each end, into a very large parterre. This is divided into quarters by gravel-walks, and adorned with two fountains and eight statues, in the several quarters ; at the end of the terrace-walk are two summer-houses, and the sides of the parterre are ranged with two large cloisters, open to the garden, upon arches of stone, and ending with two other summer-houses, even with the cloisters which are paved with stone, and designed for walks of shade, there being none other in the whole parterre.   Over these two cloisters are two terraces covered with lead and fenced with balusters ; and the passage into these airy walks, is out of the two summer-houses at the end of the first terrace-walk. The cloister facing the south is covered with vines, and would have been proper for an orange-house, and the other for myrtles, or other more common greens ; and had, I doubt not, been cast for that purpose, if this price of gardening had been then as much vogue as it is now.

From the middle of this parterre is a descent by many steps flying on each side of a grotto that lies between them (covered with lead and flat) into the lower garden, which is all fruit-trees ranged about the several quarters of a wilderness which is very shady ; the walks here are all green, the grotto embellished with figures of shell-rock work, fountains and waterworks. . . .

This was Moor Park when I was acquainted with it, and the sweetest place, I think, that I have seen in my life, either before or since, at home or abroad . . . the remembrance of what it was is too pleasant ever to forget '.

It is interesting to note in this account that a garden of moderate size contained no less than four summer-houses,

SEVENTEENTH-CENTURY GAZEBO
(Holdsworth House, near Halifax, Yorkshire)

John Rose presenting the first pineapple ripened in
England to Charles II

(After the painting by Henry Danckerts, c.1625-c.1679, at Ham House)
Victoria and Albert Museum

apart from the cloisters ' upon arches of stone ' and the grotto. Summer-houses in those days were sometimes called by the pleasing name of ' shadow houses '. In the Parliamentary Survey of the manor of Wimbledon, which had formerly belonged to Queen Henrietta Maria, five ' shadow houses ' are mentioned, one garden summer or shadow house ' in the middle of the East wall of the Lower Level . . . covered with blue slate handsomely benched and wainscotted in part, and paved with bricks ', two on the south side of the Maze, one at each end of the ' close walk ' of high thorn hedges and two in the Vineyard Garden, ' the one standing in the wall at the end of the walk that leads . . . to the hall door of the said Manor . . . and very much graces that walk ', and one ' at the end of the walk or alley that leads up the middle of the Vineyard from East to West '. Garden houses were frequently used as waiting-rooms for the coach and were therefore placed near the road. John Worlidge, the author of *Systema Agriculturæ*, *Vinetum Britannicum*, and *Systema Horticulturæ*, was evidently of opinion that their chief use was a refuge from ' your Family or Acquaintance ' !

' This small edifice may be made at some remote Angle of your Garden : For the more remote it is from your house, the more private you will be from the frequent disturbances of your Family or Acquaintance, and being made at an Angle, part within your Garden and part without, you will have the priviledges and advantages of Air and View, which otherwise you will want, and which render it much more pleasant than to be without them.

The Windows and Doors, the one or other respecting every Coast, may be glazed with the best and most transparent Glass, to represent every Object through it the more splended, with Skreens of printed and painted Sarcanet, to prevent in the day, and shutters of thin Wainscot in the Night, others from disturbing your Solitary repose '.

The illustration[1] shows a charming seventeenth-century stone-built summer-house ; this is in the garden of Holdsworth House, near Halifax. Like the house which bears the date 1680 on its porch the summer-house is adorned with stone ball ornaments. These ball ornaments, which were commonly used, are interesting, for in older times a skull was nailed to the

[1] I am indebted to Mrs. Pollit for kindly sending me this photo.

highest point, in the belief that it would ward off lightning, and the ball ornament so frequently used to adorn houses and gate posts represents the traditional skull. Over the 'house body' of Holdsworth House is the double cross of the Knights of St. John of Jerusalem, a sign that the property once belonged to that order. Tenants of these lands were not obliged to grind their corn at the lord's mill, nor to do suit at his court. These privileges continued even after the suppression of the order.

Sundials were still favourite garden ornaments. Both Sir Christopher Wren and Sir Isaac Newton were famous diallers, and Evelyn records in his Diary that when he dined with Dr. Wilkins, at Wadham College, his host showed him not only a remarkable collection of sundials but also beehives built like miniature palaces complete in every detail of their exteriors even to wind-vanes and sundials. Many of these were of his own workmanship and of 'that prodigious young scholar, Mr. Chr. Wren'. To be 'an ingenious dialler' was accounted a great accomplishment in those days. Charles I was a great lover of sundials, he always carried a pocket-dial about with him, and on the night preceding his execution he delivered it to his servant Hubert, it being his last gift to his younger son, the Duke of York. How prophetic was the motto on the garden dial Charles I gave his queen—' United in Time, parted in Time, to be reunited when Time shall be no more '.

Charles II inherited his father's love of sundials, and by his order a sundial was set up in the Privy Garden at Whitehall, which must have been one of the most remarkable in the kingdom. In Queen Elizabeth's reign there had been a large square stone sundial in the Privy Garden which Leopold von Wedel admired and noted in the account of his travels. Charles II's sundial is fully described in Father Hall's book, *An Explication of the Diall sett up in the King's Garden at London, an. 1669. In which many sorts of Dyalls are contained ; by which, besides the Howres of all kinds diversely expressed, many things also belonging to Geography, Astrology and Astronomy are by the Sunnes shadow made visible to the eye. Amongst which very many Dialls, Especially the most curious, are new inventions, hitherto divulged by None.* On ordinary dials the shadow of the style or gnomon passes over the hour-lines, but in this dial animals were painted at the bottom of the glass boxes and the shade of the hour-lines passed over the gnomons. Similarly with the portraits of the King, the Queen, the Queen Mother and Prince Rupert—'In his Majestyes picture the Hour is shewne by the shade of the Hour-lines passing over the top of the Scepter; In the pictures of the two Queens, it is shown by the like shade passing over the top of a Flower, and in the other by passing over the end of a troncheon'. Under each picture was written a chronograph for the year 1669 and suitable to the person. The dial shewed also the time at Jerusalem, Constantinople, Jamaica, etc., and also according to other methods of reckoning time —'the Ancient or Judaicall', the Babylonian, the Italian, the Astronomical.

During the latter years of the seventeenth century it was a favourite conceit to lay out living sundials, the figures being of box or of any other suitable shrub. There are illustrations of these sundials at New College, Oxford, in Loggan's *Oxonia Illustrata* and Williams' *Oxonia depicta*, and at Queen's College and Pembroke College, Cambridge, in Loggan's *Cantabrigia Illustrata*. Southey, in his *Letters of Espriella*, said that formerly at New College, there was 'a sundial in box, set round with true lovers' knots'. He observes, 'These have been destroyed more easily as well as more rapidly than they were formed, but as nothing beautiful has been substituted in their places, it had been better if they had suffered these old oddities to have remained'. William Hughes, in the 1692 edition of his *Flower Garden*, gives elaborate directions for the making of these living sundials, the figures to be cut in rosemary, hyssop, thyme or box, and he adds the interesting information that these dials were greatly in favour in the West Indies where they were planted in myrtle or cypress. Andrew Marvell gives a charming description of a sundial of this type; indeed his lines transport one straightway into an orchard of his day, with its fountain and dial, of herbs and flowers:

> Here at this fountain's sliding foot,
> Or at some fruit-tree's mossy root,
> Casting the bodie's vest aside,
> My soul into the boughs does glide:

There, like a bird it sits, and sings,
Then whets and claps its silver wings ;
And, till prepar'd for longer flight,
Waves in its plumes the various light.

．　　　．　　　．　　　．　　　．

How well the skilful gardener drew
Of flow'rs and herbs this dial new ;
Where, from above, the milder sun
Does through a fragrant zodiack run,
And, as it works, th' industrious bee
Computes its time as well as we !
How could such sweet and wholesome hours
Be reckon'd but with herbs and flow'rs.

Viticulture attracted considerable attention in Charles II's
reign. The chief writers on the subject were William Hughes
(*The Complete Vineyard*), 1665, and John Rose, whose *English
Vineyard Vindicated* was published in 1666 with a preface by
Philocepos (John Evelyn) and in 1669, 1675, and 1691, with
Evelyn's *French Gardiner*, and separately again in 1672. John
Rose, who had been in the service of the Earl of Essex, was sent
to Versailles to study under Le Nôtre and subsequently was
appointed head of the royal gardens in succession to Andrew
Mollet. Rose is always credited with having presented Charles
II with the first pineapple ripened in England, a remarkable feat
at that time. He was an enthusiast on the subject of viticulture,
another being Sir William Temple. The latter was proud of
having introduced four sorts of grapes into this country and his
statements are interesting as showing that vines were still fairly
extensively cultivated. The Burgundy, he says, never failed
once in the fifteen years he had it and he describes it as ' the
surest to ripen in our climate '.

' I have had the honour of bringing over four sorts into England ;
the Arboyse from the Franche Comte, which is a small white grape, or
rather runs into some small and some great upon the same branch ; it
agrees well with our climate, but is very choice in soil, and must have
a sharp gravel ; it is the most delicious of all grapes that are not
muscat. The Burgundy which is a grizelin or pale red, and of all others
is sweet to ripen in our climate ; so that I have never known them to

fail one summer these fifteen years, when all others have ; and have had it very good upon an east wall. A black muscat, which is called the Dowager, and ripens as well as the common white grape. And the fourth is the Grizelin Frontignac, being of that colour, and the highest of that taste, and the noblest of all grapes I ever eat in England ; but requires the hottest wall and the sharpest gravel ; and must be favoured by the summer too, to be very good. All these are, I suppose, by this time pretty common among some gardeners, in my neighbourhood, as well as several persons of quality ; for I have ever thought all things of this kind, the commoner they are made, the better '.

Conservatories began to be more commonly built in Restoration times. At the Oxford Physic Garden there was a house of tender plants 60 feet long ; it faced south and was roofed with stone slates. It is shown in the plan of the Physic Garden in Loggan's *Oxonia illustrata* (1685). Evelyn in his Diary (Aug. 7, 1685) comments on the new conservatory in the Chelsea Physic Garden :

' I went to see Mr. Watts, Keeper of the Apothecaries' Garden of simples at Chelsea . . . what was very ingenious was the subterranean heate conveyed by a stove under the conservatory all vaulted with brick so as he has the doors and windows open in the hardest frosts, secluding only the snow '.

Where there were no stoves the air was warmed with pans of charcoal. Rea, in his *Flora, Ceres and Pomona* (1665), says, ' In default of stoves you must attemper the air with pans of Charcoal '. In Gibson's account of the gardens near London[1] he refers with great interest to the conservatories—the most noteworthy being those at Hampton Court, the Queen Dowager's garden at Hammersmith, Chelsea Physic Garden, Sir Henry Capel's at Kew, the Archbishop of Canterbury's at Lambeth, Brompton Park garden (belonging to the great nurserymen London and Wise). Beddington Garden, belonging to the Carews but at that time rented by the Duke of Norfolk, he describes as having the finest orangery in England and unlike

---

[1] *A Short Account of several Gardens near London with Remarks on some Particulars wherein they excel or are deficient upon a View of them in December* 1691. Communicated to the Society of Antiquaries by the Rev. Dr. Hamilton from the original manuscript in his possession. Read July 3, 1794.

other places they were grown in the ground. These must have been amongst the oldest grown in this country.

'Beddington Garden has in it the best orangery in England. The orange and lemon trees there grow in the ground, and have done so near one hundred years, as the gardener, an aged man, said he believed. There are a great number of them, the house wherein they are being above two hundred feet long; they are most of them thirteen feet high, and very full of fruit, the gardener not having taken off so many flowers this last summer as usually others do. He said he gathered off them at least ten thousand oranges this last year. . . . The heir of the family being but five years of age the trustees take care of the orangery and this year they built a new house over them. . . . The rest of the garden is all out of order, the orangery being the gardener's chief care'.

Pepys records in his Diary (June 25th, 1666) that the first time he saw oranges growing was in Lord Brooke's garden at Hackney and he 'pulled off a little one by stealth'!

'Here I first saw oranges grow, some green, some half, some a quarter and some full ripe, on the same tree, and one fruit of the same tree do come a year or two after the other; I pulled off a little one by stealth (the man being mightily curious of them) and eat it, and it was just as other little green small oranges are—as big as half the end of my little finger'.

In the seventeenth century as in mediæval and Tudor days dovecotes were utilitarian rather than ornamental. In the *Countrie Farme* (1600) owners are instructed to perfume their dove-houses:

'Perfume oftentimes your Dove-house with Juniper, Rosemarie, and sometimes with a little fine Frankincense, for that doth mightily retaine and keepe them and causeth them to love their owne house more than anie other.

Peacocks, however, have from very early times been kept not merely for food but for their beauty. The author quoted above gives a quaint description of the bird which he accurately describes as being as good as a watch-dog:

'The Peacocke is a bird of more beautifull feathers than any other that is: he is quickly angrie . . . he is goodly to behold, verie good to eat, and serveth as a watch in the inner court ; for that hee spying strangers to come into the lodging, he fayleth not to crie out and to advertise them of the house. It is true that he is not kept with a little cost and meat, being a great eater, and quickly digesting his meat : . . . The Cocke liveth a long time, as from twentie to twentie five yeares, but the Henne somewhat lesse, both the one and the other somewhat troublesome to reare and bring up whiles they be young, but they need not have any great care taken of them after they have once left the dam, except it be in keeping them from hurting the Corne. . . .

People of old and ancient time did cast Islets on the backside of their Gardens, onely for Peacockes, and there set up some little shed for them at their pleasure to repaire unto, and another for the partie that should feed them. And in Italie unto this day they use, in places neere unto the Sea shore, to bring up Peacocks in Islets somewhat neere unto the Sea, that so they may prevent such harme as the Foxe might otherwise doe them ; which was also the drift why our auncient predecessors tooke the same course : but wee which make not so great account of them, are content to keepe them in some roome over the Hennes even in the highest part of the Henne house for they love to roost on high and in an open ayre, sitting verie often for that cause upon trees. . . .

Great attention was paid to lawns during this century. The history of the lawn is indeed an interesting by-path in the history of gardening and since Tudor days our lawns have been one of the finest features of English gardens. In mediæval times, as has already been noted, lawns were imitations of the natural meadows and like the meadows starred with flowers. It was apparently not till Tudor days that ' lawns ' in the modern sense of the word were commonly made. Green plots and alleys were as frequently planted with camomile as with grass. Possibly the lawn on which Drake played his historic game of bowls on the eve of the Armada was a camomile lawn. And it was of camomile thus planted that Falstaff said, ' the more it is trodden on the faster it grows '. The earliest description of a grass lawn and the manner of making it is to be found in Gervase Markham's *Way to get Wealth* (1613) :

' To fit a place for this manner of greene plot, it is requisite that it may be cleansed from all manner of stones and weedes, not so much as the rootes left undestroied, and for the better accomplishing hereof, there must boiling water be poured upon such endes of rootes as staying behind in the ground cannot be well pulled up, and afterwards the floor must be beaten and troden downe mightily, then after this, there must be cast great quantity and store of turfes of earth full of greene grasse, the bare earthe part of them being turned and laid upward, and afterward danced upon with the feete, and the beater or paving beetle lightly passing over them, in such sort as that within a short time after, the grasse may begin to peepe up and put foorth small haires ; and finally it is made the sporting green plot for ladies and gentlewomen to recreate their spirits in, or a place whereinto they may withdraw themselves if they would be solitary and out of sight '.

Markham enjoins that sanded or gravelled paths should always be bordered by grass as broad on each side as the breadth of the path :

' Now, you shall also understand that as you make this sandy and smooth walke through the midst of your Alleyes, so you shall not omit but leave as much greene swarth, or grasse ground of each side the plaine path, as may fully countervaile the breadth of the walke : as thus for example, if your sandy walke be sixe foote broad, the grasse ground of each side it, shall be at least sixe foote also, so that the whole Alley shall be at least eighteene foote in breadth, which will be both comely and stately '.

Stephen Blake, the author of that rare gardening book *The Compleat Gardener's Practice* (1664), gives his readers the outline of a book he intended to write ' if God permit me life '. In the contents of this book, which unfortunately he did not live to write, we find ' The expert way of laying of Grass work ' and ' How to make bowling Alleys with great care and little cost '.

John Rea in his *Flora* (1665) gives minute directions for the making of lawns, and it is interesting to remember that the wooden rails, surrounding lawns, which he describes, survived into the next century.

' All grass plots ', he says, should be marked out by ' sawed Rails five inches broad and an inch and quarter thick that have been laid straight and seasoned a year at least ; you may put them to a stone colour with white lead or London white, some charcoal and linseed oyl ground together on a painters stone but the rails and the stone colour will last much longer if they be first primed with red Lead and Timber ground as the former. Then after the colours are drie and the Rails fitted to their places nail on the insides thereof pieces of hard wood that will last, about half a yard long, placing them an inch under the upper edge : if you set them too thin the Rails will be apt to warp and turn with the Sun ; which done with discretion make holes to let these feet into the ground and so place them by a line. . . .

The next work is to prepare the places intended for Grass and to provide Turfs for them. First, level the ground, and consider the thickness of the Turfs, which when layed, must be three inches lower than the upper edge of the Rails, and the Allies four inches, so the Grass will be an inch higher, remembering still from the Rails to fetch your measure and level, to keep the whole work in order ; and if the ground under the Turfs be not barren of itself, it should be covered some thickness with hungry sand to make it so, that the grass grow not too rank. The best Turfs for this purpose are had in the most hungry Common, and where the grass is thick and short, puck down a line eight or ten foot long, and with a Spade cut the Turfs thereby, then shift the line a foot or 15 inches further, and so proceed until you have cut so far as you desire, then cross the line to the same breadth, that the Turfs may be square ; and cut them thereby ; then with a straight bitted Spade or Turving-hoe (which many for that purpose provide) and a short cord tied to it near the Bit, and the other end to the middle of a strong staff, whereby one thrusting the Spade forward under the Turfs, and another by the Staff pulling backwards, they will easily be staved and taken up, but not too many at a time for drying, but as they are laid which must be done by a line, and a long level, placing them close together, and beating them down with a Mallet, having covered the quarter or place intended, let it be well watered, and beaten all over with a heavy broad Beater. Lastly cut away by a line what is superfluous that the sides may be straight and even or in what work you shall please to fancy '.

' In Orchards ', according to Leonard Meager,

' curious green walks kept short by Mowing and Rowling in Summer are of good esteem, and such may be raised so above the common surface, that the wet may have little influence in staying on them even in winter after a shower of rain is past '.

In that quaint gardening book translated from the French, *The Solitary or Carthusian Gardener* (1706), a chapter is devoted to ' The different sorts of Green Plots and the way of making them '. The author says there are five ways of making green plots or walks, ' namely by Turfs, by Spanish Clover-Grass, by Hay-Seed, by the Seed of Sanfoïn, and by that of Medick

Fodder'. Turf he considers the best. Of Sanfoin he says: 'Sanfoin has a very pretty Aspect especially when it is in flower. When it arrives at its perfect Maturity we cut it down'. Green plots made with Medick Fodder he regarded with mild enthusiasm, but he observes that it can be planted in remote parts, 'and by consequence is less in view'. Hay seed he directs should be winnowed 'in order to clear it of the Dust, and the coarse stuff that attends it'.

Nearly all seventeenth-century garden books give directions for the treatment of camomile lawns. Under 'October', in John Evelyn's *Kalendarium Hortense*, we find: 'It will now be good to Beat, Roll and Mow carpet walks and camomile for now the ground is supple and it will even all inequalities'. They were equally popular in Continental gardens, and are described in various books, notably *Le Jardinier Hollandois*, by Van de Groen (1669). Camomile lawns continued to be a feature of English gardens at least as late as the early nineteenth century. Charles Marshall, in his *Introduction to the Knowledge and Practice of Gardening* (1805), gives directions for making camomile 'green or carpet walks' by planting the sets 'about 9 or 10 inches asunder which, naturally spreading the runners are fixed, by walking on them or rolling'. And I wonder how many of the thousands who attend the garden-parties at Buckingham Palace notice that considerable stretches of the lawn are planted with camomile? This is, as far as I know, the only garden in London with stretches of camomile lawn.

Bowling-greens were a feature of most gardens of any size. John Locke, writing in 1679, says, 'The sports of England for a curious stranger to see are horse-racing, hawking, hunting and bowling'. At Chatsworth the bowling-green was the central feature of the garden. At Cassiobury the bowling-green was in a wood, the approach to it being through an avenue of trees. The greens were as a rule surrounded with trees. In *The Solitary Gardener* we are informed that:

'A Bowling Green should be incompassed with great Trees such as Elms, Horse-chestnut trees or Acacias accompanied with Yews. They are only proper in spatious Gardens and commonly are drawn in the remotest places to prevent the confining of the prospect by the tall Trees that surround it'.

FRENCH AND DUTCH INFLUENCES

It is interesting to note the author's statement that 'A Bowling green is a Garden-Knot that the French had first from England'. He gives a plan for a green surrounded with trees at regular intervals, some of them (presumably yews) in topiary work.

One of the earliest bowling-greens in this country was the one made at Windsor Castle by order of Charles II in 1663. The accounts in the records run thus :

'May 11, 1663. To W. Herbert for making ye bowling green and walks £10, and for cutting Turfe for ye green £3 12s. in all £13 12s.

For 8 pairs of bowls and carriage and hampers £4 5s. 6d.

Sept. 26. Iron work for ye bowling green door, £1 17s. 11d.'.

An important event in Charles II's reign was the founding of the Chelsea Physick Garden by the Apothecaries' Society.[1] This Society had been founded in James I's reign, when it broke away from the Grocers' Company in 1617. In 1673 they obtained the lease of a garden about three and a half acres in extent for an annual rent of £5,[2] in the village of Chelsea, where the great hospital designed by Wren had not yet been even planned. Through the village passed the King's Road, which to this day commemorates in its name the fact that it was made in order that the King (Charles II) might pass by a short, direct way from Whitehall to Hampton Court Palace where French gardeners were employed in laying out the gardens in the new style. To this day a recess in the south-east corner of the Garden marks the spot where the Company kept their barge —a modest four-oared barge with a cabin. About 1683 the four famous cedars of Lebanon were planted ; the first in England. Two were cut down in 1771, but two remained on either side of the gates, the one till 1878, and the other till 1903. In 1685, Evelyn records in his Diary he went to see ' the Apothecaries' Garden of simples at Chelsea ', where amongst other rarities he saw the cinchona tree. In 1772 Sir Hans Sloane, who had bought the manor of Chelsea from the second Lord Cheyne, conveyed the Physic Garden to the Apothecaries'

---

[1] See *The Romance of the Apothecaries' Garden at Chelsea*, by F. D. Drewitt M.A., M.D.

[2] Lord Cheyne offered them the freehold for £400.

Society for a yearly payment of £5 for ever to ' enable the Society to support the charge thereof, for the manifestation of the power, wisdom and glory of God in the works of Creation '. A committee was formed, of which a notable member was James Sherard (brother of William Sherard who founded the Sherardian Professorship of Botany at Oxford). Philip Miller was appointed gardener and within two years published his great book, *The Gardener's Dictionary*, a book described by Linnæus as ' a dictionary not only of horticulture but of botany '. It is interesting to remember in connection with the sending of a plant collector to Georgia by the Society that Miller forwarded by him a packet of cotton seed in 1732, ' the parent stock of upland cotton ',[1] from which little packet Dr. Drewitt points out ' three-fourths of the world's cotton is descended '. Linnæus visited the garden in 1736 and at first he failed to make friends with Miller, but the latter soon gave him permission to collect plants and presented him with dried specimens from South America. Twelve years later another great Swedish botanist— Peter Kalm—visited the Garden. At Linnæus' suggestion the King of Sweden had commissioned him to visit the North American colonies. He was detained in England for six months ' for want of a vessel to cross to America ', and visited the Physic Garden several times. He describes it in his Diary as ' one of the largest collections of all rare foreign plants, so that it is said in that respect to rival the Botanic Gardens of both Paris and Leyden '. Many great names were subsequently associated with the Garden—Sir Joseph Banks, William Forsyth (who had been a pupil of Philip Miller), William Carter, John Lindley, Sir Joseph Hooker, Robert Fortune, Nathaniel Ward (the inventor of the Wardian case), to mention but a few.

The lesser writers of this period are wellnigh eclipsed by the great name of John Evelyn. His *Sylva*, his *Kalendarium Hortense*, and *Acetaria*, his translations from the French—*The Compleat Gardner* and *The French Gardiner*, the newly published *Instructions to the Gardener at Sayes Court*, are familiar to all. *The Compleat Gardner*, translated from the original by De la Quintinye, who for forty years was the Director of Louis XIV's kitchen-garden, is by far the most important of the seventeenth-century

[1] A. W. Hill, *Annals of Missouri Botanical Garden*, p. 222.

treatises on fruit-growing. With a few notable exceptions[1] books on this subject written even as late as the middle of the seventeenth quoted in all seriousness the absurd old beliefs, many of them dating from classical times. In De la Quintinye's fine book there is no mention of these beliefs. Evelyn's translation preserves the tone of precision of the original and in his faultless English the turn of every sentence is a delight. In those days a copy of this book was probably to be found in every country house of any size in England. De la Quintinye himself twice visited England, and he was in correspondence with nearly all the great horticulturists of the day. Doubtless many enthusiasts from this country visited the French royal kitchen-garden, which John Evelyn described as ' the admiration of all that see it and particularly of foreigners, who have nothing at home that comes near it '. Louis XIV had a profound respect for the ' Director General ' of his fruit and kitchen-gardens. Perrault records[2] that when De la Quintinye died, the King went immediately to offer his sympathy in person to Madame De la Quintinye. ' You and I know ', he is reported to have said, taking her hand, ' that we have to bear an irreparable loss. There will never be another De la Quintinye '.

Evelyn's *Kalendarium Hortense* has until now ranked as the earliest gardening calendar in the English language. But a manuscript has recently come into the market which contains one written in 1653. This MS.[3] is of the first importance, for it is the garden note-book of Sir Thomas Hanmer and was obviously written with a view to publication. Sir Thomas Hanmer, a Royalist, was one of the great horticulturists of his day and during the Commonwealth he devoted himself to his garden at Bettisfield[4]. He was a friend of Rea, also of Evelyn, and when Evelyn was making his garden at Deptford, Hanmer sent him

[1] William Lawson's *New Orchard and Garden* (1610), Ralph Austen's *Treatise of Fruit Trees* (1653), and Francis Drope's *Short and Sure Guide in the practice of raising and ordering of Fruit Trees* (1672) are wholly free from these errors. Austen devotes a lengthy chapter to ' Errors discovered '.

[2] Charles Perrault, *Les Hommes illustrés qui ont paru en France pendant ce siècle* (1696).

[3] This MS. will be published next spring (1933) by Messrs. Gerald Howe.

[4] See *A Memorial of the Parish and Family of Hanmer in Flintshire*, by John, Lord Hanmer (1877).

plants accompanied by a letter dated from Bettisfield August 21st, 1671, in which he says :

' I suppose your flower garden, being new, is not very large, and therefore I send you not many things at this tyme, and I wish the beares eares doe not dry too much before you receive them, they will be a fortnight at least before they come to Deptford, and theresett them as soon as may be, and water them well (if it rain not) for three or fower dayes and plant them not in too hott a sun. I thought once to have ventur'd some gilliflowers having two years since raised some very good ones from seed (wh I never did before, nor I thinke never shall againe, because the wett in England hinders the ripening of the seed more than in Holland and Flanders) but there is such store of excellent ones all about London, that I had not the confidence to adventure any to your view, and I doubted whether being soe long on the way would not kill them '.

Had Evelyn but had his way, London would have been a great garden city surrounded by square plots thirty or forty acres in extent, bordered with

' such shrubs as yield the most fragrant and odoriferous flowers, and are aptest to tinge the Air upon every gentle emission at a great distance : such as are (for instance among many others) the sweet-brier, all the periclymenas ; and woodbine ; the common white and yellow jessamine ; both the syringas or pipe trees ; the guelder rose ; the musk and all other roses ; genista hispanica : to these may be added the rubus adoratus, bayes juniper, lignum vitæ, lavender : but above all, rosemary, the flowers whereof are credibly reported to give their scent above thirty leagues off at sea, upon the coast of Spain : and at some distance towards the meadow side view, yea hops

Et arbuta passim
Et glaucas salices, casiamque crocumque rubestem
Et pinguem liliam, a ferrugineos hyacinthos.

For there is a sweet smelling sally (willow) and the blossoms of the tilia or lime tree are incomparably fragrant ; in brief whatsoever is odoriferous and refreshing '.

The ' beds and bordures ', he suggested, should be

' employ'd with pinks, carnations, clove, stock-gilly-flower, primroses, auriculas, violets, not forgetting the white, which are in flower twice a year ; April and August : cowslips, lilies, narcissus, strawberries, whose very leaves as well as fruit emit a cardiaque and most refreshing halitus : also parietaria lutea, musk lemmon, and mastick, thyme, spike, cammomile, balm, mint, marjoram, pimpernel and serpillum etc. which upon the least pressure and cutting breathe out and betray their ravishing odours '.

All these he pointed out were marketable in London, and the air ' perpetually fanned ' from so many fragrant shrubs and flowers

' the whole City would be sensible of the sweet and ravishing varieities of the perfumes . . . yielding also a prospect of a noble and masculine majesty by reason of the frequent plantations of trees and nurseries for ornament, profit and security. . . . The remainder of the fields included yielding the same and better shelter, and pasture for sheep and cattle than now ; that they lie bleak, expos'd and abandon'd to the winds, which perpetually invade them.[1]

A book commonly quoted in connection with the history of this time is Celia Fiennes' Diary. That sprightly lady toured England on a side-saddle in William and Mary's reign. In her Diary she frequently refers to the gardens she visited ; but fountains, elaborate water-works, imposing gateways, summer-houses and bowling-greens interested her apparently more than flowers and trees, and gardens in the new French fashion more than those in ' the old fform and mode '. She had a unique opportunity, and had she but described the ' old ffashioned ' gardens she saw we should feel more grateful for her records. Her notes on the Oxford College gardens are somewhat fuller. At New College she noted the mount with its rounds of green paths and summer-house and the pots of orange and lemon trees, and she was greatly impressed with the collection of plants at the Physic Garden, which she said would have entertained her a week : she was especially interested in the sensitive plant.

The accession of William III naturally brought Dutch garden architecture into favour in this country. Dutch gardens of this period were very different from the early type described by Erasmus in his *Divine Repast*, the earliest account of a Dutch garden that has come down to us.

' In form a perfect square, and walled, its contents appeal to the

---

[1] *Fumifugium : or the Inconvenience of the Aer and Smoke of London dissipated*, by John Evelyn.

pleasure of the higher senses, each sweet herb having its own parterre.
. . . Amid the scented herbs a fountain with a marble channel, divided
the garden into halves. Three covered allies or berceaux serve as out
of door studies, dining rooms, or conversation halls. . . . One alley
faces the rising, another the setting sun ; a third runs North to South.
They are paved with tesseræ or mosaic, and the walls are painted with
trees and birds . . . and also with serpents, basilisks and vipers, all
with appropriate mottoes and legends. The kitchen or herb garden
given over to wife or servant maid, as one of the provinces of their small
empire, is spacious and divided into two parts—one containing all the
edible herbs and the other the botanical plants. To the left of this is a
meadow, devoted to pasture and grazery, enclosed by a quick-thorn
hedge ; on the right an orchard, in which foreign trees are acclimatised.
Near the tall Alley is an aviary, where the birds are so tame that during
supper they perch upon the table and are fed by hand. At the end of
the orchard is a Republic or rather a Kingdom of bees '.

The phrase ' Dutch garden ' is somewhat vague. It is usually
employed in reference to the type made in this country in William
III's reign, but Dutch influence had made itself felt at a far earlier
date. This was due to the publication in 1583 of de Vries'
designs.[1] Jan Vredeman de Vries was the great Dutch garden
architect of the latter half of the sixteenth century and though it
is probable that few gardens were actually laid out from his
plans, yet they set a fashion which was generally followed in this
country.[2] The charm of the Dutch garden in its natural setting—
the Netherlands—was the skilful use made of water. The old
engravings of Hollar, Vanweerden, Petters, etc., show very
clearly the quaint beauty of the Dutch seventeenth-century homes
—gabled, and turreted châteaux, the upper part of the port-
cullis tower sometimes made a dovecot, and the pleasaunce—
orchards, herb-gardens, vegetable plots, flower-gardens, laid
out in a series of islands divided by canals and each with its little
bridge. Unlike the French, the Dutch grew flowers in abundance—the flowers that were immortalized by the great flower
painters of the country. Grimer's *Spring*[3] (see illustration) shows

---

[1] *Hortorum Viridariorumque elegantes et multiplicis formæ architectonicæ artes
norman affabre delineatæ a Johanne Vredemanno Frisio, Philippus Gallæus
execudebat Antwerpiæ,* 1583.
[2] See Inigo Triggs, *Garden Craft in Europe.*
[3] The Museum, Antwerp.

SPRING

(Abel Grimer, c.1573–c.1619)

Musée Royale des Beaux–Arts, Antwerp

PLAN FOR A SMALL GARDEN

(From *The New Art of Gardening*, 1697, by Leonard Meáger)

British Library

this type of garden and is full of interesting details. In the foreground men and women are busily digging, raking, sowing seeds, watering, etc. There are plants growing in pots and what may be a small orange tree growing in a tub. (Orange trees were frequently grown in carved tubs.) The lady of the house gives instructions to a gardener, who holds a basket of seeds, and beside her is a young girl with her pet dog ; to the right two men are working at the construction of a tunnelled arbour at the entrance to which are two carved statues. In the left background there is an interesting example of an elaborate arbour—trees trained and clipped in such a fashion as to make a room where musicians are playing. Others sit and listen and a man in front of a table pours out wine, a stairway leads to the upper story of the tree where there are also people amusing themselves, shaded by the clipped and pleached branches above them ; the summit of the tree is clipped in a ball shape. On the canal lovers are seated in a barge, and beside the tunnelled arbour on the water-side there are swans. The flower-garden in the foreground is bounded partly by a low balustrade and partly by the typical Dutch low hedge. In this we differed greatly, for in England we have always preferred high hedges, which make for privacy, but the Dutch liked to look beyond the garden to the farm and the country-side. In the right background the farmyard is depicted, two women being engaged in clipping the sheep, and to the right of the entrance with its penthouse roof are the bee-hives, protected in the fashion of the period with a sloping roof. A man enters the farmyard with a large burden on his head and to the right is the picturesque dovecote. There are pigeons on the roof and flying in the distance are the inevitable storks, for a household where there were no storks was regarded as ill-fated.

The flower-gardens were frequently somewhat elaborate and the beds edged with box. The ' Spring Garden ' from Crispin de Pass's *Hortus Floridus* (1614) shews a flower-garden of this type (see illustration). The whole enclosure is shewn surrounded with the characteristic gallery of the period ; the lady is gathering tulips (the tulip mania was then at its height) and a man leans on the balustrade watching her. There are various specimens of topiary work and the beds are shewn filled with spring flowers—

M   161

crown imperials, hyacinths, ranunculus, etc. The picturesque features of these gardens, however, were their waterways and painted barges and their elaborate arbours, made from trees (usually limes) planted in a circle and elaborately pleached.

It is small wonder that the quaint Dutch garden made so strong an appeal to English folk. Sir William Temple laid out his garden at his 'retreat' in Surrey (which he named Moor Park after the place he so much loved in Hertfordshire) in the Dutch style. This was the most famous garden in England laid out in this fashion. Unfortunately we lacked in this country the canals which made the pleasaunces in Holland so picturesque.

It is at least possible that the fashionable craze for orangeries during the latter half of the seventeenth century owed much to Dutch influence, for their cultivation had been brought to great perfection in Holland. The most important Dutch book on orange culture was Jan Commelyn's *Nederlantze Hesperides* (1676), translated into English in 1683, and published with the title *The Belgick or Netherlandish Hesperides, that is the management, ordering and use of the Lemon and Orange Trees made English by G.V.N.* Dutch methods of cultivating oranges were eagerly studied and it is interesting to recall that orange trees brought from the royal garden at Het Loo to Hampton Court were still alive at the beginning of this century.

Topiary work, as engravings and illustrations in the books of the period shew, was exceedingly popular in Holland. In what country this art was revived in western Europe is a moot point. As the writings of Bernard Palissy, Bacon, and Olivier de Serres shew, topiary work was commonly practised both in France and England during the sixteenth century. The Dutch carried the art to excess and in imitation of their style gardens in England became overcrowded with specimens of this work. The finest example remaining in England of a Dutch garden is that at Levens, where, as a plan of 1720, still preserved in the house, shews, every path and hedge with few exceptions remain as originally laid out. The topiary garden there is probably the most remarkable in the world. Levens belonged to Colonel James Grahame, Keeper of the Privy Purse to James II, and on the accession of William III he retired to the estate he had recently bought. Although Dutch in style the garden was laid out by Beaumont, a Frenchman and a pupil of Le Nôtre; he had worked previously at Hampton Court.

The Dutch carried their garden craft far afield. The first garden at the Cape was made by the Dutch East India Company, to supply their fleets on their way to and from the East with fresh vegetables. The remnant of that great enclosure planted nearly three centuries ago by Jan van Riebeeck and developed by the van der Stels (father and son) is still a famous garden. But according to the accounts by eye-witnesses in the seventeenth century, it must have been then indeed a wonderful place. Père Tachard, who visited the Cape in 1685, described it as ' one of the loveliest and most curious Gardens that I ever saw '. Unlike the French gardens he emphasizes that the interest of the place lay in the fine collection of trees and flowers brought from various parts of the world and planted in squares divided by walks between orange, lemon and pomegranate trees and sheltered from the terrible south-easterly gales by ' high and thick Hedges of a kind of Laurel which they call *Speck*, always green and pretty like unto the Filaria '. Francois Valentyn, who visited the Cape four times between 1685 and 1714, wrote of it as ' the incomparable garden of the East India Company ' and ' the matchless gardens at the Cape '. Sir William Temple in his *Gardens of Epicurus* bestowed equally high praise although he had only heard of its beauties. He, too, comments on the remarkable collection made there of ' trees, fruits, flowers, and plants that are native and proper to each of the four parts of the world so as in this one enclosure are to be found the several gardens of Europe, Asia, Africa, and America '. ' There could not be in my mind ', he adds, ' a greater thought of a gardener nor a nobler idea of a garden and may pass for the Hesperides of our age '.

In the New World also some of the earliest gardens were those made by the Dutch settlers. Adrian van der Donck's charming list of roses, gillyflowers, ' Jenoffelins ', tulips, crown imperials, white lily, anemones, ' baredames ', violets, marigolds, ' summer sots ', sunflowers, red and yellow lilies, mountain lilies, morning stars, red and white and yellow ' maritoffles ', bell flowers, etc., grown by the Dutch housewives in their gardens in the days when New Amsterdam contained only about a thousand inhabitants, is well known.

Although William III laid out his garden at Loo in imitation of the French style, Le Nôtre's influence was probably less felt in the Netherlands than in any other part of Europe.[1] Trees and avenues were a dominant feature in Le Nôtre's designs and in many parts of Holland it was impossible to grow large trees to any extent, because the roots could not penetrate far without coming to water. The leading Dutch garden designers, however—Daniel Marot, Simon Schynvoet, and Jacques Roman—copied Le Nôtre as far as they could. Marot, who was a pupil of Le Nôtre, was court gardener to William III and accompanied his royal master to England. Jacques Roman laid out the royal garden at Het Loo. There has always been the tradition that Le Nôtre visited England, his name is associated with various large gardens—Chatsworth, Wrest, etc., but there is no evidence to prove that he ever came. Lady Cecil over thirty years ago made exhaustive researches in the matter and came to the conclusion that he never came.[2] Since then no fresh evidence has come to light. He may have supplied plans to Charles II, and he certainly made plans for William III. These were brought by Le Nôtre's nephew and pupil, Claude Desgots. It is probable that the plans brought by Desgots were for the garden at Windsor, for Lady Cecil quotes a letter from the Earl of Portland to William III, dated March 7th, 1698, from Paris, in which he says ' M. Le Nôtre me fera un plan pour les jardins projettez a Windsor '.

At Hampton Court William and Mary completed the work Charles II had begun on French lines. Hampton Court became the residence of the new sovereigns, for William's health was so poor that he could not endure the smoky air of London. Gardening, as Macaulay tells us, was one of his hobbies—' next to hunting his favourite amusements were architecture and gardening '. George London[3] was appointed head of the Royal

[1] In Jan van de Groen's *Nederlandsche Hovenier* (1669), we find the best illustrations of the famous gardens of Ryswyck, Honsholredyk, and the Huis 'ten Bosch (near The Hague) as they were before they were altered in imitation of Le Nôtre's designs. In *Der Koninglycke Hovenier* (1676), by D. H. Cause, the plans are also of the old-fashioned type.

[2] See *A History of Gardening in England*, by the Honble. Lady Cecil.

[3] George London had been a pupil of John Rose and for a time he was gardener to Bishop Compton at Fulham Palace. After the Peace of Ryswick

Gardens, and he carried out the plan shown in Kip's view, a plan which is similar to the one made by Sir Christopher Wren. The great parterre was laid out in box scroll-work, the large fountain removed (to the Chestnut Avenue in Bushey Park) and the lime trees on the northern side of the semi-circular avenue replanted south of the southern row. All traces of the old Mount were swept away and no vestige of it remains, but Sir Ernest Law identified its site as a little to the west of the fountain in the King's Privy Garden. During William's frequent absences in London and Holland, Mary lived in the Water-gallery (where Elizabeth had spent part of her time during Mary Tudor's reign). Like her husband, Mary took the keenest interest in the garden and to this day the charming ' cradle walk ', as John Evelyn termed it—Queen Mary's Bower—in the Privy Garden perpetuates her name.[1] She was equally interested in the new gardens then being made in the Dutch style at Kensington Palace. ' This active Princess ', says Switzer, ' lost no time, but was either measuring, directing or ordering her Buildings, but in Gard'ning, especially Exoticks, she was particularly skill'd and allowed Dr. Pluknet £200 per ann. for his assistance therein '. Like Bishop Compton, the Queen was particularly interested in exotics. Her collection of ' tender greens ' at Kensington was housed every winter in the celebrated nurseries at Brompton, belonging to London and Wise. Whether William and Mary planted any trees either at Hampton Court or Kensington is not known. But amongst the oldest trees known to have been planted by reigning sovereigns in this country[2] are the two firs in the garden of Gayton Hall (Cheshire), planted by William and Mary on the occasion of their visit in 1689. They were entertained by the owner, Mr.

he went to Versailles with the Earl of Portland. In James II's reign he, with Moses Cook (gardener to the Earl of Essex at Cassiobury Lucre (gardener to the Queen Dowager at Somerset House), Field (gardener to the Earl of Bedford, Bedford House, Strand), founded the famous Brompton Nursery. About 1690, after the death of Lucre and Field and the retirement of Cook, Henry Wise became a partner.

[1] There are records, however, which suggest that it may have been planted earlier when it was called ' Queen Anne's Bower ' (Anne Boleyn).

[2] Probably the oldest are the mulberry trees in the West garden at Hatfield, which according to tradition were planted by Queen Elizabeth.

William Glegg, and the following morning the King knighted him.

Possibly it was Bishop Compton (then Bishop of London) who had inspired Mary with a love of gardening, for he had been tutor both to her and to Princess Anne. Henry Compton was one of the most distinguished horticulturists of the day. He was appointed to the See of London in 1675, but being an ardent Protestant he was suspended on James II's accession. He remained, however, at Fulham and devoted his time to the garden, which had been celebrated since the days of Mary Tudor, notably in the time of Bishop Grindal, who used to send Queen Elizabeth presents of fruits grown at Fulham. Compton spent altogether thirty-eight years at Fulham and made the garden during that time one of the most remarkable in England. Switzer states :

'He had a thousand species of exotick plants in his stoves and gardens, in which last place he had endenizoned a great many that have been formerly thought too tender for this cold climate. There were few days in the year, till towards the latter part of his life, but he was actually in his garden, ordering and directing the Removal and Replacing of his Trees and plants '.[1]

The great garden lovers of the day, naturally, frequently visited Fulham. John Evelyn often went there. In his Diary, October 11th, 1681, he notes that it was at Fulham he first saw *sedum arborescens* in flower. ' To Fulham to visit the Bishop of London, in whose garden I first saw the *Sedum arborescens* in flower, which was exceedingly beautiful '.

The name of the gardener at Fulham, Adam Holt, is fortunately preserved by Richard Bradley. Like his master, Holt was evidently an enthusiastic and ' curious ' gardener (it is a pity we do not revive the old meaning of ' curious '). In connection with the passion flower, Bradley writes :

' We must Plant it in very moist and cool places, where it may be continually fed with Water ; this I had from the curious Mr. Adam Holt, Gardener to the late Bishop of London, who shew'd me a letter from the West Indies, from whence I learnt it was an Inhabitant of Swampy Places '.

[1] *Ichnographia rustica* (1718).

Bradley frequently refers to plants growing at Fulham, In 1750 Sir William Watson's treatise on the trees at Fulham was published in the Philosophical Transactions. Amongst the most notable trees he listed 'the black Virginian walnut tree', 'the cluster pine', 'the honey locust',[1] 'the pseudo-acacia', 'the ash maple', the 'Virginian Flowering Maple', the 'Red Horse Chestnut', the 'Cotton Tree', the 'Evergreen Oak'. Watson concluded his report with a eulogy on Compton, 'that excellent prelate who by means of a large correspondence with the principal botanists of Europe and America introduced into England a greater number of plants, more especially trees, which had never been seen here, or before described by any author—therefore his name is mentioned with the greatest encomiums by the botanical writers of the times, to wit Herman, Ray and others '.

Bishop Compton was an intimate friend of both William and Mary ; he had been largely instrumental in bringing the Prince to England and he performed the ceremony of coronation. It is more than probable that his expert advice would have been sought by the King and Queen in connection with both Hampton Court and Kensington. At Mary's death William was prostrated with grief and Switzer records, ' Upon the death of that illustrious Princess gardening and all other pleasures were under an eclipse with that Prince ; and the beloved Hampton Court lay for some time unregarded '. After the disastrous fire which destroyed Whitehall, William turned his attention again to Hampton Court. The beautiful wrought-iron gates designed by Jean Tijou[2] and believed to have been executed by Huntingdon Shaw, were set up (these were removed in 1865, but in 1902

---

[1] The honey locust (*Gleditschia triacanthus*) mentioned by Watson survived till 1906, but very few of the trees planted by Bishop Compton remain. The best known are some of the elms in the elm avenue.

[2] The best iron-work of this period was done by Jean Tijou and the gates designed by him are still the finest in this country. A collection of his designs is preserved in *A New Book of Drawings Invented and Designed by John Tijou*, London, 1693. His best-known work is perhaps that at Hampton Court—the twelve screens of wrought iron made about 1694. Each screen is 10 ft. 6 in. high and 13 ft. 4 in. wide and in the centre of each beautiful design is one of the national emblems—rose, thistle or harp—or the royal monogram, W M (William and Mary).

they were replaced), along the river-side a terrace, a bowling-green and four pavilions were constructed, the Broad Walk was made and the famous maze.

It is interesting to note that whereas large gardens were being altered in imitation of the new French style, most of the gardening books of this period were written for owners of moderate sized gardens and give us charming glimpses into typical small pleasaunces of the period. Rea, in his *Flora, Ceres and Pomona* (1665), suggests that eighty square yards for fruit and thirty square yards for flowers is a suitable size for a nobleman, and for a 'private gentleman' forty square yards for fruit and twenty for flowers; the garden to be surrounded with a brick wall nine feet high and the flower and fruit gardens divided by a wall five feet high or a painted wooden paling. He gives various designs, most of them square with rectangular beds 'to be railed with wooden rails painted or box-trees or pallisades for dwarf trees'.

In the beds:

'the best crown imperial lilies, Martagons, and such tall flowers; in the middle of the square beds great tufts of peonies, and round about them several sorts of cyclamen, the rest with Daffodils, Hyacinths and such-like. The streight beds are fit for the best Tulips, where account may be kept of them. Ranunculus and Anemones also require particular beds—the rest may be set all over with the more ordinary sorts of Tulips, bulbed Iris and all other kinds of good roots'.

In the middle of one side of the garden, he suggests

'a handsome octangular somer-house roofed everyway and finely painted with Landskips and other conceits furnished with seats about and a table in the middle which serveth not only for delight and entertainment, but for many other necessary purposes, as to put the roots of Tulips and flowers in, as they are taken up upon papers, with the names upon them untill they be dried, that they may be wrapped up and put in boxes'.

Rea was one of the great tulip enthusiasts (tulips were still a cult), and it is therefore not surprising to find he regarded a summer-house as being not merely 'for delight and entertainment' but as a useful place for drying tulip bulbs! Rea's son-in-law, Samuel Gilbert (author of the *Florist's Vade Mecum*), describes Rea as ' the best florist of his time' and of his collection of tulips he says ' He had the largest collection of any man in England, some of which I lost by being beyond sea at his death'. Rea left everything, including his valuable collection of tulips, to his daughter Minerva (Gilbert's wife). Gilbert, in the second edition of his book, gives a plan for a tulip garden, divided into fifty square beds. He was also an iris enthusiast and he observes with pride that there are more colours in irises than in the peacock's tail. Auriculas were apparently his special flowers and he proudly states that he has the best collection in the country. He much admired those he had seen in the Physic Garden at Oxford, also those in the Palace garden at Worcester ' belonging to Mr. Thomas Newton, gentleman to my very good Lord the Right Revered Father in God, James Lord Bishop of Worcester'. The Bishop himself Gilbert describes as ' the greatest florist amongst the chiefest pillars of our Church'. Gilbert writes at considerable length on the cultivation of auriculas and it is interesting to note that enthusiasts paid as much as twenty pounds for a root. He writes also of snowdrops, anemones, daphne mezereum, candytuft, meadow saffron, columbines, cowslips, crocuses, crown imperials, violets, daffo-dils, jonquils, wallflowers, double daisies, hyacinths, dog-tooth violets, primroses, fritillaries, guelder-roses, flower-de-luce, asphodels, sweet williams, gilliflowers, honeysuckle, dittany, sweet johns, jasmines, periwinkle, bell flower, campions, ladies' slipper, lady smocks, larkspurs, lilies, roses, bindweed, marsh marigolds, peonies, poppies, marvel of Peru, nasturtium, prince's feather, African marigolds.

Gilbert's book went into many editions, for apart from his brief astrological calendar the book is thoroughly practical and, as he claims in his preface, ' each direction from the beginning to the end being an experimental Truth, and the whole fitted in a Pocket Companion to all Lovers of Flowers and their Pro-pagation'. Gilbert's arrangement of his book was novel in his day :

'I follow not the Method most Authors have, in writing of all Bulbous rooted flowers by themselves, and all Tuberous Flowers so too etc.—but as more natural, you will find the Flowers treated on successively as they blow one after another, and as they appear in each Month, under the Titles of which you will find their Names, brief descriptions and ways of their management both for their preservation, increase and procuring new Faces to each kind, the last being the greatest skill as well as satisfaction to a Florist. A Divertisement more healthful to our bodies, by often stirring in the Earth, beneficial to our Souls by our daily converse with the matter whence we were at first created, and to what we must return, each flower showing the providence of Almighty God, and that we may read Him in these His beautiful Handy-works, that so diaper our Gardens '.

Indeed these books give us a vivid idea of the many gardens in these islands whose owners had no desire to imitate the great French gardens, but were genuine flower-lovers and who, like Abraham Cowley, would say :

' I never had any other desire so strong, and so like to covetousness, as that one which I have had always, that I might be master at last of a small house and large garden, with very moderate conveniences joined to them, and there dedicate the remainder of my life only to the culture of them and study of nature '.

It is the homely type of garden also which figures in both Leonard Meager's books *The English Gardener* (1670) and *The New Art of Gardening* (1697). In the latter there is an attractive pictorial plan of a small garden and it is easy to picture it full of the pleasant old-fashioned flowers which he lists—madonna lilies, hollyhocks, elecampane, lovage, succory, clary, wall-flowers, gilliflowers, Coventry bell-flowers, heart's-ease, Melancholy Gentleman (*Hesperis tristis*), thyme, wood-sorrel, goat's rue, tansy, angelica, bugloss, marigolds, lavender, borage, comfrey and so forth. Meager was gardener for many years to Philip Hollman (of Warkworth), a member of the well-known Northamptonshire family of that name. *The English Gardener* is dedicated to his employer and is a pleasant testimony to the friendship between the two men. I like the use of the Biblical phrase ' Grace, Mercy, and Peace be Multiplied '. Indeed it would not be easy to find a simpler and more charming dedicatory letter :

FRENCH AND DUTCH INFLUENCES

To the Worshipful
>Philip Hollman Esqre

Of Warkworth in the County of Northampton
>Grace, Mercy, and Peace be Multiplied

Worshipful Sir,

   Sir, I having many years since had the advantage and opportunity in your Worship's Service to study and practice the Art of Planting, Grafting and Gardening, to which I was naturally inclin'd ; as also being in some measure countenanced and assisted by your Worship, as indeed you did all your other Servants that had any inclination or endeavour to the practice of good Husbandry ; as also having found your Worship rather as an indulgent Father than a Master to me, I being thus obliged to your Worship, in token of thankfulness, I have presented this Tract of the Art of Planting, Grafting and Gardening.
. . Thus begging pardon for my boldness, I rest
>Your Worship's most humble Servant
>in what I may
>LEONARD MEAGER.

CHAPTER VI

THE GEORGIAN PERIOD

Visualising the gardens of the late seventeenth and early eighteenth centuries as depicted in the old county histories (Dugdale's Warwickshire, Plot's Staffordshire, Atkyn's Gloucestershire, etc.), *Britannia Illustrata, Les Délices de la Grande Bretagne,* Kip's views and similar works, I think one is chiefly impressed by the extent to which we modified the new French style. We imitated Le Nôtre's ideas, but in accordance with our traditional custom we adapted them to our insular taste. As a nation we have never taken kindly to grandeur, the stateliest houses in these islands are homes rather than palaces, and homeliness has always been the characteristic feature of our gardens. Fine avenues adorned many properties in these islands, but more commonly pleasant, dignified walks between high sheltering hedges or cut trees. These walks were prominent and most attractive features of the Queen Anne garden, they differed greatly from the far less pretentious sheltered walks of Elizabethan and early Stuart times. Not only were they more extensive and in proportion to the greatly increased size of gardens, but a striking feature were the trees clipped and grown in a curious fashion. They were clipped so as to leave the trunks quite bare up to a height of about twelve or fifteen feet and then allowed to grow naturally, or their branches pleached and clipped so as to form a solid green wall. When the trees were allowed to grow naturally above a certain point, they would give pleasant shade to the walks and it is easy to picture the formal charm of avenues made in this fashion and the people in the costumes of the period. 'To make one in love with yew hedges, you need only take a walk either in Paradise or the Physick Garden at Oxford.'[1] The other fashion of clipping combined with pleaching the trees to form solid green walls above the bare trunks must have required considerable skill and is suggestive of Dutch rather than French influence. The best illustration I know of this feature is the plate of St. John's College in W. Williamson's *Oxonia depicta* (1717). What is now

[1] John Lawrence, *The Gentleman's Recreation* (1716).

the lawn beyond the Garden Front is shown divided into four gardens surrounded by yews with their lower trunks all bare and the upper clipped and trained to make a solid wall. The plan of Trinity College shows another method of clipping yews characteristic of this period. In this case the yews are depicted clipped to resemble panelling. Southey, in his *Letters of Espriella* (1807), comments on this yew panelling (at Trinity), which was still in existence at that time :

' The garden here (Trinity) is remarkable for a wall of yew which encloses it on three sides, cut into regular pilasters and compartments. . . . I should lament if a thing which is so perfect in its kind and which has been raised with so many years of care—indeed so many generations—were to be destroyed because it does not suit the modern improved taste in gardening. You would hardly conceive that a vegetable could be so close and impervious, still less that anything so unnatural could be so beautiful as this really is '.

Yet another type of clipped hedge is shown in Fairchild's *Catalogus Plantarum* (1723). In this case a broad, central walk leads between yews clipped to form arcaded walks on either side. (See illustration.) The fan in the lady's hand is noteworthy. It was customary for ladies to use fans as though they were parasols, not only in private gardens but in public places, such as the parks. It was possibly the popularity of these elaborately clipped hedges that made variegated evergreens so fashionable during this period. These hedges were a striking contrast to the simpler type described by John Evelyn, who had a great admiration for holly hedges. Of the holly hedge in his garden at Sayes Court he wrote :

' Is there under heaven a more glorious and refreshing object of the kind, than an impregnable Hedge a hundred and sixty feet in length, and seven feet high, and five in diameter, which I can shew in my poor garden at any time of the year, glittering with its armed and varnish'd leaves ? the taller Standards at orderly distances, blushing with their natural Corall. It mocks at the rudest assaults of the Weather, Beasts and Hedgebreakers '.

Clairvoyées or ornamental grilles placed between two piers of brick or stone were also attractive features during this period. They were equally common in Holland and show the desire to extend the garden beyond the range of the enclosing walls. Lead statues and vases, which had to some extent been used in English gardens since the sixteenth century, became more popular. The statues were usually classical subjects, such as Venus, Neptune, Minerva, Cupids, etc., or the seasons, or shepherds and shepherdesses, haymakers, gamekeepers and even figures of people skating. Portrait statues were also fashionable. Examples of the last-named are now rare, the best known being those at Glemham, Wilton, Wrest and Hoghton Tower. The statues were sometimes covered with stone-dust to imitate stone and sometimes gilded or painted. The most noted worker was Jan van Nost, amongst the best-known examples of his work being the statues at Melbourne (Derbyshire), the Amorini at Wilton and the lead vases on the terrace before the south front at Hampton Court, all of which were cast at his workshop in St. Martin's Lane. Caius Cibber (a Dane) and his son, Colley Cibber, were almost equally famed as sculptors. Caius Cibber's name is chiefly associated with Chatsworth, where he was employed 1687–1691, and there is a fine specimen of his low-relief carving on the east front of Sir Christopher Wren's building at Hampton Court—the ' Triumph of Hercules over Envy '. Lead cisterns also were in common use in the late seventeenth and eighteenth centuries and a large number of them are still in existence. One of the finest is at St. Fagan's (near Cardiff), an octagonal lead cistern, roughly eight feet in diameter and four feet high, the sides decorated with foliage and arcading.

Dovecotes were still indispensable though they were only seldom made actually within the garden. They were usually rectangular, either square or octagon-shaped with gable roofs : occasionally they were circular and a notable example of this type with ' dormer windows ' and a cupola may be seen at Rousham (Oxfordshire). A most curious early eighteenth-century illustration of a dovecote (the dovecote itself dated probably from the seventeenth-century) may be seen in Bade-slade's view of Sundridge Place (Kent). In this instance the dovecote is depicted in the centre of the fish-pond. The floor on the water-level for the ducks, above a room surrounded by a balcony with steps leading up to it, and the upper part pierced with holes for the pigeons.

The few dovecotes built now are small in comparison with those of olden times. One of the finest of the latter still in existence is the beautiful octagonal columbarium built in Elizabethan times at Whitehall, Shrewsbury. This unique dovecote with its fine arcaded cornice has 650 niches for nests.

An uncommon type of eighteenth-century garden is depicted in the frontispiece to the 1732 edition of Miller's *Gardener's Dictionary*. (See illustration.) The enclosure is divided in two by a long sheet of water widened from the centre to form an oval. In the foreground the water falls in a cascade of three tiers into a large basin. On either side of the main cascade the water pours through six satyr masks, three on either side of the basin, in smaller cascades and six fountains play in the basin. Ornate pots with small shrubs growing in them are ranged on the wall by the cascades. Two fountains play at the head of the cascade, one in the oval and one at the further end of the garden, in front of a wall concave in the centre with seats within its shelter. On either side of the water, the whole length of the enclosure, are straight walks flanked by high clipped hedges with arched entrances at intervals and seats facing the water, the walks beyond the central fountain being broader and adorned with single rows of topiary work. Portrait busts stand at the entrances in the foreground, a lady emerges from one entrance and a gardener on a ladder is clipping the other. The enclosed garden on the right is full of topiary work and there are two small garden-houses. Beyond is the kitchen garden, each plot enclosed by a low clipped hedge, and there is a large circular pool in the broad walk leading from the main entrance. The garden in the left foreground is divided into four squares by intersecting paths. Beyond is another enclosure with a stately orangery overlooking a large court with a fountain playing in the centre. Orange trees growing in square boxes are ranged in a double row round the fountain. Topiary work flanks this enclosure on two sides. Beyond the garden proper is the wilderness, also divided in two by the water which ends in an elaborate fountain. A mount planted with trees forms the background to the fountain.

The two commonest types of garden seats are shown in this illustration, the elaborate sheltered seat set in the concave wall

at the further end of the garden and the simple seats set along
the hedges flanking the paths by the water-side and overlooking
the cascades in the foreground. Worlidge, in his *Systema
Horticulturæ* (1677), says that garden seats should be of wood
and painted white or green, that they should be set in niches
in the garden wall or at the ends of the walks. Sometimes
they were sheltered by a cupola or a slight wooden arbour. These
simple seats continued to be the fashion till the latter half of the
century, when elaborate seats with finely panelled or trellised
work were introduced apparently by Sir William Chambers. He
also designed the elaborate small arbours with trellis-work in
the Chinese style which were so widely imitated.

The eighteenth century ushered in the ' grand period ' of
lawns. Every gardening manual of note of that period testifies
to the importance of the lawn, and it is interesting to remember
that the name was applied not only to lawns proper, but also to
deer parks, etc. John Reid, in *The Scots Gardener*, describes a
deer park as a ' lawn ', and Alexander McDonald, writing as
late as 1807, speaks of ' a lawn of eight acres or more in extent ',
and also of ' extensive lawns in parks dotted with noble trees.' In
regard to lawns proper, there was possibly no period when the
beauty of green turf without adornment of any kind was more
genuinely appreciated. ' The Parterre Garden at His Majesty's
Royal Palace of Hampton Court ', says Batty Langley in his
New Principles of Gardening, 1728, ' would have a very grand
aspect were those trifling plants of Yew, Holly, etc., taken
away and made plain with grass '. Langley's book is largely a
treatise on lawns, and there are numerous plans of them. One
plan shows the house fronting ' a parterre of grass and water ',
the water being an oval in the centre of the grass. Another plan
shows the south front of the house opening on ' a grand parterre
of grass from which over the Canal you have a boundless view
into the Country '. Yet another plan shows a garden consisting
wholly of variously shaped lawns each surrounded by magnificent
avenues and plantations of trees. The only adornment Langley
suggests are statues, and it is interesting to find that he suggests
including ' Runciana the goddess of weeding '. Le Blond was
only one of many who acknowledged that English lawns were
the finest in Europe. ' Their Grass plots ', he says, ' are of so

Exiguus spatio, parvis sed fertilis herbis.

TITLE PAGE OF CATALOGUS PLANTARUM, 1723

British Library

AN EARLY EIGHTEENTH-CENTURY GARDEN

(From *The Gardener's Dictionary*, 1732, by Philip Miller)

exquisite a beauty that in France we can scarce ever hope to come up to it '. Yet in France they devoted as great attention to lawns as in England. According to this same French authority, ' Handsome grass plots require the greatest care of the Gardener, who ought to be almost constantly attending them '.

Nearly all the gardening manuals comment on the difficulties of getting good seed. ' There is great difficulty ', wrote the anonymous author of *The Gardener's New Kalendar* (1758), ' in getting good seed ; for that from a common haystack is by no means proper'. He directs that seed should be obtained from ' the grass of a clean up-land pasture ', but turfing he prefers—' it does the business sooner and much more perfectly '.

' The only proper mixture with the grass of turf is the white trefoil. . . . These mix well with the grass and form a fine thick bottom. . . . This little trefoil has all the qualities requisite to thicken and improve the carpeting of turf ; and its being plentiful in the spot whence that is to be taken is an advantage not a hurt. But this is the only weed that should be admitted. . . . Let the gardener work with alacrity and dispatch. . . . At the same time that an inferior hand is employed in cutting up the turf, let the gardener himself be preparing the bed for it '.

In rolling the grass, he adds, ' care must be taken that the horses should be without shoes and have their feet covered with woollen mufflers '. Even as late as the early nineteenth century, however, hay seed was still used, and it was generally acknowledged that laying turfs was better than sowing seed. Alexander McDonald's *Gardening Dictionary* is one of the earliest manuals in which it is suggested that ' seed should be obtained from a seedsman ' and ' should be of those kinds which strike deep root, spread out laterally in their tops and are permanent and capable of resisting the effects of heat ; there are many of this kind '. Turves in those halcyon days cost ' about a shilling to fifteen pence the hundred according to the nature of the soil . . . a man will cut from three to five, six or seven hundred a day or more if very soft easy-cutting turf, with a person to race them out and roll them up as they are cut '.

The green lawns of these islands are still the admiration of the world. The beauty of the matchless lawns in college quadrangles remains for ever in the memory, and lawns are still the chief beauty of many of our most famous gardens. The methods of making and maintaining them lack the picturesqueness of olden days, though there are still gardens where the discordant sound of the lawn-mower is never heard, and the lawns are shorn by men who come of generations skilled in the craft of the scythe. ' Mowing 'em and rolling 'em ', is still the principal factor in the making of lawns, but they owe their beauty nowadays at least as much to the chemist as to the gardener. The foreigner admires, but even with all the resources of science he cannot hope to make lawns to compare with the deep velvety texture of our lawns. Those of us who live in the Old Country and those whose lot is cast in the great dominions beyond the seas, are equally proud of the fact that in ' the islands of the West ' we have the greenest and most beautiful grass in the world.

Great progress was made in vegetable culture during the eighteenth century, and the leading nurserymen vied with each other in producing delicacies out of season, whereas formerly these had been imported from Holland. Bradley particularly commends the gardens ' at the Neat-Houses near Tuttle-fields, Westminster ', for salads, early cucumbers, cauliflowers, melons, and winter asparagus, and he adds that it was the best place for a kitchen gardener to learn his trade. He mentions the gardens about Hammersmith as being famed for strawberries, raspberries, currants, gooseberries and such like, and for early fruits ' some months before the Natural Season ', Mr. Miller's ' at North End near the same Place '. Hot-houses were greatly improved, the outstanding triumph being the successful culture of pineapples. John Rose, in Charles II's reign, had succeeded in growing and ripening a pineapple, which he presented to the King, but he was, as far as is known, the only man to achieve such a feat in the seventeenth century. According to Bradley, the first to make the ' Anas or Pine-Apple to rejoice in our climate ' was Henry Tellende, gardener to Sir Matthew Decker at Richmond. Several treatises on the culture of this fruit were published before the end of the century, the earliest being *Ananas ; or a Treatise on the Pine Apple*, by John Giles (1767).

The early growers of pineapples in this country would certainly be surprised could they but see these fruits being hawked, sometimes for as little as sixpence apiece, in the streets of London. Indeed one of the pleasantest sights in our great cities are the piles, replenished daily, of colourful fruits in countless small shops and on barrows at prices which bring these delicious wholesome foods within reach of the poorest. Even at the beginning of this century, who would have believed that magnificent bunches of Cape grapes (sweeter and far more valuable as a food than any grown under glass) would be hawked in the streets for a few pence a pound ? The fruits, vegetables and herbs hawked in the streets of London have varied considerably through the centuries, the great features of modern times being the quantities of exotic fruits, much of it brought from remote parts of the Empire, sold so cheaply that everyone can afford to buy them. At least as early as the fifteenth century, as we know from John Lydgate's[1] ballad, strawberries and cherries were hawked. ' Hott baked Wardons, Hott ', was a well-known ' cry ' in the seventeenth century, and as Wardon pears had been grown in this country for centuries they had probably been hawked long before. ' Ripe speregas ', ' Fair Lemons and Oranges ', ' Delicate Cowcumbers to pickle ', ' Any Bakeing Peares ? ' ' Pippins ', ' Cherry Ripe ', ' Lettice ', ' Onions ', ' Rosemary ', ' Bays ', ' Buy any prunes ', ' Ripe damsons '. ' Rype chesnuts ', ' Rype walnuts ', ' Fyne potatos fyne ', ' Buy any garlick ', ' Whyte carots whyt ', ' Buy any cocumber ', were all seventeenth-century cries.[2]

From *The Common Cries of London* dated 1662, but probably written much earlier,[3] one realizes what a variety of both pot and medicinal herbs were hawked in the streets in olden days— rosemary, sage, thyme, ground ivy, feverfew, gilliflowers, rue, knotted marjoram, sweet lavender, parsley, winter savory, heart's-ease, hyssop, cinquefoil, pennyroyal, marigold, nettles, water-cress, scurvy-grass, wormwood, mugwort, southernwood, dandelion, houseleek, dragon's-tongue, wood sorrel, bear's-foot and horehound. Vegetables, fruits and nuts figure largely in this old ballad of the ' cries '—coleworts, brocoli, radishes, ' young green hastings ho ',[4] ' beans, right Windsor beans ',

---

[1] *London Lyckpenny.*
[2] See *Habits and Cryes of the City of London*, by M. Laroon (1711).
[3] See the Roxburghe Ballads.
[4] A variety of early pea.

'young carrots ho!', cauliflowers, asparagus, cucumber, spinach, French beans, parsnips, leeks, potatoes, 'ripe hautboys',[1] plums, mulberries, gooseberries, currants, nectarines, peaches, apricots, filberts.

Addison occasionally referred to the London Cries in *The Spectator*.[2] 'There is nothing which more astonishes a Foreigner and frights a Country Squire than the Cries of London. My good friend Sir Roger often declares that he cannot get them out of his Head or go to sleep for them the first Week that he is in Town'. And in the same essay—'I am always pleased with that particular time of the year which is proper for the pickling of dill and cucumbers, but alas! this cry like the song of the nightingale is not heard above two months'.

How far into the nineteenth century fruit, vegetable and flower cries survived it is impossible to say; modern traffic has long since drowned every sound but its own, yet even during the closing years of last century 'Flowers, penny a bunch', 'All a-growin, all a-blowin', 'Sweet lavender, six bunches a penny', 'Sweet primroses, four bunches a penny', 'primroses', 'Fine myrtles and roses', 'Will you buy a beau-pot?'[3] 'Green hastings', 'Southernwood that's very good', 'Rue sage and mint, farthing a bunch', 'Roasted pippins piping hot', 'Cherries two pence a pound, all round and sound', 'Fine duke cherries! Cherries O! ripe Cherries O!', 'Holly O! Mistletoe!' were still familiar cries.

A large number of new plants were introduced during the eighteenth century. Amongst those of outstanding interest were Kalmias (*K. latafolia, K. angustifolia, K. glauca*) the Carolina allspice, Catalpa (*C. bignonioides*, introduced by Mark Catesby), magnolias (*m. grandiflora* and *m. accuminata*), sumachs (*r. canadensis, r. Michauzi*), various rhododendrons, *camellia japonica* (imported by Lord Petre), hydrangeas (*h. arborescens, h. hortensis, h. radiata*), and *cydonia japonica*. Both *h. hortensis* and *cydonia japonica* were sent by Sir Joseph Banks. One of the earliest introductions

---

[1] *Fragaria elatior* : a strawberry commonly grown until the middle of the nineteenth century.

[2] *The Spectator*, No. CCLI.

[3] A word never heard nowadays. It is probably of Norman-French origin and signifies a nosegay.

from New Zealand dates from this period—the ' Glory Pea ' (*Clianthus puniceus*) collected by Banks during Cook's first voyage to New Zealand. In October, 1769, they spent a day anchored off Anaura Bay. The Maoris there were friendly and Banks was able to collect 90 specimens of plants, the ' Glory Pea ' being one ; he found it cultivated by the Maoris in the vicinity of their dwellings.

I think it is particularly interesting to realize that the most familiar and certainly the most gorgeously coloured of our autumn flowers—China asters, phloxes, chrysanthemums, and dahlias were first grown in these islands during this period. Seeds of China asters were sent by Father d'Incarville to the Royal Garden of Paris about 1730. Miller received seeds from Paris in 1731 and in 1752 seeds of the double variety. Miller was cultivating the chrysanthemum in 1764 in the Chelsea Physick Garden, but it was apparently lost, as it is not mentioned in the first edition of the *Hortus Kewensis*. Monsieur Blanchard, a merchant of Marseilles, again introduced it into Europe and it was cultivated in England in 1795. Even in cottage gardens the chrysanthemum soon became a prime favourite. The dahlia (a native of Mexico), named after Andrew Dahl, the Swedish botanist, was introduced first by Lady Bute in 1789 and again by Elizabeth, Lady Holland in 1804. Dahlias have been grown at Holland House ever since they were first flowered there. The gardens of Holland House, the only gardens in London which still retain the atmosphere of the country, seem haunted by the ghosts of the famous men and women of olden days and particularly those of the eighteenth and nineteenth centuries—Addison (whose name is commemmorated in the road and station), Charles James Fox, the third Lord Holland, Sydney Smith, Sheridan, Thomas Moore, Byron, Scott, Canning, Hallam, Macaulay, Talleyrand, Lord John Russell and Palmerston, to mention but a few. But I think the picture that appeals most to the imagination is that of the lovely Lady Sarah Lennox, arrayed as a shepherdess, hay-making, when the young King George III rode by on his way to Kew, with the not surprising result that he fell in love with her.

It is not until the early eighteenth century that we have much information about Scotch gardens. Yet the art of gardening was practised there from very early times, chiefly by the monks, and there has always been the tradition of the remarkable garden, attached to the monastery of Icolmkill in the Hebrides, said to have been established in the sixth century. The remains of the artificial lake and the broad walk raised above the water were still in existence in the eighteenth century. And it is a notable fact that the Edinburgh botanic garden was established in the same century as the Oxford botanic garden and nearly a hundred years earlier than Kew. The Edinburgh garden was founded about 1680, and in 1683 James Sutherland, the intendant, published a catalogue of the plants entitled *Hortus Medicus Edinburgensis* which contained the names of 3000 plants.

In 1767 the site of the garden was changed and a range of magnificent hot-houses erected under the direction of Dr. John Hope, the first to teach the Linnæn system in Scotland. The first book written for the owners of Scottish gardens was John Reid's *The Scots Gardener* (1683), but the finest of the early works was James Justice's *The Scots Gardener's Director* (1755). His garden at Crichton near Edinburgh was reputed to be the best in Scotland. He had travelled extensively on the Continent and introduced many florists' flowers from Holland. He spent the greater part of his fortune on his garden and was the only man in Scotland who grew pineapples. Apart from Justice the most famous garden-lovers were the Earls of Lauderdale, Stair, Haddington, and Bute and Lord Kames. Lauderdale is said to have corresponded with London and Wise. Switzer and Langley both state that they were frequently sent for to Scotland. Switzer and Langley also occasionally visited Ireland.

We have as little knowledge of gardens in Ireland in early days as of those in Scotland. In Ireland, as in this island, the Druids were renowned for their knowledge of plants, though to what extent, if any, they cultivated them is unknown. Irish traditions concerning early plant lore are particularly interesting. According to the legend there was a famous herbalist—Diancecht by name—who lived about the fourth century. He had a son and a daughter both of whom excelled him in knowledge. His jealousy became so great that he killed his son Midoch, but after the body had been burned there grew from it 365 healing herbs, each one from the part it was reputed to cure. Armida collected them all and hid them from Diancecht in her cloak, but he discovered this and kicked the cloak about so vigorously that no doctor in Ireland has ever been able to sort them again! Another herbalist of repute was one Maelodar O'Tinny, who died in 860. In the medical corps of the Fianna Fail—the Irish army of olden days—each man carried a bag of herbs in his belt.[1]

One of the earliest Irish plant lovers of whom we have definite information was Sir Arthur Rawdon. After visiting the Chelsea Physic Garden he sent James Harlow (a gardener) to Jamaica, and he returned with an immense quantity of plants, for which a hot-house was built at Moira, probably the first in Ireland. For many years Ireland was far behind England and Scotland in hot-house productions, yet during the latter half of the eighteenth century pine-apples were more commonly cultivated in the neighbourhood of Kilkenny than anywhere else. Loudon quoting Robertson, an eminent nurseryman at Kilkenny, states that in 1785 there were within twelve miles of the city ' a dozen gardens or more, each of which contained pine-stoves from fifty to one hundred feet in length ; and other forcing-houses corresponding, well stocked and managed by able gardeners from Kew, Hampton Court—and other places round London'. Loudon states further that the Countess of Ormond during this period, had her table regularly served through the winter with cucumbers raised in her pine-stoves, on trellises against the back-wall ; a practice which was not introduced into the neighbourhood round London till the early nineteenth century.

The earliest landscape garden in Ireland is believed to have been that made by Dr. Delany at Delville near Glasnevin, about 1720. As Dr. Delany was a friend of Pope's the latter is supposed to have helped his Irish friend with suggestions. The botanic garden of Trinity College was established in 1786, and that of the Dublin Society in 1790.

The great gardens in England during the early eighteenth

[1] In this connection it may be of interest to state that I have a list, kindly sent me by a doctor during the War, of the herbs which he found the French soldiers used.

century were usually under the care of George London and Henry Wise. London, in William and Mary's reign, was Superintendent of the Royal Gardens, but Queen Anne gave the appointment to Wise, and London devoted himself to private gardens, riding all about England in the course of his work. It is a thousand pities he did not write a book about the gardens he so continually visited instead of translating (in collaboration with Wise) books by French writers. It was for owners of large properties that the best-known manuals of this period were written—John James' translation of Le Blond's *Theory and Practice of Gardening* (1703), Richard Bradley's more important works (it is interesting to note in connection with his *Dictionarium Botanicum* his statement ' a work never before attempted '), Switzer's *Ichnographia Rustica* (enlarged from his *Nobleman, Gentleman, and Gardener's Recreation* (1715) and Philip Miller's authoritative works. For the owners of small gardens various unpretentious little manuals were published which are now regarded as treasures by collectors.

One of the earliest of these was Charles Evelyn's *Lady's Recreation* (1707), the only book written during the eighteenth century for women gardeners. From Tudor to Victorian times only three books were written for women gardeners—William Lawson's *Countrie Housewife's Garden* (1618), Charles Evelyn's *Lady's Recreation* (1707), and in the early nineteenth century Mrs. Loudon's volumes were the first of the spate of modern books written for women flower-lovers. This paucity is all the more remarkable because at least since mediæval days the garden had been regarded as the special province of the housewife. FitzHerbert,[1] writing in 1523, says :

' And in the begynninge of Marche, or a lyttell afore, is tyme for a wyfe to make her garden, and to gette as many good sedes and herbes as she canne, and specilly suche as be good for the potte and to eate : and as ofte as nede shall requyre it must be weded, for else the wedes wyl overgrowe the herbes '.

Tusser takes it for granted that every ' good huswife ' attends

[1] Sir Anthony FitzHerbert, *A new tracte or treatyse most profytable for All Husbandmen* (1523).

to the garden[1] and in Barnaby Googe's *Foure Bookes of Husbandry* (1577), we find :

' Herein were the olde husbandes very careful and used always to judge that where they founde the Garden out of order, the wyfe of the house (for unto her belonged the charge thereof) was no good huswyfe '.

William Coles observes quaintly, ' Gentlewomen if the ground be not too wet may doe themselves much good by kneeling upon a Cushion and weeding '. And Parkinson in his *Paradisus* says :

' Gentlewomen, these pleasures are the delight of leasure, which hath bred your love and liking to them, and although you are not herein predominant, yet cannot they be barred from your beloved, who I doubt not, will share with you in the delight as much as is fit '.

Sir William Temple in his *Garden of Epicurus* (1685) says :

' I will not enter upon any account of flowers, having only pleased myself with seeing or smelling them, and not troubled myself with the care, which is more the ladies' part than the men's ; but the success is wholly in the gardener '.

Charles Evelyn gives us a very charming glimpse into a ' lady's garden ' of the period. A walk of orange trees ' whose fragrant Smell, especially in the Blooming Season, excels that of all other Plants and Flowers ' leads to grass plots and square beds ' filled with the most beauteous Greens and Borders set off with the most delightful Flowers '. A fountain ' of the best architecture ' and ' an excellent contriv'd Statue ' adorn this enclosure and beyond a wilderness ' and being no longer pleas'd with a solitary Amusement you come out into a large Road, where you have the Diversion of seeing Travellers pass by, to compleat your Variety '. He writes simply and attractively of the flowers grown in every garden—carnations, ' the pride of the Summer as Tulips are the glory of the Spring ', gilliflowers, anemones, hyacinths, irises, peonies, lilies of the valley, ' a flower of the greatest fragrance ', wallflowers ' in scent excelled by none ', prince's feather, columbines, hollyhocks, snapdragons, crown-imperials, and cranes-bill, ' a beautiful Flower in the Day and very sweet and odorous in the Night '. He gives no direc-

---

[1] See T. Tusser, *Five hundreth points of good husbandry* (1573).

tions for growing the commonest flowers—foxgloves, garden mallows, scabious, fennel, double lady's smock and campions; for these ' every Country Dame has in her garden and knows how to sow, plant and propagate them '. Then ' for your sweet Herbs ', he adds, ' there's Marjoram, Basil, Mastick, Lavender, Thyme, Sage, and double flowered Rosemary which every Kitchen Maid is so well acquainted with that I need make no farther mention of them '.

A renowned lady gardener of the day was the Duchess of Beaufort. She figures conspicuously both in Charles Evelyn and Switzer's books. Evelyn, who describes her as having ' a Soul above her Title, Sense beyond what is common in her Sex and Greatness and good nature so agreeably mixed as to leave few Equals behind her ', says her gardens contained so many treasures that she ' could challenge any foreign Gardens to produce greater Curiosities than her own '. Switzer, in his *Nobleman, Gentleman and Gardener's Recreation* (1715), also praises her highly, commenting specially on her exotics and ' the Thousands of those foreign Plants regimented together '. He observes that when men divert themselves with gardening it is ' no more than what is from them expected ', but that when ' the fair and Delicate Sex ' garden ' it has something in it that looks supernatural, something so much above the trifling Amusements of Ladies that it is apt to fill the Minds of the Virtuous with Admiration '. John Lawrence gives his views on the subject of women gardeners in his *New System . . . a complete Body of Husbandry and Gardening* (1726). He observes rather severely :

' I flatter myself the Ladies would soon think that their vacant Hours in the Culture of the *Flower-Garden* would be more innocently spent and with greater Satisfaction than the common Talk over a Tea-Table where Envy and Detraction so commonly preside. Whereas when Opportunity and Weather invite them amongst their Flowers, there they may dress, and admire and cultivate Beauties like themselves without *envying* or *being envied* '.

In many ways the most attractive of the small manuals is John Lawrence's first book *The Clergyman's Recreation* (1714). Lawrence was at Clare College, Cambridge, and it was there he met his lifelong friend Whiston, the eccentric genius of whom Macaulay said : ' Poor Whiston believes in everything but the Trinity '. Lawrence was rector first of Yelvertoft in Northamptonshire and later of Bishop Wearmouth. Lawrence held views which were not wholly orthodox, and there is a tradition at Bishop Wearmouth that when he conducted his first service there three leading landowners rose and left the church together to show their disapproval. In spite of this Lawrence's eldest daughter married one of the three squires and his younger daughters the sons and heirs of the other two. It is not surprising that his *Clergyman's Recreation* went through six editions in twelve years, for, unlike more ambitious works, the author does not lay down rules but writes delightfully of the joys and troubles he experienced in making his own garden. When he came to his new living, he tells us he found the place in a dilapidated condition, and ' what they used to call a garden ' a wilderness smothered with couch grass, nettles and gooseberry bushes. The soil was heavy white clay within six inches of the surface. And he surveyed this prospect ' with Grief '. To add to his troubles he was assured it was hopeless to attempt to make a garden on such soil. Nevertheless he turned to and with ' the kind help of my Neighbours ' he built a brick wall and planted apricots, pears, vines, figs, plums, cherries, a peach and a nectarine. Within three years he was amply rewarded for his trouble. It is interesting to learn that even in the eighteenth century mud walls (made of earth and straw worked together) coped with straw were common in Northamptonshire and Leicestershire. Lawrence states that these old-fashioned walls (which must have been very picturesque) were best for ripening fruit and that the coping of straw sheltered the fruit from rain.

Apparently some of his parishioners objected to their rector spending so much time in his garden. To these he replies : ' I answer that it easily appears a great deal of time has not been spent in composing it. Indeed only a few leisure Hours in the Winter for want of Company by way of diversion '. ' For indeed ', he says elsewhere :

' a Clergyman whose chief and most constant Business is sitting at his Study, most wants Relaxation, and some modest Exercise, to preserve Health. For my own part I must own, that it is the best and almost only Physick I take : and if through rigour or wetness of the Season, I am denied the benefit of my Garden for some Days, and labour under Indisposition, God's blessing with a warm and Sun-shiny Day that invites me out soon sets me to rights again.

For I thank God this sort of Diversion has tended very much to the ease and quiet of my own Mind ; and the Retirement I find therein by Walking and Meditation, has helped to set forward many useful thoughts upon more divine subjects. . . . In the meantime I cannot but encourage and invite my reverend Brethren to the love of a Garden ; having myself all along reap'd so much Fruit from it, both in a figurative and literal sense '.

From the early eighteenth century dates also the first book on town gardening, *The City Gardener* (1722). The first to comment on the ill-effects of the contaminated, smoke-laden atmosphere of a city was Parkinson. In his *Paradisus* he gives it as his opinion that the worst of all ' unwholesome ayres ' is ' where there is much smoke . . . especially of sea-coales which of all other is the worst, as our Citie of London can give proofe sufficient, wherein neither herbe nor tree will long prosper, nor hath done ever since the use of sea-coales beganne to be frequent therein '.

The author of *The City Gardener* was Thomas Fairchild, the noted nurseryman, and he states in his book that he had had thirty years' experience of London gardens. His memory is perpetuated in the Fairchild sermon (he left a bequest for the purpose) preached annually at St. Leonard's, Shoreditch, on Whit-Tuesday afternoon. The subject has to be ' The Wonder-ful Works of God in the Creation ', or ' On the certainty of the resurrection of the dead proved by the certain changes of the animal and vegetable parts of the creation.' Fairchild's book is chiefly interesting as a record of what could be grown in the City itself even in the eighteenth century. In spite of increasing difficulties Londoners, as ever, were flower lovers. ' I find ', says Fairchild, ' that almost every Body will have something of a Garden at any rate '. His book was avowedly written to enable those who lived in the City ' to delight themselves in Gardening ' and to prepare them to enjoy the country when they could retire from business. From this book we learn that though apple trees blossomed freely within the confines of the

City, they did not bear fruit unless grafted on Paradise stock; that pear trees not only blossomed but gave good fruit even in such confined places as the alleys about the Barbican. Cherries did well and 'brought Fruit to perfection in most airy parts of the City'. Mulberries and figs both did well and he mentions specially the figs in the Rolls garden in Chancery Lane and Dr. Bennet's garden in Cripplegate. It was impossible to grow roses with the exception of the Provence rose; honeysuckle had ceased to flourish, but the lily of the valley could still be grown—'there is an Instance of it now in a close Place at the Back of the Guildhall'. A most interesting chapter is that entitled 'Of Court yards and close Places in the City'. It is pleasant to think of those eighteenth-century London court-yards, brightened with lilacs, jasmine, lilies, pinks, daisies, French marigolds, angelica (angelica grew wild on a waste piece of ground near the Tower of London at the beginning of this century), scarlet lychnis and wallflowers. Flowering currants, he says, grew not only in tavern-yards, but even 'on the tops of the houses amidst the Chimneys'. Balconies were adorned with apple trees grown in large pots and he mentions specially those grown at the Record Office in the Tower of London.

The list of flowers he particularly recommends for London gardens includes madonna and martagon lilies, sweet williams, evening primroses, perennial sunflowers, Canterbury bells, candytufts, lupins, nigella, sweet peas, French and African marigolds and sweet sultans, pinks and carnations. Wall-flowers he states would succeed only for a season. Fairchild's plan for a town garden is very attractive—a circular avenue of horse-chestnuts and in the centre of the space a mound covered with trees. Beyond the avenue flower beds and large quarters filled with evergreens, white thorn, flowering currants, almonds, dwarf pears, apples and flowering shrubs.

Fairchild's name stands at the head of the list of contributors to *Catalogus Plantarum* (1730), published by the Society of Gardeners; this noted Society was formed by twenty practical gardeners, most of them well-known nurserymen. They met every month at Newhall's coffee-house in Chelsea and discussed the plants brought by the various members who had grown them. After five or six years of these monthly meetings it was decided to publish a catalogue and to have all the plants ' drawn and painted by an able hand '. They engaged for the purpose Jacob van Huysum (brother of the great Dutch flower painter). Only one volume of the projected series was published, and it is now one of the treasures of garden literature. The section on the honeysuckle (with a beautiful illustration) is particularly interesting.

The most distinguished member of the Society was Philip Miller, Curator of the Chelsea Physic Garden. Miller was a Scotsman. Born in 1694, he was trained by his father, whom he succeeded as Curator in 1722. He held the appointment for nearly 60 years and died the year he retired (1771). He made the Chelsea Physic Garden the finest of its kind. Peter Collinson, who visited the place July 19th, 1764, wrote of it that it ' excels all the gardens in Europe '. Miller's industry must have been colossal. For his book, *The Gardener's Dictionary*, published in 1731, dwarfs in importance every other gardening book of the eighteenth century, not only in the English language, but any language. It was translated into Dutch, French, and German and is the only book of which it can be said that it was the standard authority for quite a century, not only in Europe, but also in America. In the seventh edition (1750) Miller adopted the Linnæan system of classification. He had first followed Tournefort's system and then Ray's. The edition enlarged by the Rev. Thomas Martyn and published in 1803–7, in two massive folio volumes, is, I believe, the largest gardening manual in existence.

One of the most noted gardens of this period was Dr. James Sherard's at Eltham. The plants grown there were described by Dillenius in one of his finest works, *Hortus Elthamensis* (1732), a book described by Linnæus as one of the most complete works of its kind. Dr. James Sherard's brother was the equally famous William Sherard, one of the greatest of English botanists and founder of the Sherardian Professorship at Oxford.

A garden as remarkable as Dr. James Sherard's at Eltham was that made by Peter Collinson[1] at Mill Hill.

Peter Collinson was the honoured friend of Lord Bute (the Prime Minister), the Duke of Argyll, Lord Holland, Lord Petre,

[1] See *The Life of Peter Collinson*, by Norman G. Brett-James.

the two Dukes of Richmond, Henry Fox, Sir Hans Sloane, to mention but a few in this country; by correspondence with Franklin, John Bartram, the Penns, Logan, and others in America; Father d'Incarville, and Père Heberstein in China, etc. Collinson was a Quaker, and came of a family who were amongst the earliest of Quakers. Like his father he was a haberdasher and mercer and he enlarged the business considerably by trading with the American colonies. Seven years after his marriage he took a small house at Peckham, and there is an interesting glimpse of his first garden in one of his letters—'a little cottage, a pretty garden well filled . . . the gay appearance of the great don't disturb me, perhaps they'd be glad to exchange their gilded shows for my real enjoyment.' Collinson was an enthusiastic collector of American plants, of which he received many from John Bartram. Peter Kalm, during his six months' stay in this country, visited Collinson and commented in his diary with enthusiasm on ' the beautiful little garden full of all kinds of the rarest plants, especially American ones, which can endure the English climate and stand out the whole winter'. In 1749 Collinson moved to Mill Hill, and the garden he made there soon became famous, although he avoided publicity. Honours were showered on him, for he was made a member of the Royal Societies of London, Sweden, and Berlin. Aiton, in the second edition of *Hortus Kewensis*, ascribed fifty-two new species of plants as either introduced or first cultivated by Collinson, but to these, L. W. Dillwyn, who published Collinson's catalogue in 1843, added 119 more, which had been assigned to Miller, Sherard, etc., but acknowledged in their own writings to have been received from Collinson.

Amongst the notable plants introduced by him were *cupressus thyoides, ailanthus glandulosa, abies canadenses, azalea viscosa, betula nigra, chionanthus virginica, dodecatheon meadia* (first grown by Bishop Compton at Fulham, lost to English gardens and re-introduced by Collinson), *Kalmia latifolia* and various lilies (*l. carolinianum, l. pensylvanicum, l. philadelphicum, l. pomponium, l. pumilum*).

Of *Kalmia latifolia*, Collinson wrote :

' The Ivy, Laurel or broad-leaved Kalmia is now in flower. Certainly it is one of the finest evergreen shrubs that is in the world. . . . I have a spray in water and it stares me in the face all the while I am writing, saying, or seeming to say " As you are so fond of me, tell my friend John Bartram, who sent me, to send more to keep me company ; for they will be sure to be well nursed and well treated " '.

Collinson persuaded Philip Miller, the Duke of Richmond and many others to join him in paying Bartram for his numerous journeys and the time he gave to collecting plants and sending them to England. The plants were named by Miller, Dr. Dillenius (Oxford Physick Garden) and Dr. Gronovius (Leyden) and later by Dr. Solander, a pupil of Linnæus. Ultimately, through the good services of the Duke of Northumberland, Collinson succeeded in his project of Bartram being appointed ' Botanizer Royal for America '.

' My repeated solicitations have not been in vain ; for this day I received certain intelligence from Our Gracious King that he had appointed thee his botanist, with a salary of £50 a year. . . . Now, dear John, thy wishes are in some degree accomplished to range over Georgia and the Florida. As this is a great work and must be accomplished by degrees, it must be left to thy own judgement how to proceed '.

The various packets of seeds sent by Bartram and presented by Collinson to the King were probably given to the Princess of Wales, who, like her husband, was a great garden-lover. Indeed, according to his own doctor (Dr. Mitchell) the Prince of Wales' untimely death was owing to his ' contracting a cold by standing in the wet to see some trees planted, which brought on a pleurisy '. After his death the Princess founded Kew as a botanic garden and she was assisted by the Earl of Bute, who acted as scientific adviser. The Garden was put under the charge of William Aiton, who had been a pupil of Philip Miller.

It is interesting to recall that even before the founding of Kew as a botanic garden, the 288 acres it now covers had previously and for many years been under the care of enthusiastic gardeners. The gardens were originally two properties—the grounds attached to Kew House and those that belonged to Richmond Lodge, the latter being the favourite residence of George II and Queen Caroline. Richmond Gardens, now incorporated in Kew, were noted, and the sylvan beauty for which Kew is to this day so justly famed is undoubtedly due to the planting done

KITCHEN GARDEN

(From *The Gentleman and Gardener's Kalendar*, 1718, by Richard Bradley)
British Library

GARDENER PRESENTING A BOUQUET
(From *The Complete Florist, or The Lady and
Gentleman's Recreation in the Flower Garden*)

THE GARDENER
(From *The New Gardener's Calendar*
by William Thompson)

A TERRACE GARDEN
(From *Campania Fælix*, 1700,
by Timothy Nourse)

TITLE PAGE
(From *The Lady's Recreation*, 1717,
by Charles Evelyn)

under Queen Caroline's supervision. It will be remembered that Scott, in the *Heart of Midlothian*, laid the scene of the interview between Queen Caroline and Jeanie Deans in these gardens.

After the death of the Princess, the Earl of Bute's place was taken by Sir Joseph Banks. Until his death Banks acted as unpaid Director of the Gardens, and it was under him that they first became noted for the magnificent collection of plants to be found there. He sent out the first collectors to distant parts of the Empire, a work which has never ceased to this day. The first collector sent out from Kew was Francis Masson, whose name will for all time be associated with the cinerarias and pelargoniums he sent home from the Cape. William Ker, who subsequently became Superintendent of the Royal Botanic Gardens in Ceylon, was one of the earliest collectors of Chinese plants. Another Kew gardener—Christopher Smith—was instrumental in introducing the bread-fruit tree into Jamaica. One of the most famous of these early collectors was Alan Cunningham, who ultimately became Superintendent of the Sydney Botanic Gardens. It was under Sir Joseph Banks also that David Nelson, one of the Kew gardeners, joined the expedition in the *Bounty* in 1787, under Captain Bligh. Nelson was one of those who remained loyal when the crew mutinied, and with Bligh and a few others was cast adrift. After enduring the terrible hardships of a journey of 3,600 miles in an open boat they ultimately reached the Dutch settlement of Timor, where Nelson died. Nelson had previously been with Captain Cook to Australia and sent home the first specimens of eucalyptus.

George III and Sir Joseph Banks both died in the same year, and from that time until the appointment of Sir William Hooker as Director, in 1841, the Gardens were kept in a very poor state, for neither George IV nor William IV took the slightest interest in them. In 1838 it was actually suggested that Kew as a scientific institution should be abolished and that it should be turned into a kitchen-garden for the use of the Royal Household. Public opinion, however, was so strongly expressed that the Government was forced to appoint a Commission, of which the most distinguished members were Sir Joseph Paxton and Dr. Lindley.

This was the genesis of the imperial side of the work at Kew. It has been said that ' as a national establishment it stands in relation to the science of botany much as Greenwich does to astronomy '. Kew is the botanical adviser to all Government departments, and as such is in touch with the Colonial and India Offices, the Board of Trade, the Board of Agriculture and Fisheries and the Foreign Office. It was under Sir William Hooker that the imperial aspect of Kew began to develop, and ever since the economic importance of the collections has become paramount. The plants of economic value which have been distributed to new centres during the last eighty years include such valuable products as tea, coffee, cocoa, pine-apples, bananas, quinine, etc. Of supreme importance was the introduction of the quinine plant (cinchona) from South America to India. Until then, quinine cost the Government of Bengal £40,000 per annum, and in this country its cost was roughly sixteen times as much as it is now. The rubber industry was a still more sensational success. Until nearly the 'eighties the world was dependent for its rubber supply on the rubber obtained from *Hevea brasiliensis* from the forests on the banks of the Amazon. Rubber seeds, as is well known, are very short-lived, but the expert collectors from Kew sent home quantities of seeds and from these hundreds of plants were raised. A thousand plants were sent to the Malay Peninsula and Ceylon. The success of the plants in Malay was phenomenal, and resulted in the remarkable ' rubber boom '. To quote the late Mr. Joseph Chamberlain's remark, ' I do not think it too much to say that at the present time there are several of our important Colonies which owe whatever prosperity they possess to the knowledge and experience and assistance given by the authorities at Kew '.

It was Sir William Hooker also who began the monumental work of describing and classifying all the plants growing within the limits of the British Empire. This work, which is not yet complete, is incorporated in the magnificent series of Colonial and Indian floras—*The Flora of Australia*, in seven volumes; *The Flora of South Africa*, in ten volumes; *The Flora of Tropical Africa*, in twelve volumes; *The Flora of British India*, in seven volumes; *The Flora of New Zealand*, etc. *The Flora of Tropical West Africa* is not yet complete, and there still remain the floras of British Guiana and Trinidad to be done. Another work of inestimable value has been the compilation of the *Index Kewensis*—the alphabetical list of every plant name published with reference to place of publication. This work is carried on by quinquennial supplements and as a work of reference it is unequalled.

The first Museum of Economic Botany was opened in 1842. It was the first Museum of its kind and has been imitated in many places both at home and abroad. The building in which it was first housed was formerly the gardener's house and store-room. The collections now fill four large buildings. The fourth Museum was opened to the public not long before the War. Part of this building was formerly Cambridge Cottage, built by the late Duke of Cambridge's father, and in this connection it is interesting to remember that Her Majesty Queen Mary spent much of her girlhood in this cottage.

Kew 'village' is associated with many famous names—notably those of Sir Peter Lely and Gainsborough. The association of the place with gardening and the science of botany dates back to early Tudor days. For William Turner, 'the Father of English botany', and the author of the first printed original work on plants in the English language, lived at Kew. Unfortunately the site of Turner's house and garden is not known. There is probably no other piece of woodland so near the heart of London, and certainly none that can compare with Kew. It is a wild-bird sanctuary, and it was recorded by Mr. W. H. Hudson that there were about eighty species in these woods. According to that authority, even in the heart of the country it would not be easy to find so great a variety in the same space. The longest life spent there would not suffice to appreciate more than a fraction of the endless interests, and from the highest to the lowest all may wander, as they please, in this great green book laid at the feet of London.

CHAPTER VII

THE LANDSCAPE SCHOOL AND THE VICTORIAN AND EDWARDIAN ERAS

The wane of the formal garden and the partial triumph of the landscape school was a slow process. In the early years of the eighteenth century, Addison and Pope led the storm of ridicule, Addison in *The Spectator*[1] and Pope in *The Guardian*.[2] Addison in an essay entitled ' The Pleasures of a Garden ' declared :

' Our British gardeners, instead of humouring Nature, love to deviate from it as much as possible. Our Trees rise in Cones, Globes and Pyramids. We see the mark of the scissars upon every Plant and Bush. I do not know whether I am singular in my Opinion but, for my own part, I would rather look upon a tree in all its Luxuriancy and Diffusion of Boughs and Branches, than when it is thus cut and trimmed into a Mathematical Figure.'

Pope's witty catalogue of topiary work sent out by ' an eminent town gardiner '—' Adam and Eve in yew, Adam a little shattered by the fall of the tree of Knowledge in a great storm ; Eve and the Serpent very flourishing ', etc.—is too well known to quote. Switzer, who had been a pupil of London and Wise, was an enthusiast for what he called ' Rural gardening ' and in his book threw scorn not only on topiary work but also the formal garden. Bridgeman, who succeeded London and Wise as Superintendent of the Royal Gardens, wrote nothing, but Horace Walpole[3] bestowed high praise on him and indeed the gardens laid out by Bridgeman must have had considerable charm, for whereas he kept the old walks with high clipped hedges for ' his great lines ' the rest was laid out in natural groves. According to Walpole, Bridgeman was the first to do away with the enclosing wall or hedge, and thereby to make the garden part of the country round it.

[1] *The Spectator*. June 25th, 1712.
[2] *The Guardian*. No. 173.
[3] *Essay on Modern Gardening, by Mr. Horace Walpole. Traduit en Français par M. le Duc de Nivernois, en MDCCLXXXIV. Imprimé à Strawberry Hill, par T. Kirgate. MDCCLXXXV.*

' As his reformation gained footing, he ventured farther, and in the royal garden at Richmond dared to introduce cultivated fields, and even morsels of a forest appearance, by the sides of those endless and tiresome walks, that stretched out of one into another without intermission. . . . But the capital stroke, the leading step to all that has followed, was (I believe the first thought was Bridgeman's) the destruction of walls for boundaries, and the invention of fosses— an attempt then deemed so astonishing that the common people called them *Ha ! Ha !* to express their surprise at finding a sudden and unperceived check to their walks '.

Walpole claims that one of the first gardens to be laid out in the new style was his father's at Houghton, by Eyre, ' an imitator of Bridgeman '. The greatest name amongst the early exponents of this school is that of William Kent, who ' leaped the fence and saw that all nature was a garden '. Kent, a Yorkshireman who had begun as a coachbuilder's apprentice, was a painter and an architect, but made his name as a garden architect. Owing to the influence of his patron, Lord Burlington, he was made Architect, subsequently Painter, to the Crown. Unlike Bridgeman, Kent disliked even the great walks between high hedges. ' Nature abhors a straight line ' was his dominating principle and Walpole describes him as the genius who ' struck out a great system from the twilight of imperfect essays '.

' The pencil of his imagination bestowed all the arts of landscape on the scenes he handled. The great principles on which he worked were perspective and light and shade. Groups of trees broke too uniform and too extensive a lawn . . .

But of all the beauties . . . none surpassed his management of water. . . . The gentle stream was taught to serpentine at its leisure ; and where discontinued by different levels, its course appeared to be concealed by thickets, properly interspersed, and glittered again at a distance, where it might be supposed naturally to arrive. Its borders were smoother but preserved their waving irregularity. A few trees scattered here and there on its edges, sprinkled the tame bank that accompanied its meanders, and when it disappeared among the hills, shades descending from the heights leaned towards its progress, and framed the distant point of light under which it was lost, as it turned aside to either hand of the blue horizon '.

' Art ', said Shenstone in his *Unconnected Thoughts on Gardening*

(1764), ' should never be allowed to set foot in the province of Nature'. Yet all this highly artificial imitation of Nature was described as ' natural ' and hailed as an escape from the bondage of the old formal style ! Kent actually went so far as to plant dead trees in Kensington Gardens to give the air of greater truth to the scene. Even this was nothing compared to the absurdities practised by the landscape school both in these islands and on the continent in later years. Paths, wandering aimlessly in all directions, were substituted for the fine old avenues and fountains and straight canals were abolished to be replaced by ' natural' winding streams or great lakes. Incidentally it was in conformity with the tenets of the new school that Queen Caroline ordered the ponds in Hyde Park to be joined into one, thereby making the Serpentine. Stowe was regarded as the height of perfection and the various contemporary accounts give an accurate idea of what was then regarded as the acme of taste. Lord Cobham, who succeeded his father, Sir Richard Temple, at Stowe, began the gardens, and by 1755 they were 500 acres in extent. Kent succeeded Bridgeman as the designer and Sir John Vanbrugh was responsible for some of the temples and other buildings. Next to Stowe, the most admired gardens were those at Claremont, at Esher ' where Kent and Nature vied for Pelham's love ', the Prince of Wales's at Carlton House (declared by Walpole to have been copied by Kent from Pope's garden at Twickenham), and the garden at Rousham, laid out for General Dormer, and described by Walpole as ' the most engaging of all Kent's works '. Other noted gardens of this period were those at Gunnersbury (bought afterwards by Princess Amelia), Pain's Hill, Surrey (belonging to the Honourable Charles Hamilton), The Leasowes, belonging to Shenstone, and Hagley, Worcestershire, where the gardens were made by Lord Lyttelton.

Kent was succeeded by that ' very able master ', Capability Brown (so called because when asked to give his opinion of any place he was asked to take in hand he was wont to say it had ' great capabilities '). He worked in Lord Cobham's kitchen-garden and became head-gardener to the Duke of Grafton at Wakefield Lodge, Northamptonshire. The lake he made there attracted attention and through the influence of his former employer, Lord Cobham, he was appointed head-gardener at Hampton Court. Loudon states that Brown planted the celebrated vine there in 1769. He was next employed by the Duke of Marlborough at Blenheim, and very soon ' the omnipotent magician', as Cowper called him, was consulted by everyone, and destroyed fine old gardens, creating in their place landscape gardens with his favourite artificial lakes for his numerous fashionable clients. Brown died in 1783. His successor, Humphrey Repton, was the first to assume the title of ' landscape gardener' and to describe the art he practised as ' landscape gardening'. To quote his own explanation ' the art can only be advanced and perfected by the united powers of the landscape painter and the practical gardener'. The first to use the expression ' landscape gardener', however, was Shenstone—' I have used the term " landscape gardener " because, in accordance with our present-day taste, every good landscape painter is the proper designer of gardens'.[1]

Brown had been omnipotent, but by this time people had become somewhat more critical of the destruction wrought by conforming with the new craze. Amongst the earliest hostile critics were Sir Uvedale Price, Richard Knight, William Gilpin and William Mason. How far Repton was influenced by these critics it is impossible to say, but his alterations were on a far less drastic scale than Capability Brown's. Repton's ' Red Books', as he called the collections of plans and notes bound in red morocco which he presented to the owners of the various properties he remodelled, show with painful clearness, however, the gardens he swept away in order to create ' landscape scenery'.

Had this school confined their energies to establishing new gardens their vagaries would have been harmless enough. But what must fill the least imaginative with horror is to think of the wanton destruction of fine old gardens, many of them established for centuries and full of interesting plants, the cutting down of trees and magnificent avenues, the wholesale destruction of orchards and so forth, perpetrated by the new school. The people who must have suffered most were the gardeners, who had to engage in the work of uprooting and cutting down their

[1] William Shenstone. *Unconnected Thoughts on Gardening* (1764).

carefully tended treasures. Why our flower-loving nation tolerated such vandalism it is hard to understand. So far from making or attempting to improve gardens the landscape 'gardeners' destroyed them, substituting fields and lawns and 'natural' lakes and streams. At its best landscape gardening as practised in Western Europe was an imitation of pictures by artists such as Claude; at its worst it was ludicrous and deplorable. The reaction against the excesses of the formal school, notably the undue prominence given to topiary work, was natural. Topiary work has its own charm, but like everything else becomes absurd when overdone. Garden lovers in every century have delighted in the beauty of plants growing naturally and had the change to a new type of garden been led by genuine gardeners and plant-lovers, instead of men such as Kent and Brown, the history of gardening in these islands during the late eighteenth and early nineteenth centuries might have been very different.

The self-styled landscape gardeners were evidently unaware that they knew nothing of landscape gardening. Certainly, no one possessed of any knowledge of the subject would have attempted to establish landscape gardens in western Europe. So far as is known, the only peoples who have practised the art and developed it to such perfection that it could justly be described as an 'art' are the Chinese and the ancient Mexicans. Chinese traditions of gardening go back to a remote antiquity, and from time immemorial they have made both formal and informal gardens, fraught with symbolism of which we understand but a particle. Their landscape gardens have no counterpart so far as is known in the civilizations of the East, but they are suggestive of the landscape gardens of ancient Mexico, a country where, as in China, both formal and informal gardening was practised, the art in both cases dating back apparently to very remote times. We know all too little of the gardens of these ancient civilizations, but sufficient to realize that landscape gardens in the West bore as little resemblance to theirs as children's first efforts with pencil and paper to the finished works of great masters.

At intervals through the centuries our Western imaginations have been dazzled with accounts of the beauty and magnificence

Princess Humay received in a garden at the Court of China

(Fifteenth-century Persian painting)

Musée des Arts Décoratifs, Paris

of Chinese gardens. During the eighteenth century two books on this subject were published, both of which attracted widespread interest. The first of these was Father Attiret's *Particular Account of the Emperor of China's Gardens near Peking.*[1] The second was Sir William Chamber's *Dissertation on Oriental Gardening.*

When Father Attiret's description was published people were still accustomed to think of Versailles as the height of splendour. They must have realized with no small amazement that in the Emperor of China's garden near Peking, Versailles, with all its great avenues, would occupy but an insignificant patch of ground. In the Emperor of China's garden there were more than 200 palaces, each one large enough for the greatest noble in Europe. Further, whereas even the wealth of Louis XIV did not suffice to furnish the gardens of Versailles with flowers, the Emperor of China's far vaster gardens were adorned with an infinite profusion of trees, flowering shrubs and plants in boundless variety for all seasons of the year. One of the lakes in the Peking garden was nearly five miles round. Most amazing of all was the fact that all the beauty and varied interest of the Pekin gardens were to afford pleasure to one man and one man only—the Emperor. No one, not even a Chinese nobleman of the highest rank, was permitted farther than the audience chamber of the chief palace. Within the vast enclosure thousands of slaves ministered to the pleasure of the Emperor and his women-folk. Naturally these gardens were a source of profound curiosity to the comparatively few white folk in Peking, but the only people who were ever allowed to enter were artists, such as Father Attiret (engaged to adorn apartments in some of the imperial palaces), and clockmakers. These men were not allowed to move even a few yards unless attended by armed guards. Father Attiret's account of what must rank for all time as one of the most remarkable gardens in the world is so interesting and his pamphlet being one of the rarities of literature, I quote a considerable section of it. Reading his soberly-written account,

[1] *A Particular Account of the Emperor of China's Gardens near Peking. A letter from Father Attiret, a French Missionary, now appointed by the Emperor to Paint the Apartments in those Gardens, to his Friend at Paris. Translated from the French by Sir Henry Beaumont* (1752).

it is plain that so far from exaggerating he found himself quite unable to give any adequate description of what he had seen. Unfortunately Father Attiret was neither a gardener nor a botanist, so he does not give even a brief list of the plants. After referring to the palaces and courts he devotes the rest of his letter to the gardens which impressed him far more than the magnificence of the palaces.

' They have raised Hills from 20 to 60 Foot high ; which form a great Number of little Valleys between them. The Bottoms of these Valleys are water'd with clear Streams which run on till they join together, and form large Pieces of Water and Lakes. They pass these Streams, Lakes and Rivers in beautiful and magnificent Boats. I have seen one 78 Foot long and 24 Foot broad with a very handsome House raised upon it.

They go from one of the Valleys to another not by formal strait Walks as in Europe ; but by various Turnings and Windings, adorn'd on the Sides with little Pavilions and charming Grottos ; and each of these Valleys is diversify'd from all the rest, both by their manner of laying out the Ground, and in the Structure and Disposition of its Buildings.

All the Risings and Hills are sprinkled with Trees and particularly with Flowering-trees which are here very common. The Sides of the Canals are not faced (as they are with us) with smooth Stone, and in a strait Line, but look rude and rustic with different Pieces of Rock, some of which jut out and others recede inwards ; and are placed with so much Art that you would take it to be the Work of Nature. In some Parts the Water is wide, in others narrow ; here it serpentizes and there spreads away as if it was really push'd off by the Hills and Rocks. The Banks are sprinkled with Flowers ; which rise up even through the Hollows in the Rock work as if they had been produced there naturally. They have a great Variety of them for every season of the Year.

Beyond these Streams there are always Walks or rather Paths, pav'd with small Stones ; which lead from one Valley to another. These Paths too are irregular ; and sometimes wind along the Banks of the Water, and at others run out wide from them.

On your Entrance into each Valley, you see its Buildings before you. All the Front is a Colonnade, with Windows between the Pillars. The Wood-work is gilded, painted and varnished. The roofs too are covered with varnished Tiles of different Colours, Red, Yellow, Blue, Green and Purple, which by their proper Mixtures and their manner of placeing them form an agreeable Variety of Compartments and Designs.

Every Valley has its Pleasure-house : small indeed in respect to the whole Inclosure ; but yet large enough to be capable of receiving the greatest Nobleman in Europe and all his Retinue. Several of these Houses are built of Cedar ; which they bring with great Expense, at the Distance of 1500 Miles from this Place. And now how many of these Palaces do you think there may be, in all the Valleys of Inclosure ? There are above 200.

Over the running Streams there are Bridges, at proper Distances, to make the more easy Communication from one Place to another. These are most commonly of Brick or of Free-stone, and sometimes of Wood ; but are all raised high enough for the Boats to pass conveniently under them. They are fenced with Ballisters finely wrought, and adorned with Works in Relievo ; but all of them varied from one another, both in their Ornaments and Design.

Do not imagine to yourself, that these Bridges run on, like ours, in strait Lines : on the contrary they generally wind about and serpentize to such a Degree, that some of them, which, if they went on regularly, would be no more than 30 or 40 Foot long, turn so often and so much as to make their whole Length 100 or 200 Foot. You see some of them which (either in the Midst or at their Ends) have little Pavilions for People to rest themselves in supported sometimes by Four, sometimes by Eight and sometimes by Sixteen Columns. They are usually on such of the Bridges, as afford the most engaging Prospects.

I have already told you that these little Streams or Rivers are carried on to supply several larger Pieces of Water and Lakes. One of these Lakes is very near Five Miles round, and they call it a Mear or Sea. This is one of the most beautiful Parts in the whole Pleasure-ground.

But what is the most charming Thing of all is an Island of Rock in the Middle of this Sea, rais'd in a natural and rustic Manner about Six Foot above the Surface of the Water. On this Rock there is a little Palace ; which however contains an hundred different Apartments. It has four Fronts ; and is built with inexpressible Beauty and Taste ; The Sight of it strikes one with Admiration. From it you have a View of all the Palaces, scattered at proper Distances round the Shores of this Sea ; all the Hills, all the Rivulets and all the Groves.

The Banks of this charming Water are infinitely varied ; there are no two parts of it alike . . . natural Terraces with winding Steps at each End, and above these other Terraces and other Palaces that rise higher and higher and form a sort of Amphitheatre. There again a Grove of Flowering-trees presents itself to your Eye; and a little farther, you see a Spread of wild Forrest-trees and such as grow only on the most barren Mountains: then perhaps, best Timber-trees with their Under-wood; then trees from all foreign Countries, some all blooming with Flowers and others all laden with Fruits of different kinds.

. . . This whole Inclosure is called Iven-ming-Iven the Garden of Gardens or The Garden by way of Eminence. It is not the only one that belongs to the Emperor; he has Three others. . . . In one of these lives the Empress his Mother and all her Court . . . and is called Tchang tchun yven or The Garden of perpetual Spring.

Thirty years later, Sir William Chambers, in his *Dissertation on Oriental Gardening*, attempted the impossible feat of describing in comparatively brief space some of the principles of gardening in China, a fine art developed through the centuries, governed by ancient traditions and complicated principles. Their gardens, so far from being natural, were made with such consummate art that they appeared natural: they were in fact the height of artificiality. Their landscape artists, as Chambers emphasized, were men who had undergone a severe training in botany, painting and philosophy. Their art was an object of legislation on account of its influence on the general culture and consequently beauty of the country as a whole. Mistakes could not be tolerated, for they were in a measure irreparable, a century perhaps being required to redress the blunders of an hour. The scenery of a garden, according to their tenets, should differ as much from Nature as a poem from a prose relation and gardeners like poets should give the rein to their imaginations. In large gardens they aimed to make scenes for different hours of the day as well as for different seasons of the year. Rare shrubs, flowers and trees were grown in glass houses built in the form of temples, and warmed with subterranean fires, and in these temples they covered the woodwork of the glass frames by growing grapes, apricots, peaches, cherries and figs. For their amusement they kept gold and silver fish in large porcelain cisterns.

In the open garden their spring scenes abounded with evergreens, interspersed with lilacs of many sorts, laburnum, limes, double-blossomed thorn, almond and peach trees, sweet briar, early roses, honeysuckles; the borders with snowdrops, wild hyacinths, wallflowers, daffodils, violets, primroses, polyanthuses, crocuses, daisies and various iris species. The seasons of March and April being scanty in flowering shrubs and trees, etc., they interspersed amongst their plantations menageries of tame and wild animals, aviaries and courts for wrestling, boxing, quail fighting and other games; and in the summer gardens lakes, streams and waterfalls of every sort, woods with deer, birds of many kinds, and summer palaces adorned with pictures, sculptures, embroideries, and frequently clocks of great value. Chambers cites also what strikes the Western mind as grotesque features, the 'scenes of terror' consisting of gloomy woods and deep valleys, dark caverns, trees ill-formed and apparently torn almost to pieces by tempests, birds of horrid aspect in the groves, wolves, tigers and jackals in the forests, the 'surprising' subterranean vaults, wherein pale images of ancient heroes could be scarcely perceived in the dim light, optical delusions and buildings seen in 'mad perspective'.

The disposition of the walks was arranged with the utmost care, and they never formed them to deviate apparently needlessly, and always so as to keep the spectator continuously entertained. The arrangement of trees and shrubs was an art in itself, guided by principles handed down through the centuries and by laws from which they seldom deviated. No tree was planted 'in discord' with those near, but always to form scenes of great beauty. Nor did they scatter flowers indiscriminately in the borders. 'They paint their way very artfully along the skirts of the plantations and in other places where flowers are to be introduced'. Flowers with straggling growth, poor foliage and harsh colours they rejected and sudden transitions both in colour and dimensions were avoided. In large plantations the flowers were grown naturally but in special flower gardens they were in pots buried in the ground, the pots being removed as soon as the blooms faded and others brought in their place, so that the place was full of flowers in perfection the year round.

Amongst the most interesting Chinese gardens mentioned by Chambers were those reserved for the ladies of the household. These were usually groves planted on hill-sides to combine the beauty of the shady trees with the views over flowery meads, lakes and open country in the sunlight. These groves were planted with evergreens, flowering shrubs, fruit trees and flowers growing between. Pheasants and partridges, deer, monkeys, squirrels, parrots and so forth were kept in these open groves for amusement. No two gardens, Chambers states, were ever alike, for the Chinese garden-artist disdained to copy, saying 'whatever bears even a distant resemblance to a known object seldom excites a new idea'. Finally he exhorted European artists not to hope to rival Oriental splendour—'yet let them look up to the sun and copy as much of its lustre as they can'.

One remark in Chambers' *Dissertation* is invariably ignored—his reference to the Chinese formal garden. 'Nor have they', he states, 'any aversion to regular geometric figures which they say are beautiful in themselves and well suited to small compositions, where the luxuriant irregularities of nature would fill up and embarrass the parts they should adorn'. Illustrations of Chinese formal gardens are most interesting. Amongst the most beautiful modern gardens of this type is the Lee-ming-koon Garden at Canton. Whether it is still in existence I do not know, but I have photographs of it showing what a masterpiece of formal gardening it must have been. The high surrounding walls are pierced so that from without charming views of the garden may be seen. Within, the small enclosure is divided by low walls pierced in beautiful and varied designs and on the walls stand ornate pots of different kinds with dwarf shrubs growing in them. Trees and small shrubs form the background of the outer beds. A straight path leads round the central enclosure—a deeply-sunk garden. Entrances to this type of garden are often circular, octagonal, or leaf-shaped, and they are never placed opposite each other lest they should invite evil spirits to enter. One of the entrances to this garden is eight-sided and shows an attractive view of the enclosure within.

Chambers himself fell a victim to the craze for copying Chinese gardens, but he was a man of great knowledge and taste and instead of destroying what he found at Kew, he improved shrubberies instead of uprooting them, planted higher ground without levelling it and opened up charming vistas. His pagoda at Kew remains as a monument to this cult for the Chinese style.

There is no doubt that the more discerning section of the public realized from Chambers' book that the landscape school was composed of the veriest tyros. Their gardens, as he pointed out, differed little from common fields. False taste had swept away old plantations, venerable trees, orchards, fine gardens and whole woods to make room for a little grass—'if devastation continues there will not be a fruit tree left standing in the whole kingdom'. The *Dissertation* undoubtedly helped to stem the tide of wanton destruction, but the landscape school, so far from being impressed with a sense of their own ignorance, developed their so-called art on a surprising mixture of 'Chinese' and English principles. What a Chinese artist would have thought of the results it is impossible to imagine. It is a pity the landscape school did not take to heart the sage warning of Sir William Temple, written the previous century, in connection with the subject of Chinese gardens :

'But I should hardly advise any of these attempts in the figure of gardens among us ; they are adventures of too hard achievement for any common hands ; and though there may be more honour if they succeed well, yet there is more dishonour if they fail, and 'tis twenty to one they will '.

There has never been a time when fashion in garden architecture was less characteristically English, yet this fantastic type of garden was named ' le jardin anglais ' in France and as such was enthusiastically copied all over the Continent, not excluding even Russia. As early as the seventeenth century considerable interest had been taken in Chinese gardens. The passage in Sir William Temple's *Gardens of Epicurus* has already been noted. Le Comte's *Nouveaux Mémoires sur l'Etat présent de a Chine* (1696) was widely read. Kampfer and Du Halde's books increased the interest, whilst Father Attiret's remarkable pamphlet was discussed in *Lettres d'une Société aux Remarques sur qualques ouvrages nouveaux* (1751) and incorporated by Latapie in his translation of Wheatley's *Observations on Modern Gardening*.

At no time have gardens been so much influenced by literature as during the eighteenth century. The cult for 'freedom', for 'nature', and for breaking away from all conventions was widespread. It was through books such as Langier's *Essai sur l'Architecture* (1753), Rousseau's *La Nouvelle Hèloïse*, the Marquis de Girardin's *La Composition des Paysages*, Saint Pierre's *Etudes de la Nature*, and Delille's *Les Jardins*, that the theories of landscape gardening were made known to the literary world. Although there were earlier gardens laid out in the new style, notably the Duchesse de Boufflers', it was the Petit Trianon that was regarded as the height of fashion. Marie Antoinette had probably only a vague idea what 'le jardin anglais' was like; the King had given her Trianon and she was determined to have a garden in the new style. An English gardener, Richard by name, was appointed and the grounds were soon adorned with a Chinese aviary, Turkish fountains and other follies. Marie Antoinette was a genuine flower lover and these failed to please her and Richard was dismissed. Later when his son, Claude Richard, was given the appointment, she was delighted, for he grew flowers for her in abundance. The rustic hamlet preserves to this day the memory of the unfortunate Queen's brief enjoyment of the 'simple' life.

In many ways the most interesting of the English landscape gardeners employed on the Continent was Thomas Blaikie. Unlike the majority of that school, he was deeply interested in plants. Blaikie was one of those remarkable Scotsmen who not only make themselves at home anywhere, but achieve success from sheer force of character.

He was sent abroad by Dr. Fothergill and Dr. Pitcairn in search of rare Alpine plants in 1775. He had apparently been in the service of the former in his famous botanical garden at Upton near Stratford. Apart from his careful botanical notes the interest of the Diary for the first year, published for the first time last year, 1931,[1] lies chiefly in his travel notes. At Chamonix his companion was Michel Gabriel Paccard, the first climber to accomplish the ascent of Mont Blanc, and at Geneva he was visited by Voltaire, then over eighty. (Voltaire's garden, Les Délices, was the most celebrated of those laid out in the English style in Switzerland.)

[1] *The Diary of a Scotch Gardener*, by Thomas Blaikie, edited by Francis Birrell.

HERBACEOUS BORDER, GLAMIS CASTLE

The following year Blaikie began the most interesting phase of his life, when he took service with that astonishing French nobleman, the Comte de Lauraguais (the first lover of Sophie Arnauld). Lauraguais never paid Blaikie his wages but he launched him on a brilliant career. Owing to Lauraguais, Blaikie entered the service of the Comte d'Artois (brother of Louis XVI) and worked under his architect, Belanger, the last great architect of the eighteenth century. From the account in his diary it is evident that Blaikie drew the original plan for the famous garden of Bagatelle, his plan being modified to suit French taste by Belanger and Lerouge (in his book *Jardins Anglais et Chinois*, Lerouge reproduces the plan as his own). The Count had made a bet with the Queen that he would rebuild Bagatelle in sixty days and that a fairy palace should be constructed there during the sixty days' absence of the Court at Fontainebleau. He won his bet at a cost of some five million livres.

Blaikie had by this time achieved fame and he passed into the service of the Duc d'Orleans (Philippe Egalité), who had a profound admiration for everything English, not least for English gardens. Plans of a few of the Duke's gardens are to be found in Lerouge's *Jardins Anglais et Chinois* (1776–1788), and in view of Blaikie's great knowledge it is more than probable that he was largely responsible for the carrying out of his employer's schemes.

Blaikie's diary is full of comments on the famous people with whom he was brought into contact, including the King and Marie Antoinette. He was no courtier and his blunt outspoken replies seem to have caused the royal circle much amusement. He had a sincere admiration for the Queen and he gives a touching account of his last interview with her. ' I know your way of thinking and shall never forget you. I have known you long ', was her farewell to him.

The Revolution reduced Blaikie almost to beggary and he wisely retired to Chauny. Loudon states that it was Blaikie who during the Consulate ' laid out Malmaison, the residence of Josephine, in the English style and richly stocked the garden with trees and shrubs from London '. In 1822 he was living at St. Germain where he had a garden of about forty acres, he and

Gabriel Thouin being accounted the most eminent of the 'Artistes Jardiniers et Architectes des Jardins de France'.

Alexandre Laborde's *Description des nouveaux Jardins de la France et de ses Châteaux* gives a series of graphic pictures of the types of 'jardin anglais' made in France during the early nineteenth century. In Germany, the landscape garden was made fashionable about twenty years later than in France, chiefly owing to Louis Sekell, who had been sent by the Elector, Max Josef IV, to study the new art under Chambers. Frederick the Great became an enthusiast on the subject and soon every German royal house had followed his example, the most notable landscape garden being perhaps that made at Wilhelmshöhe by the Landgraf of Kassel. In Russia the new fashion was introduced by Catherine II. An English landscape gardener, John Bush, laid out part of Tsarskoe Selo at her orders ; the other part being left in the old formal style. The most extravagant and absurd 'English gardens' were those made by the orders of Prince Potemkin in various parts of Russia. The work was done by Gould, a pupil of Capability Brown. Loudon states that on one of the Prince's journeys to the Ukraine he was accompanied by Gould and several hundred under-gardeners who, whenever the Prince halted, even if for only a day, laid out a garden for him, not only with trees, shrubs and winding walks, but adorned with seats and statues taken by the cavalcade the whole distance.

The most distinguished critic of the landscape school in the nineteenth century was Sir Walter Scott. So far from simplicity being their guide, 'it is not simplicity', he shrewdly observed, 'but affectation labouring to seem simple'.[1] The literature of landscape gardening in its widest aspect is a vast subject, ranging from the practical and often insignificant manuals to books by the school led by Voltaire and Rousseau, the German philosophers, notably Christian Hirschfeld, Gœthe's and Schiller's writings, the works of the English Lake School of poets and most interesting of all, the translations of the Chinese Nature-mystics.[2]

[1] See *Quarterly Review*, Vol. XXXVII, 1828, and *Criticisms*, Vol. V.
[2] The earliest translation of Lao Tzu's work is in Latin MS. and was probably made by a Jesuit missionary. It is at the India Office.

THE VICTORIAN AND EDWARDIAN ERAS

The landscape school looms largely in the annals of the eighteenth and nineteenth centuries, but there were of course thousands of gardens where their influence was not felt at all. Apart from the many distinguished gardeners who have already been mentioned (Philip Miller, Peter Collinson, etc.), there must have been many others whose names are unknown to us who were deeply interested in plants but wholly uninterested in the fashionable cult. Moreover, landscape gardening was impossible in a limited space and it is pleasant to think of the many medium-sized and small gardens of the late eighteenth and early nineteenth centuries where they kept the old formal walks shaded by clipped hedges, the fountains and the sundial, the comfortable garden house and above all the great borders where they grew the fine old-fashioned flowers, many of them known in these islands for centuries, and the old roses. There must have been thousands in the 'forties of the nineteenth century who, like William Cobbett, deplored the destruction of the lovely old gardens. He mentions specially in *The English Gardener* the garden made by Sir William Temple at Moor Place (Surrey), where as a boy he had ' for hours ' admired its beauties, especially the great borders of flowers.

It is, I think, a little difficult to realize how much the colour of flower borders has altered, even though nominally the same plants may be grown. We are so accustomed to the dazzling colouring and the large size of flowers ' improved ' out of all recognition by skilful modern professionals, that it is doubtful whether many would appreciate the quiet soft colours and the smaller blooms of a century ago. Needlework, in which flowers figure, reflects more or less faithfully the colours of the period, and there is something very restful and beautiful in the old quiet tones. The individual flowers are more accurately portrayed in the charming wreaths and bouquets which adorn so many books of the period, and it is from them that one can most easily visualise the favourite flowers commonly grown even in humble gardens—the small old-fashioned pansies, the many beautiful roses, snowdrops, crocuses, primroses, polyanthuses, violets, periwinkles, auriculas, crown imperials, hyacinths, dog's tooth violets, fritillaries, tulips, lilies of the valley, Star of Bethlehem, Solomon's Seal, narcissi, irises, madonna, tiger and orange lilies, day-lilies, foxgloves, forget-me-nots, peonies, monkshood, asphodels, the Mexican tiger-flower, lavender, bergamot, rosemary, snapdragon, musk, cherrypie (heliotrope), cyclamen, phlox, winter cherry (physalis), pinks and carnations, mullein, jasmine, campanulas, honeysuckle, woodruff, valerian, everlastings, dahlias, zinnias, the little old button chrysanthemums, sunflowers, marigolds, evening primroses, hollyhocks, mignonette, fuchsias, etc. In an attractive book of this period entitled *Favourites of the Flower Garden* (1818) there are twelve plates in which all these flowers are depicted in charming loose bouquets, the flowers themselves exquisitely and correctly drawn.

Kitchen gardens made great progress during the late eighteenth and early nineteenth centuries, though the landscape school doubtless regarded their orderliness as a necessary evil. It is interesting to picture those well-stocked gardens from the works of Abercrombie, Loudon and other writers before 1850. It is noteworthy that in the whole range of books on this subject emphasis is laid on varieties which were hardy and of good flavour. Those eminently sensible folk did not value mere size.

Of the cabbage tribe they grew the common cabbage in numerous varieties to obtain a succession from April to October; red cabbages in three principal varieties (the large, the dwarf, and the Aberdeen red 'with an open leafy head found in cottage gardens in the north of Scotland'), and of savoys about five good varieties, the dwarf and the yellow being considered the best for flavour. The Portugal cabbage, *couve Tronchuda*, was introduced in 1821 and the dwarf variety in 1822. In the Highlands of Scotland cabbages were preserved by burying the entire plants, and not allowing them to touch each other in dry soil, so deeply as to be out of the reach of frost. In peaty soil this kept them in perfect condition till the following spring or summer. Brussels sprouts were naturally highly esteemed. 'In Great Britain the seed used is generally procured at least every second year from Brussels, as the plants are found to degenerate if grown two seasons from British seeds'. About fourteen varieties of borecole were grown, and Russian kale was sometimes blanched like seakale. Cauliflowers were preserved by lifting the entire plant, hanging it up in a cellar or cool shed, covering the flower with the leaves and removing any part that decayed immediately. Broccoli were preserved as they are now by disturbing the roots as little as possible and laying the plants in a sloping position with their heads towards the north. They grew about eighteen varieties of peas, including the sugar pea. Of broad beans about ten varieties and several varieties of kidney beans and scarlet runners.

Potatoes, when they were first introduced, were regarded as delicacies for the wealthy, but in the early years of the eighteenth century they were somewhat despised. London and Wise do not mention them in their *Complete Gardener* (1719) and Bradley regarded them as inferior to skirrets and radishes. Loudon states that the cultivation of potatoes was very little understood in gardens in Scotland till about 1740 and that they were not cultivated in fields in that country till twenty years later. 'It is stated in the *General Report of Scotland*, Vol. II, p. 111, as a well-ascertained fact that in the year 1725–6 the few potato plants then existing in gardens about Edinburgh, were left in the same spot of ground from year to year, as recommended by Evelyn; a few tubers were perhaps removed for use in the autumn and the parent plants were then well covered with litter to save them from the winter's frost'. Since the middle of the eighteenth century, however, Loudon adds, the cultivation of the potato had made great progress in Scotland and in the early nineteenth century they were grown in every cottage garden. Jerusalem artichokes were less esteemed as potatoes became more commonly grown. They were served not only boiled but baked in pies. Turnips were commonly used and the young seedlings were an ingredient in salads. Loudon mentions a 'violet' carrot as a new sort recently obtained from M. Vilmorin —'a very large and exceedingly sweet variety sent to him from Spain'. Parsnips were apparently not so popular as formerly. In the north of Ireland the roots were brewed with hops. Beetroots were used not only as they are now but dried and ground and mixed with coffee to lessen the cost of the latter.

Skirrets, which Worlidge, writing in 1682, described as 'the sweetest, whitest and most pleasant of roots', were still commonly grown; in the north of Scotland they were called crummocks. Scorzonera and salsify were both grown and, apart from the roots which were used in the same way as now, the stems of salsify were sometimes used like asparagus in spring. Radish seed-pods, when young and green, were put into vegetable pickles or used as a substitute for capers. Spinach, white beet, orach, wild spinach (Good King Henry) and New Zealand spinach were all grown. New Zealand spinach had been introduced by Sir Joseph Banks. It was found growing wild in bush, sandy places, in New Zealand, but not used by the natives. As it resembled Good King Henry it was considered safe and some was boiled every day for breakfast and dinner on board. When first introduced into this country it was treated as a greenhouse plant. Sorrel too was commonly grown in gardens and used in soups, sauces and salads. Of the onion tribe onions, leeks, chives, garlic and shallots were all grown. Asparagus, Loudon says, ' is cultivated in London to a greater extent than anywhere else in the world and chiefly at Deptford and Mortlake.' Some growers in these places had over 100 acres under cultivation. In some parts of Gloucestershire the flower stalks of *ornithogalum pyrenaicum* were sold in the market under the name of ' Prussian asparagus '. ' Hop-tops ' (the young shoots of hops) were another substitute. Asparagus was one of the earliest vegetables to be forced. Leonard Meager in his *English Gardener* says ' Some having old beds of asparagus which they are minded to destroy and having convenience of new or warm dung lay their old plants in order on the dung and the heat doth force forward a farewell crop '.

Seakale, which is a native of our coasts, has been used from time immemorial, but when it was first cultivated in gardens is unknown. William Turner and Lobel sent roots to the Continent, but Philip Miller was the first to write of its culture. It was grown by Dr. Lettsom at Grove Hill about 1767 and by him popularized in the neighbourhood of London. It was cultivated in the gardens near Dublin at least as early as 1764. William Curtis wrote a pamphlet on it and Loudon says that Curtis ' has done more to recommend it and diffuse the knowledge of it than any of his predecessors '. Seakale is one of the very few vegetables which is better flavoured when forced than when grown naturally. Globe artichokes were grown in three varieties, the French conical, the globe, and the dwarf globe. The flowers were sometimes used instead of rennet to coagulate milk. The Orkney Islands were celebrated for the culture of these artichokes, due doubtless to the quantities of sea-weed they used as manure. Cardoons (introduced in the seventeenth century) were more commonly grown than they are now, but not nearly so much as on the Continent. Rampion was grown as a salad herb, the root, which has a nutty flavour, being eaten raw like radish and the leaves being valued in winter salads. Alisander was beginning to go out of favour, celery being preferred. Celery, known in its wild state as smallage, is another native plant, improved almost out of recognition by cultivation. Celeriac was chiefly cultivated for use in soup. Quite fourteen varieties of lettuce were grown. Endive, introduced in the sixteenth century, was highly esteemed. Chicory (succory) was used as it is now and the young leaves in salads. Little is known concerning the history of mushroom culture. The earliest book in which its culture is mentioned is *The Solitary Gardener* (1706). Loudon states, ' Its peculiar habits and the method of propagating it are so unlike those of any other culinary vegetable, that gardeners, till lately, seem not to have generalized on its culture. For a long period back, it seems never to have been produced in any other way than on ridges of warm dung ; no one appearing to advert to the circumstance of its being indigenous, and that it may be grown in the open ground in the warmer months '. Market gardeners, however, gradually adopted the culture of them in the open air during the warmer months. As early as about 1830 this method of growing them was practised by Cunningham, an Edinburgh nurseryman. In 1831 Ellis, gardener to the Archbishop of Armagh, grew them in this fashion and in an article in the *Gardener's Magazine* (Vol. IX, p. 229) stated that he found it the best of all methods. In the neighbourhood of Paris mushrooms were commonly grown in the caverns formed by exhausted lime quarries. Mustard and cress, lamb's lettuce, water-cress, burnet, wood-sorrel, purslane, parsley, tarragon, fennel, chervil, dill, horse-radish, nasturtiums, marigolds, borage, balm, thyme, sage, clary, samphire, wormwood, liquorice (introduced according to Stowe early in Elizabeth's reign), mint, marjoram, savory, basil, rosemary, angelica, anise, coriander, rue, caraway, hyssop, camomile, elecampane, tansy and costmary were grown for salads, flavouring and garnishing, pickles and medicinal use, and lavender for perfuming linen. Lavender was extensively cultivated at Mitcham (Surrey) and Maidenhead (Berkshire) for distillation. Tomatoes and egg-plants (treated as a greenhouse annual) and capsicums were grown for salads and flavouring. With what scorn the cooks of that period, accustomed to such a range of excellent herbs, would regard the bought sauces and flavourings of to-day! People who were children in the 'sixties say that bought crystallised angelica and fruits began to supplant the home-preserved about that time, but the bought stuff was regarded with contempt by the older generation and considered a sign of inferior housekeeping.

William Forsyth who succeeded Philip Miller as Curator of the Chelsea Physic Garden devoted much attention to the improvement of fruit trees. In the Catalogue of Fruits published by the Royal Horticultural Society in 1831, 1400 sorts of apples are listed. The fruit was used not only as now, but for making pomatum, and the bark in dyeing (it produces a yellow colour). About 400 sorts of pears were grown, the Jargonelle and Marie Louis being the most esteemed. Quinces were used for quince marmalade and syrup, for flavouring apple-pies and medicinally. Medlars, as in mediæval days, were eaten ' bletted ' and used for making jelly. The fruit of the service tree was regarded as somewhat inferior. About 140 varieties of peaches and nectarines were grown, about seven apricots, about 100 of plums, and over forty varieties of cherry. The most important novelty amongst plums was the ' Victoria ' still so commonly grown. Myatt, the well-known nurseryman, whose name is commemorated in Myatt's Fields, Camberwell, found this plum as a seedling in a Sussex cottage garden. Mulberries were grown under glass as well as in the open. Among small fruits gooseberries were said to be better grown in Britain (particularly Lancashire) than in any other country. In Lancashire, to quote Loudon, ' almost every cottager who has a garden cultivates the gooseberry, with a view to prizes given at what are called gooseberry-prize meetings : of these there is annually published an account, with the names and weight of the successful sorts, in what is called the *Manchester Gooseberry Book*, or *Gooseberry Growers' Register*. The prizes vary from £105 to £5 or £10, the second, third, to the sixth and tenth degrees of merit receiving often proportionate prizes'. Black-currants in Ireland were put as a flavouring into whisky and the dried leaves were mixed with tea by cottagers. Currants were grown in about fifteen varieties and raspberries in about nine. The old hautbois strawberry (*fragaria elatior*) was still grown as well as alpine and wood strawberries, and the larger varieties obtained by crossing the Virginian and Chilean species. Myatt's ' British Queen ' was held to be the finest strawberry. Cranberries were grown merely for interest. To quote Miller : ' they can only be cultivated for curiosity in gardens, for they will not thrive much, nor produce fruit out of their native swamps and bogs '. The cranberry was introduced into this country by Sir Joseph Banks, and in the *Horticultural Transactions* (Vol. I, p. 71) he gave an interesting account of the cranberries he grew in 1813 on a bed about 18 feet square. He gathered 3½ Winchester bushels of berries, enough for 140 cranberry pies. Of nuts five varieties of walnuts were commonly grown, the sweet chestnut and filberts.

Great progress was made in the culture of fruit under glass. According to Loudon twelve varieties of pines were grown— ' the fruit is reckoned the most delicious of all and in Britain gardeners are valued by the wealthy in proportion to their success in its cultivation'. William Speechley, gardener to the Duke of Portland, was the author of the most authoritative treatise on the culture of pines and vines. The pines grown by Barnes, gardener to Lady Rolle at Bicton (S. Devon), were noted both for their size and flavour. Between 1840 and 1850 the culture of the pine was so much improved that instead of the three years formerly considered necessary to produce fine fruit fifteen months or less proved ample to produce even finer fruit. In those spacious days this fruit, produced with so much cost, was used not only for dessert but for making conserves. Equally great advances were made with the culture of grapes, peaches, melons, figs, and cucumbers under glass. Orangeries had declined since the latter years of the eighteenth century. The trees planted in the open by Sir Francis Carew at

Beddington (Surrey) in 1595, and only covered during the winter, were greatly neglected, according to Evelyn, in his day, and ultimately they were killed during the severe winter of 1739-40. These were generally accounted the first orange trees planted in this country, but Loudon describes as the largest in Britain in his time (early nineteenth century) the celebrated trees at Smorgany in Glamorganshire, which he states were of immense size and still bore abundantly. According to tradition these were still older than Sir Francis Carew's, for they were said to have been procured from a wreck off the coast of Glamorganshire in Henry VII's time. Amongst other fine trees of the citrus family growing in the open in this country he mentions the orange and lemon trees at Wormleybury (Herts) and Shipley Hall (Derbyshire), the three trees in boxes ' not surpassed by any so grown in Europe,' in the Marquess Camden's garden, the collection of all the citrus species trained against the back wall of forcing houses and producing large crops of fruit at Woodhall near Hamilton, the citron tree at Castle Semple near Paisley, various gardens at Salcombe (Devonshire), where there were trees all over a hundred years old and producing fruit ' as large and fine as any in Portugal ', and the trees at Coombe Royal. The date of the introduction of the citron into England is unknown. It may have been at the same time as the lemon, which was cultivated in the Oxford Physick Garden in 1648. Miller states that the finest fruit in his time was that produced in the Duke of Argyll's garden at Whitton, the trees there being covered during the winter. The shaddock (a native of China and Japan) was introduced into England in 1739 and was brought to the West Indies by Captain Shaddock, after whom the fruit is named. Loudon states that figs were grown only out of doors until Philip Miller's day. Miller introduced over a dozen new sorts from Italy and in time their culture was taken up under glass. Some of the most celebrated of the old fig trees planted in the open were still in existence in the middle of the nineteenth century. Notably the trees brought by Cardinal Pole from Italy in Henry VIII's reign and planted at Lambeth Palace. They were of the white Marseilles kind and in the early nineteenth century covered a space 50 feet high and 40 feet broad, two of the trunks having a circumference of 28 inches and another of

21 inches. They were injured in the severe winter of 1813–14 and the principal stems had to be cut nearly to the ground. The fig trees at Arundel Castle were amongst the largest standards in England and at Tarring there were orchards of standard figs. About twenty varieties were grown in England generally. Pomegranates and olives were as little grown as they are now and usually only under glass. According to Philip Miller, ' both the single and double pomegranate are hardy enough to resist our most severe winters in the open air ; and if planted against the walls the former will often produce fruit, which ripen tolerably well in warm seasons, but ripening late, are seldom well tasted '. Mr. Bean[1] quotes a letter preserved at Kew from Lady Rolle of Bicton in which she stated that in 1874 a magnificent tree that covered the whole front of a house in Bath was laden with fruit. Loudon states that six varieties of olive were grown in English nurseries and he mentions the trees planted against a warm wall at Campden House (Kensington), which in 1719 produced fruit fit for pickling. The olive is still grown in a few gardens, notably Lord Mount Edgecumbe's near Plymouth, where it has borne fruit.

Vineyards were few in the eighteenth century and in the nineteenth century apparently none were still in existence. At Arundel Castle there was a vineyard from which in 1763 over sixty pipes of excellent burgundy were made. Switzer mentions several vineyards, amongst them one at Waltham Green, from which good wine had been made for thirty years. The most celebrated vineyard was apparently that at Pain's Hill (Surrey), and in Philip Miller's time excellent champagne was made from the grapes grown there. Before 1850, however, the site of this vineyard was almost covered with a grove of Scots pines. Switzer was the first author to give a plan of a vinery with directions for growing the fruit under glass.[2] Canon Ellacombe, writing in 1878,[3] states, ' It is certain that as the Gloucestershire Vineyards were among the most ancient and best in England, so they held their ground till within a very

[1] *Trees and Shrubs hardy in Great Britain*, by W. T. Bean, formerly Curator, Royal Botanic Garden, Kew.
[2] *The Practical Fruit Gardener*, 2nd edition, 1763.
[3] *The Plant Lore and Garden Craft of Shakespeare.*

recent period '. He quotes Rudge's *History of Gloucestershire* to the effect that there was ' satisfactory testimony of the full success of a plantation in Cromhall Park from which ten hogsheads of wine were made in the year. The Vine plantation was discontinued or destroyed in consequence of a dispute with the Rector on a claim of the tythes '. H. Phillips in his *Pomarium Britannicum* (1820) says, ' There are several flourishing Vineyards at this time in Somersetshire ; the late Sir William Basset, in that county, annually made some hogsheads of wine which was palatable and well bodied. The idea that we cannot make good wine from our own Grapes is erroneous ; I have tasted it quite equal to the Grave wines and in some instances when kept for eight or ten years, it has been drunk as hock by the nicest judges '. Canon Ellacombe, however, was unable to find any confirmation of this statement. The only effort to establish a vineyard during the nineteenth century was that made by the Marquis of Bute at Castle Coch near Cardiff.

The great nurserymen of the latter half of the eighteenth and early nineteenth centuries were James Gordon, who had his nursery at Mile End (at one time he was gardener to Lord Petre : his name is chiefly associated with *sophora japonica* and the gingko tree, which he introduced), James Lee, whose nursery was at Hammersmith, and Conrad Loddiges, whose nursery was at Hackney. Loddiges' name is chiefly associated with his magnificent *Botanical Cabinet* (1818–33), the most celebrated illustrated book on flowering plants in the English language. It contains 2000 hand-coloured plates and was issued in twenty volumes.

Many important books were published during the latter years of the eighteenth and the early years of the nineteenth century. William Curtis published his *Flora Londinensis* in two folio volumes between 1777 and 1799 and in 1787 he began his celebrated *Botanical Magazine*. After 1826 it was continued by Samuel Curtis (his son) and Sir W. J. Hooker to 1858. James Sowerby's *English Botany* was published in thirty-six numbers between 1790 and 1820 and remained throughout the nineteenth century the standard authority on the subject. George and John Lindley (particularly the latter) were amongst the greatest authorities on everything pertaining to horticulture and botany.

The names of John Lindley's books fill two columns in small type in the *Bibliographer's Manual*. Robert Kaye Greville's *Scottish Cryptogamic Flora* (published in six volumes between 1822 and 1828) is the earliest specific work on that subject. The two most beautifully illustrated rose books in the English language were published before 1828—Miss Lawrence's magnificent volume *Roses* in 1799 and H. C. Andrews' *Roses* in 1827. Together with Redouté's splendid books I think they may be justly described as the most beautiful books of garden interest extant. They are now very costly treasures. It is noteworthy that all these fine books were produced during what is usually regarded as the period when gardening was at a very low ebb.

Amongst gardening manuals Abercrombie's works were the standard books throughout the latter half of the eighteenth and first half of the nineteenth century and gradually supplanted Philip Miller's. Abercrombie as a young man witnessed Bonnie Prince Charlie's victory at the battle of Prestonpans, when the Highlanders, charging sword in hand, proved more than a match for the English cavalry, artillery and infantry. They claimed that the battle lasted but five minutes. Abercrombie became gardener to Sir James Douglas and married a relative of that family. Thomas Abercrombie is one of the many Scotch gardeners who have made their name not in their own country, but in this. He started a nursery garden near Hackney three years after writing his first book—*Every Man his own Gardener* (1767). Fearing the book might be a failure he paid Thomas Mawe (gardener to the Duke of Leeds) £20 to put his name on the title-page before his own and the book was issued under their joint names, although Mawe had contributed nothing.

An unimportant little manual published during this period is worthy of mention for its quaintness—*The Florists' Manual* by Maria Jackson. Together with Lady Charlotte Murray's *British Garden* (1799) and Mrs. Henrietta M. Moriarty's *Viridarium or Greenhouse Plants* (1806) it is one of the earliest gardening books written by a woman. Two books only, as already noted,[1] had been written in earlier centuries for the benefit of women

---

[1] See pp. 125 *et seq.* and 184 *et seq.*

gardeners. (Elizabeth Blackwell's fine book[1] is purely a herbal.) Yet the care of the garden had always been considered the province of the lady of the house[2] and at least since early mediæval days women had been employed as gardeners, though apparently never for anything of greater importance than weeding and watering.[3] Maria Jackson's book was published in 1816 and is entitled *The Florist's Manual or Hints for the Construction of a Gay Flower Garden. With Observations on the best methods of preventing the depredations of insects. By the authoress of Botanical Dialogues and Sketches of the Physiology of Vegetable Life.* The book is dedicated to the authoress's ' highly esteemed friend Lady Broughton, as a tribute to the taste and ingenuity which she had displayed in the formation and arrangement of her peculiarly beautiful flower garden '. The book deals solely with the planting of beds with herbaceous plants and annuals, with a view to securing a pleasing display of colour from February to October. The list of plants at the end of the book is divided between those flowering between February and May, and those flowering between May and August. In small gardens, even as late as 1816, the autumn was regarded as a time when but few plants were in flower, for the authoress merely adds the names of a few in a note—dahlias, sunflowers, asters, marigolds, etc. A few pages are devoted to insect pests and the authoress observes with wisdom doubtless learned by experience—' The simple and laborious mode of picking away the animal, is the only one to which recourse can be had with permanent advantage '. It is difficult to picture a lady in elaborate Georgian costume and using such high-flown language, destroying slugs !

The earliest gardening manual in the English language published outside Britain was Bernard McMahon's *American Gardener's Calendar* (1806), the first gardening book published in America. It has a lengthy title :

[1] Elizabeth Blackwell, *A Curious Herbal* (1737).

[2] See pp. 184 and 185.

[3] Apparently the earliest records of women working as paid labourers in a garden (in this case a vineyard) are the entries in the fourteenth-century rolls of Ely Cathedral where women figure in the wages list for digging the vines and weeding.

The names and wages of the women employed at Hampton Court in Henry VIII's reign have all been preserved.

' The American Gardener's Calendar; adapted to the climates and seasons of the United States. Containing a complete account of all the work necessary to be done in the kitchen-garden, fruit-garden, orchard, vineyard, nursery, pleasure-ground, flower-garden, green-house, hot-house and forcing frames, for every month in the year; with ample practical directions for performing the same. Also general as well as minute instructions, for laying out or erecting, each and every of the above departments, according to modern taste and the most approved plans; the ornamental planting of pleasure-grounds in the ancient and modern style; the cultivation of thorn-quicks and other plants suitable for live hedges, with the best methods of making them etc. To which are annexed extensive catalogues of the different kinds of plants, which may be cultivated either for use. or ornament in the several departments or in rural economy; divided into eighteen separate alphabetical classes, according to their habits, duration and modes of culture; with explanatory introductions, marginal marks, and their true Linnæan or Botanical as well as English names; together with a copious Index to the body of the work '.

The author states in his preface that American gardeners have to resort to books published in other countries ' and however excellent and useful these works are in the regions to which they are adapted they tend to mislead and disappoint the young American Horticulturist, instead of affording him that correct, judicious and suitable instruction, the happy result of which would give impulse to his perseverance '. I have a copy of this bulky, large octavo volume and I like to think that the stray pressed petals and leaves in it belonged to the original owner. Bernard McMahon was a Philadelphia nurseryman with thirty years' experience and he had every reason to be proud of the book he wrote. To the modern reader, the most interesting part is the general catalogue at the end, giving the names of nearly three thousand species and varieties of plants, for this list is probably the most trustworthy in existence of what plants were grown in American gardens in those days. To lovers of the old roses, the rose list is particularly interesting. It is also interesting to find the very large number of medicinal herbs grown apart from the aromatic, pot and sweet herbs. Amongst other rare early American books are Major John Adlum's *Cultivation of the Vine in America,* and Thomas Bridgeman's *Young Gardener's Assistant.* There were two editions of John Adlum's book

(1823 and 1828) and the British Museum copy of the second edition has on the title-page the inscription ' The Honourable George C. Washington with the respect of the author '. In this same copy, between pages 12 and 13, is attached a facsimile copy of a letter dated April 11, 1823, from Thomas Jefferson (third President of the United States) thanking the author for the home-made wines he had sent him and adding :

' Of your book on the culture of the vine it would be presumption in me to give any opinion because it is a culture of which I have no knowledge either from practise or reading. Wishing you very sincerely compleat success in this your laudable undertaking I assure you of my great esteem and respect.
MAJOR JOHN ADLUM
TH. JEFFERSON.

Thomas Bridgeman's *Young Gardener's Assistant* (1829) is a slender little volume and treats solely of flowers and vegetables. The author describes himself on the title-page as ' Gardener, Seedsman and Florist. New-York, Brooklyn '. I have his presentation copy inscribed ' Thomas Eastmond's Book given by the author Mr. Thomas Bridgeman '. At the end of the book is a note in the same handwriting ' Mr. Thomas Bridgeman went to America in the year 1819 '.

Early American gardening books are already rare and the earliest published in British dominions beyond the seas are equally rare. There were some magnificent gardens in eastern Canada in the early nineteenth century. For instance, a Mr. Henry Atkinson had a garden at Carouie, near Quebec, part of which was on the top of a precipice 200 feet high and flanked by a wooded mountain range. Part of the grounds called Spencer Wood had been occupied by General Wolfe's troops before the attack on the city. The kitchen-garden was four acres in extent. An horticultural society was started at Montreal about 1830 and a botanic garden was established there in 1832. In Toronto an horticultural society was established in 1834. It seems a far cry from those early days to such leading societies as the Rose Society of Ontario. A charming contemporary description of the small gardens near Montreal of a century ago is to be found in *The Gardener's Magazine* for 1833 :

' It is by no means an uncommon sight in passing through the suburbs of this town (Montreal) in winter, to see a dozen or twenty Canadian houses, in fact almost every house with the front windows decorated with roses, carnations and pelargoniums (particularly the countess seedling and pine-apple pelargoniums) in full bloom and flowering in a style that would not disgrace the most scientific gardener. Their gardens are in summer generally graced with a few showy hollyhocks and roses, particularly the cabbage rose, together with the large crimson peony, and perhaps a few plants of bachelor's buttons and a few annual flowers. Two things are always found in these gardens; a lilac in one corner and flower beds full of mignonette '.

The earliest Canadian gardening manual (apart from sections in books such as Pickering's *Emigrant's Guide*) appears to be a French book—L. Provancher's *Le verger, le potager et le parterre dans la province de Quebec* (Quebec 1874).

The earliest gardens in Australia seem to have been those at Sydney. Almost all the trees and shrubs introduced into Australia from Europe were first grown in the Sydney Botanic Garden. Amongst the largest of the first gardens there were Elizabeth Bay, belonging to Mr. McLeary, and Lyndhurst, belonging to Dr. Bowman. In Western Australia the government garden at Perth was celebrated. Tasmania, then called Van Diemen's Land, was from early times a land of gardens. One of the first of which an account has been preserved was of that belonging to a Dr. James Ross, at Hobart. He described it as

' commanding heavenly views of the Derwent, the harbour and shipping. One part of the ground is so steep that 100 wooden steps are required to facilitate the ascent. . . . My arbours of " cool recess " and serpentine walks, formed out of the native shrubbery, are clothed in perpetual green, which borrows vernal freshness from a copious spring gushing forth at the highest point and visiting in its descent every plant and flower '.

The earliest gardening manual published in Australia was D. Bunce's *Australian Manual of Horticulture* (1849). The earliest treatise on the culture of the vine was published in 1825. *A Treatise on the Culture of the Vine* . . . by James Busby (1825) The book is dedicated to Major-General Sir Thomas Brisbane, ' Governor and Commander-in-Chief . . . of New South Wales and its Dependencies'. The place of publication is given simply as ' Australia '.

It is a striking testimony to the love of flowers amongst the earliest settlers in New Zealand that the Wellington Horticultural Society was established at Port Nicholson before the settlement was two years old. The first body of settlers landed at Plymouth, Taranaki, in March, 1841, and in December, 1842, they formed a horticultural society. According to Loudon the first nursery in New Zealand was that established early in 1844 by Mr. William Trotter in the valley of the Hutt River, a place he described as ' one of the sweetest spots that ever was beheld by the eyes of man '. He states that in this estate he grew the first grapes in the colony.

The immense number of half-hardy plants which had been introduced may have accounted for the ' bedding-out ' system which was such a marked feature of the majority of gardens throughout the nineteenth century. People soon tired of the flowerless landscape style and the great lawns were cut up into beds, round, square, diamond and so forth, and planted to make a display during the summer months with flowers such as lobelias, calceolarias, geraniums, antirrhinums and ageratum. The flat, closely bunched Victorian bouquet reflected the fashionable beds of the period. In 1863 a book was published containing no letterpress, except a brief preface, and consisting wholly of plans for these ugly beds—*Geometrical Flower Beds*, by Charles Francis Hayward. (The attractive part of the book is the cover, on which pleasing Victorian wreaths are depicted.) Other features of early-Victorian gardens were the rustic baskets and beds planted so that the flowers in bloom presented the appearance of a multi-coloured cone. The ' rustic basket ' were beds surrounded with iron or woodwork to resemble basket-work or vast pottery baskets placed on stands and filled with growing plants, or circular tiers of wood diminishing in size with pots of growing plants arranged on them. The custom of growing flowers in a perfect cone is described in Swinden's *Beauties of Flora* (1778). He gives careful lists of plants growing from 8 to 12 inches high, from 12 to 18 inches, from 20 to 24 inches, from 2 feet to 3 feet, from 3 to 4 feet and from 5 to 10 feet. Arranging these curious beds must have required no little patience. Loudon observes gravely that this sort of gardening may appeal, to persons in remote districts, to residents in the colonies 'and to infant and female gardeners'. People who lived in remote districts and colonials, amongst whom were probably as many good gardeners as elsewhere, were doubtless not best pleased to find themselves classed with infants and females. Another 'conceit' of the period was to make a dial bed containing plants which opened and closed at successive hours. Linnæus had made a list in his *Philosophia Botanica*, and Loudon gives a list 'sufficient to complete a botanist's dial in Britain'. His list is as follows :

	Opens in the morning.		Shuts from noon to night.	
	Hrs.	Min.	Hrs.	Min.
Tragopogon pratensis	3	5	9	10
Leontodon serotinus	4	0	12	1
Helminthia echioides	4	5	12	0
Borkhausia alpina	4	5	12	0
Cichorium Intybus	4	5	8	9
Papaver nudicaule	5	0	7	0
Hemerocallis fulva	5	0	7	8
Sonchus laevis	5	0	11	12
Agathyrsus alpinus	5	0	12	0
Convolvulus arvensis	5	6	4	5
Lapsana communis	5	6	10	0
Leontodon Taraxacum	5	6	8	9
Achyrophorus maculatus	6	7	4	5
Nymphæa alba	7	0	5	0
Lactuca sativa	7	0	10	0
Tagetes erecta	7	0	3	4
Anagallis arvensis	7	8	2	3
Hieracium Pilosella	8	0	2	0
Dianthus prolifer	8	0	1	0
Calendula arvensis	9	0	3	0
Arenaria purpurea	9	10	3	3
Portulaca oleracea	9	10	11	12
Malva caroliniana	9	10	12	1
Stellaria media	9	10	9	10

The 'rockeries', or 'rockworks' as they were commonly called, must have looked very odd, and some writers disapproved of them—'I must venture to disapprove the extended manner

in which this rock work is used . . . the unnatural appearance
of artificial crags of rock and other stones interspersed with
delicate plants to the culture of which the fertile and sheltered
border is evidently necessary, being decided that nothing of the
kind should be admitted that is not manifestly of use to the
growth of some of the species therein exhibited'. Shrubberies
were very much the vogue and Loudon lists as ' select shrubs '
rhododendrons, azalea, kalmia, andromeda, vaccinum, erica and
daphne. A tree that attracted great attention when first introduced was the Monkey Puzzle (*araucaria imbricata*). Judging
from the numbers one sees, at least one specimen of this tree
must have been planted in every garden of any size in these
islands. In the gardens belonging to wealthy folk pineta
were a new feature, established mostly during the 'fifties, to
accommodate the vast numbers of pines sent by David Douglas
and William Lobb. Sir Joseph Paxton and Sir Charles Barry
reintroduced the Italian garden and many examples laid out
during this period remain to this day. The gardens of Osborne
House were laid out in this style under the direction of the
Prince Consort. Another notable garden laid out in the Italian
fashion was Harewood. Bowling-greens were still a feature,
but the game became less popular with the advent of croquet,
and in the 'seventies of sphairistike (invented by Major Wing-
field) and lawn tennis. The accounts of early lawn tennis with
hour-glass-shaped courts, lines marked out with tape, nets
higher at the sides than in the middle and the lop-sided rackets
make those days seem as remote as the Middle Ages.[1]

The Victorian garden has been so persistently abused and its
worst features, notably the geometric beds and ribbon borders,
held up to such ridicule, that succeeding generations may perhaps
imagine that this was the only type of garden made in those
days. This, of course, is very far from the truth, for the old
formal garden, although considerably modified, persisted until
nearly the close of the last century. Those of us who were
children even in the late 'nineties, remember very well the two
kinds—the dull gardens laid out with a magnificent display of
bedding plants during the summer (and even as a child one
perceived dimly that between the owner and the garden there was

[1] See *Tennis, Origins and Mysteries*, by Malcolm D. Whitman.

a great gulf fixed) and the other delightful sort, so often associated in one's memories with cathedral and remote little country towns—gardens with mellowed walls where the broad, generous beds were full of fine old hardy plants and flowers with rich soft colours and delicious scents and hoary with traditions of centuries. Each garden had its characteristic atmosphere and the owner knew every tree and flower as a shepherd knows his sheep. It is to those gardeners and to cottagers that we owe the preservation of many treasures amongst the old herbaceous plants despised by the enthusiastic admirers of bedding-out plants. A large number of discerning gardeners are now doing their utmost to retrieve the lost treasures of those days, for with all the wonderful new introductions we cannot afford to lose the old denizens of our gardens. There are many humble plants too, all too seldom seen nowadays, but commonly grown in the 'old-fashioned' type of Victorian gardens. To mention but a few—the double sweet rocket,[1] which in Tudor and Stuart days was called Dame's Violet or Queene Gilliflower (one of the most deliciously perfumed of all the night-scented flowers), lovage (not only a handsome border plant, but the leaves have a most uncommon scent), elecampane (called after Helen of Troy), sweet Cicely, costmary or Maudeline (the only plant called after Mary Magdalene), mandrake, and that 'goodly plant' (to quote Parkinson's phrase), dittany. The finest clump of dittany I know is in St. John's garden, Oxford. Dittany has always had the reputation of being a mystic plant and was formerly used by witches in their concoctions. The leaves emit an inflammable gas and hence the old name 'burning bush'. The flowers of dittany are curiously attractive, and it is strange that this plant is so seldom seen in modern borders. Think of the old roses too that we have lost. William Paul's *Rose Garden* gives the long lists of provence (of which the old cabbage rose was still the favourite), damask, gallica, etc., grown in those days.[2] No modern roses can compare with the old aristocrats

---

[1] The double sweet rocket is not only difficult to get but also to keep. The only practical instructions I know to keep this plant are to be found in early nineteenth-century manuals.

[2] In *The Scented Garden* I devoted a lengthy chapter to the old roses and am therefore not recapitulating the substance of it here.

immortalised by the great artists and poets and rich with centuries of traditions.

An important event in the first decade of the nineteenth century was the founding of the Horticultural Society by Thomas Andrew Knight, with the help of Sir Joseph Banks, in 1804. The Society was incorporated by Royal Charter in 1809. Their earliest gardens were at Kensington, Ealing, and then at Chiswick until Wisley was acquired. By the middle of the century numerous provincial societies had been founded and now their number is legion. Soon all the ' florists' flowers ' will have their special societies. The Botanic Society was founded in 1839. Various important publications were established during the same period, notably Edwards' *Botanical Register*, Maund's *Botanical Garden*, Paxton's *Magazine of Botany*. John Loudon edited *The Gardener's Magazine* (which he founded) from 1826 to 1843, and in 1841 Lindley and Paxton[1] founded *The Gardener's Chronicle*.

The interest of the nineteenth century centres in the vast numbers of new plants collected from all parts of the world. It is manifestly impossible in the space of a chapter to do more than refer briefly to a few of the great collectors. For the tales of adventure and tragedy, apart from the interest of the plants themselves, would fill a large volume and the numerous books written by the collectors themselves are familiar to garden-lovers throughout the world. The history of the great plant collectors goes back to early days. One's mind goes back to Captain Winter, who accompanied Sir Francis Drake and brought back from the Magellan Straits the aromatic bark of Drimys Winteri (named after him when the living plant was collected in 1827), and to far older days when Adelard of Bath, of whom we know so little, was sent to the Near East, partly at

---

[1] Joseph Paxton, one of the most noted gardeners of the day, entered the service of the Duke of Devonshire as an assistant gardener. In 1826 he was made head-gardener. His name at Chatsworth is chiefly associated with the remarkable palm-house he designed, which was begun in 1836 and finished in 1840. This palm-house, which was 300 feet long, 123 feet wide and 67 feet high, was regarded as one of the most remarkable achievements of the age, for in it a tropical garden could be enjoyed even in the depth of winter. It inspired Paxton himself with his plan for the Crystal Palace in 1850 ; a plan which earned him his knighthood.

the royal expense, in Henry II's reign. During the late eighteenth and early nineteenth centuries an immense number of what are now familiar plants in our gardens and greenhouses were brought from South Africa—ixias, agapanthus, the arum lily, some species of nerines, heaths (Loudon, writing in 1830, says that over 400 species had been introduced), pelargoniums, Cape geraniums and, quite late in the nineteenth century, freesias and montbretias. The 'Barberton daisy' (*gerbera Jamesonii*) was introduced after the South African War. Early in the nineteenth century various treasures had been sent from the Himalayas by directors of the Botanic Garden at Calcutta—Buchanan, Hamilton, and Wallich. The greatest name in this connection, however, is that of Sir Joseph Hooker. He collected for Kew between 1847 and 1851 ; amongst his best known introductions being the Sikkim rhododendrons. Hundreds of plants were introduced during the late eighteenth, the nineteenth and early twentieth centuries, from China. The introduction of some well-known treasures is associated with Lord Macartney's embassy, notably the Macartney rose. William Kerr was sent out from Kew in 1803 ; his name is chiefly associated with *Kerria japonica* and the Chinese juniper. But the greatest of the early names is that of Robert Fortune, sent to China by the R.H.S. in 1843. His remarkable books and the tale of his adventurous life are known to all. Apart from the many plants with which his name is associated (Fortune's rose, *anemone japonica, dielytra spectabilis*, various azaleas, chrysanthemums and viburnums, *jasminum nudiflorum*, etc.), his greatest claim to fame lies in the fact that he founded the tea industry in India. In 1877–1879 Charles Maries collected in China for Messrs. Veitch, his name being chiefly associated with *styrax obassia* and *Hamamelis mollis*. Later we benefited as much as France from the work of the French Jesuit missionaries, notably David, Delavay, and Farges. The great collectors in China of the late nineteenth century were Dr. Henry, who collected for Kew for nearly twenty years. He sent over 15,000 dried specimens to Kew, of which about 5000 were different species. On his return he studied forestry in France and afterwards wrote his great book in collaboration with Henry John Elwes—*Trees of Great Britain and Ireland*. In 1899 Messrs. Veitch, on the advice of Sir William

Thiselton-Dyer (then Director of Kew), sent the late Mr. E. H. Wilson. Mr. Bean[1] states that Mr. E. H. Wilson had (by 1914) introduced some 1200 species of trees and shrubs, amongst which about 400 were new species and four new genera, and had collected about 65,000 sheets of herbarium specimens. Mr. E. H. Wilson's name is popularly connected, however, chiefly with lilies, notably *lilium regale*. The most recent great name associated with China is that of the late Mr. George Forrest. Captain Kingdon Ward's plant collecting has been chiefly in Tibet. The great collector of the early nineteenth century in Japan was Philipp Siebold. In 1830 he published his beautifully illustrated *Flora Japonica*. In 1860 John Gould Veitch went to Japan. Japanese lilies, notable *lilium auratum*, irises, maples, and hardy bamboos were amongst the most important introductions of the late nineteenth century. With the exception of André Michaux all the great plant collectors in North America during the late eighteenth centuries were Scotsmen. John Fraser's name is chiefly known in connection with *rhododendron catawbiense*, the chief parent of the garden race of rhododendrons. John Lyon also worked chiefly in S.E. United States. In 1824 the R.H.S. sent David Douglas to Western N. America. Apart from many trees, notably the Douglas fir, his name is also associated with the American currant (*ribes sanguineum*), which attained such instant popularity. Douglas came to a terrible end in the Sandwich Islands, for he fell into a pit constructed by the natives to catch wild bulls and was gored to death. The first to explore Chile in the interest of horticulture was William Lobb, sent out by the firm of Messrs. Veitch. The best-known trees associated with Lobb's name are the Wellingtonias and the monkey puzzle. The next great collector in Chile—Richard Pearse—was sent out by the same firm and worked out there 1859–1866. His name is chiefly associated with *eucryphia pinnatifolia*, to many one of the most beautiful of all shrubs. In the middle of the nineteenth century the Oregon Association (Edinburgh) sent out John Jeffrey; he worked chiefly in California. In 1872 the Arnold Arboretum was founded under the joint auspices of Harvard University and Professor

[1] *Trees and Shrubs hardy in the British Isles*, by W. J. Bean, formerly Curator, Royal Botanic Gardens, Kew.

THE SCENTED GARDEN, FRIAR PARK

Sargent, to whom English and American gardens are equally indebted.

So many new alpines were introduced during the late nineteenth century that rock gardens began to be established in the 'eighties. One of the first was that made at Kew in 1882. It included the collection of over 2000 plants left in his will by George Joad. Wild gardens soon became very popular, owing to Mr. William Robinson's book, *The Wild Garden*. Subtropical gardening was first attempted on a large scale in Battersea Park as early as 1864, by the superintendent, John Gibson. It was Mr. Robinson also who did much to popularize this type of garden, now to be seen in perfection in various parts of Cornwall, Dorset, and Hampshire. 'Japanese gardens' (so-called, for they bore no resemblance to the symbolic gardens of Japan) were a later cult.

The two last decades of the nineteenth century will always be celebrated for the rise of the new landscape school led by that great veteran, Mr. William Robinson. It is a pity that no new name was adopted, for the new had nothing in common with the early landscape school. The new school were gardeners of the first rank, and their names are honoured throughout the gardening world in all countries. Unlike the early landscape school, who destroyed gardens to make parks, the new school turned parks into vast gardens. They retaught the almost lost art of gardening to a nation who were all eagerness to learn. It would be presumptuous to attempt to say anything of the services rendered by gardeners such as the late Mr. Vicary Gibbs, to mention but one great name. Miss Jekyll's books are familiar to English-speaking people the world over, whilst Miss Willmott's monumental book on roses is the standard one on this subject. The opposition to the new landscape school was led by Sir Reginald Blomfield, who drew attention to the beauties of the old formal gardens in his book, *The Formal Garden*.[1] Incidentally the phrase 'formal garden' is modern. In mediæval Tudor and Stuart times it was never used, doubtless for the excellent reason that no other type of garden was known. So far as I can discover, the phrase was coined by Sir Reginald

[1] *The Formal Garden*, by Reginald Blomfield, with illustrations by Inigo Thomas, 1892.

Blomfield, and has ever since been in common use. The controversy raged well into the twentieth century.

It is obviously impossible to treat of modern developments. Every branch of gardening has its own vast literature. The cultivation of plants never seen in these islands before is the dominant interest of the scientific gardeners of to-day. They do not concern themselves greatly as to the lay-out of a garden, but they are profoundly interested in the plants grown in it. There is, I suppose, no part of the earth's surface as small in area as these islands where such a diversity of plants can be grown. In these richly blessed 'isles afar off' we can grow plants ranging from the Arctic circle and the Roof of the World to plants from tropical swamps. In what the catalogues describe as 'favoured parts' they can grow almost anything The opening of the most notable gardens to the public, in connection with the Queen's Institute of District Nursing, has been an inestimable boon, for it has given thousands opportunities to see rare plants, to say nothing of the varied beauties of the hundreds of remarkable gardens in these islands usually so carefully screened from the public gaze.

The English-speaking peoples are indisputably the most garden-loving nations of the world. I do not know whether the amount spent on plants in this country has ever been estimated, but the total must be stupendous. Apart from the vast sums disbursed by the wealthy, there is surely no other country where people with very small incomes spend so large a proportion on their gardens. Gardening is the absorbing hobby of thousands. Gardening papers have a larger circulation in this country than in any other. It is rare to find a house with even a few square yards of garden where one of the well-known weekly papers is not taken. In what other country would nurserymen and seedsmen find it profitable to distribute broadcast such large and frequently beautifully got-up catalogues ? Nearly anything else in the nature of an advertisement is consigned to the waste-paper basket, but these catalogues are eagerly studied even by those who can only afford to buy very little. Many of the modern catalogues are so first-rate that they can only be justly described as garden literature. They cater for every rank, ranging from the high-brow to the humble beginner. Not only are we inundated with catalogues from British firms, but foreign growers, notably those in America, France, Holland, and Japan, send their catalogues to their numerous customers in these islands. It is estimated that on the Continent over 15,000 acres are under cultivation to supply bulbs for British gardens.[1] Gardening clubs range from the Garden Society, of which every member is a distinguished horticulturist, to societies for those whose activities are in many cases confined to a few square yards of ground. The plucky attempts made in the slums of our great cities to grow anyhow something under conditions which at least the majority of gardeners would regard as impossible appeal to the sympathy of all and are splendidly encouraged by societies such as the London Gardens Guild. In what other country are annual competitions held for the best railway station garden? Not only stationmasters and their staffs but the general public take the keenest interest in their local lines. On the G.W.R. alone 500 stations were entered for the competition this year. The gardens range from fair-sized plots of ground to boxes, tubs and white-washed drain-pipes. It is amazing what can be done with the three last-named.

One type of garden in these islands has changed but little through the centuries—the cottage garden. What the cottager's plot was like in mediæval days is unknown, but it is more likely that it resembled the cottage garden of to-day than the elaborate mediæval enclosure, familiar to us from the illuminations and miniatures in the old manuscripts. For the pleasaunces of the wealthy in those far-off days were, like the gardens of classical days, suggestive of the town rather than the country. The town still symbolized security and protection and the mediæval garden reflected in no small measure the sense of security of a walled town. In common with towns, the gardens of wealthy folk had walls and turrets ; the alleys and fountains, the clipped walls of verdure, all suggested a town in miniature, even the flowers were safely enclosed in plots surrounded with small

[1] In the 'eighties of the last century Mr. Dorrien Smith started the bulb industry in the Scilly Islands which has been so successful, and the campaign 'Buy British grown' has already given an immense impetus to all British growers who have to compete with cheap foreign imports.

hedges, rails or trellis-work. The very word 'garden' in all its forms—garth, yerd, yard—is derived from an Aryan root signifying an enclosure, i.e. protection. But the humble country-man had little to fear, for he had nothing to lose. His garden reflected, doubtless, this sense of freedom and he grew his roses and lilies, his jasmine and honeysuckle, his cabbages and beans as best pleased his individual fancy. For that has ever been a feature of cottage gardens—no two are ever alike. Further, the cottager has always had a marked preference for the aristo-crats of the plant world—roses and lilies, and those royal flowers are at home in the smallest plot. The 'betwixt and be-tweens' of the plant world would look out of place grown amongst cabbages and onions, but the aristocrats are serenely at home. When some people were foolish enough to destroy their beautiful old gardens, many of them centuries old, the cottager did not imitate them. He did not cut down roses and uproot flowers in order to turn his plot into something resem-bling a field. Like his forefathers, he pursued the even tenor of his ways and grew the old-fashioned flowers beloved of our nation through the centuries.

Four introductions of the late eighteenth and early nine-teenth centuries captured the cottagers' fancy—the American currant, the fuchsia, the scarlet geranium and musk. One of the earliest fuchsias to flower in England was a plant on a cottage window-sill. James Lee, the great nurseryman of the late eighteenth century, saw a pot of it in flower in a small house in Wapping. The woman refused at first to listen to his offers to buy it, for it had been brought her by her husband, who was a sailor. Ultimately she reluctantly parted with it for eight guineas (a large sum for those days) coupled with the promise of two of the first plants raised from it. Geraniums and musk were grown on almost every window-sill. The great name of David Douglas is chiefly associated with pines, but he intro-duced also the humble little musk which achieved such wide-spread popularity. For about a century it was a universal favourite and then came tragedy, for the musk lost its scent. The fact attracted the attention of botanists and scientists all over the world, but even the most distinguished were unable to give any satisfactory reason. And now (August, 1932) comes the welcome news that scented musk has again been found. Botanists sent out from the Provincial Museum, British Columbia, found it at North East Cape on Texada, one of the islands in the Gulf of Georgia. There is little doubt that when the Texada musk, as it will probably be popularly known, comes into the hands of the nurseryman, everyone will buy it. Will it, one wonders, have the old fragrance ? To the cottager we owe the preservation of many of our most charming flowers—notably the old English cottage tulips (diligently sought out by the late Mr. Peter Barr) and the sturdy button chrysanthemums, the best flowers in the border in late November, but only lately grown again in large gardens. Nothing daunts these flowers. Through the worst late autumn weather they produce their cheery masses of little old-fashioned blooms when every other flower is dashed and splashed with rain.

Our cottage gardens are the envy and admiration of every intelligent foreigner, and no foreigner can imitate them. The characteristic features of the true cottage garden (as distinct from the imitation of the small suburban plot) are difficult to describe because there is no type. They vary from the thrifty little gardens in the West of Scotland with their delightful fuchsia hedges to those Devonshire and Cornish gardens where everything grows in such rich luxuriance, from the remarkable little plots so often to be found in northern parts to the characteristic sunny gardens of the South, from those of East Anglia, usually rich in roses and lavender, to those hidden in remote Cotswold villages and parts of the West and Wales known only to folk who love these silent places where Time has apparently stood still. The cottage garden has much in common with hand-needlework, for there is always the individual touch and lack of regularity. Edgings are regular up to a point, but the line of London pride or thrift, etc., will be interrupted by perhaps a clump of pinks or a stray Canterbury bell. The arrangement of the flowers is never drearily precise, they suggest an old-fashioned posy and are indicative of the owner's taste. Paths do not twist needlessly, but for some sensible reason—to avoid the water-butt perhaps, or an overgrown gooseberry bush. The bit of grass is seldom of any particular shape but strays off into unexpected corners and usually ends somewhat vaguely in the much trodden path by the clothes-line. Nor is the owner disturbed when in April the grass is starred with daisies; the children are told that when they can put a foot on seven at a time summer has come. Dandelions too grow on the paths with a cheerful, instead of an abashed air; their golden flowers are welcome. The flowers most grown in Victorian days were, amongst roses, the cabbage rose, moss roses, Cottage Maid, Maiden's Blush, Seven Sisters and sweet briar; honeysuckle and jasmine for their porches; the American currant and lilac, daffodils, wallflowers, peonies, forget-me-nots, snapdragons, polyanthuses, double daisies, gardener's garter, columbines (the old 'granny bonnets'), the old red Dusty Miller (auricula) and the yellow Dusty Miller, the madonna lily, pansies, clove carnations, stocks, southernwood, which they called 'lad's love' or 'old man', balm, rosemary, pinks, especially the old laced pinks and the old white pink (*dianthus fimbriata alba*) with demure blooms like soft little Maltese crosses, sweet-Williams, sweet rocket, phlox, hollyhocks, bergamot, thyme, marigolds, Aaron's rod, and the old cottage chrysanthemums. There is always something interesting at all seasons of the year in the cottage garden and it is at its loveliest perhaps when the apple blossoms and the wallflowers fill the air with fragrance and the bees with music. In common with all gardens in these islands their chief fascination lies in their everchanging loveliness. From days in midwinter so warm that the garden is full of bees and the open cups of the crocuses brimming with golden sunlight, to days in midsummer of drenching rain and strewn petals, and then in half an hour cloudless blue skies and sunshine, the flowers radiantly fresh after the rain and their scents richer than before.

> ' So, some tempestuous morn in early June,
>   When the year's primal burst of bloom is o'er,
>   Before the roses and the longest day—
> When garden-walks and all the grassy floor
>   With blossoms red and white of fallen May
>   And chestnut-flowers are strewn—
> So have I heard the cuckoo's parting cry,
>   From the wet field, through the vext garden-trees,
>   Come with the volleying rain and tossing breeze:

Soon will the high Midsummer pomps come on,
   Soon will the musk carnations break and swell.
Soon shall we have gold-dusted snapdragon,
   Sweet-William with his homely cottage-smell,
     And stocks in fragrant blow ;
Roses that down the alleys shine afar,
   And open, jasmine-muffled lattices,
   And groups under the dreaming garden-trees,
And the full moon, and the white evening-star.'

CHAPTER VIII

AMERICAN GARDENS

By Mrs. Francis King.[1]

I who have lived for many years in a garden, have therefore lived principally in the present and the future. 'On this earth', says the writer of *Days Spent on a Doge's Farm,* 'one season is usually spent in looking for signs of the next'. What have I to do then with gardens of the past, how write of gardens that have been ? Only by turning to sources from all parts of America, sources happily many in number and variety, engrossing in their curious charm.

In so brief a sketch as this it is impossible to do full justice to early gardening in America. I take therefore but a few of these seaboard states, Massachusetts, New York, Pennsylvania, Virginia, reminding the reader that in New Hampshire, Rhode Island, New Jersey, Maryland, Maine, Connecticut, were early gardens of great importance in their time. It is likely that the first mention of the word 'Garden' in any news from this continent was made by Captain John Smith, in his *Description of New England,* in 1614 ; 'sandy cliffes and cliffes of rock, both which we saw so planted with Gardens and Cornefields'. And again

'the winter is more cold in these parts wee have yet tryed nere the Sea side then we finde in the same height in Europe or Asia ; Yet I made a Garden upon the top of a Rockie Isle in forty-three and a half (latitude) foure leagues from the Main, in May, that grew so well, as it served us for sallets in June and July'.

' The fertility of the soil is to be admired at ', writes Higginson,

'as appeareth in the abundance of grass that groweth everywhere both very thick very long and very high in divers places. . . . But the abundant increase of corn proves this country to be a wonderment. Thirty forty fifty sixty are ordinary here. . . . They have tried

---

[1] One of the Founders and formerly one of the Vice-Presidents of the Garden Club of America, Honorary President of the Women's National Farm and Garden Association. Author of *Pages from a Garden Note-book, Chronicles of the Garden, Variety in the Little Garden, From a New Garden,* etc.

our English corn at New Plymouth Plantation, so that all our several grains will grow here very well and have a fitting soil for their nature. Our Governor hath store of green pease growing in his garden as good as ever I eat in England. . . . Our turnips parsnips and carrots are here both bigger and sweeter than is usually to be found in England with store of roots of great variety. Here are also store of pompions cowcumbers and other things of that nature which I know not, Also divers excellent pot-herbs grow abundantly among the grass as well as strawberry-leaves in all places of the country, and plenty of strawberries in their time, and pennyroyal, winter savory, sorrel, brookline, liverwort, carvel and watercresses ; also leeks and onions are ordinary and divers physical herbs. Here are also abundance of other sweet herbs delightful to the smell, whose names we know not, and damask roses, very sweet, and two kinds of flowers, very sweet, which they say are as good to make cordage or cloth as any hemp or flax we have. Excellent vines are here up and down in the woods. Our Governor hath already planted a vineyard with great hope of increase. Also mulberries, plums, raspberries, currants, chestnuts, filberts, walnuts, small nuts, hurtleberries and haws of white thorn, near as good as our cherries in England, they grow in plenty here '.

This then was the soil and climate, these the plants found by our earliest settlers in New England, this the surrounding, the yield which gave heart to those in a new land whose thoughts flew back with longing to the cultivation of gardens in England, to the English countryside. In his visits Josselyn made lists of plants which he had seen in America thus, with these headings :

' 1. Such plants as are common with us in England.
2. Such plants as are proper to the country.
3. Such plants as are proper to the country and have no names.
4. Such plants as have sprung up since the English planted and kept cattle in New England.
5. Such Garden Herbs among us as do thrive there and of such as do not '.

To quote Josselyn again in *New England's Rarities :* ' The plants in New England for the variety, beauty, number and vertues, may stand in competition with the plants of any countrey in Europe '. ' In the flower gardens of that period were to be found already, the White Satten, Gillyflower, Holly-hocks, the whole surrounded', says a writer in *Garden and Forest*,

'by a hedgerow composed of English Roses, Eglantine, Barberries and Privet for the planting of which Josselyn gives full directions. The Lilacs and Snowballs were reserved for the modest adornment of the dooryard as precious souvenirs of Old England'.

Not, however, until about 1650 were any gardens known to have been laid out in patterns of any kind. The settlers were too busy growing crops, too much occupied by the heavy duties of the pioneer to have leisure for the art which was to follow hard upon the cultivation of their farmlands. Governor Bradford, it is set down in *Old-Fashioned Gardens*, concludes somewhat tartly his account of gardening in Massachusetts by saying that

'the women went willingly into the field, which before would aledge weakness and inabilities whom to have compelled would have been thought great tiranie and oppression'.

Among the earliest New England gardens were those of Governor Winthrop at Salem and of Edmund Quincy at Milton near Boston. Of the latter there is a description, written about 1750, which shows it to have been a charming garden and to have had an orchard decoratively planned as in the Elizabethan time. Thomas Brattle of Cambridge, near Boston, had a notable place about 1792. Says Grace Tabor, 'Gamaliel Wayte's place in Boston had a court paved with blue and white cobblestone, and a garden of box with shrubs, not flowers, growing in the beds'. 'Roses, seringa, honeysuckle and snow-drops' are named as in these gardens much later. Downing in his *Landscape Gardening* comments on the beauty of the estate of Theodore Lyman at Waltham, near Boston, which stands untouched to this day.

It is impossible to go into detail concerning old gardens of New England; but I commend to the reader as the important books on Northern and Southern gardens, *Gardens of Colony and State* for the former, and *Historic Gardens of Virginia* for the latter, and *Old-Fashioned Gardening* on the whole subject.

Among the gardens which have been made to-day with great

feeling for the past is a highly interesting small one, that of the Mission House, Stockbridge, Massachusetts, the first house built in that town and now set up and perfectly furnished for its period. Miss Mabel Choate has restored this house and placed it in its garden as a Memorial to her parents, Mr. and Mrs. Joseph H. Choate. John Sergeant, builder of the house, was a teacher of the Indians in the year 1735 and the house dates from 1739. A simple but beautiful small dwelling, it has only one decorative architectural feature, the doorway of the illustration opposite page 261. But it is the garden around the house which more concerns us here; and this has been done after much study and with great success by Fletcher Steele, Esq., of Boston, one of our most distinguished landscape architects. The Mission House stands on a piece of ground of 120 by 150 feet on the old wide street of Stockbridge.

' It is close to the street and near one side of the lot. Between it and the highway is a small fenced-in herb garden. Behind the house is a little yard with woodshed, (weaving-room and garage) well and well-sweep and grape-arbour. Still further on is the caretaker's house, where once the barnyard would have been. Between street, house and barn is the old-fashioned garden with its straight walk lined with fruit trees and flower borders, its vegetable plots, bush fruits, and casual rose bushes and beds of striped grass '.

This garden of the Mission House is not a restoration but a recreating of an early American garden as it was supposed to exist. We have no actual authorities to turn to for such gardens, but must build on what we think those gardens were.

The Dutch settlers in New Amsterdam, later the city of New York, from 1640 on had each ' A patch of cabbages, a bit of tulips '. Adrian van der Donck's *Description of New Netherland*, in 1655, contains lists with such headings as these : ' Of Fruit Trees Brought Over from the Netherlands ', ' Of the Flowers ', ' Of the Healing Herbs ', and ' Of the Products of the Kitchen Garden '. Records show that the women of New Netherlands tended the vegetable and flower gardens themselves, and among the so-called Pennsylvania Dutch, really of German descent, in the central part of that state to-day where farms and gardens are in great perfection it is interesting to notice that tradition and custom both keep the women at work out of doors. Women there are constantly found with hoe and fork in hand; the milking too is their province.

'Long ago, the care of plants, such as needed peculiar care or skill to rear them, was the female province. Everyone in town or country had a garden. Into the garden no foot of man intruded after it was dug in the spring. I think I see yet what I have often beheld—a respectable mistress of a family going out to her garden in an April morning, with her great calash, her little painted basket of seeds, and her rake over her shoulders to her garden of labours. A woman in very easy circumstances and abundantly gentle in form and manners would sow and plant and rake incessantly'.

Manors, as large country estates were called, were granted to individuals between 1671 and 1701, and the gardens of those great houses are still, some of them, to be seen. Philipse Manor, the Van Cortlandt Manor at Croton-on-the-Hudson, where for generations were beautiful gardens; Sagtikos Manor at Islip, Long Island, Sylvester Manor on Shelter Island, a part of Long Island, with beautiful gardens of box and box trees of great age to-day. 'From these times', says Mrs. Luke Vincent Lockwood of the gardens of Sylvester Manor,

'flowers had a charming way of reappearing in the grassy hedges—grape hyacinths, with the delicious fragrance that the modern ones have lost, Stars of Bethlehem, Lady's Delights, tall red lily-like tulips, larkspurs from which the mid-Victorian ladies made little blue wreaths to put in their Bibles and Books of Beauty'.

Beautiful gardens were made on the banks of the Hudson River by men with goodly estates. Landscape gardening began early in this country, with the advent of the great Andrew Jackson Downing. In the three decades between 1825 and 1855, Downing, disciple of Repton, planned many beautiful places along the banks of the Hudson River and elsewhere, estates which still stand in wonderful dignity and beauty. Downing's book, *Landscape Gardening*, published in 1841, was for years a standard work. Frederick Law Olmstead, the next great land-scape architect, planner of parks and gardens, 'continued the traditions of Downing and was the first man in America to organize and practice his profession on a large scale'. Central

Park, New York, and many other parks in the large cities, as well as grounds and gardens of private properties, remain to show his genius.

Loudon's *Encyclopædia of Gardening*, published in 1834, makes mention of various aspects of American gardening from that year on. Mrs. Trollope wrote of the villa of Hyde Park on the Hudson in these words :

' Hyde Park is the magnificent seat of Dr Hosack ; here the misty summit of the distant Kaatskill begins to form the outline of the landscape ; and it is hardly possible to imagine a more beautiful place '.

All travellers were impressed by the magnificence of the trees here at that period, especially by the arborvitæ, the weeping willow and the Lombardy poplar.

At Fort Ticonderoga, New York, between Lake George and Lake Champlain, is the beautiful ' King's Garden ' of Mr. and Mrs. Stephen H. T. Pell. Mr. Pell has written for me the following paragraphs ending with the sonnet by Mrs. Gilchrist.

' The garden at Ticonderoga was laid out in 1756 under the instructions of Michel Chartier, afterwards Marquis de Lotbinière, probably by Captain de Pont le Roy, afterwards Chief of Engineers. It was named the Jardin du Roi, which, however, is not as romantic as it sounds as it means something like King's Highway and was reserved for the officers. It was probably originally a vegetable garden but the French maps of the period show that it was laid out in formal design. The American troops in 1775–77 cultivated the garden. When William Ferris Pell built his second house, the present pavilion, in 1826, he enclosed what had been the middle section of the old Jardin du Roi with a cedar hedge and following the old lines which were still discernible made a beautiful flower and vegetable garden out of it. The *Northern Traveller*, published in 1828, mentions it in the following terms :

" A little further east, and under the bank, is an old stone house, formerly a store belonging to the fort, and now occupied by the tenant of Mr. Pell, the proprietor of the whole peninsula of Ticonderoga. On a spot formerly occupied as the King's Garden, Mr. Pell has a fine garden, abounding in the choicest fruits imported from Europe, and transported from the celebrated nurseries of Long Island. Mr. Pell has been a very successful propagator of the locust tree, (Robinia Pseudo Acacia of Linnæus) thousands of which are growing on the grounds in the most flourishing manner : here is also the Magnolia Grandiflora, never before cultivated in so high a latitude ; the Horse Chestnut (Castanea Equinus), and upwards of 70 varieties of the Gooseberry from Europe. Here also we find the beautiful Catalpa, and the Liriodendron Tulipefera. The grounds are laid out with good taste, and are kept with care and in excellent order ".

During the long period when the family did not come to Ticonderoga and the house was turned into a hotel, the garden was entirely neglected. The hedge had practically disappeared, having been patched up with boards, and there was not much of the original garden to be seen when Mr. and Mrs. Stephen H. P. Pell bought off the other heirs in 1909.

The old garden was then rebuilt partly after the old French maps, a high wall of brick enclosing it. Miss Marian Coffin laid out a planting plan within the lines of the old garden and that is the garden as it exists to-day.

While not much of the original garden is there except the soil, it has been a garden for 176 years.

LE JARDIN DU ROI

On guard to hold the heights of Carillon
For that far king of France who banished them
To outposts of his realm, the tide to stem
Of Iroquois and English pressing on,
They longed for home, those pioneers of France,
Their dear land's gracious ways of sun and flowers ,
Garrisoned here through long, dull winter hours,
Or watching green spring tread a slow advance,
They made a garden, thinking of the lanes
And terraced greenery of old Versailles,
And in the sun, and through the warm June rains,
They smiled to see rose and French lily vie.
Their love of home it was that, blossoming,
Made fragrant here the garden of the King.

HELEN IVES GILCHRIST.'

To-day the King's Garden is a picture of grave and quiet beauty, the atmosphere of its own period fragrant within it. I lately saw this garden in the twilight of a summer's evening. A portico of the ancient house gives directly upon it. The whole garden is walled with brick, its centre a great *tapis vert* with a reflecting pool. The corners of the green space are marked by four magnificent elms, a seat beneath each tree. This tranquil central space of turf throws into telling relief the flowery sections of the garden which surround it. One notices particularly the beauty of an ox-blood red poppy with copper-coloured snapdragon, and along the high walls, below green creepers, are seen echinops' silver-blue balls rising above fronds of fern. In the beds too is scarlet verbena in profusion with the deep red of monarda didyma, a very dark red coreopsis and wine-coloured snapdragon. Great tangles too of Frau Karl Druschki roses, tall ageratum and salvia farinacea are there, while what one might almost call hills of superb phloxes in rich hues give deep colour to the picture. On a small marble tablet above a gate in the wall leading to an orchard are these words of Mrs. Montagu carved long ago but how pertinent to-day :

I MARVEL THAT THE
GREAT MEN
OF THE EARTH PREFER
TO REAP
THE IRON HARVEST OF WAR
TO THE RICH GIFTS OF
CERES.

That wise Quaker, William Penn, enjoined it upon those commissioned so to lay out the city of Philadelphia in 1682 that

' every house be placed, if the Person pleases, in ye middle of its place as to the breadth way of it, that so there may be ground on each side, for Gardens, or Orchards, or fields, yt it may be a greene Country Towne, wch. will never be burnt and will allwayes be wholesome '.

What more auspicious beginning for gardens ?

In Germantown, near Philadelphia, the houses had large grounds about them ; sometimes as much as twenty-five acres ; and the beautiful houses along the Delaware and Schuylkill Rivers, Stenton, and Chew House, were once surrounded by small parks. Some of these places remain almost as they were in Colonial days. Stenton, the beautiful mansion in Philadelphia, built in 1718, by James Logan, Chief Justice of the Supreme Court of Pennsylvania, has a charming garden, kept in order now by the Pennsylvania Society of Colonial Dames, who have restored both house and garden to their original condition. Andalusia dates from 1795, with its magnificent box and the walls of its vineries and its eight small ' stoke houses ' where were fires for the winter warmth of grapes ; Tockington with box brought from England in 1740 and whose descendants in vegetation are still there as is the garden's inheritor with her much loved collections of rare primulas and narcissi.

John Bartram's is a name familiar to all who know of botanical and gardening beginnings in this country. His house and garden, ' near the City of Philadelphia ', but now in the midst of it, constantly visited, were established in 1731 ; and here lived one who was our first great botanist, who was the friend and correspondent of men like Dr. Fothergill, Lord Petre, Collinson, Sir Hans Sloane and above all, Linnæus. In the garden to-day are some of the trees set there by Bartram, notably the Petre pear. Linnæus gave it as his opinion that John Bartram was the best self-made botanist known. His travels over this country to the limits then known were constant and fruitful. His garden became a place of pilgrimage for botanists from other parts of the world ; here he set out many indigenous trees and shrubs. ' A seat under an Ohio Buckeye (*Aesculus pavia*) around which once twined a luxuriant Tecoma was a favourite resort of Washington while he lived in Philadelphia '. Bartram was a member of the Royal Societies of London and Stockholm and his correspondence extended to the most distinguished savants of Europe. Linnæus, Collinson, Gronovius, Fothergill, Sir Hans Sloane, and many others were constantly receiving from him the productions of the New World ; and thousands of the finest trees in the parks of Europe have been raised from seeds sent from Bartram's Botanic Garden. In a letter to Colonel W. Byrd of Virginia in 1739, Bartram writes :

' I have made several successful experiments of joining several species of the same genus whereby I have obtained curious mixed colors in flowers, never known before '.

This was undoubtedly the first experiment in hybridizing made in this country. Bartram's garden was filled with native plants, and after him his two sons, John and William, continued his activities. Other notable botanic gardens there were but Bartram's was the first.

Benjamin Franklin, the friend of Bartram and of Peter Collinson, was usually at the bottom of any far-reaching and beneficent movement in this country. In 1785 he was partly responsible for the organization of the Philadelphia Society for Promoting Agriculture; and it is likely that this society played a part in founding the second oldest horticultural society in America, that of Pennsylvania, in 1827. Franklin thus made here the first organized beginnings of scientific study of agriculture and horticulture. He also took American apples to the British Court, where they were so much liked that from that time to this our apples have sold in England. In ' Poor Richard's Almanac' his fundamental knowledge of horticulture was thus used as a social admonition :

> ' I never knew an oft-transplanted tree
> Nor yet an oft-removèd family
> That throve so well as those that settled be '.

A nice echo of old gardens of Philadelphia was heard in the setting up of little gardens at the Sesqui-Centennial International Exposition in that city in the summer of 1926. Here the Women's Committee decided to reproduce eighteen of the old houses which stood a century and a half before upon High Street in Philadelphia, as the present Market Street was then known. The names of these buildings give the character of the street; the Friends' Meeting House, the Slate Roof House, the First Infirmary, the Indian Queen Inn, the Franklin Print Shop, Dr. Shippen's house, the Robert Morris and Washington houses, and the Girard Counting House. Five garden clubs of Philadelphia took the work of planting the gardens here, all in a very short time in spring. ' The street was divided into five sections laid out on blueprints. The clubs drew lots and each designed a garden or gardens appropriate to the houses in their section'. Due to building delays these gardens could not be actually made and planted till June 26th, but thanks to a great quantity of box lent to the committee for the summer, to the planting of many annuals which were in reserve and late perennials, to the careful moving of deciduous shrubs such as forsythia and viburnum, an effect of flowery gaiety was quickly got, and an atmosphere of an older day in gardens pervaded the green surroundings of the lovely little buildings.

Towards the end of the seventeenth century arose the great plantations of Virginia, owned by Englishmen accustomed at home to broad lands and well-kept parks. The garden for vegetables and flowers was always near the dwelling, and fenced; among the flowers grown in these Virginia gardens were ' gillyflowers, hollyhocks, sweet bryer, lavender cotton, white satten or honestie, English roses, fether-few (feverfew), comferie (comfrey) and celandien'. These earliest gardens of Virginia were all inspired by the Elizabethan gardens of England, and the boxwood gardens often had no flowers in them; but were designed to be patterns of green and nothing more. The flowers were planted in borders or in the so-called ' open knots '.

' Gardens ', says Mary Johnston the novelist in her exquisite preface to the best of all guides to these gardens, *Historic Gardens of Virginia*, ' began early in Virginia. At Varina in 1614, lived that wedded pair John Rolfe and Pocahontas, daughter of Powhatan. Rolfe experimented with tobacco and who shall say that in turn he did not show the young wonderful Indian woman how they set flowering bushes, how they made beds of flowers in Norfolk, in England? In 1625 on the banks of the James, George Sandys translated Ovid's *Metamorphoses*. Surely he had some planting of flowers about his door? In 1642 at Greenspring Sir William Berkeley had a garden of extent and colour. When, a little later, the King's men, the Cavaliers, fled with their families to Virginia from an England no longer Stuart, there came with them garden ideas and garden seeds and slips and cuttings. Washington and Mason, and Lee, Pendleton, Randolph, Cary, Madison, Monroe, Brodnax, Skipwith and many others—these men and their wives and sisters soon had their sun-lighted, their moonlighted gardens in Virginia. English squires, English and Scots merchants turned Virginia planters—near their houses of wood or of brick rise gardens with fruit trees, with old fair shrubs, with low formal beds of blossom, with paths winding or straight, with arbours and summer-houses. Jamestown is burned and Williamsburg arises and there are gardens still in Williamsburg, gardens of lilac and daffodils, violets and roses.

In 1732 leaving his own garden at Westover, William Byrd travels to Germanna and with Governor Spotswood takes " a turn in the garden . . . Three terrace walks that fall in slopes, one below another ". The valley is settled and gardens arise about the homes of Lewises and Campbells, and McDowells and Gays and Prestons and Wilsons and Alexanders and many another. And there is Greenway Court where the young surveyor George Washington walks and talks with Lord Fairfax. And in March 1774, in Northumberland county, young Mr. Philip Fithian, the tutor at Nomini Hall, " had the honour of taking a walk with Mrs Carter through the Garden. . . . We gathered cowslips in full bloom and as many violets. The English honeysuckle is all out in green and tender leaves ". Presently he rides to Mount Airy, in Richmond County, and finds " a large well-framed and beautiful garden, as fine in every respect as any I have seen in Virginia. In it stand four large beautiful marble statues ".'

In the time of Charles II there came to Virginia an English gentleman named Tayloe ; two generations later Mount Airy on the Rappahannock River was built by Colonel John Tayloe in 1747. To-day a brother and three charming sisters carry on the name and the ancestral tradition in this most beautiful of all Virginia houses, love and keep the garden, now much changed from its old state, but having still its glorious trees and terraces toward the river. ' The present owners of Mount Airy ', writes Miss Gresham,

' use the three sides of the bowling green for flowers, and also below the terraces to the brink of the hill. The borders of the bowling green are a glowing mass of jonquils, narcissi, iris in the spring. In summer these are followed by peonies, pansies, roses, poppies, hollyhocks, snapdragon, larkspur, phlox, Sweet William, Canterbury Bells, ragged robin and madonna lilies '.

The original plan of the gardens of Mount Airy, and their relation to the whole house was one of the finest ever made in America. The building itself, of brown and grey sandstone, a Palladian house, superb in beauty and dignity and perfect in condition to-day, has two smaller stone buildings flanking it, connected with the main house by covered curving passages. This group has a forecourt of turf, a terrace, with stone piers surmounted by the hospitable pineapple in stone, where the steps lead down from the terraced house—site to the entrance—drive and circle. In this circle stands an old sundial.

The other side of the great house has a green terrace, dropping to a bowling green: on either side of this, the original plan shows what might be called knot gardens; two squares geometrically planned for walks and flowers, and below these and the bowling green again was a walk on the axis of house and garden leading toward the river and a balanced design of eight squares on either side, perhaps outlined long ago with box and also flower-filled.

Words cannot convey the dignified beauty of this classic house, this magnificent house of Mount Airy. One feels in England there, and those who have been welcomed by the owners of the estate, who have sat beneath the portraits in the high-ceiled dining-room, who have sipped from little crystal glasses the rose-leaf cordial made by the ladies of the house from their own damask roses, have the feeling that here in Virginia is one of the most untouched of all the great places made by English families in our land.

As one thinks of the gardens of Virginia the word that comes to mind with that thought is always and ever 'box'. For in no gardens anywhere perhaps has the use of box over the years been so common, so generous, and so successful as in this state whose mild climate and clay soil give the conditions favourable to both the tree and dwarf box; and is there anywhere a plant whose scent carries the mind back into the past as does the smell of box? At Hickory Hill the box is remarkable both because of its magnificent growth and generous use. The original plan of Hickory Hill showed a central axis two miles long, as long as that of Versailles. The pear-shaped drive on the order of that at Mount Vernon, but far more important because of scale, may have been copied from that. The estate 'came into the possession of the Carter family on the 2nd of March, 1734, and was long an appendage to Shirley-on-the-James'. The garden was not made until 1820, but then were planted the cedar avenues, and the box bushes and trees, also the-pleached walk of box which runs through the centre of the garden whose trees (*buxus sempervirens*) are now more than thirty feet in height above a walk fifteen feet wide. . . . Another broad walk edged with dwarf box (*suffruticosa*) lies between flower-filled beds with low box hedges about them ; and here, writes Colonel Wickham the present owner, are some of the

' original roses brought by Anne Carter from Shirley in 1820 ; the Noisettes, Champney's Blush Cluster, Seven Sisters, La Touterelle and the ever-blooming Pink Daily. To the left extends a small maze of box, with beds of lilies of the valley, and hardy begonia, at the foot of tall magnolia trees. The inner circles of the maze contain, carefully cherished, La Reine, Dr Marx, Baron Provost, Rivers', George IV, the White Rose of Provence, and other old-fashioned remontant roses, planted by Mrs W. C. Wickham when she came as a bride in 1848 '.

At Brandon there is the long low house of old brick, a superb growth of trees fronting its pillared portico on the James River side. Box in waves and billows grows close to the house. The wide grass walk bordered by tall trees and lower shrubs leading from the house to the river's edge is the outstanding feature. But the glory is in the plan. No garden lies more superbly placed than this, and all its squares are bordered with cowslips and violets. Lilacs, Japanese quince and great trees, especially one huge pecan, were in young leaf and bud (when last I saw Brandon) with all the freshness and innocence of spring. No lovelier legacies were ever left to men than these gardens of Virginia.

It is an interesting fact that two of our Presidents have possessed a remarkable gift for landscape gardening, Thomas Jefferson and George Washington. Jefferson's own plan for Monticello was noble in scope and design. He took off the top of a mountain to get the site he needed for his fine house, and the view to the University of Virginia far distant, that beautiful group of his own designing. Washington's plans for the gardens and general planting of Mount Vernon were his own and drawn by his own hand.

I am happy to lay before the reader the following paragraphs concerning our beloved garden of General George Washington at Mount Vernon, lately sent me through the kindness of Colonel H. H. Dodge, the Director of the estate for The Ladies' Association of Mount Vernon, that choice group of American women, one from almost every state, whose happy privilege it is to care for this national possession. This memorandum, the work of Mr. Harold T. Abbott, is both fresh and authoritative. No garden is more dear to the hearts of Americans than this; in no spot can one family be more easily imagined in its own surroundings; and the First President's devotion to his garden is repeatedly shown by paragraphs in his letters and diaries. While the garden is familiar to every Englishman stationed or visiting in Washington, the account here gives certain details which may be welcome.

THE FLOWER-GARDEN AT MOUNT VERNON

Little documentary evidence is as yet available concerning the early days of the flower-garden at Mount Vernon, Virginia. The Diaries of General Washington give a number of references to the garden, and from these allusions we are obliged to draw our conclusions. The first of these references to the flower-garden in its present form is in the diary for February 4, 1786:

'Having assembled the Men from my Plantations, I removed to the garden Houses which were in the middle of the front walks to the extreme points of them; which were done with more ease and less damage than I expected, considering the height one of them was to be raised from the ground'.

The next information on the development of the garden is recorded for April 10, 1786. Washington mentions here the construction of the fence surmounting the wall.

'Began my brick work to-day, first taking away the foundations of the Garden Houses as they were first placed, and repairing the damages in the Walls occasioned by their removal; and also began to put up my pallisades (on the Wall)'.

The houses referred to are the seed house in the kitchen garden and the schoolroom in the flower-garden.

Washington's account of tree planting in the flower-garden gives one the impression that a portion of the garden was in the form of a nursery. His mention of 'nursery' in the following instance does not mean the experimental garden west of the Spinning House, where he was accustomed to try out small lots of seeds.

' Planted the young peach Trees which I brought from Mr. Cockburn's in the No. Garden, viz. 4 on the South border of the second walk (two on each side of the middle walk), 2 in the border of the walk leading from the Espalier hedge towards the other cross walk, and 3 under the South Walk of the Garden ; that is two on the right as we enter the gate and one on the left. The other Peach tree to answer it on that side and the two on the West Walk, parallel to the Walnut trees were taken from the nursery in the Garden '.

Monday, March 14, 1785. Again on April 1, 1785, Washington records :

' Grafted 12 Duke, 12 May Duke, and 12 black May heart Cherries and 12 Burgamy pears. The Cherries were chiefly on stocks wch. had been taken up a considerable time, and the roots covered with Earth. These Cherries and pears are planted on the left of the area leading from the Gate to the Green House in the following manner : next the cross walk are the Duke Cherries, then the May Duke, then the black May Heart, and lastly the Burgamy Pears. A peg is driven between each sort, the last being nearest the back Wall '.

The picture we receive, that along the north wall of the garden on axis with the gate walk, was the greenhouse. To confirm this viewpoint there is the earlier statement from the General in February 9, 1785 :

' Transplanted an English Walnut from the Corner near where the old School house stood to the opposite side wch. with the one that was moved in the fall, were intended to answer the two remaining ones, but from their size and age, I have little expectation of their living. Also moved the Apricots and Peach Trees which stood in the borders of the grass plots, which from the same causes litt'e expectation is entertained of their living. These were placed under the Wall in the North Garden on each side of the Green House, and an old pear tree was mo(ve)d at the same time into the lower square of the South Garden, from which less hopes of its living were entertained than of any of the others '.

The next record of tree planting in the garden is for February 11, 1786 :

' Transplanted the following trees to the following places in the North Garden, viz ; the first on the left, looking eastward from the garden house, along the walk in front of it, is a peach tree transplanted the 14th of last March from the Gardeners Nursery, to the South Side of the Walk by the English Walnuts. The 2d and 4th, on the same side are burgamy pears, grafted the first of April last year by the green House. The 3rd on the same side, is a black May heart cherry, grafted at the same time, in the same place. The 5th on the same side is a Duke cherry, Do. Do. The 3d tree from the same house, on the right Side (looking the same way) is also a Duke cherry, grafted as above. By the stumps of the Coronation Cherry, and Apricot, which were removed into the same garden on the 26th of last October, (not expecting either of them to live), I planted a white heart cherry; and one of the small cherries that used to grow in the walk, in front of the House; the White heart was placed by the stump of the Coronation Cherry '.

In June and July of 1786, Washington informs us that he has received seeds of various unusual plants grown in France. These seeds, the gift of André Michaux, Botanist to the Court of France, were prized treasures in those days. Michaux had been sent by the Court to establish a botanic garden on Long Island and, through the recommendation of Lafayette, he paid Washington a short visit at Mount Vernon in June 1786. From this time Washington does not allude to the flower-garden in any way according to the Diaries. Whatever changes have taken place since the days of the General, we do not know. Since the Mount Vernon Ladies' Association have been the owners of the estate, we do know that preservation has been their aim. The large boxwood hedges are original as far as we know. It is said that Washington obtained the plants from England. In front of the servants' quarters on each side of the palm house there are unique boxwood parterres. These hedges, about ninety-five years old, replace, on the original lines, hedges which were destroyed by the fire of 1835. On each side of the walk leading from the palm house to the gate, there are oak-leaf hydrangeas (*Hydrangea quercifolia*) said to have been planted by Lafayette during his visit in 1824. These shrubs are fine examples of this unusual variety of the hydrangea. During the latter part of June the fragrance from the snowy panicles is very marked in the vicinity of the garden. Not far from these two old shrubs and in the hedge extending towards the schoolroom, is a large sweetshrub (*calycanthus floridus*) claimed to be the gift of Thomas Jefferson. In front of the east end of the palm house is a *magnolia soulangeana*, said to have been the gift of Lafayette. In one of the curved perennial borders at the west end of the garden is an old *multiflora* rose planted by the General and named for his mother. This rose is a small semi-double white and is a profuse bloomer. Many rooted cuttings are sold at Mount Vernon each year. Another *multiflora*, around which has grown up a pleasant story, is the Nelly Custis rose. This shrub, possessing a good deal of the noisette character, is now growing in one of the beds of the east parterre. Two units of the flower-garden now used as rose gardens have symmetrically arranged members edged with boxwood, but each member varies in its use of plant materials. The rose beds are to consist of old roses, the more modern varieties giving place to the old types. Among the old roses now growing at Mount Vernon, there are : old Damasks, including the York and Lancaster ; the Scotch briers, Austrian Copper and Harrison's Yellow ; the centifolias, rugosas, and muska. In the spring the beds are brightened by clumps of tulips, hyacinths, pansies, narcissus, and many other familiar spring blooms. Later in the season, as the mass of perennials begin to lose colour, annuals are introduced to keep a continuing interest throughout the garden. The old true lavender (*lavandula vera*) acts as a strong accent in the rose beds. Its greyish foliage is a pleasing contrast to the more yellow tinge of the rose leaves. Perhaps the most interesting part of the garden, with the exception of the boxwood hedges, is the large expanse of perennial borders. It is the purpose of the Mount Vernon Ladies' Association to introduce into these borders specimens of all the old flowers with which Washington might have been familiar. Nowhere in the Diaries does the General mention the sort of herbaceous flowering plants which were growing or which he planted in his garden. During the summer months a number of the tubbed trees and shrubs are moved from the palm house to the garden. Among those now placed in prominent positions are : lemons, oranges, oleanders, agaves, a cycas, and crape myrtles. At the west end of the garden is the ' Schoolroom ', a small octagonal pavilion. It was here in this room, scarcely more than six feet in diameter, that George Washington Parke Custis and Nelly Custis received instructions from Tobias Lear. The house, situated as it is at the western end of the garden area, acts as a focal point for three major paths. Along the wall south of the school are a number of large fig bushes planted by Washington. These, as well as the fig trees in the kitchen garden, are vigorous and produce a great quantity of fruit. The old pear trees in the garden have all disappeared. It is, however, the aim of the Association to replace a number of the pear trees, using if possible varieties mentioned by the General.

South Carolina gardens were among the earliest. Those of Charleston and the plantations round about were the special pleasure of their owners.

‘ The first person who cultivated a garden on a large scale was Mrs Lamboll. About 1750 her garden was richly stored with flowers and other curiosities of nature as well as useful vegetables. She was followed by Mrs Martha Logan and Mrs Hopton. The former wrote at seventy, a treatise on gardening called *The Gardener's Kalendar*, which was published after her death in 1770 and as late as 1808 regulated the practice of gardening in and near Charleston. She was a great florist and uncommonly fond of a garden ’.

An important merchant of South Caroline, Henry Laurens, introduced into his garden in the same period ginger, Guinea-grass, the Alpine Ever-bearing strawberry, olives, limes, capers, also the white Chasselas grape. André Michaux, the French botanist, collecting plants for his government in 1786, created, ten miles out of Charleston, a botanic garden. . . . The William-sons’, later the Champneys’, garden contained ‘ every species of flowering tree and shrub, native and foreign, with pecan nut trees and pears ’. The gardens of Charleston were thus referred to in Flint’s *Geography and History of the United States :*

‘ The houses of the suburbs are for the most part surrounded by gardens, in which orange trees with most splendid ripe fruit, monthly roses in full bloom and a variety of other flourishing plants display themselves. Upon the walls and columns are climbing vines and a great number of passion flowers ’.

The Pride of India tree (*Melia Azedarach*) caught the attention of all travellers in Charleston and Savannah, as they saw it along the streets of these towns. William Logan of Stenton had among his correspondents John Hopton and Henry Laurens of Charleston. An excellent medical botanist of Charleston, Dr. Garden (for whom the Gardenia was named by Linnæus), wrote a *Flora Carolina*.

To-day, outside of Charleston, two gardens are greatly visited; one the garden of Middleton Place, the other the Magnolia Garden on the Ashley River, magnificent from mid-March with its towering trees of flowers, a glory of colour reflected occasionally in still black waters below. Magnolia-on-the-Ashley is the ancestral home of the Drayton family, and here to this day flower the great magnolias, the camellias, the crape myrtles. But it is the azaleas, some of them now 20 feet wide and 15 feet high, it is these banks of colour in flowers that are so amazing and so lovely. Set out eighty years ago by the Reverend John Grimke Drayton, who is said to have brought the first *azalea indica* to this country from the Orient, these gardens are now the delight of thousands every spring, who motor from afar to see them. The colour is indescribably fine ; imagine the soft yellow of the Banksia rose, the wisteria's lavender, with those other brighter hues of the great banks of azalea, the whole overhung by the mist of greyness from the darkness of the live-oak . . . ' Nothing ', says John Galsworthy, ' so free and gracious, so lovely and wistful, nothing so richly coloured yet so ghostlike, exists, planted by the sons of men. This is the most beautiful spot in the world '.

The gardens of the old plantations on the Cooper River, not so often seen, some of them fortunately known only to a few, are among the loveliest. Medway is one of these, another is Mulberry Castle. ' In the old days ', writes a friend,

' this region was honey-combed with gardens. Every plantation seems to have had a flower-garden for its lady. One has the ruins of a Temple of Love and of a vast water garden, now all overgrown '.

Plans of old gardens of early Spanish settlement in Florida show formal treatment, according to the European idea ; any other type would have been out of the question in a new and barbaric land, when walls must be built for protection from the Indian, as well as from the beasts of the forest. To-day in St. Augustine traces are everywhere of these little Spanish gardens ; old fig trees, guavas, limes, the Pride-of-India tree,

the camphor, crape myrtles which flower in June, palms of varying types, especially the palmetto—for the palm flourishes if
removed from the Atlantic winds—pecan trees, the indigenous
live-oak, the oleander, jasmines, azaleas, camellias as in Charleston further north. Everyone has a garden, fenced occasionally
with Spanish Bayonet, and one of the little town's chief charms
is its walled gardens, those walls often covered with *ficus repens*,
closest of all climbers. Annuals here prosper exceedingly in the
gardens, and roses, old roses like Belle of Portugal, Lamarck, the
Pink Daily; while the hedges are sometimes of Australian
cypress and sometimes of pittosporum, a rich subject for this
use. The roses of St. Augustine were always many; 'carnations
there were and heliotrope, blue and white violets, oleanders,
rosemary, lavender, honeysuckle, jessamine, iris, tulips, narcissus,
poppies', all these are there to-day too in the gardens in this
old (perhaps oldest) town of America.

Only in recent years have Americans generally had a realiza-
tion of the manner in which houses and gardens of the past
were slipping from them. In consequence a movement to save,
to rehabilitate, to restore, to reproduce is now in full swing.
The gardens mentioned or described in these pages such as
Mount Vernon, and that of the Old Mission House, at Stockbridge, are two notable examples of restoration and recreating,
and are of untold value to our people.

Looking backward into the history of our gardens several
observations may be made. One, that the persistent love of
beauty crops out in men and women under the most adverse
circumstances; another, that the leading men and women of
earlier times invariably had and loved their gardens; a third,
that garden history, like that of the race, repeats itself. We
have many variants on the older forms of plants, shrubs and
trees to-day, but ever and always there will be found in our
gardens the types beside hybrids from those types. The present
revival of interest in old roses is proof of this fact. An amateur
on the Hudson River has formed a superb collection of moss and
species roses; a small nursery in Maryland devoted to these
same plants has lately been started by two women, and a committee on old roses has sprung up within that very active body,
the American Rose Society.

HERB GARDEN, MISSION HOUSE, STOCKBRIDGE, MASSACHUSETTS

As for old flowers and plants, Alice Morse Earle gives a nice list of seeds advertised for sale in the *Boston Evening Post* of March 1760 :

' Hollyhock, Purple Stock, White Lewpins, Africans, Blew Lewpins, candy-tuff, cyanus, pink, wallflower, double larkin-spur, venus navelwort, brompton flock, princess feather, balsam, sweet-scented pease, carnation, sweet williams, annual stock, sweet feabus, yellow lewpins, sunflower, convolvulus minor, catchfly, ten week stock, globe thistle, globe amaranthus, nigella, love-lies-bleeding, casent hamen, polianthus, canterbury bells, carnation poppy, india pink, convolvulus major, Queen Margrets (adding that the Queen Margrets are our asters) '.

Coming now to the gardens of to-day let me preface some descriptive paragraphs by the following. In the second issue of *Garden and Forest*, in 1888, the sentences occur under the heading, ' The Future of American Gardening '.

' It is not surprising that few examples of the gardeners' art in its highest development should be met with in America, especially in the more recently settled portions of the country. Even where the designing and planting of a garden are good the element of time is needed to produce that ripeness and repose which are so satisfying to the contemplative mind. . . . A new country or one of shifting population not only lacks the interest which accompanies long continued human association but nature itself is not subdued into that tranquil and homelike aspect which is won only where generation had succeeded generation, each impelled by a strong local attachment to its birthplace to conserve and develop its native beauties with affection and intelligence. . . . The future of gardening in America then is bright with promise. Our country offers to the landscape gardener wonderful advantages in its endless variety of scenery, the unrivalled richness of its Flora and such diversity of soils and climate that somewhere within its borders every extra-tropical plant will grow. The imagination can conceive of nothing more lovely and refreshing than spring in New England when vegetation bursts suddenly forth from the restraints of a long winter ; nothing more glorious than the colour that flames through New England woodlands when trees and shrubs and humbler plants are preparing for their season of rest. And what a field for the artist is offered in the warm rich valleys of the southern Alleghanies, the home of the most beautiful deciduous forest of the world. And as trees and shrubs which have developed under the same sky, blend in softer and more perfect harmonies of colour than those brought together from different climates and continents, here where the American forest culminates in its great beauty and richness of composition, the artist capable of using all this wealth of vegetation will find his greatest opportunity. . . . And here too he can collect, if Nature has not supplied him with sufficient material for his pictures, the plants of all the temperate zones—the evergreens of China and Japan, the Rhododendrons of the Himalayas, the trees of Europe and the Conifers from the highlands of Mexico. Another ideal garden could be made on our north-west coast where plants which luxuriate in the moist regions of the temperate zone would be at home ; while in southern California could be gathered the trees of the Mexican plateau, of the Mediterranean basin, of Australia, and of all the dry countries of the world and here gardens might be made surpassing in richness and variety of interest even those of the Riviera '.

This prophecy of high knowledge and enthusiasm and of more than forty years ago was written by no less a pen than that of Professor Charles Sprague Sargent. He lived to see his words take form in gardens, some of them to-day of supreme beauty ; to see a great engulfing wave of garden interest sweep the country ; to see the Arnold Arboretum, his wonderful garden of trees and shrubs, whose loveliness is mainly due to his knowledge and labour, a place of pilgrimage not only for Americans but for devotees of botany, arboriculture and horticulture from all parts of the world.

Two modern gardens I shall now describe in the hope that these may convey some impression of what exists to-day in America, The first is a small town garden in Pasadena, California, the garden of Mrs. W. W. Phillips, landscape architect. This garden is really minute. The piece of ground whereon its three divisions lie is 172 feet by 50. It lies between two other town lots of about the same size. The house here is a little one, lived in only by the owner. The little garden has much more chance for charm than the large ; and when a very little one like this of Mrs. Phillips' is showered with pleasant adverbs by all who see it, a triumph has surely been achieved. The decision to wall or hedge the whole space stands as the first reason for its success ; next the judicious spacing of the three small gardens within these walls and the long narrow walk to the right connecting them as one walks through, and last the decorating of these spaces by beautiful and ingenious planting and the perfect setting about of plants in pots. Those who have seen these garden pictures in March or April will bear me out when I declare it to be one of the most fascinating of all the small gardens we possess. The short walk from the street to the house is flanked by two parterres whose clipped hedges are of Italian myrtle. The parterres in spring are masses of daffodil and tulip. Emerging from the dining-room at the back of the house (the building practically filling the width of the property) one comes upon a little terrace and crosses it to step immediately into the first little garden, French in feeling. This first garden is severely formal. Box and ivy lend their dark greens, standard roses in each square of this very simple design give April brilliance of colour, while the curving edges toward the centre of each bed are outlined by irises. A stone ornament on its pedestal completes the box-edged brick-paced little garden, focussing its beauty in fit fashion. This ornament is a basket of fruit in stone, while the four standard plants in each quarter are Los Angeles roses.

To the south of this first garden and along the wall to the west are borders of such plants as calla lilies, white nicotines and yellow hemerocallis, with a border of pale-coloured cyclamens. The pepper tree of the patio has its sphere of influence of light and shadow upon this garden too : box bushes accent the corners of the borders, a delightful Spanish seat is recessed against a wall among the flowers, and in the angle of darkly-painted fence with a festoon-like top stands a crimson-flowering peach tree.

The central garden is one of pink roses flanked by hedges of heliotrope, and of yellow roses and calla lilies, the last two growing together. The rich pittosporum fills in the designed space at the south end of this garden ; a recessed piece of sculpture stands against this green background ; the floor is brick-paved, unlike that of the two gardens on either side.

The Spanish garden has a beauteous arrangement for water, a fine octagonal pool. Here are petunias which have succeeded the primula malacoides flowering in the pots on the basin's edge. At the left is a bay tree in a large pot, while to the right are standard roses. Blue primulas also rise from other pots near a sculptured figure against the wall; and potted oleanders are in evidence here. One lemon and one orange tree are set most judiciously in the paving. These, having had careful clippings, are in beautiful condition, and the earth beneath the little trees is planted to rincospermum jasminoides, whose white flowers are very fragrant and appear with the blossoming of lemon and orange. Beyond these three gardens, the walk is covered for all its length by a pergola of rough wood, saplings forming the cross-beams of its light roof, the whole flanked to the north by a hedge of clipped cypress 15 feet high.

The second garden, that near Philadelphia, is the possession and delight of Mr. and Mrs. J. Franklin McFadden, the garden of Ithan House at Rosemont. This part of Pennsylvania was settled largely by Welsh and the farm in which the house and garden stand is Radnor Valley Farm. The garden has long called forth admiration as unique in situation and in beauty. The house stands at the edge of a steep slope running down to Ithan Creek, a fine house of the blue limestone of the region, Pennsylvania Colonial in type, the garden falling from its house in a series of terraces and at the foot of the fall spreading out into what has been named the Fan Garden, descriptive of its form. Mr. McFadden has given me in almost the words below a description of this plan and of the planting.

The estate was planned in 1913 by Olmsted Brothers while Charles Borie laid out the flower-garden; the whole measuring from the house terrace to the edge of the fan about 340 feet, with four different levels beautifully treated for variety and with good planting. The upper level is the House Terrace, 27 feet wide; a ramp with brick-paved descent (as slippery as any in England with moss and weather!) leads to the Box Terrace about 9 feet below, where the old box is magnificent in growth and condition; 7 feet lower is the Sunken Garden. Below this again and eight feet down comes the Rose Garden; three feet lower still is the Fan Garden. The dominant feature of the garden is the centre axis with its two lines of evergreens. On the Box Terrace on either side of this line and close by the wall are two tall arbor-vitæ and in the Sunken Garden two on each side at the two ends of that garden; lower down stand four very tall Retinosperas, about 25 feet high ; other old aborvitæ at the edge of the pool continue the line of lofty evergreens, and an opening in the trees by the stream below (Ithan Creek) carries the eye to the field beyond, fringed with deciduous trees. When the garden was first made it could all be seen from the house terrace. To correct this a row of white dogwood trees was planted along the edge of the second or Box Terrace. The same objective, mystery and new views and effects wherever one went, led to the making of the two green rooms of the Sunken Garden with arborvitæ hedges. These 'rooms' are roughly 40 by 30 feet. The garden on its long axis is almost east and west from lower to higher levels.

The north side of the Sunken Garden is bounded by a pergola of white wood pillars hung with climbing roses and the walk slopes gradually to the foot. Outside of the pergola to the north are many Japanese flowering cherries. Beneath the pergola posts are narrow beds with ferns on the shady north side, and Carolina phlox and aquilegia on the south or sunny side. On the south side of the Sunken Garden, which is on a higher level than the Pergola Walk, is a pleached walk or alley with two varieties of Japanese crabs ; in May these give fragrant bloom for two weeks. This walk ends in a square with four Norway maples, one at each corner, making a shady place. The steps from the end to the Sunken Garden are now almost entirely covered with moss and the walks under the trees are practically all moss from the shade and acid of the crab-apples. A low hedge of common barberry borders the stone coping of the dry wall on that side of the garden.

From the Sunken Garden a semicircular sloping terrace leads to the level of the pool and Rose Garden. This sloping place, with central steps of stone, is planted with hemlocks and rhododendrons and various semi-wild plants. The pool is surrounded with irregular paving of reddish stone with small rock things like tunica growing between. This pool has water-lilies and a few cat-tails. The whole length of the central walk from the top to the bottom of the garden is edged with dwarf box (*suffruticosa*) 4 feet high and 2¼ thick and edging the beds under the perpendicular dry wall is more old box, now about seventy years old.

265

On either side of the Rose Garden are two alleys of white dogwood which in spring are lovely and in summer part of the scheme to make a shaded walk entirely around the garden. This walk is carried on on the fourth terrace or Fan Garden by Oriental planes on the three sides of the Fan Garden. (I think these very poor trees for the purpose as they are the last out and first home, writes Mr. McFadden.) The east end of the Rose Garden has a five foot arborvitæ hedge, a little dull and not so good for the roses as it keeps out air. Climbing roses are in a circle at each side of this garden growing on high-hooped supports. Some of the rose beds have been replaced with grass. The Fan Garden has a tall hemlock hedge. This is the cutting and perennial garden. The general idea is that beginning with the foot of the steps from the Sunken Garden to the Rose Garden a fan is opened out, the wider part of the fan holding the flower-beds of this garden. The wall below the House Terrace is dry and perpendicular, planted in many places with alpines and here and there ivy and large-flowering clematis while roses fall over as well. The wall at the west end of the Sunken Garden is battened with a gentle slope and the stones so set as to allow of planting in the crevices. Here cerastiums, aubretias, alyssum saxatile, aquilegia and phlox subulata flower under the masses of white dogwood bloom in spring. Pink dogwoods arch the centre steps from the Sunken Garden to the Rose Garden and again at the steps from the Rose to the Fan Garden and are effective there against the cool green of cedar.

At the very foot of this whole garden on its slope and across a driveway, is the Shrub Garden through which runs Ithan Creek. The paths are broad and converge upon an open space where stand two large oaks, one a magnificent white oak 12 feet in circumference. An old sundial is in the centre of this open space. In 1913 all this was an open field with oaks and beeches; now it is a continuation of the garden which from the end nearest the house gradually grows less formal till it ends at the stream with Nature alone in charge. There is of course a long vista from the sundial upwards towards the house, some 600 feet. Shrubs best fitted for the climate are used in the Shrub Garden together with flowering trees such as early magnolias, and laburnums. ' Like all shrub planting', writes the owner, ' the distances apart for the individual shrubs and trees were much too short and the effect would have been better with half as many. It was the old theory of plant thickly and thin later. I have yet to meet the man or woman who did not do the first or did the second '.

For ornament or accessory in the gardens of Ithan House, there are seats of old teak, some lead vases, old oil jars from New Orleans brought long ago from France; all as rich and mellow as the garden itself, seeming to have grown with it.

Let no one in England speak the last word on American gardens until they shall have seen this, one of our best in a comparatively new land,—seen it too in that time of supreme loveliness, the American spring.

To-day wherever the traveller in America may find himself, east, west, north, south, he will never be far removed from some garden worth the seeing. The gardens of Florida, as for example at Mountain Lake Club, in Palm Beach, at and near Jacksonville, the gardens of Georgia and the Carolinas—modern gardens—are many and most lovely. Well-designed, delightfully planted, always with a feeling for suitability of locality, they have often a sensitiveness to beauty which is quite enthralling. I venture to say that taste in the good present-day garden here has never been surpassed in gardens anywhere. We have had all the world to draw upon for suggestion, we have by no means always imitated. Our variety of climate, soil and plant subject is limitless. As an imaginative people it would be strange if in the past years with the *furor hortensis* raging on all sides we had not accomplished something good in gardens. In the Pacific North-west are delightful gardens, in Portland, in Seattle; here conditions are like those of England, the heaths and rhododendrons are at home. Around San Francisco are gardens unparalleled for beauty. Those of Santa Barbara have long been renowned for the same quality. In Lake Forest near Chicago are gardens great and small, some of incomparable loveliness. Cleveland and Detroit gardens are legion, among them those of major importance and charm. No garden unit is more impressive than that of Cornish, New Hampshire, where a group of sculptors, architects, painters, writers have created such gardens as reflect their own atmosphere. Newport's gardens are of many varying types adapting themselves to the lives led by their owners from the small quiet garden of great charm to the highly formal and sumptuous one. Everyone knows of the outburst of spring beauty in the gardens of Long Island, gardens superbly planned and planted, and which thread those shores like jewels. Here are dogwood, wisteria, azalea, forsythia, lilac, philadelphus, with tulip, iris and every early flower in ' bright array '. These gardens, with a soft climate and perfect care, hold their own in rivalry with those of England in everything but age. Boston, Philadelphia, and Baltimore, seats of our earliest gardening, still more than hold their own and everywhere around these cities are their enchanting pleasaunces ' spreading to the moonlight '.

Have I permitted our eagle to flap his wings too noisily ? I hope not ; but as an antidote let me touch upon the little garden in America. As for this, our suburban type, it is sadly alike for the most part. It is easy to see why this standardization has entered even into the garden ; it is because of the great amount of printing which has been done on gardening, much of it dull and stereotyped ; it is because many are more ready to imitate than to think. Certain horticultural plagues have swept through this country from time to time ; once it was spirea van Houttei which clothed the land as with a blanket ; now hydrangea arborescens seems to be an obsession. Set out in unimaginative fashion the eye turns away for relief, as it does too from the masses of Crimson Rambler and now from that even brighter and therefore more fatal subject, Paul's Scarlet Climber, when these hang in unmeaning curtains of colour in a place where they are simply a spot. The bird bath of concrete, the seat of concrete in more or less classic design have become commercialized in this country, to the immense detriment of taste in the little garden. With these forces of a modern time working against the sweeter side of gardening, there will still be found however among the lesser types, here and there, a plot that is a delight, that shows individuality, that has a touch of the owner's spirit and ability to plant, to place, to grow well. The garden movement spreads apace. Garden clubs are legion, since the founding of the Garden Club of

LOOKING SOUTH IN THE GARDEN OF ITHAN

America in 1913, whose objects are to stimulate the knowledge and love of gardening among amateurs; to share the advantages of association, through conference and correspondence in this country and abroad; to aid in the protection of native plants and birds; and to encourage civic planting. The influence of this group of women, looked to as most active instigators of the best gardening in their localities, cannot be overestimated and spreads to-day for good into every town and village. From our gardening forebears, English, Dutch, Spanish, we have a great inheritance of interest in this art, an art which, with Maurice Hewlett, I hold is almost divine.

Sources for this chapter are as follows and are gratefully acknowledged:

The Encyclopædia of Gardening; J. C. Loudon; Longmans Green, London.
Old-fashioned Gardening; Grace Tabor; McBride; New York, 1925.
Gardens of Colony and State ; Mrs. Luke Vincent Lockwood; published for The Garden Club of America, by Charles Scribner's Sons, New York, 1931.
Historic Gardens of Virginia; edited by Edith Tunis Sale; published for the James River Garden Club, by the William Byrd Press, Richmond. Va.
Bulletins of the Garden Club of America; Mrs. T. H. B. McKnight, Editor.
Cyclopædia of American Horticulture; 6 Vols.; L. H. Bailey; Macmillan and Co.
Old Time Gardens ; Alice Morse Earle; Macmillan.
Portraits of Philadelphia Gardens ; Bush-Brown; Dorrance.
Chapter by Professor F. A. Waugh, 'Landscape Architecture in North America', in *A History of Garden Art*, by Marie Luise Gothein; J. M. Dutton and Co., New York.
History of the Massachusetts Horticultural Society; 1829–1878; Boston; printed for the Society.

APPENDIX I

(Abbrevation: B. & H.:=Britten and Holland *Dictionary of English Plant Names*, 1878.)

Adderstong: Ophioglossum vulgatum or Arum maculatum (B. & H.).
Affody: Narcissus Pseudo-narcissus.
Appyl: Apple: Pyrus Malus: and garden varieties.
Asche tre: Ash: Fraxinus excelsior.
Auans: Geum urbanum, Avance or Avens (B. & H.).
Betony: Stachys Betonica.
Borage: Borrago officinalis.
Bryswort: Bruisewort, Brusewort, or Brisewort: Bellis perennis, Saponaria officinalis or Symphytum officinale (B. & H.).
Bugu: Bugle: Ajuga reptans (B. & H.).
Bygu: Bigold: Chrysanthemum segetum (B. & H.).
Calamynte: Calamintha officinalis.
Camemyl: Chamomile: Anthemis nobilis.
Carsyndylls? 'Cars or Carses: cress' (B. & H.), a name applied to many cruciferous plants.
Centory: Great Centaury: Centaurea nigra and Little Centaury: Erythræa centaurium Centaury: C. negra or E. centaurium (B. & H.).
Clarey: Clary: Salvia sclarea.
Comfery: Comfrey: Symphytum officinale.
Coryawnder: Coriander: Coriandrum sativum.
Cowslippe: Cowslip: Primula veris.
Dytawnder: Dittander and Dittany: Lepidium latifolium, or Origanum Dictamnus (B. & H.).
Egrimoyne: Egremoyne: Agrimony: Agrimonia Eupatoria.
Elysauwder: Smyrnium Olusatrum: Alysaunder (B. & H.).
Feldwort: Felwort and Fieldwort: Gentiana Amarella (B. & H.).
    Feltwort: Verbascum Thapsus (Mullein) (B. & H.).
Floscampi? Lychnis Flos-cuculi: or Lychnis diurna: Campion?
Foxglove: Digitalis purpurea.
Fynel: Fennel: Fœniculum vulgare.
Garleke, Garlick. Allium sativum or Allium ursinum (B. & H.).
Gladyn: Iris fœtidissima or Iris Pseudacorus (B. & H.).

[1] From 'A Fifteenth Century Treatise on Gardening'. *Archæologia.* By kind permission of the Honble. Lady Cecil.

APPENDIX

Gromel: Gromwell: Lithospermum officinale.

Growdyswyly: Growndyswyly: Groundswyll: Groundsel: Senecio vulgaris.

Hasel tre: Hazel tree: Corylus Avellana.

Haw thorn: Hawthorn: Cratœgus Oxyacantha.

Henbane: Hyoscyamus niger.

Herbe Ion: A variety of Hypericum or St. John's Wort.

Herbe Robert: Geranium Robertianum.

Herbe Water: Herb Walter. Cannot identify.

Hertystonge: Hartystonge: Hart's tongue: Scolopendrium vulgare.

Holyhocke: Althæa rosea or Malva sylvestris or Althæa officinalis.

Honysoke: Honeysuckle: Lonicera periclymenum.

Horehound: Marrubium vulgare.

Horsel: Horselle: Horsehele: Inula Helenium (B. & H.).

Hyndesall?: Hind-heal. In Gerard's appendix it is entered 'hynd-heele is Ambrosia'. Many plants were known as Ambrosia, Chenopodium, Botrys and Ambrosia maritima and Teucrium scorodonia (B. & H.).

Hyndberry was a name for Rubus Idæus. Hind is a local name in Norfolk for a kind of sedge: Carex divisa?

Langbefe, generally supposed to be Helminthia echioides, but Turner (Lib.) intends it for Echium vulgare (B. & H.).

Lavyndull: Lavandula vera.

Leke: leek: Allium porrum.

Letows: Lettuce: Lactuca sativa.

Lyly: Lily. Lilium candidum and other species of Lilium.

Lyverwort: Agrimonia Eupatoria, Anemone Hepatica or Marchantia Polymorpha (B. & H.).

Merege. Cannot identify, ? Apium graveolens.

Moderwort: Motherwort: Artemisia vulgaris or Leonurus Cardiaca or Lysimachia nummularia (B. & H.).

Mouseer: Mouse ear: Hieracium Pilosella or Cerastium triviale (B. & H.).

Myntys: Mint. Various species of Mentha (B. & H.).

Nepte: Nep or Neppe or Nept: Nepeta Cataria or flowerheads of Lavandula vera or a turnip (B. & H.).

Oculus *Christi*: Salvia verbanaca (B. & H.).

Orage: Atriplex hortensis: Arage or Orage.

Orpy: Orpies: orpine or orpyn: Sedum Telephium.

Ownyns and Oynet: Onion—Allium cepa.

Parrow. Cannot identify, ? mistake for Yarrow.

Pelyter: Pellitory: Parietaria officinalis.

Percely: Perselye: parsely: Petroselinum sativum.

Pere : Pear : Pyrus communis and all its garden varieties.
Peruynke : Periwinkle : Vinca major and V. minor.
Primrole : Primrose : Primula vulgaris or Ligustrum vulgare or
    Bellis perennis (B. & H.).
Polypody : Polypodium vulgare.
Pympernold : Pimpernel. Pimpinella saxifraga—Poterium sangui-
    sorba. Prunella vulgaris or Anagallis arvensis (B. & H.).
Radysche : Radish : Raphanus sativus.
Redenay. Red Ray : Lolium perenne.
Rewe : Rue : Ruta graveolens.
Rose : Rosa, red and white.
Rybwort : Ribwort : Plantago lanceolata.
Saferowne : Saffron : Crocus sativus.
Sage : Salvia officinalis.
Sanycle : Sanicle : Sanicula Europæa.
Sauerey : Savory : Satureja hortensis or Satureja montana.
Scabyas : Scabious, varieties of Scabiosa.
Seueny : Seniue : Sinapis nigra, S. Alba or S. arvensis.
Sowthrynwode : Southernwood : Artemisia abrotanum.
Sperewort : Spearwort : Ranunculus Flammula.
Spynage : Spinach ; Spinacia oleracea.
Strowberys : Strawberries : Fragaria vesca.
Stycheword : Stichewort Stellaria Holostea (B. & H.).
Tansay : Tansy : Tanacetum vulgare.
Totesayne : Tutsan : Hypericum Androsæmum (B. & H.).
Tuncarse : Town cress : lepidium sativum.
Tyme : Thyme : Thymus serpyllum.
Valeryan : ' A general name for Valeriana, especially V. officinalis,
    also Polemonium cœruleum (B. & H.). or Centranthus ruber '.
Verueyn : Vervain : Verbena officinalis.
Violet : Viola : generally V. odorata.
Vynys and Vyne tre : Vine. Vitis vinifera.
Walwort : Parietaria officinalis or Sedum acre or Sambucus Ebulus
    or Cotyledon umbilicus (B. & H.).
Warmot : Wormwood : Artemisia Absinthium.
Waterlyly : Water lily : Nymphæa alba or Nuphar luteum.
Weybrede : Plantago major.
Woderofe : Woodruff : Asperula odorata.
Wodesour : Woodsour : Oxalis acetosella or Berberis vulgaris
    (B. & H.).
Wurtys or Wortys : Brassica oleracea.
Wyldresyl : Teazel : Dipsacus sylvestris or D. fullonum.
Ysope : Hyssop : Hyssopus officinalis.

APPENDIX II. BIBLIOGRAPHY

(Arranged chronologically. In the case of more than one author's books being published during the same year the authors are listed alphabetically. Translations are listed under the name of the translator. The titles of books published after 1550 are given as briefly as possible. On account of their numbers it is impossible to include modern books, i.e. *those published in Victorian and subsequent times.)*

1495. BARTHOLOMÆUS ANGLICUS. De proprietatibus rerum.
(The seventeenth book of the above—containing nineteen chapters—is on herbs. It was the first original work on plants by an English writer to be printed, and the woodcut at the beginning of the book was probably the first botanical illustration to be printed in an English book. There is the following note on a slip in the copy of this edition in the British Museum. ' This is generally considered to be the finest copy known of a work which is certainly the *chef d'œuvre* of Winkin de Worde's press. The paper on which it is printed is said to be the first ever made in England for the press. *See* Douce, ii. 278, Dibdin Typt. Ant. ii. 310 '.)

1535. Bartholomæus de Proprietatibus Rerum. Londini in Ædibus Thomæ Berthelete Regii Impressoris.

1582. Batman uppon Bartholome His Booke De Proprietatibus Rerum. Newly corrected, enlarged, and amended . . . London. Imprinted by Thomas East dwelling by Paules Wharfe.
(The book was first printed at Basle about 1470, and went through at least fourteen editions before 1500. Besides the English and French translations, it was also translated into Spanish and Dutch.)

?1503. IN THIS BOOKE is Conteyned the names of yᵉ bailifs Custos mairs and sherefs of the cite of londō . . . wyth odur dyuers mat's good and necessary for euery Citezē to understond and knowe.

?1521. Second edition.
(Contains a small section on gardening.)

1516. THE GRETE HERBALL. Imprinted at London in Southwark by me Peter Treveris. MDXVI the XX day of June. (Described by Ames. No copy in any of the chief British libraries and no other record of it.)

?1525. The Grete herball which is translated out ye Frensshe into Englysshe. With the mark of Peter Treveris. Undated.
(Mentioned by Hazlitt, who ascribes the date 1525–6. No other record of it.)

1526. The grete herball, which geveth parfyt Knowledge and understandyng of all maner of herbes and there gracyous vertues. . . . Also it geveth full parfyte understandynge of the booke lately printed by me (Peter Treveris) named the noble experiens of the vertuous handwarke of Surgery. Imprentyd at London in Southwark by me peter Treveris. In the yere of our Lorde god MDXXVI. the XXVII day of July.

1527. The grete herball. MDXXVII. 18 April. (Mentioned by Ames.)

1529. The grete herball. . . . Imprynted by me Peter Treveris. MDXXIX the XVII day of Marce.

T   273

1539.   The great herball newly corrected. Londini in edibus Thome Gybson.
MDXXXIX.
(This edition contains no cuts.)

1550.   Edition mentioned by Ames & Pulteney. No other record.

1561.   The greate Herball . . . newly corrected and diligently oversene.
MCCCCCLXI. Imprynted at London in Paules churchyarde at the
signe of the Swane by Jhon Kynge. MDLXI.

1523.   'FITZHERBERT'S HUSBANDRY.' Here begynneth a newe tra&e or trea-
tyse moost profytable for all husbande men : and very frutefull for all
other persons to rede. Imprinted at London in Fletestrete by Rycharde
Pynson printer vnto the Kynges noble grace. With priui- lege to hym
graunted by our sayd souerayne lorde the Kynge.
Subsequent editions (?)1525, 1532, 1534, 1537, 1546, 1548, 1560, 1562,
1576, 1598, 1767.
(Commonly known as FitzHerbert's Husbandry. In the British
Museum catalogue it is suggested that John FitzHerbert (Sir Anthony
FitzHerbert's brother) was the author. See reprint of the treatise by
W. W. Skeat printed by the English Dialect Society in 1882 and
paper read by Sir Ernest Clark before the Bibliographical Society in
1896.)

1525.   HERE BEGYNNETH a new mater . . . an Herball Imprynted by me
Rycharde Banckes dwellynge in London . . . ye XXV day of Marche,
MCCCCC & XXV.
(Formerly this book was frequently ascribed to Walter Cary. In
Notes and Queries, March 29, 1913, Mr. A. L. Humphreys proved
conclusively that this supposition was erroneous.)
Later editions issued by various printers, 1526 (only known copy in
Cambridge University Library), 1530, 1532–1537, 1530, 1535, 1540
(all approximate dates assigned in British Museum catalogue), 1541,
1546 (only known copies of the two latter in Bodleian Library),
1548 (only known copy in library of the Manchester Medical Society),
1550, 1552 (approximate date assigned in British Museum catalogue),
two editions mentioned by Ames, one published by Anthony Kitson
and the other by Richard Kele), 1550 (' gathered by Anthonye Askham '), one printed by Wyllyam Powell and the other by Jhon Kynge,
1555–1561 (approximate date assigned by Mr. H. M. Barlow), edition
printed by John Kynge.

1527.   LAURENS ANDREWE. The vertuose boke of Distyllacyon . . . by
Master Jherom bruynswyke. And now newly Translate . . . Imprinted at London by me Laurens Andrew . . . MCCCCXXVII
[*sic*] the XVII daye of Apryll. Second edition MCCCCCXXVII. the
XVIII daye of Apryll.
(This edition, although professedly printed a day later, varies considerably from the preceding.)

?1530.   MACER'S HERBAL . . . Translated out of laten into Englysshe . . .
R. Wyer, London.

BIBLIOGRAPHY

?1535. A newe Herball of Macer . . . R. Wyer.

1538. WILLIAM TURNER. Libellus de Re Herbaria novus . . . Londinii apud Ioannem Bydellum . . . 1538.
(Reprint edited and with life of author by B. D. Jackson. London, 1877.)

1544. Historia de Naturis Herbarum Scholiis et Notis Vallata. Printed at Cologne.
(Mentioned by Bumaldus but not otherwise known.)

1548. The names of herbes in Greke, Latin, Englishe, Duche and French with the commune names that Herbaries and Apotecaries use. . . . Imprynted at London by John Day & Wyllyam Setes.
(Reprint edited by J. Britten, published for the English Dialect Society, 1881.)

1551. A new Herball . . . Imprinted at London by Steven Myerdman . . . 1551.

1562. The second part of Vuiliam Turners herball . . . Imprinted at Collen by Arnold Birckman . . . MDLXII.

1568. The first and seconde partes of the Herbal of William Turner. . . . Imprinted at Collen by Arnold Birckman . . . MDLXVIII.
(See also John Hollybush, 1561.)

?1540. ANDREW BORDE. The boke for to Lerne a man to be wyse in buylding of his howse. . . . Robert Wyer.
(This book is always ascribed to Andrew Borde, as it was republished with his name in *Compēdyous Regyment*.)

1550. ANTHONY ASKHAM.
(See 1525. Here begynneth a new mater . . . an Herball. 1550 edition.)

1557. THOMAS TUSSER. A hundreth good pointes of husbandrie.
(The copy of the above in the British Museum is believed to be unique.)
Subsequent editions, 1561, 1562, 1564, 1570.

1573. Five hundreth points of good husbandry vnited to as many of good huswiferie, first deuised, & nowe lately augmented.
Subsequent editions, 1576, 1577, 1580, 1585, 1586, 1590, 1593, 1597, 1599, 1604, 1610, 1614, 1620, 1638, 1672, 1692, 1710, 1744, 1810, 1812, 1834, 1848, 1878, 1931.

1558. WYLLYAM WARDE. The secretes of Alexis of Piedmont. . . .
Later editions, 1562, 1568, 1580.

1559. PETER MORWYNG. A new book of Destillation of Waters.
Later edition, 1565.

?1560. ALBERTUS MAGNUS. The boke of secretes of Albartus Magnus.

1561. JHON HOLLYBUSH. A most excellent & perfect Homish Apothecarye.
(Said to be the pseudonym of either Miles Coverdale or William Turner; it is more likely to be the latter.)

1562. WILLIYAM BULLEYN. Bulleins Bulwarke of defēce. . . .
Second edition, 1579.

1563. THOMAS HYLL. A Most Briefe and pleasaunt treatyse.
A Most Briefe & pleasante Treatise. . . . Imprinted by Jhon Day for Thomas Hyll.
(In the bibliography of her *History of Gardening in England* (1892), Lady Cecil states that a book with this title was in the Amherst Library and was probably the second edition.)

1568. The proffitable Arte of Gardening, now the third tyme set fourth.
The above is the third edition of *A Most Briefe and pleasant treatyse*.
Subsequent editions, 1572, 1574, 1579, 1586, 1593, 1608.

1577. The Gardeners Labyrinth : by Dydymus Mountaine.
(Dydymus Mountaine, a play on his own name, was a pseudonym of Thomas Hyll. The book was completed by Henry Dethicke.)
Subsequent editions, 1586, 1594, 1608, 1651, 1656.

1567. JOHN MAPLET. A greene Forest. . . .
(The dedicatory epistle is to the Earl of Sussex, ' Justice of the Forrestes & Chases from Trent Southward ; and Captaine of Gentlemen Pensioners, of the house of the Queene our Soveraigne Ladie Eliz.)

1570. PIERRE PENA & MATHIAS DE L'OBEL. Stirpium Adversaria Nova. . . .

1605. Dilvcidæ simplicium medicamenorum. . . .

1654. Matthiæ de L'Obel . . . Plurimas elaborantes inauditas plantas . . .
(I am not listing de l'Obel's works printed by Plantin at Antwerp, as this bibliography is confined to books printed in England or in the English language.)

1572. LEONARD MASCALL. A Booke of the Arte and maner, howe to plant and graffe.
Later editions, 1575, 1582, 1592, 1596, 1656.

1574. REYNOLDE SCOT. A perfite platforme of a Hoppe Garden. . . .
Later editions, 1576, 1578. See also *The Countryman's Recreation*, 1653.

1577. BARNABY GOOGE. Foure Bookes of Husbandry.
Later editions, 1578, 1586, 1601, 1614, 1631, 1658.

1577. JOHN FRAMPTON. Joyfull Newes out of the newe founde worlde.
Later editions, 1580, 1596.
(The Spanish original was published in 1569. The book was translated into Latin, Italian, Flemish, and French before 1620.)

1578. HENRY LYTE. A Niewe Herball. . .
Later editions, 1586, 1595, 1619.

1579. WILLIAM LANGHAM. The Garden of Health. . . .
Second edition, corrected and amended 1633.

1586. JACQUES LE MOYNE. La Clef des Champs . . . 1586. . . .
(The only two known copies are in the British Museum.)

1587. THOMAS NEWTON. An Herbal for the Bible. . . .
(The dedicatory epistle is to the Earl of Essex.)

1589. J.B. The Booke of Thrift. . . .

1591. ANONYMOUS. A Short instruction veric [*sic*] profitable . . . for the better ease of the Gardner.
(The only known copy is in the library of Mr. Lownes of Providence.)

BIBLIOGRAPHY

1592. ANONYMOUS. A Short instruction very profitable and necessary, for al those that delight in gardening.
(The only known copy of the above is in the Marquis of Crewe's library.)

1594. SIR HUGH PLATT. The Jewell House of Art & Nature. . . .
1608. Floræs Paradise. . . .
1653. The Garden of Eden. . . .
(The above is the second edition of *Floræs Paradise*, and was brought out after the author's death by his kinsman, Charles Bellingham.)
Later editions, 1654, 1659, 1660. Sixth edition is dated 1675.

1596. JOHN GERARD. Catalogus arborum fruticum ac plantarum. . . .
(The only known copy is in the British Museum.)
Second edition, 1599. (Excessively rare.)
1876. Reprint with notes by B. D. Jackson.
1597. The Herball. . . .
Second edition, 'very much enlarged and amended by Thomas Johnson', 1633. Last edition, 1636.

1597. ANONYMOUS. The Orchard, and the Garden.
Second edition, 1602.

1599. RICHARD GARDINER. Profitable Instructions for Kitchin Gardens.
(The only copy I have seen was in the late Mr. J. Jacobs' library.)
Second edition, 1603. (The only known copy is in the British Museum.)

1599. A New Booke of good Husbandry . . . by Janus Dubravius.
(The translator's name is not stated.)

1600. RICHARD SURFLET. Maison Rustique, or The Covntrie Farme,
Later editions, 1606 and 1616 (augmented by Gervase Markham).

1600. JOHN TAVERNER. Certaine Ex- periments con- cerning Fish and Frvite.

1604. N.F. The Frviterer's Secrets.
1608. The Husbandman's fruit- full Orchard.
(The above is the same book as *The Fruiterer's Secrets*.)
Second edition, 1609.

1606. WILLIAM RAM. Rams little Dodoen. . . .
(The above purports to be an epitome of Lyte's 'Dodoens', but though some of the matter has been abridged from Dodoens it is in reality a compilation of recipes unworthy of the great name it bears.)

1607. NICHOLAS GEFFE. The perfect use of silk-wormes, and their benefit.
1609. W.S. Instructions for the increasing of Mulberie Trees. . . .
1612. R.C. An Olde Thrift newly revived. . . .
(Mentioned by Hazlitt.)
1613. GERVASE MARKHAM. The English Husbandman.
1614. The second Booke of the English Husbandman.
1635. The English Husbandman.
1616. Maison Rustique. See 1600. Richard Surflet.
1631. The Whole Art of Husbandry. See 1577. Barnaby Googe.

1638. A Way To Get Wealth . . . the last (book) by W. L.
W.L. was William Lawson (q.v.).

1615. CRISPIN DE PASSE. A Garden of Flowers.

1617. WILLIAM LAWSON. The Covntrie Hovswifes Garden.
Later editions, 1623, 1626.
Also issued with separate title-page but not separate pagination with
A New Orchard and Garden, 1631, 1638, 1648, 1656, 1660, 1668, 1683.

1618. A New Orchard & Garden.
Later editions, 1623, 1626, 1631, 1638, 1648, 1656, 1660, 1668, 1683.
Modern reprint with introduction by Eleanour Sinclair Rohde, 1928.

1623. ANONYMOUS. Certaine excellent and New inuented Knots and
Mazes, 1623.

1624. SIR HENRY WOTTON. The Elements of Architecture. . . .

1625. FRANCIS BACON. The Essayes or Covnsels, Civill and Morall, of
Francis Lo. Verulam Viscount St Albans.

1627. Sylva sylvarum. . . .
(Numerous later editions.)

1626. ADAM SPEED. Adam out of Eden. . . .
Second edition, 1659.

1626. SIMON HARWARD. The Art of Propagating plants.
(Printed in 1626 edition of William Lawson's *New Orchard and Garden*.)

1629. JOHN PARKINSON. Paradisi in sole Paradisus Terrestris.
Reissued 1635. Second edition, ' corrected & enlarged ', 1656. Facsimile reprint from the edition of 1629 published by Messrs. Methuen
in 1904.

1640. Theatrum Botanicum.

1629. THOMAS JOHNSON. Iter Plantarum investigationis ergo susceptum
. . . in Agrum Cantianum.

1632. Descriptio Itineris Plantarum.

1633. The Herball. See John Gerard.

1634–41. Mercurius Botanicus.

1639. GABRIEL PLATTES. A Discovery of Infinite Treasure.

1639. A Discovery of Subterraneall Treasure.
Second edition, ' Whereunto is added . . . what colour any berry,
leaf or wood will give ', 1679.

1644. The Profitable Intelligencer.

1640. ANONYMOUS. The Expert Gardener.
(The only known copy is in the library of St. David's College,
Lampeter. Reprinted in *The Countryman's Recreation*, 1640, and again
in 1654. Ascribed by Johnson & Watt to C. de Sercy.)

1640. ANONYMOUS. The Country-man's Recreation.
Later editions, 1653, 1654.
(The above is a compilation of the works of Leonard Mascall and
Reynolde Scot. With the exception of the title-page it is identical with
The Orchard and the Garden (1597).

1640. I.H. Δενδρογια Dodona's Grove.

BIBLIOGRAPHY

?1645. ISAAC DE CAUS. Wilton Garden.
   Reprinted by Bernard Quaritch, 1895.

1659. A New & Rare Invention of Water-Works.

1648. JACOB BOBART. Hortus Medicus Oxoniensis.
   (Published anonymously by J. Bobart. Republished at Copenhagen by
   Simon Paulli in his *Viridaria varia regia et academica*. The book was
   published with the author's names, P. Stephens and W. Brown, in
   1658.)

1649. WALTER BLITH. The English Improver.
   Third edition, 1652.

?1650. PETER STENT. A booke of Flowers Fruicts Beastes Birds and
   Flies.

1650. WILLIAM SIMPSON. The second booke of Flowers Fruicts Beastes
   Birds and Flies.

1661. The second booke of Flowers Fruicts Beastes Birds and Flies. With
   additions by John Dunstall.

1650. WILLIAM HOW. Phytologia Britannica.

1651. LEONARD SOWERBY. The Ladies Dispensatory.

1651. SAMUEL HARTLIB. Samuel Hartlib his Legacie.
   Later editions, 1652, 1655.

1651. An essay for the advancement of Husbandry-Learning.

1652. Cornucopia.

1652. A Designe for Plentie.
   Later edition, 1654.

1653. A Discoverie for Division or setting out of Land.

1652. NICHOLAS CULPEPER. The English Physician, 1652.
   (This is the edition repudiated by the author in later editions as incorrect
   and unauthorised.)
   Later editions, 1652, 1653, 1661, 1693, 1695, 1714, 1725, 1733, 1784,
   1792, 1814, 1820.

1818. Welsh Translation.
   Second edition, 1862.
   1932 edition with corrections, etc., by W. J. Ferrier and a Foreword by
   H.R.H. Princess Louise.

1652. ROBERT PEMELL. Tractatus, De facultatibus Simplicium.

1653. Second part of the above Treatise.

1653. ANONYMOUS. A Book of Fruits and Flowers.

1653. RALPH AUSTEN. A Treatise of Fruit-Trees.
   Later editions, 1657, 1665. The *Spiritual use of an Orchard* was issued
   separately in 1847.

1658. Observations upon some part of Sir Francis Bacon's Naturall History.
   (Also issued with the 1665 edition of the *Treatise of Fruit-trees*.)

1676. A Dialogue betweene the Husbandman, and Fruit-Trees.
   (Excessively rare. No copy in the British Museum. The only copy
   I know is in the R.H.S. Library.)

1653. JOHN BEALE. A Treatise on Fruit Trees.

1657. The Hereford Orchards.
1677. Nurseries, Orchards, Profitable Gardens, and Vineyards Encouraged. The first letter from Anthony Lawrence; All the rest from Iohn Beale.
1677. General Advertisements concerning Cyder . . . London, 1677.
1656. WILLIAM COLES. The Art of Simpling, 1656.
Second edition, 1657.
1657. Adam in Eden.
1656. JOHN TRADESCANT. Museum Tradescantium.
1658. SIR THOMAS BROWNE. Hydriotaphia.
1658. JOHN EVELYN. The French Gardener.
Later editions, 1669, 1672, 1675, 1695.
1664. Sylva.
Second edition, 1670, various later editions that of 1786 (with notes by A. Hunter York), 1801.
1664. Kalendarium Hortense (second edition).
(The first edition appeared in *Sylva* in 1664.)
Subsequent editions, 1664, 1666, 1669, 1671, 1673, 1676, 1683, 1691, 1699, 1706.
1676. A Philosophical Discourse of Earth . . .
1673. Of Gardens . . . by Renatus Rapinus, now made English by J.E.
1693. The Compleat Gard'ner. From the French original by J. de la Quintinye.
Later editions, 1699, 1701, 1704, 1710.
1699. Acetaria. Second edition, 1706.
1658. J. B. PORTA. Natural magic, etc.
1659. THOMAS DUCKET. Proceedings concerning the improvement of land . . .
1659. ROBERT LOVELL. Παμβοτανολογια.
Second edition, 'with many Additions', 1665.
1660. JOHN RAY. Catalogus Plantarum circa Cantobrigium nascentium.
1663. Appendix ad Catalogum.
(Published anonymously.)
1670. Catalogus Plantarum Angliæ et insularum adjacentium.
1673. Catalogus Stirpium in exteris regionibus, 1673.
1686–1688, 1704. Historia Plantarum.
1690. Synopsis methodica Stirpium Britannicarum.
Second and enlarged edition, 1696.
1694. Stirpium Europæarum extra Britanniam nascentium Sylloge, 1694.
1718. Philosophical Letters, 1718.
1660. ROBERT SHARROCK. History of the Propagation of Vegetables.
Later editions, 1672, 1694.
1661. SIR KENELM DIGBY. A Discourse concerning the vegetation of plants.
1661. M. STEVENSON. The Twelve Moneths.
(Excessively rare.)
1664. STEPHEN BLAKE. The Compleat Gardeners Practice.

BIBLIOGRAPHY

1664. JOHN FORSTER. England's Happiness Increased.
1664. The manner of ordering Fruit Trees . . . by the Sieur de Gendre.
. . . London, 1664.
(The translator was John Forster.)
1664. JONATHAN GODDARD. Observations concerning the texture and similar parts of a Tree.
1664. The Fruit Tree's Secrets.
(Papers read before the Royal Society. Printed in John Evelyn's *Sylva* in 1664.)
1665. WILLIAM HUGHES. The Compleat Vineyard.
Second edition, 1670.
1671. The Flower-Garden.
Later editions, 1672, 1683.
1672. The American Physitian.
1665. JOHN REA. Flora : seu, De Florum Cultura.
Later editions entitled *Flora Ceres and Pomona*, 1676, 1702.
1665. Philosophical Transactions (published by the Royal Society), first published in 1665.
1666. JOHN ROSE. The English Vineyard Vindicated.
Later editions, 1669, 1675, 1691 (with John Evelyn's *French Gardener*), and 1692.
1667. ABRAHAM COWLEY. The Garden.
1669. S.B. (Samuel Blagrave or as some say Billingsly). The Epitome of Husbandry, 1669.
(Mentioned by Johnson, who describes it as a complete plagiary, the first 181 pages being copied from FitzHerbert and the rest from Mascall, etc. See 1685, J. Blagrave.)
1669. FRANCIS DUDLEY (LORD NORTH). Observations & Advices œconomical . . . 1669.
1669. RICHARD RICHARDSON. De cultu Hortorum Carmen.
(Mentioned by Johnson.)
1669. [JOHN WORLIDGE.] Systema Agriculturæ.
Later editions, 1675, 1677, 1681, 1687. (In the 1687 edition the engraved frontispiece has the date 1681, the letterpress title that of 1687.)
1676. Vinetum Britannicum.
Later editions, 1678, 1691.
1677. Systema Horti- culturæ.
Second edition, 1682.
1670. ILIFFE. The Compleat Vineyard.
(Mentioned by Johnson.)
1670. LEONARD MEAGER. The English Gardener.
Numerous later editions. The twelfth edition is dated 1721.
Undated. The New Art of Gardening, with the Gardener's Almanack.
Second edition, 1697.
1697. The Mystery of Husbandry.

1670. ANDREW MOLLET. The Garden of Pleasure.
(The only known copy of the above is in Captain the Hon. R. Legh's library. A French translation of this work, *Le jardin de plaisir*, was published in Stockholm in 1651.)

1670. CAPTAIN JOHN SMITH. England's Improvement Reviv'd.
Second edition, 1673.

1672. FRANCIS DROPE. A Short and Sure Guid.
(See *Philosophical Transactions of the Royal Society*, No. 86, pp. 10, 49.)

1672. NEHEMIAH GREW. The Anatomy of Vegetables begun.

1682. The Anatomy of Plants.

1672. JOHN JOSSELYN. New England's Rarities Discovered.

1672. ROBERT MORISON. Plantarum Umbelliferarum Distributio.

1680. Plantarum Historiæ Universalis Oxoniensis Pars secunda . . .

1699. Pars tertia . . . explevit & absolvit Jacobus Bobartus.
(The first part was never published.)

1674. Icones et descriptiones rariorum Plantarum Siciliæ, etc.
(A translation of Paolo Boccone's Manifestum Botanicum.)

1676. MOSES COOK. The Manner of Raising, Ordering, and Improving Forest-Trees.
Later editions, 1717–1724.

1675. CHARLES COTTON. The Planters Manual.

1681. T. LANGFORD. Plain and Full Instructions.
Second edition, 1696.

1681. The Practical Planter of Fruit Trees.
Second edition, 1696.

1682. SAMUEL GILBERT. The Florist's Vade Mecum. To which is added The Gardeners Almanack.
Later editions, 1683, 1690, 1693, 1702.

1683. G.V.N. The Belgick, or Netherlandish Hesperides.

1683. JOHN REID. The Scots Gard'ner.
Later editions, 1721, 1766.
(This is the first book on Scottish gardening.)

1684. RICHARD HAINES. Aphorisms upon the new way of improving Cyder. London, 1684.

1685. J. BLAGRAVE. The Epitomie of the Art of Husbandry.
(I think this must be the book ascribed by Johnson to 'Samuel Blagrave or as some say Billingsly'.)

1685. WILLIAM ELLIS. The Complete Planter.

1685. SIR WILLIAM TEMPLE. Upon the Garden of Epicurus.

1685. ANONYMOUS. The Art of Pruning Fruit-Trees.

1690. LEONARD PLUKENET. Phytographia.

1694. SIR DUDLEY CULLUM. A new invented Stove for the Green House.

1694. JOHN PECHEY. The Compleat Herbal.

1699. GEORGE LONDON & HENRY WISE. The Compleat Gardiner.
Later editions, 1701, 1704, 1710.

1706. The Retired Gardner.

1706.   Le jardinier Solitaire.
        (The same work with a different title.)
1699.   N.F.D. Fruit walls improved by inclining them to the Horizon. By a
        member of the Royal Society. N.F.D., 1699.
1700.   TIMOTHY NOURSE. Campania Felix.
1700.   Adam Armed.
1702.   T. SNOW. Apopiroscopy.
1703.   JOHN JAMES. The Theory and Practice of Gardening, translated
        from the French of A. Le Blond.
        Later editions, 1712, 1728.
1703.   HENRY VAN OOSTEN. The Dutch Gardener.
        Second edition, 1711.
1704.   ANONYMOUS. Dictionarium Rusticum et Urbanicum.
        Later edition, 1726.
1706.   RICHARD BRADLEY. Paintings of succulent plants, with accounts
        of them.
1710.   A treatise on Succulent Plants.
1716–27.   Historia Plantarum succulentarum.
1717.   New Improvements of planting and gardening.
        Later editions, 1718, 1720, 1724, 1726, 1731, 1739.
1718.   The Gentleman and Gardener's Kalendar.
        London, 1727.
1721.   A Philosophical Account of the Works of Nature.
1721.   A Philosophical Treatise of Husbandry and Gardening by G. A.
        Agricola, M.D., translated and with preface by R. Bradley. London,
        1721.
1722.   The Monthly Register of Experiments and Observations in Husbandry
        and Gardening.
        (Two parts, April and May, 1722, are in the Sturtevant Library, St.
        Louis, Mo., U.S.A.)
1726.   A General Treatise of Husbandry and Gardening.
1725.   A Survey of the Ancient Husbandry and Gardening.
1727.   Ten practical discourses.
        Second edition, 1733.
1728.   Dictionarium Botanicum.
1729.   The Riches of a Hop Garden explained.
1747.   A Dictionary of Plants.
1757.   A general treatise . . . displaying the arts of . . . gardening.
1707.   CHARLES EVELYN. The Ladies' Recreation.
        Later editions, 1717, 1719 .
1707.   WILLIAM FLEETWOOD, Bishop of St. Asaph and Ely. Curiosities
        of Nature and Art.
1707.   JOHN MORTIMER. The Whole Art of Husbandry.
        Later editions, 1708, 1712, 1721. The sixth edition (1761) edited by his
        grandson Thomas Mortimer.
1708.   J. PHILIPS. Cyder . . . (a poem containing much practical information).

1710. WILLIAM SALMON. Botanologia.

1712. JOSEPH ADDISON. An Essay on the Pleasures of the Garden (*The Spectator*, No. 477).

1712. PIERRE POMET. A Compleat History of Drugs. Done into English. Later editions, 1725, 1737, and the fourth ' carefully corrected with large additions ', 1748. London.
(The French original *Histoire Generale des Drogues* was published in 1694. Second edition, 1735, contains ' A catalogue of the seeds lately brought from the American Islands '.)

1713. ALEXANDER POPE. Essay on Verdant Sculpture (*The Guardian*, No. 173).

1713–1715. JAMES PETIVER. A Catalogue of Mr. Ray's English Herbal.

1715. Hortus Peruvianus Medicinalis.

1764. Historia naturalem.

1714. JOHN LAWRENCE. The Clergyman's Recreation.
Later editions, 1715, 1716, 1717, 1726.

1716. The Gentleman's Recreation.
Second edition, 1717.

1718. The Lady's Recreation.

1718. Gardening Improved.

1718. The Fruit Garden Kalendar. London.
Second edition, 1736.

1726. A new system of Agriculture.

1715. STEPHEN SWITZER. The Nobleman, Gentleman and Gardener's Recreation.

1718. Ichnographia Rustica.
Second edition, 1742.

1724. The Practical Fruit-Gardener.
Second edition, revised by Laurence and Bradley, 1724.

1727. The Practical Kitchen Gardiner.
Second edition, revised by Laurence and Bradley.

1729. A compendious Method for the raising of Italian Brocoli, etc.

1729. An introduction to . . . Hydrostaticks.

1731. A Dissertation on the true Cytisus of the Ancients, etc.
Second edition, 1735.

1715. C. J. WOLFE & JAMES GANDON. Vitruvius Britannicus.

1716. REV. HENRY STEVENSON (Master of the Free School at East Retford). The Young Gardener's Director.

1716. The Gentleman Gardener instructed.
Numerous later editions, the eighth dated 1769.

1717. GEORGE ANDREW AGRICOLA. The Artificial Gardener.

1717. The Experimental Husbandman and Gardiner.
Second edition, 1726.

1721. A Philosophical Treatise of Husbandry and Gardening.
See Richard Bradley, 1721.

1727. On Planting.

BIBLIOGRAPHY

1717. JOSEPH CARPENTER. The Retir'd Gardener.
1717. SAMUEL COLLINS. Paradise retriev'd.
1717. GILES JACOB. The Country Gentleman's Vade Mecum.
1718. REV. JAMES GARDINER. Rapin of Gardens.
    (See also John Evelyn, 1658.)
1719. TOURNEFORT. The Compleat Herbal.
1720. PATRICK BLAIR. Botanick Essays.
1723–1728. Pharmaco-Botanologia.
1722. THOMAS FAIRCHILD. The City Gardener.
1724. The different and sometimes contrary motion of the sap in plants.
    Phil Trans, 1724.
1730. Catalogus Plantarum. See A Society of Gardeners, 1730.
1722. JOSEPH MILLER. Botanicum Officinale.
1724. PHILIP MILLER. The Gardener's and Florist's Dictionary.
1730. Catalogus Plantarum.
    See A Society of Gardeners, 1730.
1731–1739. The Gardener's Dictionary, 1731.
    Numerous editions, that of 1735 being the first in octavo.
1732. The Gardener's Kalendar. London, 1732.
    Numerous editions, the eleventh dated 1757, the thirteenth 1782.
1758. The Method of Cultivating Madder.
1760. Figures of the most beautiful Plants described in the Gardener's Dictionary.
    Later edition, 1771.
1764. The Elements of Agriculture, translated from Duhamel du Monceau.
  . ANONYMOUS. A Discourse on the Irritability of some Flowers.
1726. BATTY LANGLEY. Practical Geometry applied to the useful Arts . . . Gardening, etc.
    Second edition, 1729.
1728. A Sure Method of improving Estates.
1728. New Principles of Gardening.
1729. Pomona.
    (Coloured copies of this book are rare.)
1741. The Landed Gentleman's Useful Companion (reprint of 'A Sure Method', etc.).
1726. BENJAMIN TOWNSEND. The Complete Seedsman.
1727. ROBERT FURBER. Catalogue of English and Foreign trees.
    (Mentioned by Watt.)
1732. Fruits for every month in the year.
1733. An Introduction to Gardening.
1727. S.J. The Vineyard.
    (Mentioned by Johnson.)
1728. ROBERT CASTEL. The Villas of the Ancients.
1728. The Theory & Practice of Gardening, London, 1728.
    (Published apparently in rivalry with Batty Langley's book of same year.)

1729. PETER COLLINSON. Article in the Philosophical Transactions, 1729.
1729. JOHN COWELL. A true Account of the Aloe Americana.
1730. The Curious and Profitable Gardener.
Second edition, 1732.
The Curious Fruit and Flower Gardener. 1732.
1730. A SOCIETY OF GARDENERS. Catalogus Plantarum. Part I.
(The only part published.)
1733. BENJAMIN WHITMILL (one of the authors of Catalogus Plantarum).
Kalendarium Universale Calendar.
Second edition, 1733. (Numerous later editions, the seventh dated
1765.)
1731. MARK CATESBY. Natural History of California, Florida, etc.
1767. Hortus Europæ Americanus.
1732. J. J. DILLENIUS. Hortus Elthamensis. London, 1732.
1732. WILLIAM HARPER. A Sermon of Gardening.
1732. The Flower Garden Displayed.
Second edition, 1734. With 'A Flower Garden for Gentlemen and
Ladies'.
1732. ANONYMOUS. An Essay concerning the best methods of pruning
Fruit Trees.
1732. ANONYMOUS. The nature and method of planting a Vineyard.
1732. ANONYMOUS. The great Improvement of Commons.
(The three books listed above are mentioned by Johnson.)
1736. GEORGE HUMPHRYS. Nature Displayed as were thought most
proper to excite the curiosity and form the minds of youth. Translated
from the French of N. A. Pluché.
(The second volume is devoted to gardening and husbandry.)
1737-1739. ELIZABETH BLACKWELL. A curious Herbal.
1738. CHARLES DEERING. A catalogue of plants growing and commonly
cultivated.
1738. STEPHEN HALES. Statical Essays.
Third edition with amendments. Vol. I, 1738, Vol. II, 1740.
1738. Public Gardens. Collection of Notes about Ranelagh, etc. (Guildhall
Library.)
1738. SAMUEL TROWELL. A New Treatise of Husbandry, Gardening,
etc.
Second edition, 1739. (Johnson states he had never seen the writings
of this ' celebrated garden artist '.)
1747. The Farmer's Instructor or Husbandman, and Gardener's useful
Companion. Edited by William Ellis. (Mentioned by Johnson.)
1739. ANONYMOUS. An Essay upon Harmony.
1740. CHRISTOPHER GRAY. A Catalogue of Trees and Shrubs . . . for
sale.
1744. ANONYMOUS. Adam's luxury and Eve's Cookery.
1744. Curious Experiments in Gardening, etc.
(The four books listed above are mentioned by Johnson.)

BIBLIOGRAPHY

1744. JOHN WILSON. Synopsis of British Plants, in Ray's Method.

1745. J. SERLE. A plan of Mr. Pope's Garden and Grotto, etc.

1746. GEORGE BICKHAM. The Beauties of Stowe. 1753.

1746. DAVID STEPHENSON. The Gentleman's Gardener's Director. Several later editions.

1746. REGAUD & BERNARD BARON. Stowe Gardens.

1746. ANONYMOUS. The Beauties of Stowe.

1746. ANONYMOUS. A description of the Gardens of Lord Viscount Cobham at Stowe.

1748. ANONYMOUS. A dialogue upon the Gardens at Stowe.

1751. ANONYMOUS. The Gardens of Stowe.

1747. ANONYMOUS. The Compleat Florist. (Excessively rare.)

1747. ANONYMOUS. The Complete Florist. (A different book from the above and not so rare. Two later editions, both undated.)

1748. SIR WILLIAM WATSON. Papers published in the Philosophical Transactions. Accounts of the remains of John Tradescant's Botanic Garden at Lambeth, 1750. Account of the Bishop of London's Garden at Fulham, 1751, etc.

1724. A Letter to Andrew Ducarel.

1750. WILLIAM & JOHN HALFPENNY. Rural Architecture in the Chinese taste. Later edition, 1805.

1750–1773. D. C. J. TREW. Plantæ selectæ.

1752. SIR HARRY BEAUMONT. A Particular Account of the Emperor's Gardens near Pekin, by F. Attiret (a French missionary). Translated by Sir Harry Beaumont.

1752. JAMES NEWTON. Compleat Herbal.

1753. FRANCIS COVENTRY. Essay in The World (April 12th, 1753). ' Strictures on the absurd Novelties introduced in Gardening '.

1775. BARTHOLOMEW ROCQUE. A Treatise on the Hyacinth.

1753. W. WEBB. A Catalogue of Seeds and Roots.

1754. JAMES JUSTICE. The Scot's Gardener's Director. Second edition, 1759.

1759. The British Gardener's Calendar.

1765. The British Gardener's new director.

1754. EDWARD KNIGHT. Dover's Legacy (containing ' The Gardener's Legacy ', by Edward Knight).

1754. ANONYMOUS. The Useful Herbal.

1755. JOHN DALTON. Some thoughts on Building and planting.

1756. JOHN HILL, M.D. (' SIR ' J. H.). The British Herbal. (Some copies of this book are coloured.)

1757. Eden, or a compleat body of gardening, 1757. (Some copies of this book are coloured.)

1757. The Sleep of Plants. A letter to C. Linnæus, 1757.

1758. A method of producing double flowers, 1758. Dutch translation, 1804.
1758. An account of a stone . . . which on being watered produces excellent mushrooms, 1758.
1759. Exotic Botany.
1759. The Vegetable System.
1770. Virtues of British Herbs.
1777. The Construction of Timber from its early growth, explained by the Microscope.
1756. TIMOTHY SHELDRAKE (THE ELDER). The Gardener's Best Companion in a Greenhouse.
1756. TIMOTHY SHELDRAKE. Botanicum medicinale.
1756. ANONYMOUS. On the Heat and Cold of Hot-houses.
1756. T. HALE. A compleat body of husbandry.
1757. Eden, or a compleat Body of Gardening . . . compiled by Sir John Hill from the MS. by Hale.
Later edition, 1812.
1757. THOMAS HITT. A Treatise of Fruit Trees.
Second edition, 1757, third edition, 1768.
1760. A Treatise of Husbandry.
1757. EDWARD LISLE. Observations on Husbandry.
1757. WILLIAM MASON. An Heroic Epistle to Sir W. Chambers.
1758. An heroic Postscript.
1772. The English Garden.
Later editions and an edition with Commentary and Notes by W. Burgh, 1783.
1757. ROBERT MAXWELL. The Practical Husbandman.
(Papers taken from ' Select Transactions of the Honourable the Society of Improvers in the knowledge of Agriculture in Scotland '.)
1757. JAMES THOMPSON. Ten distinguishing properties of a fine Auricula.
1758. The Dutch Florist.
1757. FRANCIS HOME. Principles of Agriculture and Vegetation.
1758. O. BARNES. A new method of Propagating Fruit Trees, etc.
Later editions, 1759 and 1762.
1758. REV. WILLIAM HANBURY. An Essay on Planting.
1758. The gardeners new Kalendar.
1770–1771. A complete body of planting and gardening.
1759. JOHN MILLS. A Practical Treatise on Husbandry, translated from the French of Duhamel de Monceau.
1762. A new and complete System of Practical Husbandry.
1759. RICHARD NORTH. A Treatise on Grasses and the Norfolk Willow.
1759. The Gardener's Catalogue of Hardy Trees, etc.
(Mentioned by Johnson.)
1759. BENJAMIN STILLINGFLEET. Miscellaneous Tracts. Translated from the Latin of various Swedish authors.
Second edition with the addition of the Calendar of Flora, from the Swedish of Berger.

BIBLIOGRAPHY

1767.   A Discourse concerning the irritability of some Flowers, from the Italian.
1760.   JAMES LEE. An Introduction to Botany.
1774.   Catalogue of Plants and Seeds sold by Kennedy and Lee.
1760.   SAMUEL PULLEIN. Observations towards a method of preserving the seeds of Plants in a state of Vegetation during long voyages.
1760.   ANONYMOUS. The London Gardener.
        (Mentioned by Johnson.)
1762.   T. LIGHTOLER. The Gentleman and Farmer's Architecture.
1763.   SIR WILLIAM CHAMBERS. Plans . . . of the Gardens and Buildings at Kew.
1772.   A Dissertation on Oriental Gardening.
        Second edition, 1773.
1761.   CHARLES KNIGHT. The Gardener's Legacy. Printed in *The Family Treasury* compiled by P. Montague.
1763.   THOMAS MARTYN. Plantæ Cantabrigiensis.
1763.   A Short Account of the Donation to the Botanic Garden by Dr. Walker.
1771.   Catalogus Horti Botanici Cantabrigiensis.
1766.   Rousseau's Letters. Translated from the French. London.
        Later editions, 1785, 1794, 1796.
1788.   Thirty-eight Plates, with Explanations.
1792–94.   Flora Rustica.
        Another issue N.D. in one volume.
1793.   The Language of Botany.
1803–7.   The Gardener's and Botanist's Dictionary of the late Philip Miller, corrected and newly arranged with additions.
        Papers contributed to the Transactions of the Linnæan Society.
1763.   GEORGE RITSO. Kew Gardens : a Poem.
1763.   JAMES WHEELER. The Botanist's and Gardener's New Dictionary.
1763.   An Essay on the Theory of Agriculture.
1764.   REV. WALTER HARTE. Essays on Husbandry.
        Second edition, 1764, 1770.
1764.   The Dutch Florist, from the Dutch of Van Campen, 1764.
        (Mentioned by Johnson.)
1765.   WILLIAM SHENSTONE. Unconnected thoughts on Gardening.
1766.   JOHN LOCKE. Observations upon the growth of Vines and Olives.
1767.   JOHN ABERCROMBIE. Every Man his own Gardener.
        Several later editions.
1770.   A general system of trees and shrubs.
1778.   The Universal Gardener and Botanist.
1779.   The Garden Mushroom.
1779.   The British Fruit gardener and Art of Pruning.
1781.   The Complete Forcing Gardener.

1783. The Complete Wall-Tree Pruner.
1784. The Propagation and Botanical Arrangement of Plants.
1786. The Gardener's Pocket Dictionary.
1789. The Gardener's Daily Assistant.
Gardening, etc.
Later edition, 1794.
1789. The Universal Gardener's Kalendar.
1789. The Complete Kitchen Gardener.
1789. The Gardener's Vade-Mecum.
1789. The Hot-house Gardener.
1789 The Gardener's Pocket Journal.
Second edition, 1891.
1767. G. DIONYSIUS EHRET. Of a new Peruvian Plant.
Philosophical Transactions, 1767.
1767. JOHN GILES. Ananas ; or a Treatise on the Pine Apple.
1767. JAMES RUTTER & DANIEL CARTER. Modern Eden.
1767. W. WRIGHTE. Grotesque Architecture.
Later edition, 1790.
1767. The rise and progress of the present Taste in planting Parks, etc.
1768. JOHN GIBSON (?) The Fruit Gardener.
(The book is usually ascribed to John Gibson, though the book was
published without author's name.)
1768. GEORGE MASON. An Essay on Design in Gardening.
Later revised edition, 1795.
1768. THOMAS WILDMAN. A Treatise on the culture of Peach Trees.
Translated from the French, 1768.
1769. JOHN DICKS. The New Gardener's Dictionary.
Second edition, 1771.
(John Dicks was gardener to the Duke of Kingston.)
1769. JAMES GARTON. The Practical Gardener.
Second edition, Dublin, 1770.
1769. THE HON. DAINES BARRINGTON. On the Trees which are
supposed to be Indigenous in Great Britain.
1771. Chestnut Trees not Indigenous in Great Britain, 1771.
1777. Mr. Pegge's observations on the Growth of the Vine.
1782. On the Progress of Gardening.
1769. ANTHONY POWELL. The Royal Gardener.
1769. ADAM TAYLOR. A Treatise on the Ananas, or Pine Apple.
1769. RICHARD WESTON. Tracts on practical Agriculture and Gardening.
Second edition, enlarged, 1773.
1770–1777. Botanicus universalis et hortulanus.
1773. The Gardener's and Planter's Calendar.
Second edition, 1778.
1775-80. Flora Anglicana.
1779. The Gardener's Pocket Calendar.
Bell's edition. N.D., *circa* 1779.

BIBLIOGRAPHY

1770. J. BOWLES. Flora or a curious collection of ye most beautiful Flowers. London.
(There is only one known complete copy.)

1770. JOHN DOVE. Strictures on Agriculture.

1770. JOHN ELLIS. Directions for bringing over Seeds and Plants from the East Indies.

1773. Description of the Mangostan and Bread Fruit Tree.

1774. An Historical Account of Coffee.

1770. THE REV. COLIN MILNE. Institutes of Botany.

1770. HORACE WALPOLE. Essay on Modern Gardening, 1770. Printed with a French translation by the Duc de Nivernois. 1785.

1770 THOMAS WHATELY (or WHEATLEY). Observations on Modern Gardening.
Later editions, 1770, 1771, 1777, 1793, 1795, 1801.

1770. A Botanical Dictionary.
Second edition, 1777; supplement, 1778. Third and enlarged edition, 1850.

1770. The Gardener's Alphabetical Calendar. (Author's name not given.)

1770. The Pocket Kitchen Gardener. (Author's name not given.)

1770. The Pocket Flower Gardener. (Author's name not given.)
(The three above-mentioned books are mentioned by Johnson.)

1771. WILLIAM CURTIS. Flora Londinensis. Two vols. added by Sir W. J. Hooker, 1828.

1787. The Botanical Magazine (begun by W. Curtis).

1771. JOHN REINHOLD FORSTER. Floræ Americæ Septentrionalis.

1776. Characteres generum Plantarum.

1771. JAMES MEADER. The Modern Gardener.

1779 The Planter's Guide.

1772. JOHN COAKLEY LETTSOM. The natural history of the tea-tree.
Hortus Uptonensis. N.D., circa 1774.

1784. Grovehill.

1772. LOUIS DE ST. PIERRE. The Art of planting and cultivating the Vine, etc.

1773. ANDREW DUCAREL. A Letter to Wm. Watson, M.D.

?1773. N. WALLIS. The Carpenter's Treasure.

1773. Fables of flowers. By the author of China Emblems.

1775. WILLIAM BOUTCHER (nurseryman at Comely gardens, Edinburgh).
A Treatise on Forest Trees.
Later editions, 1776, 1778.

1775. JOHN EDWARDS. A Select Collection of one hundred plates.

1775. JAMES JENKINSON. British Plants; translated from the Genera et Species Plantarum, of Linnæus; with Notes by James Jenkinson.

1776. THOMAS ELLIS (gardener to the Bishop of London). The gardener's pocket calendar.
Second edition, 1779.

1776. WILLIAM WITHERING. A Botanical Arrangement of all the vegetables, etc.
Later editions, 1778–90, 1796, 1830.

1785. An account of the Foxglove.

1777. JAMES ANDERSON. Thoughts on Planting, by Agricola.

1804. A Description of a Patent Hot-House, etc.

1777. JOSEPH HEELEY. Letter on the Beauties of Hagley, etc.

1777. A description of Hagley Park.

1777. JOHN KENNEDY (Gardener to Sir Thomas Gascoigne, Bart.). A Treatise on Planting.

1777. A Treatise upon Planting and Gardening.
Second edition enlarged 1777.

1777. CONRAD LODDIGES. Catalogue of Plants and Seeds sold by Conrad Loddige at Hackney.
Orchideæ in the collection of Loddiges & Sons. No date.

1818–1833. The Botanical Cabinet.

1777. JOHN MILLER. An Illustration of the Sexual System of Linnæus.
Later edition, 1779.

1777. WILLIAM WILSON. A Treatise on the forcing of Early Fruits.

1778. N. SWINDEN. The Beauties of Flora.

1778. ANONYMOUS. The Practical Gardener.

1779. GILBERT BROOKES. The Complete British Gardener.

1779. ADAM NEALE. A Catalogue of Plants in the garden of John Blackburne, Esq.

1779. WILLIAM SPEECHLEY. A Treatise on the culture of the Pine Apple.

1790. A Treatise on the culture of the Vine.
Later editions, 1805 and 1821. (The third edition contains the author's *Treatise on the culture of the Pine Apple*.)

1779. A General Dictionary of Husbandry, Planting, etc.
Selected from the best authors by the editors of the *Farmer's Magazine*.

1780. JOHN TRUSLER. Practical Husbandry.
Later editions, 1785, 1790, 1799.

?1800. Elements of Modern Gardening.
Neither name nor date on title-page. British Museum catalogue ascribes the book to John Trusler and 1800 as the date. Johnson gives no author's name and dates the book 1784.

1780. ALEXANDER WILSON. Some Observations relating to the Influence of Climate.

1781. SAMUEL FULLMER. The Young Gardener's best Companion.

1781. WILLIAM HOUSTON. Reliquiæ Houstounianæ.

1782. WILLIAM RALEY. A Treatise on the Management of Potatoes.

1783. CHARLES BRYANT. Flora Diætetica.

1790. A Dictionary of Ornamental Trees, etc.

1783. MALTHUS. An Essay on Landscape. From the French of Ermenonville.
(No name on title-page. Johnson ascribes it to Mr. Malthus.)

BIBLIOGRAPHY

1783. WILLIAM FALCONER. An Historical View of the Taste for Gardening.

1783–1809. WILLIAM GILPIN. Observations relative chiefly to Picturesque Beauty.
(Eleven volumes containing accounts of tours in England with accounts of gardens, etc.)

1783. THOMAS KYLE. A treatise on the management of peach & nectarine trees. Edinburgh 1783. Second edition, 1787.

1783. A catalogue of plants sold by Lucker and Smith, Dalston, 1783.

1785. JAMES BOLTON. Filices Britanniæ. Leeds, 1785.

1785. JOHN, EARL OF BUTE. Botanical Tables.

1785. JAMES DICKSON. Fasciculus Plantarum Cryptogamicarum Britanniæ.

1785. SAMUEL FELTON. Miscellanies on Ancient and Modern Gardening. (No author's name on title-page.)

1828. On the Portraits of English Authors on Gardening. Second edition with considerable additions, 1830.

1829. Gleanings on Gardens.

1785. WILLIAM MARSHALL. Planting and Ornamental Gardening. (No author's name on title-page.) (Second edition, with the title *Planting and Rural Ornament*. London, 1796. Third edition, 1803.

1786. ROBERT BROWNE (gardener to Sir Harbord Harbord, Bt., at Gunton, Norfolk. A Method to preserve Peach and Nectarine Trees.

1786. REV. PHILIP LE BROCQ. A Description of certain methods of Planting, etc.

1786. FRANCIS XAVIER VISPRE. A Dissertation on the growth of Wine in England.

1787. GEORGE WINTER. A new and compendious System of Husbandry.

1787. ANONYMOUS. The Compleat Herbal.

1788. SIR JAMES EDWARD SMITH. Some observations on the irritability of Vegetables.

1789–91. Plantarum Icones.

1790–93. Icones Pictæ.

1791–2. Spicilegium Botanicum.

1800. Flora Britannica. London, 1800.

1804. Exotic Botany.

1807. An Introduction to Physiological and Systematic Botany.

1817. Review of the Modern State of Botany.

1821. A Grammar of Botany.
WILLIAM AITON. Hortus Kewensis. Second edition enlarged by his son, William Townsend Aiton, 1810–13. Epitome of the second edition, 1814.

1789. JOHN GRAEFER. A Descriptive Catalogue of Herbaceous Plants.

1789. ANTHONY POWELL. The garden. From the original by the Abbé de Lille. (Anthony Powell was gardener to George II.)

1789. LEWIS MONTOLIEU. Translation of the Abbé de Lille's poem (cited above) with 8 head and tail pieces by F. Bartolozzi.

1790. BRULLES. Hints for the management of Hot-beds.
1790. E. O. DONOVAN. The Botanical Review.
1790. RICHARD PULTENEY. Historical and biographical sketches of the progress of Botany.
1790. Decorations for Plants and Garden. *Circa* 1790.
1805. General view of the Writings of Linnæus, 1805.
1790. WILLIAM WOODVILLE. Medical botany.
1791. ERASMUS DARWIN. The Botanic Garden.
1800. Phytologia.
1791. WILLIAM FORSYTH. Observations on the Diseases in Fruit and Forest Trees.
1802. A Treatise on Fruit Trees.
Later editions, 1803, 1818, 1824.
1791. RICHARD ANTHONY SALISBURY. Icones Stirpium Variorum.
1796. Prodromus stirpium in Horto ad Chapel Allerton irgentium.
1805–8. Paradisus Londinensis.
1791. JAMES SOWERBY. The Florist's Delight.
1792–1803. Figures of English Fungi.
1790–1820. (with Sir J. E. Smith). English Botany.
1791. The Linnæan Society's Transactions, first publication, 1791.
1792. JAMES MADDOCK. The Florist's Directory. (Translated into German in 1798 by A. W. Manteuffel.)
Second edition improved by S. Curtis, London, 1810. Third edition with appendix on the culture of the dahlia, chrysanthemum, lobelia and tree mignonette by S. Curtis, 1822.
1793. JOHN MASON. Double Hyacinths.
1793. RICHARD STEELE. An Essay upon Gardening.
Later edition, 1800.
1794. ADRIAN HARDY HAWORTH. Observations on the genus Mesembryanthemum.
1831. Narcissinearum monographia.
1812.–1819. Synopsis Plantarum Succulentarum.
1794. SAMUEL HAYES. A practical Treatise on Planting.
1794. RICHARD PAYNE KNIGHT. The Landscape.
1795. Review of the Landscape.
1794. WILLIAM MAUNSELL. Letter on the Culture of Potatoes.
1794. JAMES McPHAIL. A Treatise on the Culture of the Cucumber.
Second edition, 1795.
(This book contains a full description of the weather in London for every day of 1793.)
1803. The Gardener's Remembrancer. Second edition, 1807.
1794. SIR UVEDALE PRICE. An Essay on the Picturesque.
1795. A Letter to H. Repton, Esq.
1801. A Dialogue.
1842. On the Picturesque ; including a Letter to H. Repton, Esq. Edited by Sir Thomas Dick Lauder.

BIBLIOGRAPHY

1794. HUMPHREY REPTON. A Letter to Uvedale Price, Esq.
1794. Sketches and Hints on Landscape Gardening.
1803. Observations on Landscape Gardening.
1806. An Enquiry into the changes of taste in Landscape Gardening.
1808. On the introduction of Indian Architecture and Gardening.
1810. On the supposed effects of Ivy on Trees. Translated Linnæan Society.
1817. Fragments on the Theory and Practice of Landscape Gardening.
1840. The landscape gardening & landscape architecture of the late Humphrey Repton; with introduction by J. C. Loudon.
(Coloured copies of this book are very rare.)
1794. JAMES SHAW. Plans of Forcing houses.
1794. JOHN SIBTHORPE. Flora Oxoniensis.
1806–40. Flora Græca, 1806–1840.
1795. JEDEDIAH SIMMONS. Valuable secrets relative to Gardening. Second edition, 1795.
1796. FRANCIS BAUER. Delineation of Exotick Plants cultivated at Kew. London, 1796.
1796. JAMES DON. Hortus Cantabrigiensis.
1796. GEORGE LINDLEY. The plan of an Orchard.
1796. An Account of the Culture of Potatoes in Ireland.
1831. A guide to the orchard & kitchen garden. Edited by J. Lindley 1831.
1796. REV. CHARLES MARSHALL. An Introduction to the Knowledge and Practice of Gardening.
Later editions, 1798, 1800, 1805, 1813.
1796. JOHN PLAW. Ferme Ornee.
1797. FRANCIS DUCKENFIELD ASTLEY. A few minutes advice.
1807. Hints to Planters.
1797. HENRY C. ANDREWS. The Botanist's Repository.
1801. A Review of Plants.
1802. Coloured Engravings of Ericas . . . with full description. . . .
(The fourth volume begun in 1809 and completed 1830 is excessively rare.)
1804. The Heathery, or a Monograph of the genus Erica. Second edition, 1845.
1805. Geraniums.
1805–28. Roses. (Copies containing full number of plates—130—are very rare.)
1797. THOMAS SKIP DYOT BUCKNAL. The Orchardist. Second edition, 1805.
1797. STRICKLAND FREEMAN. Select Specimens of British Plants.
1797. THOMAS ANDREW KNIGHT. Treatise on the Culture of the Apple and Pear.
Later editions, 1801, 1809, 1813, 1818.
1802. Some doubts relative to the efficacy of Mr. Forsyth's Plaister.
1805. Report of a Committee of the Horticultural Society of London.
1806. A Letter on the origin of Blight.
1811. Pomona Herefordiensis.

1797. WALTER NICOL. The Scotch Forcing Gardener.
1799. The Practical Planter.
1809. The Villa Garden Directory or monthly index of work.
Later edition, 1810, 1814, 1822.
1810. The Gardener's Kalendar or monthly directory.
Later editions, 1814, 1822.
1812. The Planter's Kalendar, &c.
Second edition edited and completed by E. Sang, 1820.
1797. WILLIAM SALISBURY. Hortus Paddingtonensis, &c.
1816. The Botanist's Companion, &c.
1816. Hints to the Proprietors of Orchards.
1822. The Cottager's Agricultural Companion, &c.
1798. CLEMENT ARCHER. Miscellaneous Observations.
1798. W. SOLE. Menthæ Britannica.
1799. MISS LAWRENCE. Roses.
1799. LADY CHARLOTTE MURRAY. The British Garden.
Later edition, London, 1809.
1799. ROBERT JOHN THORNTON. A new Illustration of the Sexual System of Linnæus.
1805. The Temple of Flora.
1810. A new Family Herbal. (Engravings by Bewick.)
Second edition, 1814.
1810. Botanical Extracts.
1811. A Grammar of Botany.
Second edition, London, 1814.
1800. MRS. MONTOLIEU. The Enchanted Plants.
The Gardens, a Poem. From the French of L'Abbé de Lille, 1798. (For earlier translation see 1789 Anthony Powell.)
1803. J. DONN. Hortus Cantabrigiensis. Cambridge 1803.
Numerous later editions.
1805. WILLIAM PONTEY. The Profitable Planter.
Later editions 1808, 1809, 1814.
1805. The Forest Pruner, or timber owner's assistant, &c.
Second edition, 1808.
1822. The Rural Improver.
1814. The rotten reviewers . . . as exemplified in their remarks on the forest pruners.
1802. WILLIAM TURTON. A general system of Nature through the three grand kingdoms of animals, vegetables and minerals.
Translated from Gmelin's last edition of the Systema Naturæ of Linnæus.
1802. Rural Recreations, or the Gardener's Instructor. By a Society of Practical Gardeners.
1803. AYLMER BOURKE LAMBERT. A Description of the Genus Pinus.
Second edition, 1832.
1803. J. C. LOUDON. Observations on laying out the Public Squares of London (*Literary Journal*, 1803).

BIBLIOGRAPHY

1804. Observations on Plantations.
1805. A short Treatise on Hot-houses.
1806. A Treatise on Country Residences, &c.
1812. Hints on Gardens and Pleasure Grounds, &c.
1817. Remarks on the Construction of Hot-houses, &c.
1818. Sketches of Curvilinear Hot-houses.
1818. A comparative view of the Curvilinear mode of roofing Hot-houses.
1822. The Encyclopædia of Gardening.
      Several later editions.
      The different modes of cultivating the Pine Apple, &c.
1829. The Encyclopædia of Plants.
      Several later editions.
      Hortus Britannicus, 1830.
      Several later editions.
1826–34. The Gardener's Magazine ; conducted by J. C. Loudon, 1826–34.
      Second series, 1835–43.
1838. Arboretum et Fruticetum Britannicum.
1838. The suburban gardener, 1838.
      Hortus Lignosus Londinensis, 1838.
      Trees and Shrubs.
      The suburban horticulturist, 1842.
      Self instruction for young gardeners, 1845.
      Later edition, 1875.
1840. MRS. LOUDON. Instruction in Gardening for Ladies.
      Numerous later editions.
1840. Flower Garden of Ornamental Annuals.
1841. The Ladies' Companion to Flower Garden, London, 1841.
      Several later editions.
1843. The Ladies' Flower Garden of Ornamental Perennials.
1846. The Ladies' Country Companion.
      Second edition, 1846.
1847. The Amateur Gardener's Calendar, London, 1847.
1803. SAMUEL CURTIS. Florist Lectures on Botany.
1819. Monograph of the genus Camelia.
1820. Beauties of Flora.
1804. R. W. DICKSON. Practical Agriculture.
1805–7. EDWARD RUDGE. Plantarum Guianæ rariarum.
1806. WILLIAM GRIFFIN. Treatise on the cultivation of the Pine Apple.
      Later edition, 1810.
1806. P. HENDERSON. The Seasons or Flower Garden.
1806. WILLIAM HOOKER (Botanic painter). Paradisus Londinensis.
      The Descriptions by Richard Anthony Salisbury, the figures by Wm.
      Hooker. Vol. I, 1806; Vol. II, 1807. Some plates dated 1808.
      (The full number of plates is 119, though Lowndes mentions 114 and
      Putzel 117.)
1818. Pomona Londinensis.

1806. MRS. HENRIETTA M. MORIARTY. Viridarium; or Green House Plants.

1806. W. WALLIS MASON. Experiments on the Culture of Carrots. Nicholson's Journal, XV, p. 57, 1806.

1807. ALEXANDER MACDONALD. A complete Dictionary of practical Gardening.
Johnson states that the writer of this book was R. W. Dickson, author of Practical Agriculture or a Complete System of Modern Husbandry, (1804).

1807. WILLIAM SHAW. The Practical Gardener.

1807. GEORGE TODD. Plans of Hot-houses.

1807. WILLIAM WATSON. On the Culture of Turnips.
Nicholson's Journal, XVI, p. 14.

1808. Catalogue of plants in the Botanic Garden at Liverpool.

1809. J. ACTON. On the Germination of Seeds.
Nicholson's Journal, XXIII, p. 214.

1809. JAMES DEDE. The English Botanist's Pocket Companion.

1809. SYDENHAM EDWARDS. Sixty-one Plates, representing about 150 rare plants.

1812. The New Botanic Garden. See below.

1812. The New Flora Britannica.
(On title-pages of some copies the book is described as ' The new botanic garden '.)

1815–1827. The Botanical Register. Shrubbery.
The continuation to 1847 was edited by J. Lindley.

1809. MRS. AGNES IBBETSON. Contributions to *Nicholson's Journal* on Plants, Seeds, &c.

1809. JOSEPH KNIGHT. An Essay on the cultivation of the Plants belonging to the Order of Proteæ.

1809–10. J. C. KRAFFT. Plans of picturesque Gardens in France, England, and Germany.

1810. THOMAS HAYNES. Improved System of Nursery Gardening. Interesting Discoveries in Horticulture.

1810. A Treatise on the improved culture of the Strawberry, etc.
Second edition, 1814.

1821. An essay on the Soils and Composts.

1811. PETER LINDEGAARD. On the mode of forcing the Vine in Denmark. London. (Mentioned by Johnson.)

1811. WM. TIGHE. The Plants. A Poem, with notes and observations by Wm. Tighe.

1811. W. J. TITFORD. Sketches towards a Hortus Botanicus Americanus. Another edition, 1812.

1811. W. WADE. Salices.

1812. GEORGE BROOKSHAW. Pomona Britannica.
Later edition, 1817.

1816. A Treatise on Flower Painting. Part II, 1819.

BIBLIOGRAPHY

1817. The Horticultural Repository . . . of English Fruit.
Later edition, 1823.

1812. THOMAS HOGG. A concise and practical Treatise on the Carnation, etc.
Second edition, 1822.

1812. JOSEPH TAYLOR. Arbores Mirabiles.

1836. The Bible Garden.

1812. Transactions of the Horticultural Society begun in 1812.

1813. T. HORNOR. Description . . . landscape gardening in England.

1813. PETER LYON. Observations on the barrenness of Fruit Trees.

1816. A Treatise on the Physiology and Pathology of Trees.

1813. Comely Garden, Edinburgh.
(Mentioned by Watt.)

1813. ANONYMOUS. The Modern Practice of English Gardening, in a concise Monthly Display.

1814. P. P. CARNELL. A treatise on family wine making.

1814. JOHN CUSHING. The Exotic Gardener.
Later edition, 1822.

1814. T. D. W. DEARN. Designs for entrances to . . . pleasure grounds in the Gothic style, 1814.

1814. JOHN LUNAN (of Jamaica). Hortus Jamaicensis.

1814. LEONARD PHILLIPS, JUN. A Catalogue of Fruit Trees for sale.

1815. Transactions in the Fruit Tree Nursery. Vauxhall.

1814. FREDERICK PURSH. Flora Americana Septentrionalis.

1814. SIR JOHN SINCLAIR. General Report of the Agricultural state, and Political circumstances of Scotland.

1820. Account of some experiments.

1835. SIR JOHN SINCLAIR & J. FREEMAN. A history . . . of pansies in British gardens, 1835.
(Excessively rare.)

1814. E. WEEKS. The Forcer's Assistant, &c.

1815. I. EMMERTON. A plain and practical treatise on the culture . . . of the Auricula.
(Excessively rare.)
Second edition, 1818.

1816. MARIA E. JACKSON. The Florist's Manual.
Second edition (with additions on Guernsey lily, etc.), 1822. Third edition, 1827.

1816. J. SALTER. A Treatise upon Bulbous Roots, &c., 1816.

1816. GEORGE SINCLAIR. Hortus Gramineus Woburnensis, &c.

1825. Hortus Ericæus Woburnensis.

1826. An Essay on the Weeds of Agriculture, 1826.

1817. JAMES MEAN. The Practical Gardener.

1818. The Gardener's Companion. London, 1818.
Both books by John Abercrombie, edited and enlarged by J. Mean.

1817. W. B. PAGE. Page's Prodromus.

1817. HENRY SMITH. Flora salisburiensis.
1818. T. BALDWIN. Short direction for the culture of the ananas.
1818. JOSEPH HAYWARD. The Science of Horticulture.
Second edition, 1824.
1825. The Science of Agriculture.
1818. JOHN BUONAROTI PAPWORTH. Rural Residences.
1823. Hints of Ornamental Gardening.
1818. ROBERT SWEET, F.L.S. Hortus Suburbanus Londinensis.
1820. The Hot-house and Green-house Manual, &c.
Second edition, 1825.
1821. The Botanical Cultivator, 1821.
Several later editions.
1820–30. Geraniaceæ.
1823–29. The British Flower Garden.
Second series, 1831–8.
1826. Hortus Britannicus, &c.
Later editions, 1830, 1839 (edited by G. Don).
1827–32. The Florists Guide & Cultivators Directory.
1830. Cistineæ, 1830.
1820. HENRY FIELD. Memoirs . . . of the Botanic Gardens, Chelsea.
Later edition, continued by R. H. Semple, 1878.
1820. CUTHBERT WILLIAM JOHNSON. An Essay on the uses of Salt.
1825. Observations on the employment of Salt, 1825.
Numerous later editions.
Our house and garden.
1820. JOHN LINDLEY. Rosarum monographia.
1823. Instructions for collecting and planting seeds and plants.
1828. Pomological Magazine (edited by J. Lindley and R. Thompson), 1828–30.
Introductory lecture on Botany, London, 1829.
1829. A Synopsis of the British Flora.
1830–40. The Genera and Species of Orchidaceous Plants.
1830. An Introduction to the Natural System of Botany.
1832. An Introduction to Botany.
1832. An Outline of the first principles of Horticulture.
1834. Ladies' Botany, &c.
1835. A Key to structural, physiological, and systematic Botany.
1838. Flora Medica.
1838. Sertum Orchidaceum.
1893. School Botany.
1840. Theory of Horticulture.
1841. Pomologia Britannica. Assisted in Vol. III by R. Thompson.
1846. Orchidaceæ Lindenianæ.
1846. The Vegetable Kingdom.
1848. A Glossary of the technical terms used in Botany.
1852–59. Folia Orchidacea.

BIBLIOGRAPHY

1854. The Symmetry of Vegetation.
1858. Descriptive Botany.
1820. RICHARD PIGOTT. A Short, plain Treatise on Carnations and Pinks.
1821. A. DE CANDOLLE. Elements of the Philosophy of Plants, from the German translation of Theorie Elementaire, with additions by K. Sprengel.
1821. WILLIAM COBBETT (M.P. for Oldham). The American Gardener.
1825. The Woodlands, 1825.
1825. WILLIAM BILLINGTON. A series of facts, etc.
1829. The English Gardener. Later editions, 1833, 1838.
1830. Rural Rides.
Later edition, edited by James Paul Cobbett, 1853.
1821. REV. & HONBLE WM. HERBERT. Appendix to the Botanical Magazine and Botanical Register, 1821.
1837. Amaryllidaceæ.
1821. SIR WILLIAM JACKSON HOOKER. Flora Scotica.
1822–27. Exotic Flora.
1825. A Catalogue of Plants in the Royal Botanic Garden, Glasgow.
1830. The British Flora.
1830–33. Botanical Miscellany.
1835–36. Companion to the Botanical Magazine, 1835–36.
1836. Icones Plantarum.
1837. Botanical Illustrations.
1840. Flora Borealis Americana.
1842. Genera Filicum.
1849. Niger Flora.
1857–59. Filices Exotica.
1862. Garden Ferns, 1862.
1820. HENRY PHILLIPS. Pomarium Britannicum.
New edition, under the title Companion to the Orchard, 1821. Third edition, 1823.
1822. History of Cultivated Vegetables, 1822.
New edition, under the title, Companion to the Kitchen Garden, 1831.
1823. Sylva Florifera.
1823. Flora Domestica.
(The authorship is sometimes attributed to Miss Kent, sister-in-law of Leigh Hunt.)
1824. Flora Historica.
Second edition, 1829.
1825. Floral Emblems.
1825. Sylvan Sketches.
1821. Outline of a General History of Gardening.
1822. Hortus Anglicus.
(Mentioned by Johnson.)
1822. F. D. LEVINGSTON. A Practical Treatise on the Gooseberry.

1823. CHARLES HARRISON. A Treatise on the Culture of Fruit Trees.
Second edition, 1825.

1831–36. Horticultural Register (with Sir Joseph Paxton), 1831–36.

1823. PATRICK NEILL. Journal of a Horticultural Tour.

1823. Plan for cultivating Grapes in the Field.
(Mentioned by Johnson without author's name.)

1823. WILLIAM STONES. The gardens of Norfolk. (Describes gardens of
W. Hardy of Letheringsett.)

1824. WILLIAM DEAN. Hortus Croomensis.

1824. THOMAS FORSTER. The Perennial Calendar and Companion to the
Almanac.

1827. Pocket Encyclopædia of Natural Phenomena. Containing 'Flora
Spectabilis '.

1824. THOMAS GREEN. The Universal Herbal (2nd edition), 1824.

1824. THOMAS WATKINS. The art of promoting the growth of the
Cucumber and Melon.

1824. Memoirs of the rose and a series of letters to a lady, 1824.

1824. ANONYMOUS. The Greenhouse Companion.
Second Edition, 1825.
Third edition, 1832.

1824. The Topography of all the known vineyards . . . translated from the
French.

1824 (*circa*). ANONYMOUS. Greenhouse Favourites.

1824 (*circa*). ANONYMOUS. William Billington. A series of Facts, with
experimental remarks upon Fruit Trees.

1825. G. BLISS. The Fruit Grower's Instructor, &c.

1825. N. CARLISLE. Hints on rural residences, 1825.

1825. T. F. HUNT. Half a dozen Hints on Picturesque Domestic Architecture.

1828. Designs for Parsonage Houses, &c.

1825. B. MAUND. The Botanic Garden (published monthly), including the
Auctorium, the Fruitist, also Floral Register.

1839. B. MAUND & H. HENSLOW. The Botanic Album.

1825. RICHARD MORRIS. Essays on Landscape Gardening.

1825. P. W. WATSON. Dendrologia Britannica.

1826. CHANDLER & BUCKINGHAM. Camellia Britannica.

1826. WILLIAM WITHERS, Jun. A Memoir on the Planting of Forest
Trees.
Second edition, 1847.

1828. A Letter to Sir Walter Scott, Bart.

1842. The Acacia Tree.

1826. A Practical Essay on the culture of the Vine, by an experienced
gardener.

1826. WILLIAM CLARK. Flora Conspicua.

1826. Lithographic coloured flowers with botanical descriptions . . . by a
Lady. Edinburgh, 1826.

BIBLIOGRAPHY

1827. H. W. BURGESS. Eidodendron, 1827.
Studies of Trees, 1834.

1827. W. COLLYNS. Ten minutes advice to my neighbours on the use and abuse of Salt as a Manure, 1827.
(Mentioned by Johnson.)

1827. R. HUISH. Alphabetical . . . domestic adviser, 1827.

1827. JAMES MITCHELL. Dendrologia. (Treats of medicinal plants, bees, etc.)
Catalogue of Fruits cultivated in the garden of the Horticultural Society of London, at Chiswick, London, 1827.

1828. CHARLES McINTOSH. The Practical Gardener and Modern Horticulturist. London, 2 vols., 1828–1829.

1828. The new and improved practical gardener.
Second edition, 1859.

1829. Flora and pomona.

1838. The Flower garden.
Second edition, 1844.

1839. The orchard and fruit garden.

1853–55. The Book of the garden.
(One of the most noteworthy mid-nineteenth century manuals. The author was curator of the King of the Belgians' gardens.)

1828. JOHN SAUNDERS. The Kitchen-Garden Directory, &c.

1828. SIR WALTER SCOTT. On Ornamental Plantations and Landscape Gardening. (Quarterly Review.)

1828. SIR JAMES SINCLAIR, Bart. On the Culture and Use of Potatoes.

1828. J. STEPHENSON & J. M. CHURCHILL. Medical Botany.
Second edition edited by G. T. Burnett, 1834–36.

1828. SIR HENRY STEUART OF ALLANTON, Bart. The Planter's Guide.
Third edition, 1848.

1828. JAMES GRAHAM TEMPLE. The Scotch Forcing Gardener.

1828. ANONYMOUS. Practical Instructions for the formation of the Tree Rose.

1829. GEORGE DON. Encyclopædia of Plants.

1832–38. A General System of Gardening and Botany.

1831–38. A General History of the Dichlamydeous plants.

1829. J. FORBES. Salictum Woburneuse, 1829.

1839. Pinetum Woburnense.

1829. GEORGE WILLIAM JOHNSON. A History of English Gardening.

1843. The Gardener's Almanack.

1845. The Principles of Practical Gardening.

1846. The Potato Murrain and its Remedy.

1846. A Dictionary of Modern Gardening.

1849. The Cottage Gardener. Conducted by Johnson.

1852. The Cottage Gardener's Dictionary. Numerous later editions.

1856. Gardening for the Many (*Circa* 1856).

1857. British Ferns Popularly described.
1857. The Garden Manual.
1862. The Science and Practice of Gardening.
1829. JOSHUA MAJOR. A Treatise on the Insects most prevalent on Fruit Trees.
1852. The Theory and Practice of Landscape Gardening.
MRS. EDWARD ROSCOE. Floral illustrations of the Seasons. Engraved by R. Havell, Jnr.
Later edition, 1831.
1829. G. SPRATT. Flora Medica.
1829. The Domestic Gardener's Manual. By a ' Practical Horticulturist '.
?1830. E. A. BROOKE. The Gardens of England. (N.D.)
1833. JAMES MAINE. Illustrations of Vegetable Physiology Applied.
1830. The Villa and Cottage Florist's Directory.
Second edition, 1835.
Illustrations of Vegetable Physiology.
1830. J. MANTELL. A Chapter on Floriculture (in Baxter's Library of Agricultural and Horticultural Knowledge).
1830. The Domestic Gardener's Manual. By a Practical Horticulturist.
1831–36. SIR JOSEPH PAXTON. The Horticultural Register (with Charles Harrison). 1831–36.
1833. The Magazine of Botany. Edited by J. Rennie and J. Burnett.
1838. Practical Treatise on the Dahlia.
1840. Pocket Botanical Dictionary.
1831. H. RONALDS. Pyrus Malus Brentfordiensis.
1832. ANONYMOUS. Useful, ornamental planting.
1833. JOSEPH HARRISON. Floricultural Cabinet.
1833. The Gardener's & Forester's Record . . . edited by J. Harrison. (J. Harrison was gardener to Lord Wharncliffe at Wortley Hall.)
1833–37. The Magazine of Botany and Gardening. Edited by J. Rennie and new series by J. Burnett.
1835. JOHN DENNIS. The Landscape Gardener.
1835. CLEMENT HOARE. Practical Treatise on the cultivation of the Grape Vine.
1835. T. WILLATS. The Florist Cultivator.
1835. J. WALLIS. Dendrology.
1836. M. DOYLE. The Flower & Fruit Garden.
1836. R. MARNOCK. The Floricultural Magazine. (1836–41.)
1836. LOUISA ANNE TWAMLEY. The Romance of Nature.

INDEX

INDEX

INDEX

INDEX

INDEX

INDEX

INDEX

INDEX

INDEX

INDEX

*Printed in Great Britain
at the University Printing House, Oxford
by David Stanford
Printer to the University*